A PLACE OF DREAMS

A Place of Dreams

Desire, Deception and a Wartime Coming of Age

Alison Twells

https://www.openbookpublishers.com

©2025 Alison Twells

This work is licensed under the Creative Commons Attribution-NonCommercial 4.0 International (CC BY-NC 4.0). This license allows you to share, copy, distribute and transmit the text; to adapt the text for non-commercial purposes of the text providing attribution is made to the authors (but not in any way that suggests that they endorse you or your use of the work). Attribution should include the following information:

Alison Twells, *A Place of Dreams: Desire, Deception and a Wartime Coming of Age.* Cambridge, UK: Open Book Publishers, 2025, https://doi.org/10.11647/OBP.0461

Further details about CC BY-NC licenses are available at
https://creativecommons.org/licenses/by-nc/4.0/

Copyright and permissions for the reuse of many of the images included in this publication differ from the above. This information is provided in the captions and in the list of illustrations. Every effort has been made to identify and contact copyright holders and any omission or error will be corrected if notification is made to the publisher.

All external links were active at the time of publication unless otherwise stated and have been archived via the Internet Archive Wayback Machine at https://archive.org/web

Digital material and resources associated with this volume are available at
https://doi.org/10.11647/OBP.0461#resources

Information about any revised edition of this work will be provided at
https://doi.org/10.11647/OBP.0461

ISBN Paperback: 978-1-80511-566-3
ISBN Hardback: 978-1-80511-567-0
ISBN Digital (PDF): 978-1-80511-568-7
ISBN HTML: 978-1-80511-570-0
ISBN Digital ebook (epub): 978-1-80511-569-4

DOI: 10.11647/OBP.0461

Cover image: Norah Hodgkinson, 1941, W.W. Winter, Derby. A selection from Norah's archive, Alison Twells, 2025. Cover design: Jeevanjot Kaur Nagpal.

For my mum, Jean, and Ruby and Maddy, my daughters, with all my love,

*and in loving memory of the Hodgkinsons of Hill Top and Moira Dale:
Tom (1880-1945), Milly (1887-1964), Dennis (1912-1992), Helen (1913-1986),
Richard (1920-1990), Frank (1922-1985)
and Norah (1925-2009).*

And: the Archive is also a place of dreams.
— *Carolyn Steedman*

Contents

List of Illustrations	xi
Note on Names and Sources	xiii
Prologue	1
I	**3**
1. Norah's Suitcase	5
2. Norah's Story: Writing History from the Inside	19
3. Norah Hodgkinson, Schoolgirl Diarist	35
II	**63**
4. A Poke in the Eye for Hitler	65
5. Jim Gilbert, Royal Navy Stoker	85
6. Dearest Dimples	91
7. I Believe You and I Have a Few Things in Common	101
8. Where Is That Photo? A Summer of Snaps and Studio Portraits	109
9. I'm in Love with Him and I Don't Care a Scrap	115
10. The Erotics of War	123
11. Poor Jim?	131
12. Went over Daleacre: The Likely and the Plausible	139
13. If You Love Danny He Is Yours	147
14. Glorious Letters from My Sweetheart	157
15. Danny Told Me a Thing or Two	161
16. Unconditional Surrender?	169
17. Please God ... Waiting for Danny	175

18. Danny	187
19. Our Night of Love	197
20. A Terrific Surprise	203
III	**209**
21. Son of Danny	211
22. Men's Regrets	217
23. Still Part of Me	221
IV	**251**
24. A Mum's Book?	253
25. Writing Norah's Story	263
26. A Place of Dreams	271
Endnotes	275
Bibliography	307
Index	337
Acknowledgements	345

List of Illustrations

1	Hodgkinson family tree, A. Twells, 2025.	p. 8
2	Tom and Milly Hodgkinson, J. H. Turnham, Winslow, 1908. Private papers of Norah Hodgkinson.	p. 9
3	Norah's suitcase. Photo: A. Twells, 2025.	p. 12
4	LGHS scarf, beret and hat-band. Private papers etc. of Norah Hodgkinson. Photo: A.Twells, 2025.	p. 27
5	1938 *Letts's School-girl's Diary*. Private papers of Norah Hodgkinson. Photo: A. Twells, 2025.	p. 35
6	Norah's 'crazes', 1938 Diary. Private papers of Norah Hodgkinson. Photo: A. Twells, 2025.	p. 43
7	Bira's autograph. Private papers of Norah Hodgkinson. Photo: A.Twells, 2025.	p. 45
8	Map of Hill Top, John Glenn and Alison Twells, 2014.	p. 47
9	The Nag's Head, Hill Top, Castle Donington. Photo: A. Twells, 2025.	p. 47
10	Norah, John and friends, Hill Top, c. 1937. Private papers of Norah Hodgkinson.	p. 48
11	The Hodgkinson family, Webb's farm, Hill Top, 1938. Private papers of Norah Hodgkinson.	p. 50
12	Helen and Norah, Webb's farm, Hill Top, 1938. Private papers of Norah Hodgkinson.	p. 50
13	Pop's antlers, courtesy of Castle Donington Museum. Photo: A. Twells, 2025.	p. 53
14	Tom and Milly at Moira Dale, c. 1940. Private papers of Norah Hodgkinson.	p. 56
15	Norah in the back garden at Moira Dale, c. 1940. Private papers of Norah Hodgkinson.	p. 56
16	'Gentleman seeks lady' ad. Private papers of Norah Hodgkinson. Photo: A.Twells, 2025.	p. 60

17	Moira Dale. Number 18 is second from the left. Photo: A. Twells, 2025.	p. 68
18	Norah's diary, early September 1939. Private papers of Norah Hodgkinson. Photo: A. Twells 2025.	p. 72
19	Mary Belton's autograph, 1938. Private papers of Norah Hodgkinson.	p. 80
20	Jim's first letter, February 1941. Private papers of Norah Hodgkinson. Photo: A. Twells, 2025.	p. 90
21	Norah as bridesmaid at her sister Helen's wedding, August 1939. Private papers of Norah Hodgkinson.	p. 93
22	Royal Navy silk handkerchief. Private papers etc. of Norah Hodgkinson. Photo: A. Twells, 2025.	p. 94
23	Extract from Norah's diary, April 1941. Private papers of Norah Hodgkinson. Photo: A. Twells, 2025.	p. 99
24	Norah, W. W. Winter, Derby, 1941. Private papers of Norah Hodgkinson.	p. 112
25	'Between two fires' cartoon, 1941, enclosed in Jim's letter postmarked 17 August 1941. Private papers of Norah Hodgkinson. Photo: A. Twells, 2025.	p. 116
26	Jack of Spades. Private papers of Norah Hodgkinson. Photo: A. Twells, 2025.	p. 137
27	Snippet from Danny's letter, April 1942. Private papers of Norah Hodgkinson. Photo: A. Twells, 2025.	p. 150
28	Norah, W. W. Winter, Derby, 1945. Private papers of Norah Hodgkinson.	p. 196
29	Norah, 1948. Private papers of Norah Hodgkinson.	p. 222
30	Freddie, Norah's 1951 diary. Private papers of Norah Hodgkinson. Photo: A. Twells, 2025.	p. 225
31	Jean, Milly and Norah, Breedon-on-the-Hill, 1952. Private papers of Norah Hodgkinson.	p. 226
32	Newspaper cuttings. Private papers of Norah Hodgkinson. Photo: A. Twells, 2025.	p. 231
33	Norah, Birdy (left) and friends, Kirby Mallory, 1958. Private papers of Norah Hodgkinson.	p. 233
34	Norah and Eddy on a cruise, 1964. Private papers of Norah Hodgkinson.	p. 236
35	Norah and Eddy, Crete, 1971. Private papers of Norah Hodgkinson.	p. 237

Note on Names and Sources

A Place of Dreams is a true story, crafted from and faithful to the diaries and wider archive of Norah Hodgkinson and other archival sources. Norah's diary entries are presented in italics throughout the book. Apart from changing some personal and place names and other identifying details, in order to preserve anonymity, I have not edited the letters or diaries in any way. Spelling mistakes, errors of punctuation and any stylistic quirks remain as they are in the original documents; neither have I used the adverb [sic] to indicate errors that have been transcribed from the originals. All real names are used with permission, including those where individual interviewees are no longer living.

The quotations that introduce the sections of the book are from the following sources: Carolyn Steedman, 'The Space of Memory: In an Archive', *History of the Human Sciences*, 11:4 (1998), 65-83, p. 67; Alexis Okeowo, 'How Saidiya Hartman Retells the History of Black Life', *The New Yorker*, 19 October 2020, https://www.newyorker.com/magazine/2020/10/26/how-saidiya-hartman-retells-the-history-of-black-life; Mass Observation diarist (M-OA: 64 US no. 9, 29 March 1940, p. 77) quoted in Philomena Goodman, *Women, Sexuality and War* (Basingstoke: Palgrave, 2002), p. 130; Mary Wesley, *Toronto Globe and Mail*, 9 May 1995, cited by Patrick Marnham, 'Siepmann [*née* Farmar], Mary Aline [*other married name* Mary Aline Eady, Lady Swinfen; *pseud.* Mary Wesley]', *ODNB*, 5 March 2009; Colm Tóibín, 'One Minus One', *The Empty Family* (London: Viking, 2010), p. 8; Annie Ernaux, *Shame*, trns. Tanya Leslie (New York: Seven Stories Press, 1998), back cover; Laurent Binet, *HHhH* (London: Vintage, 2013), chapter 150 (no page numbers); Adrienne Rich, 'Cartographies of Silence', 1975, in Rich, *The Dream of a Common Language* (New York: W. W. Norton, 1978). The image of a handwritten X in Chapter 1 was created by Alex Muravev (Noun Project, https://thenounproject.com/icon/cross-970602/).

Prologue

Norah felt oddly lost in the vast leather armchair, her gymslip and thick lisle stockings slipping against the shiny seat. She sensed the headteacher scrutinising her face as she took the envelope, glanced at the post mark – Harwich, 12th Feb 1941 – and carefully removed and unfolded a pencil-written note inside.

The words 'Smilin Thro' looped across the left-hand corner.

J. Gilbert
2 Mess
HMS Elgin
GPO London

Dear Friend,
    I have just received a lovely pair of hand knitted socks, from our Naval Base comfort fund. Seeing your name attached to them, I wish to convey my thanks and you can be assured the socks are much appreciated for warmth and use aboard this minesweeper.
    I remain
    Yours truly
    Jim Gilbert

It was indeed a grand thing for her 'gairls' to knit comforts and write letters of encouragement to the brave servicemen who were defending our freedoms, Miss Bristol said in her Belfast burr. She was so very proud of them all. But she needed to be sure that Norah would tell her mother about this correspondence. There was to be no underhand messing around with these sailor boys, did she understand?

Norah nodded. She really couldn't see what the fuss was about. It was only a letter from a sailor, a short, scrappy thing. She'd knit for her own brothers when they joined up, just like she'd knitted for this chap. She almost shrugged and then thought better of it, as Miss Bristol continued to hold her gaze.

17th February 1941: Received a letter from a minesweeper, Jim Gilbert H.M.S. Elgin. There is no note of excitement in Norah's diary entry for that day, no sense of awe or pride stirred by the name of Jim's ship. Maybe the tone of Miss Bristol's 'interview' put paid to that. But what dreams and fancies pricked her imagination later that night? What unthought adventures began to hover in her mind? Or did she feel it in her body first of all, with a quickening step and a private smile? Three days later, Norah took possession of Jim as her correspondent. *20th February 1941: Wrote back to my minesweeper.*

Within days, a second letter arrived, this time at her home address. A navy cap-band bulked out the envelope. Friendlier but still quite formal and reserved, Jim thanked Norah for 'such a nice letter, which I must say was rather unexpected'. He apologised for his writing: the *Elgin* was 'cruising along' somewhere in the North Sea, which was 'everything but calm'. He asked about her school life, her hobbies and interests and requested 'snaps', promising to return them with his next letter.

'Cheerio', he wrote, signing his name 'Jim A. Gilbert', then adding in a P.S. that 'only 1½ d stamp is required when writing to HM Ships'.

She would be writing again.

I

Are we to be consigned forever to tell the same kinds of stories?
 – Saidiya Hartman

1. Norah's Suitcase

Paid milkman. If truth be told, I didn't have high hopes for Norah's diaries. *Had perm.* My grandmother, Norah's elder sister, had kept a similar set, her sparse entries simply confirming that she was of that class and generation that didn't dwell on feelings. Even the day in September 1965, when she discovered her unmarried daughter was pregnant – with me, as it happens – my grandmother marked the page not with words but with a single black ✕.

There was every chance that Norah's diaries would be more of the same. Her life was more exotic, that much was true. *Booked taxi to airport* would appear at least once each year. *Bought lovely new high-heeled shoes* would crop up with some frequency too. But like her sister, Norah wasn't one for shows of emotion. In the forty or more years that I knew her, I never once saw her composure disturbed. Her tiny pocket diaries, their daily windows smaller than the side of a matchbox, would allow for nothing more than the barest bones of her life.

Norah had mentioned her diaries to me a few times over the years, including on the last occasion that I saw her – an impromptu visit a few weeks before she died. We had started calling in more frequently that autumn. She had suddenly become very tired, sometimes too weary to even meet up with her friends. She relied on the lunches and outings that structured her weeks to keep the loneliness at bay. That Sunday, we phoned *en route* to instruct her to put the kettle on and then stopped at a farm shop on the outskirts of town to pick up a chocolate sponge and a pint of semi-skimmed.

'It's a rum carry-on', she said, clearly pleased, 'when your visitors have to bring their own cake and milk'.

Sitting in the middle of the settee in her mauve jumper, resting her long calves neatly to one side, Norah looked at least a decade younger than her eighty-four years.

'When I'm gone, you'll have all this lot to sort out', she said.

There was nothing untoward about this comment or the accompanying chuckle as she surveyed her living room: the colourful ornaments and mementoes that dotted the rosewood sideboard, the red Moroccan table runners, a Thai Buddha and an assortment of Egyptian figurines. Nor even in the way she leant forward, her tea cupped in her hands, to give me a meaningful look.

'And then there's my diaries'.

I already knew that Norah had kept a daily diary, starting when she was a schoolgirl before the Second World War. But when I asked her again what she wrote about, she just laughed.

'My life', she shrugged, as always giving nothing away.

Norah's enigmatic mix of fond familiarity and aloofness foxed me. While her friendly demeanour and her sing-song voice gave the impression that she didn't have a care in the world, we were vaguely aware that behind her poise was a guard that she wouldn't let down. I can't imagine now why my curiosity hadn't driven me further, to try to coax her out from behind her cool self-possession, her polish and reserve.

I regret it now, of course I do.

***

If you'd asked me then, before her wartime diaries got me in their grip, I'd have been quite certain that the period of Norah's life that most intrigued me was the 1960s, just before I was born. These were the years in which she met and moved in with Eddy, her German lover. We didn't much care for him, nor he for us. That he had fought on the 'wrong side' during the war had been a factor early on. That he was separated from his second wife but remained a married man was more unsettling. My mum and gran thought that Norah had ended up with him because she had been afraid of being left on the shelf.

'Lord only knows what she sees in him', my grandmother would say, well-versed herself in marital disappointment.

On car journeys to visit Norah when I was a child, my mum and gran would whisper about the silences surrounding her marital status and speculate about Eddy's possible war criminal past. As we neared their suburban bungalow, stern warnings would issue from the front of our Ford Cortina as I sat unbelted in the back. Once inside, my glass of orange squash balancing on my lap, legs dangling above the pale carpet, my curiosity would start to spill. My eyes were drawn to the shelf of books written in German, the photographs of unfamiliar children and, neatly placed on a polished table to the side of the sofa, a sepia portrait of a dead first wife. 'Uncle Eddy' watched me looking, curled-lipped and red-faced in his armchair throne, while Norah made small-talk, nervously serving up a madeira cake she'd baked that afternoon.

We preferred it when she came to us; alone, of course. At first, you'd hear high heels tap-tapping down the path at the side of the house. Then she'd glide in with her Grace Kelly elegance, her lilting voice and kindly eyes.

Norah and my mother had been close. As a child, my mum had spent long days at Norah's family home, helping her with the dusting and making tea. When my mum passed the 11-plus in 1952, it was Norah who lent my grandmother the money to buy her school uniform. Later, aunt and niece became companions – on walks in the country lanes around the village, Sunday evenings in front of the newly acquired television, shopping trips to Derby and Blackpool holidays. When it became clear that my mother, unmarried, was pregnant, Norah was a confidante for both her sister and niece. And when my mum reneged on an earlier adoption plan, returning from a mother and baby home with a new white and gold carrycot with me inside, Norah became my godmother.

There was a distance between them during the 1970s and 1980s. Norah's 'husband' was a jealous man who demanded her attention and (we believed) thought us beneath him. But after he passed away in the mid-1990s, Norah and my mum settled into years of comfortable companionship, with outings to stately homes, visits to well dressings and weekly chats over cups of tea. After my daughters were born, Norah would spend birthdays and Christmases, and some lunches and Sunday dinners in between, with us in Sheffield. The hour-long journey up the M1 was filled with laughter as she and my mum imagined the cake fashioned by the girls, usually more sculpture than cuisine, or placed bets on what time I'd have dinner on the table. Once here, while my mum helped in the kitchen, Norah's chat drifted through from the front room, as she delighted in her great-grand-nieces' rapturous welcome.

For Norah's 80th birthday in 2005, I arranged for her extended family to converge from all corners of the country on Donington Manor Hotel. The best photograph shows her sitting at the top of the table like a duchess, wearing a smart green suit and a composed smile.

Five years later, in the late November week when I'd begun planning for her 85th celebration the following spring, Norah suddenly died. She had chosen the cemetery at Castle Donington as her final resting place. Her plot, occupied by Eddy, was just down the path from her mother and father and three of her siblings.

Although our family were chapel-goers, we held her funeral service in the thirteenth-century Anglican church which, elegant, with a needle spire, stood on elevated ground at the heart of the village; Norah had long been an admirer. My daughters, nine and six, read a poem and a made-up prayer. My eulogy sketched the surface of her life: her love of family history and the village, her travel adventures, gardening, years with Eddy. While it was better than a thin tribute by a vicar to whom she was an unknown, it felt unsatisfactory, like I was merely wrapping up her life in a tidy way. I didn't really know her at all.

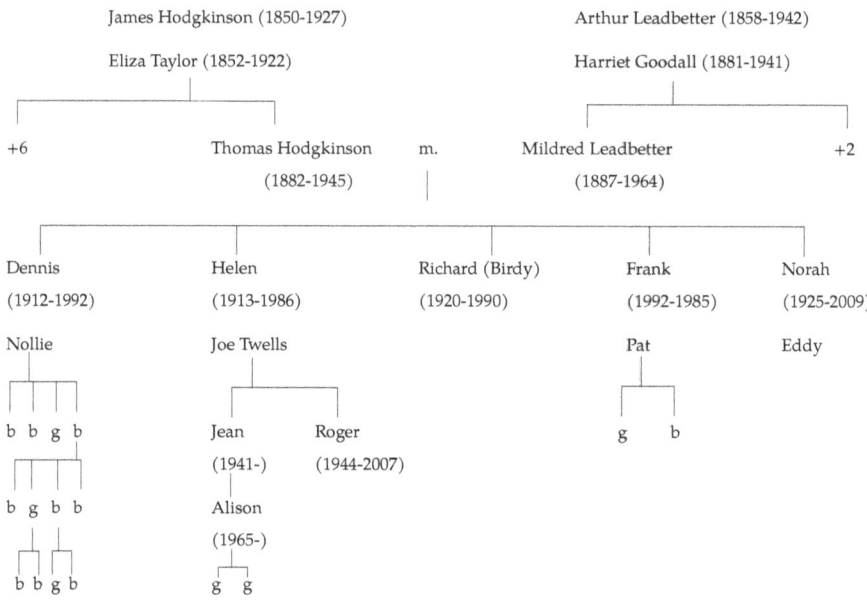

Fig. 1 Hodgkinson family tree, A. Twells, 2025.

***

My mum reminded me about the diaries when we arrived at Norah's bungalow in the evening after she died. She had been called that afternoon by a vigilant neighbour who, noticing that Norah's curtains remained drawn, had knocked and then let herself in, to find my great-aunt slumped on the bathroom floor. Norah had died, quickly it seems, during the night.

The undertaker had already been and gone and the place was shrouded in stillness. We were there to pick up precious family photographs, Norah's funeral plan, solicitor's details and her will, the contents of which we already knew: the house left to charity, small amounts of money to family, and all possessions to my mother to dispose of as she saw fit.

Overwhelmed by the task ahead, we sat down for a last cup of tea in the living room, now in cold contrast to the sub-tropical heating Norah had favoured. I reached across to the sideboard to pick up a framed photograph of her parents, my great-grandparents, Tom and Milly Hodgkinson, taken on the occasion of their engagement in 1908:

Fig. 2 Tom and Milly Hodgkinson, J. H. Turnham, Winslow, 1908. Private papers of Norah Hodgkinson.

Tom, a postman, recently discharged from the Grenadier Guards after service in the South African Wars (his papers describe him as 'clean, smart and sober'), wears a dark suit and checked waistcoat, a pocket watch nestling beneath his jacket. He is handsome with dark curly hair, a moustache and a mischievous twinkle in his eyes that has reappeared, an appealing flash of blue, in various grandchildren and great-grandchildren.

Milly is seated far enough forward to allow her new fiancé to rest a protective arm on the back of her chair. The daughter of a lockkeeper on the Trent-Mersey canal, she had been in service since the age of twelve, working in big houses in Loughborough, London and now Derby. Tall and graceful, her features are strong, her heavy jaw and brow balanced by the shiny sweep of a loose chestnut bun and offset by delicate, pretty eyes and a general air of shyness. Her pale, embroidered blouse with its fine lace collar will have been sewn by her own hand. The photograph was so familiar to me and yet, suddenly, with Norah gone, it all seemed so long ago.

'Here they are', my mother said fondly, as she returned from the dining room with the two large boxes of photographs that Norah would bring out at family gatherings. The youngest of five, she had outlived all of her siblings. She needed to make sure that we – my mum and I, our cousins and now my own daughters – appreciated our roles as responsible heirs.

'I wonder where her diaries are?' my mum pondered. I'd forgotten about Norah's diaries until that moment. We soon found the grey cardboard suitcase, resting against the teak wardrobe in Norah's bedroom. I laid it flat on the floor and flicked the locks.

'Blimey! Look here!' Dozens of coloured spines – red, blue, brown, green – were packed neatly in rows. I picked out one at random and flicked through the pages.

> *18th April 1942: Laval set up new cabinet in France. Twelve Lancasters made raid on southern Germany & lost seven of them.*
>
> *20th: Received a beautiful letter from my dearest beloved & answered it & Jim's too.*

'*My dearest beloved*? Who was that, then, when she was …' I looked at my mum as we both worked out the years – 1925 to 1942 – 'just seventeen?'

'It'll be that airman', my mum stated, matter-of-factly.

'What airman?' I frowned.

'You've never heard about Norah's boyfriend? The one who disappeared? You must have done!' My mum shot me a dubious look before telling me that Norah had a boyfriend during the war who was in the RAF and whom she had expected to marry. I remembered a story that Norah had been disappointed in love as a young woman. 'It was all a bit of a mystery, one of those things you knew not to ask about as a child'. My mum paused. 'Or since, for that matter. Now what was his name?' As my mother wrestled with her memory, I read on:

> 21st April: Mum came to Derby. Went up to Kemp's. I'm starting on Friday. Helen has pleurisy. Bought Pride & Prejudice 3/6.

'Kemp's was the secretarial college, where she did shorthand. Your gran was really poorly with pleurisy'.

> 22nd: Posted my letters. I love my Danny very much.

'Danny, that's him. Something odd happened. I'm not sure anybody knew exactly what, but it derailed her life somehow, for a while. We always thought he was the root of it'.

'The root of what?' I asked, slightly taken aback.

'How she was. With men. With life'. I had more than a vague sense of what my mum meant. In my lifetime, Norah had been on the edge of our family, her self-imposed distance received as both a puzzle and a minor affront. 'Let's just say, there was a lot we didn't know'.

A quick inspection revealed a mixture of Letts's School-girl's, Railway Clerical Workers' Association, Collins' and gardening diaries, seventy in all, stacked in order of year from 1938, when Norah turned thirteen, to 2008 when she was eighty-three. Tucked in the corner of the suitcase was a stash of letters with 1940s postmarks. A pile of photographs beneath them were of the same two men, one in Royal Navy uniform and the other RAF. I turned over a portrait. It was signed in pencil on the back: 'Danny'. And another: 'Jim'. Both: 'with love'.

My mum glanced across. 'She'd prefer the airman of course. A better *class* of serviceman'. She lengthened the 'a' in class to make it more Queen's English. That wasn't the way Norah spoke, but she did have aspirations.

As I closed the lid and lined up the locks, clicking them into place, my mother turned sharply to face me, her expression frozen and grave.

'Do you think we should burn them?'

'Not a chance', I replied. I knew that this was an archive, an extraordinary document of the century that had seen the most profound changes in women's lives. Seventy-one years of pocket diaries, following the life of a girl who lived in a council house and passed the scholarship exam; an ordinary woman who worked as a clerk, who loved glamour, travel and men, and who ended up in a 'marriage' of which no-one approved. What a gift!

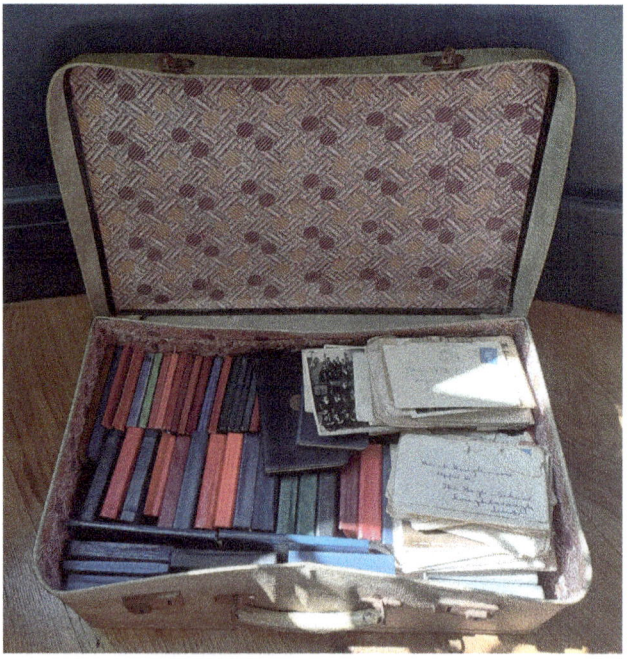

Fig. 3 Norah's suitcase. Photo: A. Twells, 2025.

***

'Where shall we start?' I asked as we settled down in my mum's back room with Norah's diaries and two dry sherries. I didn't know what her choice would be – family life at Moira Dale, maybe, for which she was so nostalgic, or Norah's early years with Eddy and her decision to live with him as man and wife. But no, neither of these.

'1965', she replied in a flash, like the question didn't need to be asked. My mum wanted to hear Norah's record of the scandalous pregnancy that she – my mum – had brought to our family as a young unmarried woman. 'September. That's when they all found out; when the shit hit the fan'. We laughed guiltily at our haste. A few hours on and here we were. Nothing could now knock us off this course.

We bond over family history, my mum and I. Life, education mainly, had drawn me away, provoking in her a definite pride, but suspicion too. There is a space between us that can prickle with unease, impatience on my part met by a 'you-clever-bugger' look on hers. My twenties had seen us at a distance – me at a south coast university, then settling in Yorkshire, her leaving Donington briefly, to marry. But my babies' births in the following decade had brought a new kind of kinship, an embeddedness in each other's lives. Family stories and regular reports on Norah's family tree-ing adventures became part of our daily phone calls and weekly visits.

Families are where we first learn about history, about change over time. They are also where we start to sense, in Suzannah Lessard's words, 'how short time is, how close the generations are, how powerfully lives reverberate [...], deeply affecting each other'. But the 'genealogical imaginary' – how we use kinship to place ourselves in time – is always selective.[1] Norah favoured her Hodgkinson ancestors – agricultural labourers over centuries in the Derbyshire Dales, dispersed into urban life with her police sergeant grandfather's generation, his daughters, Norah's aunts, marrying up and moving south. My mother and I, by contrast, were most at home with the women on Norah's maternal side. Norah's granny, Harriet Leadbetter, a member of the Independent Labour Party on its formation in 1893, famously neglected housework to pore over Robert Blatchford's *Clarion* and recite Walt Whitman's poems.[2] Self-educated and something of a 'seeker', she and her lock-keeper husband became so utterly disillusioned with religion that they refused to enter a church, even when dead. Milly, their loving daughter and a gentle rebel, disapproved of her parents' domestic distractions and lack of faith, joining the Christadelphians as a young teenage girl in service. With no interest in the trappings of modern life, she found her pleasures in gardening, sewing, crocheting, walking in the lanes around her home and reading her Bible.

'A true Leadbetter', my mum will say, surveying my scrappy lawn and runner bean canes, while casting a critical eye over the breakfast pots, still unwashed at lunchtime. The relaxed approach to housekeeping skipped a generation with her tidiness and cleanliness, a dab of antiseptic from the Twells side, perhaps. But for me, it's come straight down the maternal line.

While my mum and Norah kept family photographs and other mementoes safely stored in boxes and drawers, my house is home to the heirlooms: my gran's green Lloyd Loom chair and ottoman, carefully re-covered; a bookcase and an embroidered stool that Norah crafted at a woodwork class she and my gran had attended in the 1950s – though not my gran's television table, its hilariously too-long legs cut down lest the family permanently crick their necks. On a shelf in my living room, my gran's Singer sewing machine is a thing of beauty – black japanned cast iron with gold filigree engraving – and a reminder of her creativity and capacity for making. And her sideboard, bought from Loughborough Co-op in 1939: on my first weekend alone after a break-up with a man who disliked my ancestral furnishings, I dragged the 'dresser' from its attic storage place to the living room and painted it a glorious teal blue. My mother, more wedded to the idea that an original should not be tampered with, doesn't always approve of my domestic re-imaginings. But these family pieces feel to me to be constitutive of *now* rather than museum-like remnants of the past.[3]

Gardeners, knitters, sewists all, makers of light and airy sponge cakes and perfect trifles. Over the years, Norah and my mother added other talents to this list, decorating, upholstery and car maintenance among them. When Norah relayed the story of a female relative who had exclaimed in some awe and envy that 'you Leadbetter women are just so *capable*', she and my mum had cackled like crones, knowing it to be true. They congratulated each other ever after – on Herculean achievements in the garden, perhaps, or fighting off a flu bug: 'well, what with us being strong Leadbetter women ...'

Norah and my mother were in a quieter kind of cahoots over what we might call their 'relationship histories'. For both, their most intimate experiences – 'living in sin' (was Norah married or not?), an unwed pregnancy by a married man – were shaped by secrecy and shame. My mum, in later life an enthusiastic interviewee for a history of unmarried mothers,[4] was less guarded than Norah. Her oft-told story of her return from the mother and baby home in December 1965, the very next day being marched (by another aunt) down the main shopping street with me in the pram and her head held high, was, to her, two fingers to judgement and shame. It was a tactic she repeated with other women, cowed by varied disgraces. But despite her more buttoned-up approach to her life, Norah too refused to be tethered to norms of respectability when they got in the way of other wants and passions.

And me, writing this? In his 2006 Nobel lecture titled 'My Father's Suitcase', Orhan Pamuk suggests that the starting point for many writers is 'the secret wounds that we carry inside us, wounds so secret that we ourselves are barely aware of them'.[5] It is a long time since the shame of my birth has felt like a wound for either my mother or myself, but Pamuk is surely right and this is the root of our mutual fascination with all matters sex and transgression.

And there's another thing: the way family history is commonly pursued – father's name, male line, 'traditional' family structures – can silence the experiences of women. 'We think back through our mothers if we are women', wrote Virginia Woolf in *A Room of One's Own*, evoking an alternative matrix of remembrance.[6] Perhaps in so doing we catch courage from them.[7]

***

In those early weeks after Norah's death, my mother lived in what we came to call 'diary time'. It became a compulsion that pinned her to her gold two-seater settee, her arthritic limbs stiffer than ever, keeping her from her routine and from seeing her friends.

'I've been diarying all afternoon', she'd tell me wearily over the phone. 'I'll be glad when I've finished them'.

Less than a month after Norah's funeral, my mum arrived with a brown A3 envelope bulging with diaries. Marooned on the sofa on Christmas night, she offered bulletins from Norah's daily life in the 1940s. She had already read the diaries from my birth in 1965 forwards, through Norah's relationship with Eddy, to the end of her long life, and had now gone back to the beginning, to Norah's schooldays, her early years as a clerk at 'the railway' and the mystery of her wartime love affair with Danny the airman.

On Boxing Day evening, she arrived at the event she'd been waiting for. 'She's just fallen in love with Danny', my mum announced. And later: 'Danny's been to stay for the weekend'.

'What happened to him?' I asked, shuddering inwardly at the thought of the fighter pilots who were to the Second World War what soldiers in trenches were to the First. 'We never knew. Norah expected to marry him. I think he just disappeared.'

I left her to the diaries and went to clear up in the kitchen.

'You won't believe this!' My mum's voice was high with excitement when, a short time later, she joined me. 'Listen to this! *5th September 1943: Things got hot with Danny in bed in the morning.* And then a week later: *Had a beautiful time in bed with my cherub'*. My mum was incredulous. 'Where was Marsie when all that was going on?!' Marsie was the name given by her children to Milly, Norah's mother and my mum's grandmother. She also sounded a bit put out. 'I thought I was the first person in our family to do anything like that', she said, 'as an *unmarried mother*'. She over-enunciated the last two words, Les Dawson style. 'But look at her! It could have been *her*!'

When my mum picked up with Norah's diaries the following afternoon, Danny had not been in touch for a few months and appeared to be missing. Norah was writing a short prayer for him every night: 'Please God take good care of my Danny and bring him home safely to me'. In early 1945, he was back, only to disappear again after his demob later that year.

'I think he's gone for good this time', my mum lamented. 'I wish I could remember more.' She paused for a moment, wrapped in her thoughts. 'I wonder if there is there anything in the letters?'

The letters! I'd brought them back to Sheffield in a shoebox, leaving the suitcase of diaries with my mum. I was saving them for when I could give them my full attention. I was also a tiny bit afraid that they wouldn't contain anything of interest. I already knew just from flicking through that they weren't written by Danny but by someone named Jim.

'Oh Jim!' my mother exclaimed as if he were an old acquaintance of hers. 'Jim's the sailor. You remember the photographs? He's the one she knitted some socks for, while she was still at school. Schools "adopted" ships, you know. The girls knitted for them and wrote letters'.

I liked the image of teenage Norah knitting socks. It reminded me of the cardigans she had made for my newborn babies and a Christmas afternoon in more recent years when she helped me with the first sleeve of a chunky jumper, chuckling at my unwieldy size 10 pins.

I fetched the box from the bookshelf. The photographs lay on top. A portrait of Jim reveals his open, symmetrical features, his lips and eyebrows full. A second formal snap shows him standing in line with a crew of boyish sailors. Norah's collection of photos of Danny was more extensive: a boy sporting a big flat cap, a suave young man in a clutch of pre-war snaps, and the slender twenty-something whom Norah knew, bright-eyed and smiling in his RAF uniform.

Beneath the photos, the letters were a jumble. Some were not postmarked, while others, many undated, were out of their envelopes. I picked one out, unfolding the unexpectedly thick sheets. It opened with a brief account of Jim's life at sea, but mid-way down, the tone changed.

'Listen to this!' I squeaked.

> Norah if you want Danny don't be afraid to let your feelings go or are you shy. I wish you would tell what you and Danny do when he stays with you, or don't you get the opportunity, meaning being alone. Have you had more than a parting kiss? Norah perhaps I have no right in butting in your private affairs, but you can depend on me and I will do anything to help you. I wish also you would ask me a million questions. Next letter then I will expect a real –?

My mum was wide-eyed. 'Bloody hell! What was she doing getting letters like that?' A pause: 'I wonder if she had romances with both of them?' And then quietly, as a child came into earshot: 'What a bugger she was!'

***

Alarmed by her absorption in Norah's revelations, my mother's own diaries didn't see the New Year in.

'I'm not having you lot poring over *my* life like this', she announced in my kitchen one weekend in early January. Her blue eyes flashed at me accusingly, seemingly oblivious to the fact that, at this point in time, she was the only one to have read Norah's diaries. My ten-year-old daughter looked up from the picture she was sketching at the table, horrified. Inspired by her great-great-aunt, she had asked for her first diary as a Christmas present and had begun writing every night before she went to sleep.

'You can't do that, grandma!'

'I can and I have', my mother replied, pursing her lips. 'When I got back home after Christmas, I shredded the lot'.

2. Norah's Story: Writing History from the Inside

But was Norah, as my mother exclaimed, 'a bugger'? I suspected that my mum was seeing her aunt in the light of Norah's later years, when we'd been endlessly entertained by her interest in men. But this correspondence took place in the early 1940s when Norah, the daughter of a devout Christian mother, was in her mid-teens. My immediate reaction was to wonder if it was a reciprocal exchange, whether Jim's intimate questioning was wanted by Norah. It was surely not commonplace, during the war or at any other time, for a grown man to write such letters to a young woman.

I found myself musing whether this odd wartime correspondence was in any way related to Danny's later disappearance. Whether the sexually forward letters to schoolgirl Norah from Jim the sailor had any bearing on the mystery of the great-aunt I knew: the woman who lived 'in sin' with her married German lover, and who kept her distance from us, her poor-relation family, and the ever curious yet faintly disapproving village of her birth. Was this anything more than a vaguely insalubrious personal story or – the historian in me – might Jim's letters and Norah's diaries tell us something about sex and romance in WW2, now well-established areas of enquiry, but persistently tricky?

I have lost count of the number of people who, on hearing the barest of outlines of Norah's story, have responded with 'well it was the War and they didn't know if they were going to live to see another day'. To some extent, the evidence bears this out. This is especially the case in stories told by men. A Canadian soldier in London just prior to the Normandy Landings recalled the scenes and sounds of Hyde Park and Green Park at dusk and after dark. 'They just can't be described', he said 'You can just imagine, a vast battlefield of sex'. More movingly, an American combat

©2025 Alison Twells, CC BY-NC 4.0   https://doi.org/10.11647/OBP.0461.02

engineer in London described meeting a young woman while on a four-day leave, and talking, walking, sightseeing, making love while rockets exploded. Raised as a Southern Baptist, he acknowledged that 'by most peoples' standards we were immoral, I suppose. But we were young and lonely and could die tomorrow'. His time with her, he said, was 'one of the loveliest and cleanest experiences of my life'.[1]

Young women received endless cautions about their wartime behaviour. Their entry into men's jobs and other public spaces aroused many anxieties – that their economic independence would de-sex them, their new-found freedoms leave men wondering what they were fighting for. The government and mass media tasked them with what historian Philomena Goodman has called 'patriotic femininity': the job of reassuring men and boosting their morale through gentle allure and looking good. But it was a fine line: too much glamour and flirtation saw them hastily condemned as irresponsible, a threat to the war effort. The last thing our servicemen needed was the worry that their women were having a wild time without them.[2]

Yet despite the efforts to reign them in, many women pursued romantic and sexual encounters in a no less than revolutionary manner. Studies from Australia and Britain, Germany, Denmark and the USA, show young women rejecting the domestic drudgery and self-sacrifice of their mothers' generation and embarking instead on quests for erotic adventure. 'It was the wilfulness of girls and young women that contemporaries remarked upon, their agency in "picking up" men', writes historian Marilyn Lake. Colonel Geoff Calway of the United States Army charged that Australian women – who called themselves 'Yank Hunters' – 'waited on street corners' for his troops. 'When the girls go up to our boys, saying "Come on, sweetie," said film star Carol Landis, 'the boys have to beat them off with clubs'. Reporting the increase of sexually transmitted diseases among young women between sixteen and twenty, Dr Cooper Booth, Director of Social Hygiene in Sydney, told the Housewives' Association in 1943: 'Don't get the idea that these girls are of one class only. Many of them come from the best homes and have a good education... The girls simply have a desire for sexual life'.

Looking back, it was the Americans' difference from Australian men that the women enjoyed: their interest in dancing, their uniforms and personal care, their almost-feminine conversation and clear enjoyment of the company of women. Their reputation as lovers preceded them, Hollywood style. 'I wanted to fall in love with a Yank, badly', remembered Maureen Meadows of Brisbane. 'All the other girls were falling in love with Yanks, lots of them... I was all set to fall in love, really in love. Not the quiet, respectable, lukewarm affair I had known with Robert, but the sort of love I had always associated with Americans – tender, thrilling, tempestuous, and no half measures'.[3]

We see a similar story in Denmark, where social workers' reports reveal young women and girls, some no older than fourteen, roaming the streets of Esbjerg, looking for German men. As one explained, 'she simply did not know what had happened, but since 9 April [1940, the first day of the occupation] she had not been able to control herself and stay away from German soldiers. Now she feared for her own sanity'. Other incidents saw girls discovered in houses with half-dressed soldiers. 'One of the Nazi fronts is the erotic one', a local paper stated, and 'the Germans are having too much luck in this particular area'.[4]

Young Danish women, eager for fun, adventure and sexual experience, found the Germans to be polite and attentive lovers. Meanwhile, German women claimed to prefer the French. As relationships with prisoners of war were illegal in the Third Reich, women's words are revealed in statements made in court. 'Germans make love like bulls, but the French and Belgians know how to make love without making children', one woman said in front of the judges. A married farmwoman encouraged her friends to 'supply themselves with a Frenchman' because they 'know how to do it much better than the Germans'. With her new experience of cunnilingus, she claimed to finally have learned what 'real love' was.[5]

And in England? Among scant evidence, there is a vivid report from the *Sunday Pictorial* of late August 1945: 'The scene was Bristol, most English of all English cities', it opens. 'The time was 2 a.m. yesterday. The actors were a mob of screaming girls between 17 and 25' who, on learning that the four companies of African American soldiers currently in the city were leaving for home, had 'besieged the barracks', waiting through the night in pouring rain, singing "Don't Fence Me In". 'This was too much for the coloured men who began to break down the barbed wire', the report continued. 'In a few minutes hundreds of girls and U.S, soldiers were kissing and embracing..."I don't mind getting wet," said one 18-year-old. "I intend to give my sweetie a good send-off".'[6]

The Danish press decried women's behaviour as morally lax, an insult to national honour. An African American newspaper denounced girls who 'roam the streets, loving men for a night or an hour. They search for the bright lights and bars; seeking the thrills of new faces and new sensations. Patriotism to them is a cheap affair'. The moniker used in Britain – 'good-time girls' – was relatively benign compared to the US Feds' term of choice; women who crossed the all-too ambiguous line were known as 'patriotutes'.[7]

The 'experts' – social workers, sociologists and manifold psychologists – saw such girls simply as wrongdoers; lawless and unruly. 'None of the dozens of schedules, studies, questionnaires, or interviews designed to help authorities understand why so many girls and young women defied social conventions by having sex outside of marriage asked their subjects about their sexual feelings', writes US historian Amanda Littauer.[8] In stark contrast to their approach to male sexuality, it was assumed that girls who engaged in premarital sex did so because they were delinquent, not on account of desire.

Yet women around the world were peeling off the husks of traditional femininity, discarding layers of respectability, censure and shame, embracing a new kind of self-expression, an autonomous, erotic self-assertion. 'Today, seeing the 1940s and 1950s as a time of "sex anarchy" seems strange', writes Littauer, 'but worried observers at the time used this term – as well as "sex revolution," an "addiction to promiscuity," and a "morals revolt" – to describe changes in sexual culture'. 'Little is still known [...] about women's and girls' own motives for entering into relationships with occupation soldiers', writes Lulu Anne Hansen of Danish women. Yet '[i]n the midst of all the conservative efforts of social workers and nationalist resistance rhetoric, the beginnings of a sexual revolution can be glimpsed'.[9]

With her risqué letters from Jim and the *hot times* in bed with Danny that so shocked my mother, where, I wondered, did Norah fit into this picture?

***

A second set of questions lie at the heart of this book: how best do I uncover, and then convey, Norah's story?

Norah's diaries, I knew, were an unexpected treasure. Historical accounts of the lives of ordinary girls and women, written on their own terms and in their own words, are a rarity. Historians are commonly forced to rely on sources written *about* such women: newspaper articles, claxoning fears about lax morality, or the commentaries of social workers, probation officers, the police, the records of juvenile court proceedings and government departments, the concerns of which are usually very far from the girls' own, and where disclosures may be prompted by a line of questioning and expressed in words chosen to justify or play down their part in a transgression.[10]

Yet despite being written in her own words, Norah's diaries are a challenge to read. It is not simply that much of what she wrote about was very mundane. Norah's daily concerns – the weather, her routines and household chores, the comings and goings of family and friends, her health, love interests and occasional world events – were shared with other diarists, like the women who wrote for Mass Observation during the war.[11] But Norah's entries – written in tiny squares that allow for no more than twenty words a day – are more akin to almanacs and pocketbooks than to the discursive, introspective diaries that find their way to publication.[12] Laconic and telegraphic, they have little in the way of plot, dramatic tension, character development or self-reflection. Her use of parataxis, the juxtaposition of unrelated daily events, gives the ordinary and extraordinary an equal value within any given daily window. The personal pronoun, the 'I', is almost entirely absent. Full sentences too. Norah relies on phrases composed of verb/object pairings ('wrote to Danny'), with an occasional adjective thrown in ('beautiful letter from my love'). Her style is so terse as to seem almost coded, her disjointed, staccato sentences hard to decipher without insider knowledge.

'There's nothing in them, no detail, no context', my then-partner Mark had insisted that first Christmas after Norah's death. 'The way she combines personal and national events can be quaint and funny. But most of it is very mundane'. He shook his head. 'You're going to make a right fool of yourself if you start trying to write history from these. What exactly would you talk about? Who Norah sat with on the school bus in 1939?'

'But that's the point', I had retorted. 'The world is awash with historical accounts of the lives of well-heeled men and women. These are ordinary diaries, the kind kept by people who rarely find themselves in history books. That's their charm. I just need to find a way of letting them speak, that's all'.

That's all. I sounded so confident, more than I really felt. Historians have long been wary of the diary as a reliable source. And pocket diaries like these...[13] I knew as I argued that I had delayed reading Norah's diaries precisely because I feared that they would turn out to be lacking: too trivial, too tweet-like, too terse.

Such dismissals, made with even greater certainty, have long been the fare of women's historians. When women at a History Workshop event at Ruskin College, Oxford, in 1969 declared that they planned to embark on a new brand-new venture, researching the histories of women as workers, wives and mothers, their suggestion was met by 'a gust of masculine laughter'.[14] What had women ever done, except keep houses and have children? And how did these timeless and commonplace activities warrant a history?

When Laurel Thatcher Ulrich was reading the diaries of New England midwife Martha Ballard in the midst of the first wave of women's history writing in the 1980s, a fellow historian expressed his impatient wish that she should get back to some 'real' history and stop wasting her time and talents on this little women's stuff. Even a feminist scholar, committed to recovering women's lives, had dismissed Ballard's diaries as unimportant and uninteresting, filled with mundane entries about domestic chores and routines, insufficiently 'epic' to warrant attention. Philippe Lejeune, scholar of girls' diaries, found the same: 'When I talk about my research, I can see that people pity me'.[15]

'What you notice first [...] is all that it lacks', Jennifer Sinor writes of the diary of her great-great-great-aunt, Annie Ray, a homesteader on the late nineteenth-century Dakota Plains. Written 'in the days rather than of the days', Annie's short, fragmented entries, composed in the pages of a ledger, are dull, repetitious and bare. They take their shape from her everyday tasks and routines: setting and hoeing beans, baking bread and churning butter, making and mending clothes, the time spent waiting for her unfaithful husband and the baby she failed to conceive. Writing like Annie's 'everyday' entries – the closest we can get to daily life – is rarely preserved in an official archive. Like shopping lists and other daily scraps, such 'ordinary writing' is destined instead for a garden bonfire or house-clearance skip.[16]

Yet as Ulrich makes clear in her Pulitzer Prize-winning book, *A Midwife's Tale*, diaries like Martha's, like Annie's, like Norah's, while sparse and disjointed, are 'unparalleled documents', revealing whole worlds, often female and familial, so frequently absent from the historical record. 'My effort to recover the significance of Martha Ballard's life was in large part an enterprise in recapturing the historical significance of "trivia"', Ulrich writes. 'For her, living was to be measured in doing. Nothing was trivial'.[17]

And Norah's diaries, when read alongside her letters from Jim? An atypical turn of events – what micro-historians term the 'exceptional normal' – can illuminate big themes and throw light on the culture at large.[18] Like the hidden histories of sex and love contained in Bertrande de Rols' acceptance and then betrayal of the (kinder, more loving? status-conferring?) man who, on his return from war in sixteen-century France, assumed the identity of her husband. Or the insights into frontier life gleaned from the unexpected choices of Eunice Williams and Esther Wheelwright, two girls abducted in childhood during the French and Indian Wars, to remain with their adoptive Native American families rather than return to their Puritan homes of birth.[19]

Norah Hodgkinson's 1938 and 1939 *Letts's School-girl's* diaries, her *Spratt's Game Foods* diaries from 1941 and 1942 and her 1943–1946 *Railway Clerks' Association of Great Britain and Ireland* diaries, and all of those that follow, composed every day over seven decades: they hold a life. Her teenage diaries, seemingly unpromising, are an extraordinary first-hand account of an ordinary girl in wartime. Not simply a transparent 'chronicler of the everyday',[20] Norah writes on a social stage, her daily happenings and personal feelings interacting with wider cultural themes. Alongside the 'exceptional normal' of Jim's lewd letters, what insight might Norah's diaries provide into sex, romance and working-class young womanhood in Britain during the Second World War?

***

But how to bring them to life?

Norah's story doesn't tell itself. Like many private diaries, her writing is not artful or crafted.[21] She wrote without an audience in mind and had no need to explain her abrupt but sundry storylines or develop her barely-drawn characters. Her gaps and silences are inconsequential.

She does not even have to finish her sentences; an ellipsis or em dash refers to a context with which she is wholly familiar and has no need to elaborate for the benefit of readers. Things happen between her entries, not in them.[22] It will not be enough for me, therefore, to respectfully enter her diaries and carefully listen to her words. I have to engage in detective work, attend to her silences, omissions and repetitions, deploy what Elizabeth Hampsten terms 'a special inventive patience' if I am to flesh out her days.[23]

The best way to do this, it seemed to me, was to draw on the insider knowledge that comes with close acquaintance with Norah's life. My mother, Norah's eldest surviving relative and her niece, could remember any person, item or place given even the most cursory of mentions in her early diaries. Long-dead family members, neighbours and friends and their quirks of character: she knew them all. The lay-out of the garden at Moira Dale, the colour of Norah's eiderdown (pea-green), the cardigan (also green) that Norah knitted in 1946: so vivid were they in her mind's eye, she might have seen them just yesterday.

Norah's wider archive, the half-curated 'stuff' that she left behind, sparked further memories, many entangled with family stories that I have heard since childhood. These stories, which came in the main from my mum's conversations with her mother, Helen, Norah's sister, were at times inextricable from their 'explanations' of Norah's life; the way she was, her difference from us. Her wartime love affair with Danny the airman that had knocked her life off course. That she'd shacked up with Eddy because she was 'on the shelf' – and – slightly contradictorily, perhaps? – that she'd been too-easily impressed by a sharp suit, a nice car, a sister in Bordeaux. That despite her unhappiness, snobbery and shame conspired to compel her to stay. And at the root of it all, 'that school', that gave Norah high ideas and led her away.

It is striking how many of the mementoes that Norah kept throughout her life come from her High School years. A sturdy brown box tucked away in her wardrobe held her navy winter beret, the red-and-white ribbon and badge that once adorned her summer boater and, neatly folded, her red and white scarf, hand-knitted in an attractive basket-weave rib with N. I. HODGKINSON embroidered above the tassels:

Fig. 4 LGHS scarf, beret and hat-band. Private papers etc. of Norah Hodgkinson. Photo: A. Twells, 2025.

Packed away in her small blue ottoman, we found her Upper V French exercise book, a second-hand copy of *The Merchant of Venice*, *Practical Pattern-Making for Schools* and its companion *Garment Making*, the latter still covered in brown paper to keep it clean. Alongside them were Oxford School Certificate exam papers, some decorated with ink doodles of film stars, a homemade pattern for a dress, sewn up by Marsie (I assume), and an autograph album with messages from family, teachers and friends.

Norah took custody of other 'orphaned objects'[24] saved from her mother's belongings when Marsie died in 1964: photographs of Hodgkinson and Leadbetter extended family members – grandparents, siblings and cousins – stretching back a century or more; a bundle of letters from Marsie's friends from her service days; wartime mementoes – ration books, identity documents, Birdy's Bevin Boy card.

And more schooldays' 'stuff'. Two letters, typed on thick, quality paper, from Leicestershire County Council Education Committee in 1923 and 1934, inform the parents – 'Sir (Madam)' – that their sons, Norah's brothers, Dennis Vernon Thomas Hodgkinson and Francis Edward Hodgkinson, had been awarded a 'Special Place' at Loughborough Grammar School, which included payment of all tuition fees. Dennis's letter spells out in more detail that although the numbers of free scholarships were restricted for that year, it was recognised that 'he would otherwise be debarred from receiving a Secondary Education through inability to pay fees'. An attached sheet contains a warning that the parents must understand that the child is to remain in school until the end of the school year in which he turns sixteen; and that they will be fined £10 for removing him sooner.

A letter from a Mr Taylor in 1929, the year after Dennis finished his schooling, reveals that the postponement of the Civil Service exam had temporarily scuppered his plans. They – his parents included here, possibly in recognition of sacrifices made – had been 'exceptionally unlucky' in this matter, the schoolmaster wrote, as 'neither the Co-operative Society nor the Railway have any place for your boy'. However, he had contacted the manager of Boots the Chemists, who had an immediate vacancy for a four-year pupilage. 'The position is not for a dispensing chemist, but the manager tells me he would have a chance of working up to an assistant managership, if he did good work'.

Working up. Working up, up and away. This little archive is testimony not only to the place that 'getting into the Grammar' held in Norah's family, but to its later resonance in her life. For my mum and gran, it acquired new meanings, as the source of family differences, between those who left for white-collar jobs and the two siblings who failed to make the grade and stayed in Castle Donington for the rest of their days. Birdy, Norah's middle brother, was happily blue-collar, settling down after the war to work as a coachbuilder at Willowbrook. Helen, my gran, had been on the reserve list for the High School, but never got in, and left the council school at the age of fourteen in April 1927 to start work at Gibson's hosiery manufacturers ('the long-john factory') in the village. (Marsie and then Norah kept her school exemption certificate too. My gran – who lamented for the rest of her life her failure to pass the scholarship – would've binned it many moons ago.)

Indeed – another story – if I had to pinpoint a moment when I became passionate about history, it is this: sitting in our kitchen at

Garden Crescent, listening to my gran's stories of Hill Top and the school assembly in 1924 when 'Gaffer Wes'on' read out the scholarship pass list and her name wasn't on it. This was the same year that she was told she couldn't join the Girl Guides; with Dennis to kit out for the Grammar, Marsie and Pop hadn't a hope of affording the uniform. Even if she had passed the scholarship, it is quite possible that the lack of funds would have meant that she was unable to take her place. I wonder if Marsie breathed a heavy-hearted sigh of relief when her daughter returned from school that day, tearful and dejected but able to start work a few years earlier and contribute to the family coffers. Helen's feeling of having missed out deepened as the years got longer and I remember vividly how she received with pleasure and tears my own school reports and academic successes.

Despite telling stories of my own, I haven't always been fully on board with our family folklore. Tales about Norah's life were fuelled by a whole load of emotion – my grandmother's feeling that Norah 'had it easy', our universal dislike of Eddy and his angry, superior ways, and our wider incomprehension about her chosen life and the vague threat it presented to those left behind. Academic snobbery no doubt played a part here. Academic historians' sense of themselves as professionals has long excluded those designated 'amateurs', family historians prominent among them. Family history has been commonly dismissed as self-indulgent, too subjective, too parochial, concerned with small stories adrift from big historical themes. Memory too is notoriously unreliable; as any historian of the Second World War will confirm, not only do we forget so much, but we 'remember' things that didn't happen at all.[25]

While residual suspicions remain,[26] this hierarchy has been challenged in recent years.[27] We see now how the exploration of family trees, memories and stories enables better understandings of the histories of communities, nations and the world. We see too how public archives are 'assembled',[28] collections given shape by families, estate executors, archivists; by ideas of value that are rarely extended to the lives of men and women like Norah, those who wind up as little more than ever-receding figures in family photographs and sets of official certificates – birth, marriage, death. But how to attend to this absence, to find ways of moving beyond what Ivan Jablonka calls the 'pulse of silence',[29] to write histories of those excluded from 'outside' repositories or whose lives feature in such partial ways?

For so many people, family history is all that we have. As Alison Light writes in her study of her own working-class family, family stories are histories 'from the inside', histories 'from within', passed down to form a kind of 'emotional and psychological inheritance' across the generations. History may be 'the enemy of memory', writes Richard White as he reflects on his mother's stories of her early life in County Kerry between the wars, 'but there are regions of the past that only memory knows'. Women like his mother, like Norah, like my mother, are 'kin-keepers', who cherish, curate and pass on these family inheritances, keeping memories alive.[30]

A Place of Dreams is a kind of inter-generational history. My conversations with my mother have been key to my exploration of Norah's life. As well as drawing on her memories, I choose to put my mother's voice on the page. She can be funny, my mum, her sense of humour on the camp side of banter: playful, ironic, with an eye for the transgressive, the ever-so-slightly-in-bad-taste. It is my view that the history we write needs some of that.

∗∗∗

In *A Place of Dreams*, I seek to take Alison Light's idea of 'history from within' a little further, to tell Norah's story 'from the inside' too.

I knew from the start of this project that I didn't want to accept that the form of Norah's diaries – disjointed, unstoried and unpublishable – meant that I could only write *about* them. Despite its difficulties, Norah's diary-writing voice has a delightful immediacy to it. I wanted to somehow get inside her daily entries, to feel her emotion, to see the world as she saw it, to coax her life from the bare bones of her days.

I felt sure that my training as an academic historian wouldn't stretch to this. Academic history has much to commend it. It is trustworthy, for starters. Our skills of research mean we know our sources: their strengths and shortcomings, how they came into being, what they might mean. We are good at probing beneath the surface, steering clear of simplicity, unsettling false certainties.

But academic history is history from the outside. A hangover from claims to scientific status, detachment and distance are central to what we do. Our points of reference are external. We open our studies with an explanation of how our research builds on what has come before; what Louis Masur calls 'reciting the begats'. We engage with this body of work in a combative manner, our findings conveyed by a 'hidden narrator' – the 'I' erased – in a voice which is solemn, remote, argumentative, expository. Story is drummed out of us. Despite our twentieth-century scepticism about the possibility of scholarly objectivity, we purport neutrality. We have no interest in inspiring empathy, emotion and imagination. Even in cross-over books written for a non-specialist audience, we have little truck with variety in point of view, cadence and tone. 'Tough, tight, filled with fact and source, stripped of personal intonations', academic history is 'scholarship served cold'.[31]

'It's nice to have on the shelf, but you wouldn't actually want to *read* it', my mother said of the book I published the year that Norah died. I had laughed at her cheek. This is a woman who lapped up historical novels and enjoyed regular visits to country houses, museums and history-themed community events, and she couldn't be bothered to read her only child's published book! Yet her comment pithily captures the gap between lay person interested in history and stolid academic tome. While historical novels, period films and television programmes from *A House Through Time* to *Who Do You Think You Are?* are testimony to the popularity of history, the public passion does not extend to academic texts. History 'continues to fascinate', writes Hayden White, 'but its academic variant always fails finally to satisfy our curiosity about the objects of study to which it draws our attention. The dead can be studied scientifically, but science cannot tell us what we desire to know about the dead'.[32]

Despite more than sixty years of 'history from below', we still have so few ordinary peoples' histories, at least those told in their own voices and on their own terms. The diaries of a working-class girl are a rare find. But what if I want to know the girl who wrote Norah's diaries? If I want to weave her words into my writing, capture her voice, write *from within* her diaries as well as *of them*,[33] tell a story she would recognise as her own? Putting Norah's archive through the academic mill, subjecting her daily entries to an unrelenting outside *telling*, cannot get close to her life as she lived it.

I went AWOL for a while and signed up for a course in life writing and then, a full creative writing MA. I wanted to see if the techniques of the novelist – the appeal to the senses, a striking image, a nifty piece of dialogue, an imagined scene, a character for whom we feel a degree of warmth, a voice that doesn't pretend to neutrality – would allow me to get closer to Norah and move beyond an 'outside' rendition of her life. Whether thinking about voice and form, even 'troubling the line between history and imagination', in Saidiya Hartman's words, would make her more knowable, allow me to glean her desires and dreams from her tiny, symmetrical windows, give them a shape, bring them to life.[34] Could I do this and still call it history?

I was confronted from the off with unfamiliar claims about fiction and getting closer to life. I discovered that novelists, those masters of making it up, often believe they are telling not only the truth, but a deeper truth than the facts of history can reveal; that 'story-truth is truer sometimes than happening-truth', in Tim O'Brien's words. 'You don't become a novelist to become a spinner of entertaining lies', said Hilary Mantel in her Reith Lectures of 2017. 'You become a novelist so you can tell the truth'. After following the historical evidence, Mantel explained, she performed another act, putting the past into action, imagining not just what happened but what it felt like, from the inside.[35]

I got lost here for a while, playing around with story-truth vs historical truth, story-fiction vs history-fiction, fact vs imagination, imagination vs invention. I came to see the fault-lines more clearly, the places where literary aesthetics threaten to trump historical accuracy, or the novelist's promise of neatness and closure not available in honest historical investigation. *To historicise* is different from *to dramatise*. Creative writers are generally not interested in the thing that most motivates historians: our curiosity not just about what happened in the past and how people felt about it then, but how close we might get to the truth of it, and with a sense of what else could have happened, how we judge what any of it means.[36]

But when historical sources are so one-sided, as with the 'outsider' accounts from which Hartman tried to wring African American women's lives, or are so sparse and abrupt, like Norah's diary entries... how else might we hear, and tell, their stories?

A Place of Dreams is a history. I place Norah's diaries and Jim's letters alongside archival sources, published diaries, newspaper reports, oral history interviews and more. I build on, am in conversation with and kept in check by the research of many historians – scholars of diaries, of women's lives, the Second World War. But if I am to do anything more than tell the same old story – another 'outside' rendition of a working-class life – I have to try to enter Norah's diary entries, to make 'imaginative incursions' into her days.[37] My sometime-use of memories, dialogue and dramatised scenes does not detract from the truth of history, I argue, but allows me to *write with* Norah, to amplify her voice on the page, to draw out the vitality in her diary fragments and reach 'into the marrow' of her life.[38]

Like the life writer, I make my reading of Norah's diaries and Jim's letters part of the story. Confessing to what I don't know (what can't be known), revealing my doubts, dead ends, my minor jubilations, I try to make visible my workings out. As I cut and arrange her life, I select from her archive (I can't tell it all), make narrative decisions to include some diary extracts or letter segments over others. I can only speak openly of the mysterious process I find this to be, how consciously and unconsciously, a range of factors – the enigma that was Norah, her diary entries about Danny, Jim's dodgy letters, my knowledge of women's history, my role as the mother of teenage girls – come together to shape the story (my story) of her life. As Maria Tamboukou writes, the way historians are 'drawn to certain storylines, topics, characters or themes and not to others' is 'more than pure serendipity'. Something resonates with our life experience, leads us to 'feel it, in a narrative, in the vibration of an archival fragment in our hand'.[39] Showing my means of production in this way seems to be a preferable way of writing: warmer, more *felt*, more human, more honest.

Writing with an honest, authorial 'I' means telling you too about the impact of Norah's diaries on my own life. *A Place of Dreams* explores the meaning of Norah's story, for her and also for me, as a historian and a feminist, a daughter, a great-niece, and a mother of girls. I tell you too how, as my daughters approached adolescence and young womanhood, I placed Norah's wartime experience alongside present-day questions, about sex, desire and danger, modesty and shame.

***

This is not too slight a tale, too obscure a life. We know that the smallest of stories can move us; can pack a mean punch. A story can crack the world open, slow it down long enough for us to get a good look inside, ask questions, lose ourselves briefly, allow us to contemplate emotion, uncertainty and fleeting possibilities.[40]

A young woman's coming of age, her appetite for life amidst unexpected dangers, the insistent presence in all our lives of love and hope and longing, of pain and sorrow, memory, ageing and regret.

3. Norah Hodgkinson, Schoolgirl Diarist

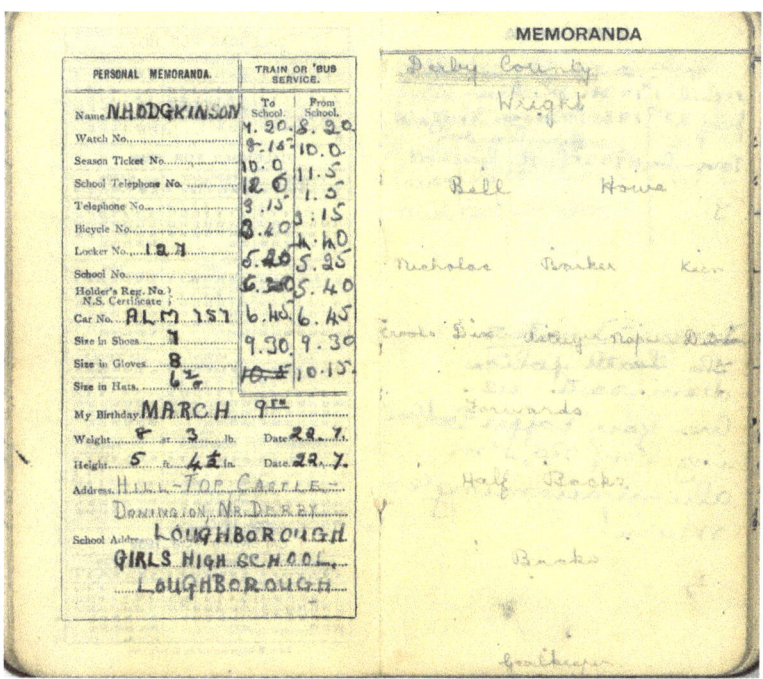

Fig. 5 1938 *Letts's School-girl's Diary*. Private papers of Norah Hodgkinson. Photo: A. Twells, 2025.

Perhaps it was on one of those oft-dull days between Christmas and New Year that Norah picked up her brand-new diary and pencilled in her surname and first initial (*N.Hodgkinson*, the space too small for *Norah Isabel*), her date of birth (*9th March*) and addresses at home (*Hill Top, Castle Donington*) and school (*Loughborough Girls' High School*). She later inked over all but her home address. Marsie and Pop had put in for one of the new council houses that were being built across the village and Norah had every faith that they would be on the move in the coming year. Other details she left blank. Norah had no use for a Watch No., Season Ticket No., Telephone No. or even Bicycle No., although, rather fancifully, she filled in a car registration plate: *ALM 757*. She created two columns for bus times, to and from school. She inserted her sizes for shoes (*7*), gloves (*8*) and hat (*6⅞*), adding her height (*5 feet 4½ ins*) and weight (*8st and 3oz*) a few months later, after she was weighed and measured at school. She doesn't elaborate in 1938, but the following year – 22nd July 1939, when she had shot up to 5 feet 5¾ but was still some way off her adult height of 5 feet 8 in her stockinged feet – she noted proudly that she was *3rd heaviest & 2nd tallest [...] The doctor said I have a 'wonderful physique'*.

***

Norah's first diary sits neatly across my palm and fingers, the rusty-red cover crisp and crinkly to the touch. Inside an oval frame of gently embossed croquet mallets, tennis rackets and hockey sticks, the name 'Charles Letts' is emblazoned in a fancy, looped script, the words 'SCHOOL-GIRL'S DIARY' printed in a plainer font below. At three inches by five, the diary is just small enough to have fitted inside Norah's Christmas stocking, no doubt bulging with clementines and nuts, which hung at the foot of the bed that she shared with her elder sister, Helen. But I imagine it wrapped in thin paper – decorated with holly, perhaps – and lying under the small spruce in the front room.

The schoolgirl's and schoolboy's diaries had been part of a new venture by Charles Letts, grandson of John, the London stationer who had printed his first diary in 1812. They marked the launch of the new special interest range that from the 1870s saw a change in the fortunes of the firm. Letts was soon catering for all manner of hobbies and livelihoods, with diaries for motorists, gardeners, ramblers, wireless amateurs, boy-scouts, girl-guides, textile workers, poultry keepers, pigeon fanciers and more, totalling four hundred overall. A new interwar diary craze saw sales rise again from just under a quarter of a million in 1900 to three million in the mid-1930s. Encouraged by radio broadcasts and popular newspapers, newly published anthologies of

British diarists, biographies of John Evelyn and Samuel Pepys and the launch of the new Mass Observation project in 1937, these years saw an unprecedented interest in the 'ordinary life'.[1]

Norah's 1938 diary, *bound in cloth* and selling for one shilling, is the cheapest on offer. Marsie and Pop, on his postman's wage, were unable to stretch to the sturdier, more elegant, *fine quality leather* version (3/-) with a pencil, pockets, world maps and gilt edges. While their eldest son, Dennis, had moved away for a white-collar job, their four other children still lived at home. Helen and Birdy, elder daughter and middle son, were poorly paid in local factories. Frank and Norah were both at grammar school and seemingly in endless need of items of uniform, sports equipment, books and pens.

An opening page reveals the results of a competition whereby Letts had canvassed schoolgirls on ways in which the diary might be improved. Replies had come in from all over the globe, including Australia, South Africa and Iraq. The winner, Joan Wisdom of north London, was promised a leather-bound set of Rudyard Kipling's novels as her prize.

After that, fifty-seven printed pages are stuffed to the gills with facts and lists. Compiled by Jersey school-master and French language teacher Marc Ceppi, they open with Daily Wants, listing term dates, Bank Holidays, postage rates, sizes of sports grounds, the temperature at which water boils, the costs of various licenses (driving, dog). A lengthy section on Careers for Women details jobs in the Civil Service, nursing, teaching, domestic science, librarianship, as well as some less predictable suggestions: positions in horticulture, engineering, and as chemists. Examinations come next, including the Oxford School Certificate that Norah will pass in 1941, followed by sovereigns of England, British Prime Ministers from 1721, the lighting-up table, world time, Latin verbs (seven pages of them), French verbs (eight pages), German strong verbs, the metric system, tables of weights and measures. The list of Books to Read – on natural history, gardening and nature study, photography, crafts, travel and more – are billed as 'supplements to the classics which you will hear in school and mainly intended as helps to various hobbies and interests'. Five pages on recent sporting triumphs – the winners of the boat race, champions in skating, cricket, lawn tennis, rugby, athletics, golf and swimming – are rounded off by two more printed lists: the Seven Wonders of the Ancient World and Some Wonders of the Modern World.

***

It is heavy-going, all this *matter*. Norah squeezes in her own term dates, adds *Oxford* to the boat race winners, and updates the list of Prime Ministers to include *Neville Chamberlain* (*1937*). On the line above, next to the name of Stanley Baldwin, the outgoing PM, we start to see her. She writes a single, unexpected, bracketed word: (*Fool*).

The inspiration for this minor piece of political commentary is surely Tom Hodgkinson, Norah's father. A ferocious socialist, his regular political altercations with local grandees were already becoming the stuff of family legend. Major Dalby, the Vicar of Diseworth and Gillies Shields, formerly agent to Lord Donington and now the owner of Donington Hall: all would wait for him on his postal round, eager to engage in political debate. Other family stories see him dashing down High Street at election time, ripping 'Vote Conservative' banners from the old oaks in Dalby's field; or, wild with anger when Labour formed the National Government in 1931, tearing the poster of Prime Minister 'Ramsay Mac' from their cottage wall. 'You turncoat! You blasted turncoat!' he roared, shoving a poker through MacDonald's eye, trampling the picture on the ground before screwing it up and throwing it on the fire.

Norah would have been six at the time. By that first-diary Christmas of 1937, she knew all about Stanley Baldwin (*Fool*).

We see more of Norah under the headings at the back of the diary, where she lists her Pocket Money (*1½d*, then *3d* after her fourteenth birthday, from *Mam*), Timetable, Presents, Exam Results and Marks, Letters (Received and Sent) and Books Read, each with a short 'review'. Among her early reading in 1938 was a memoir of Lloyd George, most likely ordered by her father as part of his *Daily Herald* subscription. She failed to finish it, moving on to *Elinor in the V* by Winifred Darch (*very good*) and Charles Dickens, *A Tale of Two Cities* (*Very, very good*). For the best read of the year, it was a toss-up between *Goodbye Mr Chips* (*Excellent*) by James Hilton and J. B. Priestley's *They Walk in the City* (*Lovely*). The worst, by far, was Rudyard Kipling's historical fantasy, *Rewards and Fairies* (*No good*).

Under Films Seen, Norah records her thirteen trips to the village picture house and her sole outing to Derby's new Coliseum cinema. *Dodging the Dole* was *absolutely awful*, she wrote, while *Maytime* with Jeanette Macdonald and Nelson Eddie was *excellent*. Disney's romanticised adaptation of the Grimms' *Snow White* came tops: *absolutely the best ever*. At the end of her diary, after pages of Match Results – tennis, swimming, hockey (the words 'or lacrosse' struck through) and netball, where Norah played a capable Goal Defence – followed by Birthdays, Addresses and Engagements, Norah stuck a cut-out photograph of the French actress Simone Simon, whom she had seen when *Girls' Dormitory (Very G)* was showing in the village.

If the list of Prime Ministers provides a small and unexpected insight, and the end-matter shows us more of Norah, it is the diary's blank Memoranda pages that give her free reign. Here, she remedies Letts's neglect of her twin sporting loves, football and motor-racing. She prints the words DERBY COUNTY atop a faint pencil pyramid of footballers' names:

Wright

Bell   Howe

Nicholas   Barker   Keen

Crooks   Nix   Astley   Napier   Duncan

Overleaf, after a half-hearted column for Girls in our School who Left and a couple of Tongue-twisters ('The Leath police dismisseth us' and 'Are you copper-bottoming 'em?' 'No I'm aluminiuming 'em, mum!'), she pencils in Derby's results over the 1937 festive period, Stoke City's Christmas fixtures and devotes a full page to Races at Donington Park.

Next comes her list of 'crazes', the local lads and sporting heroes in whom she'd had a romantic interest that year. We'll come back to them.

***

One of the pleasures of Norah's 1938 diary is the way in which her lists and insertions, her marginalia and crossings out, chafe cheekily against Letts' attempts to steer her interests. While we have access to vast amounts of material *about* children's lives in the past, historical sources that present a child's-eye view of the world are so much harder to find.[2] The information pages might be striking for their confidence about what a teenage schoolgirl needed to know, but we have no idea whether Letts's readers read them or skipped them, or whether the Kipling box-set would have been Joan Wisdom's choice of prize. So to find a girl who lets us know that in her view Stanley Baldwin was a (*Fool*) is... unusual, to say the least.

More than that, Norah's commentary offers little glimpses into a life that isn't quite contained by Letts's template for grammar school girlhood. The *School-girl's Diary* was aimed at that very small number of girls – just 12.2% of Norah's age group, girls born between 1910 and 1929 – who stayed on at school beyond the age of fourteen.[3] These were mainly the daughters of the middle class, girls who had been weaned on *The Water Babies* and raised on the classics, who had the means to take up photography as a hobby and might one day visit a wonder of the world. Girls whose continued education was not reliant on the free pass that came with success in the scholarship exam and for whom biding their time at the local council school until their fourteenth birthday and the commencement of blue-collar work was never a consideration.

While this business of missing out and having to make do with what life doles out to you could be painful, success – getting into the Grammar – could come at a price too. So many working-class girls like Norah did not stay the course. It wasn't just that their families, however proud and hopeful, were unable to sustain the cost of the uniform, books and various extra-curriculars, or simply needed them to bring in a wage if there were younger mouths to feed. For many, their location at what Richard Hoggart has called 'the friction point of two cultures' was too bewildering; the personal transformation required at such a school too difficult, like being a saltwater fish plunged into a freshwater pool. In Pierre Bourdieu's evocative phrase, grammar school involved a *habitus clivé*, a rift within oneself. Valerie Avery, the schoolgirl author of an astonishing wartime autobiography, *London Morning*, later described her movement away from her working-class roots – both physically, due to bombings, and educationally, as a grammar school girl – as heralding 'a state of disintegration of me as a person'. Just as violently, historian Rob Colls felt he was 'being trained to purge himself of who he was and where he came from'. It was 'a form of Inquisition', writes Ken Worpole;

the working-class pupil 'could either recant and embrace a new faith – or be broken on the wheel'.⁴

The breezy tone of Norah's diaries, the lack of evidence of any culture clash at school, intrigues me, and I realise this is my obsession, not hers. Ever since I read David Storey's *Saville,* on the English Literature A-level syllabus in 1982, about a boy adrift from his Yorkshire mining family after getting into a grammar school and his wider sense of never fitting in, I've been intrigued by this double estrangement: from one's new classmates by virtue of background and, through education, from family and community at home.⁵ (Not that Storey prepared me. At Sussex University in the '80s, I was utterly stunned, for the full three years. More than the specifics – the private schools, second homes and pony club pasts, the bonding over backpacking in Peru – it was the oblivious, effortless coming-from-money comfort. The blasé ease: kids totally at home on what for them were well-trodden paths, successful lives set out and ready to drop into, whenever they chose.)

But if the *Letts's School-girl's Diary* worked as a kind of shoehorn into an elite education – this is what is valued, it told its readers, this is what you will need to know to succeed – there is no suggestion that Norah felt anything other than at home there. Her grammar school brothers had paved her way, no doubt. Her parents' unshakable belief that no badge of inferiority should be attached to their social origins and that a good education was their children's natural right will surely have rubbed off. Perhaps the Letts's School-girl's Diaries of 1938 and 1939 helped ease Norah into her grammar school life, shaping her schoolgirl self, bringing her into being. With a foot in both worlds, she makes her confident little interjections, supplementing the long list of sporting triumphs, correcting the heading for Hockey or Lacrosse, the latter not played at her school. She reads without discrimination, with no special reverence afforded to 'highbrow' culture or the classics. Charles Dickens is *very, very good,* of course he is, but her favoured authors of middle-brow fiction and social commentary novels deserved a mention too.

Norah and her siblings remained proud of their school attendance throughout their lives. I remember visits when my uncle Dennis made his annual pilgrimage from his Hertfordshire home. Dennis was like a centripetal force, a jovial giant of a man, warm and playful, who drew us all in as he strode round his old school grounds with his impossibly long legs, reminiscing loudly about this teacher and that, this classroom and the other. 'Norah, Norah, do you remember..? Norah, Norah, whatever happened to..?' Norah would quietly admire the cloister windows and attractive red brick of the girls' school next door, marvelling at the new buildings, remembering where she had sat in the grassy central quad, talking and laughing with her friends.

We might see diaries as a kind of 'template for personal change', a technology for discipline and self-fashioning.[6] Norah was already well aware, in 1938, that she was 'on the up'. She wouldn't find herself in Gibson's factory making 'long-johns', like her sister. Nor would she spend her adult life in a poky, damp house overflowing with children, as her mother had done.[7] She would leave school to work in an office and – fingers crossed – find herself a handsome, affable, white-collar husband. They would enjoy holidays in neat, bright guest houses at Bournemouth and Torquay, day-trips out in the car – a Morris Eight, maybe – and most important of all, a new house with a nice kitchen and all mod cons.

For Norah, the future was looking grand.

Or would be, if that Hitler fella kept out of the way.

***

Might we drop in on Norah in mid-December 1938, at the end of her first year of diary-keeping, when she is bed-ridden and enjoying a second week off school after her clumsy middle brother Birdy has tipped the scalding contents of a pan over her left foot? I imagine her snuggling down under her pea-green satin eiderdown scattered with newspapers as she resists parental pressure to exercise, her skin now scabby and stiff rather than blistery and red raw. She wishes they'd all clear off and leave her alone. She'll sort her foot, soon enough. But before then, she has sports reports to devour on the wonders of Stoke City's star striker, Frankie Soo. His passing skills are stupendous, the papers say. And with his gentle features and those dark eyes with a hint of the Orient, he really is a beauty.[8] *Crazy over him.*

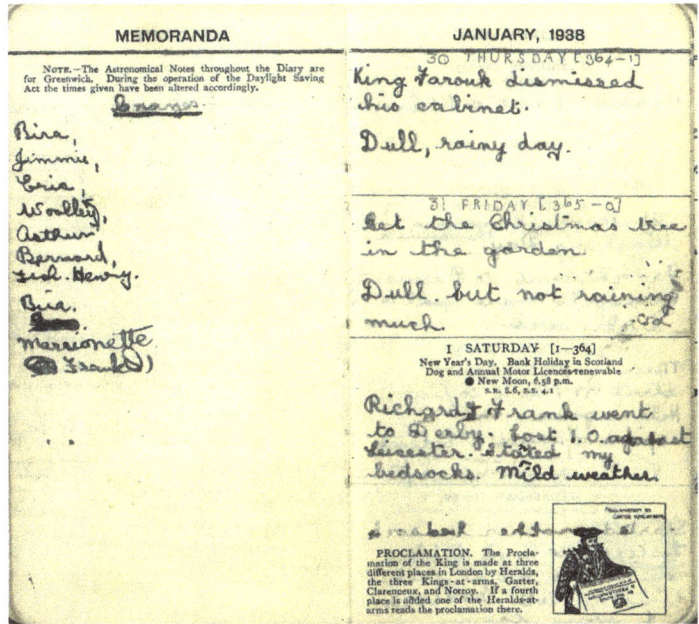

Fig. 6 Norah's 'crazes', 1938 Diary. Private papers of Norah Hodgkinson. Photo: A. Twells, 2025.

1938 had been quite the year for crazes. Bira was first. He had been Norah's best heartthrob since 1935, the year he shot to fame driving a Riley Imp at Brooklands and raced his first Grand Prix at Donington Park. Beautiful Bira, slender and broad-shouldered, with glossy black hair and golden skin. He cut a dashing figure in the pitstop and the paddock, his silk overalls dyed the same pale blue and yellow of his cars. (Norah wouldn't know that he was inspired in this choice by the evening dress of a young female acquaintance, or that these would soon become the national racing colours of his native Siam.) 'Bira blue': Norah had wanted it for a cotton frock Marsie made that summer but had to content herself with duck-egg, the closest they could find on Derby market. Still nice, though.

Does Norah thumb through her diary to find her entries about Bira's visit that glorious spring? If she does, she will see that she had sunned herself in Webb's orchard, browsing copies of *Picturegoer* and sketching her favourite film stars. That's when she had buried Dum-Dum (her cat?) in the garden, garlanding his grave with forget-me-nots. She and Audrey had gone bluebelling over the fields, usually coming home laden with common-or-garden ladysmocks, mayblobs and cowslips instead. Some nights they skipped until dark.

Bira had won the Crystal Palace Trophy Race at the start of April and just days later, here he was, at Donington Park. *Cars practising on the track all day,* Norah wrote. She loved the whirring backdrop of the distant engines, the noise building as the cars took the Melbourne hairpin, swarming round the bend towards Coppice Corner before shooting down Starkey's Straight. She could still hear it here, in the new house, but nothing like at Hill Top, the little hamlet on the south-westerly edge of the village where their cottage adjoining the Nag's Head pub had been just a short walk from the main racetrack gates.

They all loved the races. The opening of the Park had brought some life to the village. Before the middle of the nineteenth century, Castle Donington had been a thriving market town, making the most of its position on the southern escarpment of the Trent, near to the confluence with the Soar and the Derwent, and on two major roads: Derby to Leicester and Nottingham to Birmingham, the latter of which ran straight past the Hodgkinsons' gable end. But by the time Tom and Milly had moved to Hill Top in 1911, the collapse of the lace trade and reorganisation of hosiery into factories in nearby towns had seen Donington reduced to no more than a village.[9] The racetrack felt like it was part of a new beginning, a resurgent entry into the modern world.

Norah's sister Helen was thrilled by it. She was always over there. This time, for the British Empire Trophy handicap race in April 1938, she had walked Norah up to the high sloping pastures at Isley Walton to get a better vantage of the cars whizzing round the track as they practiced for the race the following day. Norah thought that might be it, the sum total of her Park adventures that year, but then Marsie had miraculously relented and promised to let her go with her older sister in pursuit of a famous 'gap ticket' to watch the big race itself. *Went to bed early. Felt excited,* Norah wrote.

Crossing the fields towards Donington Hall, she and Helen kept the walled edge of the track close by to their left until they were safely out of sight. Seeking toe-holes in the red brick, scrambling carefully so as not to scuff their shoes or snag their frocks, they pushed themselves up like gymnasts on a beam. Hearts thudding, catching their breath and scanning the scene, they swung their legs over the top before dropping cleanly into the grounds like burglars in the night, brushing their skirts and making for the crowd. On this occasion they were almost thwarted by a vigilant official, but Helen gave him some chat and they slipped otherwise unnoticed into the event. *9th April: Went to Park with Helen. Man stopped us. Saw Bira and got his autograph. Saw his wife. Dodson won, Bira second. Close, dullish.*

Afterwards, when Bira had finished as runner-up and they were pushing and shoving in the crush, Norah held out her brand new autograph book, a present from Helen. 'B. Bira', he signed himself, on the first page:

Fig. 7 Bira's autograph. Private papers of Norah Hodgkinson. Photo: A.Twells, 2025.

It was here that Norah's lifelong love of motor-racing was born. My mum and I found newspaper cuttings about Formula One champions inside her kitchen cupboards in the days after she died.

The following day, after a late start due to Daylight Saving, Norah *saw Bira and his wife going home*. How utterly perfect to be Ceril Heycock, the young Englishwoman whom Bira had met at Art School in London. Just an ordinary girl and now Princess Ceril, Mrs Birabongse Bhanudej Bhanubandh of Siam. (After a late-in-the-day spot of Googling, I discover that the number plate at the front of Norah's diary – ALM

757 – belonged to a Park Ward Rolls Royce owned by Bira's cousin and sponsor, Prince Chula. Might this be the car that took him and his princess-wife past Norah's house and home from Donington Park?).[10]

Bira first. And next? Jimmie, surely. She'd been sweet on him all year. Still was, if truth be told. They had played cricket together that summer with a crowd of neighbourhood lads, inspired by the arrival in Derbyshire of the Australians, here to defend the Ashes. Mr Robinson, one of the dads, who made cricket bats for Gunn and Moore in Nottingham, would often come out and umpire. *Lovely but Jimmie can't play*, Norah wrote on 20th May. He was hopeless! She was a much better batswoman. It didn't put her off him though. A few weeks later, he had come with Marsie to see her gym display at school. They weren't very good and the audience had laughed, the rude beggars. But Jimmie had been so sweet. *Jimmie sat with us and made me want to kiss him. Love him. Rainy, cold.*

***

'She played with us lads all the time', John Glenn recalls as we sit in his front room one sultry August afternoon. 'Cricket mainly. She was a lovely girl, nice natured, even tempered, gamey'. John adds 'played cricket' to the map he is drawing of Hill Top, the outline of the field directly opposite the opening to Diseworth Road, in his and Norah's day a pretty rural lane that ran round the southerly edge of the village. On the corner, two red-brick cottages adjoined the Nag's Head. The Hodgkinsons' was the first of these, flush with the main road, the Glenns next door sharing an entry with the pub. Beyond the yard and drying area out the back was the orchard, allotments ('the garden'), farmyard and slaughterhouse where the kids spent so much time. ('That's where we used to congregate', John says. 'It does seem a bit odd, looking back'. He enjoys my rendition of a family story that the abbatoir is where my gran and grandad did their courting. 'Where's Helen?' someone would ask, to be answered by Marsie: 'She'll be up at that slaughter house, hanging around Joe Twells.')

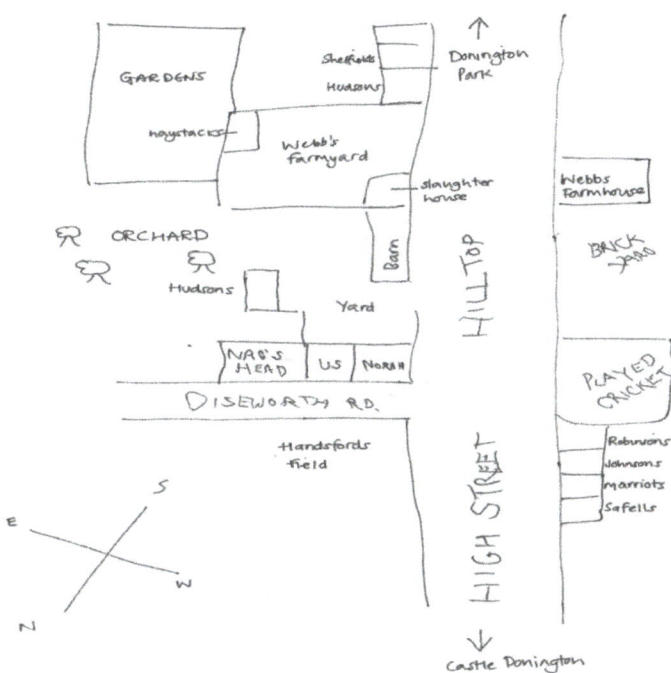

Fig. 8 Map of Hill Top, John Glenn and Alison Twells, 2014.

Fig. 9 The Nag's Head, Hill Top, Castle Donington. The Hodgkinsons' cottage stood to the right of the pub. Photo: A.Twells, 2025.

Surprisingly, no photograph seems to exist of the pre-war Nag's Head, now a revamped gastro-pub, white-washed and bedecked with hanging baskets throughout the summer. The cottages, which once adjoined the pub, are long demolished, their footprint and shared backyard now arranged with wooden benches and umbrellas. A few faded snaps in Norah's collection show children playing as geese peck at the ground and washing blows in the breeze. On one, Pop can be seen through the window, concentrating hard as he peels spuds or washes pots. Another shows a clutch of Hill Top kids clustering in and around a car.

'That's Mr Mitson's sports car!' John says, delighted. The well-to-do son-in-law of the publican ('his daughter married up'), he used to visit from somewhere near Coventry and take the local kids for a spin. I focus on Norah, bob-haired and smiling broadly, looking younger than her twelve years, sitting in the back behind a young driver.

'That's me!' John exclaims, pointing to a tall, slender lad standing beside the driver's door. Thirteen years old, he is well kitted-out in his boots, knee-length socks, shorts, jacket, waistcoat and cap. The sun picks out his cheekbones and his gentle dark eyes smile straight at the camera. In the background is his little dog, name forgotten but much loved and last stroked over seventy years ago.

Fig. 10 Norah, John and friends, Hill Top, c. 1937. Private papers of Norah Hodgkinson.

The remaining Hill Top photos in Norah's collection were taken on Webb's farm during the Hodgkinson family's last days there in July 1938. On one snap, Frank, Marsie, Norah, Helen, Pop and Birdy line up in front of a farmyard gate; only eldest son Dennis is missing. Another sees Helen, my gran, standing slightly behind Norah, who straddles a piece of farm equipment. ('The old Bamford mower', John says fondly.) Looking straight at the camera, Norah is smiling, playful, confident. I note her long, strong, suntanned legs, the calves that give them all – my mum, gran, Norah and now, it seems, my ten-year-old daughter Ruby – that extra inch of height over me.

'I think Webbie took these', I say. 'They were his gift to the family, after 27 years of neighbourliness. And rent'.

John laughs. 'They were damp, flea-ridden holes, those cottages', he says. 'But I do remember it as a very happy time'.

'Do you think you're romanticising?' I ask. I'm interested because Norah and her siblings had similar reflections on their 'idyllic' childhood.

'Yes', he concedes, 'I may be. We were dirt poor. My grandmother couldn't afford to kit me out for the grammar school. She didn't have two ha'pennies for a penny and was always worrying about how to make ends meet'.

'And the narrow morality', I add. He's already told me about his unmarried mother.

'Yes, that as well. But there was something in the innocence, the neighbourliness, the simplicity. It was a healthy outdoorsy life. It was good'.[11]

And it's all here, in Norah's 1938 diary. Norah fetching eggs from the farm, her early morning mushrooming and blackberrying in the late afternoon. Norah knitting bed socks, a blue jumper and a vest for Marsie. And then the cricket, the sledging, the lounging in the orchard reading her books and magazines. And Jimmie.

One Christmas Day, not so very long ago, sometime between the pudding and the game of 'Sorry' with my young daughters in the front room, Norah told me about Webb's orchard, the garden up the lane and the interior of the Hill Top cottage: the front sitting room and back kitchen, the rag rugs, the position of the dresser and the piano. The sitting room wallpaper was cream, patterned with delicate grey-black diamonds.

Fig. 11 The Hodgkinson family, Webb's farm, Hill Top, 1938. Private papers of Norah Hodgkinson.

Fig. 12 Helen and Norah, Webb's farm, Hill Top, 1938. Private papers of Norah Hodgkinson.

The floor was uneven, the memory of it prompted by her recollection of a china tea set, received with pride and pleasure for her fifth Christmas, and which, placed on a tray balanced on a wooden chair, smashed to smithereens when one leg wobbled a devastating half-inch above the floor.

It pains me now that I didn't ask for more detail: the flashes of colour, the extent of Marsie's untidiness, whether there was much drama from the pub, the position of the poster of Lord Kitchener, concealing the damp patch on Norah and Helen's bedroom wall and the precariousness of the loose window frame, permanently tied to the frame of their shared bed, to stop it falling out into the street below.

***

Norah thought back to that summer's day in June 1938, when she and her family had left Hill Top forever; that had been a day of heartbreak. She remembered then another brief crush: Arthur, the driver of the van that took their worldly goods all the way across the village on that blustery Saturday morning to a brand-new council house on Moira Dale. *25th June: Left our old house in Co-op [van]. I like Arthur the Remover. Called me 'sweetheart'. Mrs Robinson and Mrs Bostock gave us flowers. Emma cried. Didn't want to leave them & Jimmie. Sunny, rainy, windy.* ('They had a van?' my mum says, incredulous. 'When we moved to Garden Crescent in 1951, we went by coal lorry, all our possessions piled high for the world to see'.)

Did Norah feel her heart grow heavy as she read her diary entries for the next few days and weeks? She missed Jimmie, terribly.

> *1st July: Revised French. Practised the Gym. Felt terribly lonely. Had a return for science but didn't sign it. Rainy cold.*
>
> *2nd: Got up rather late. Worked a lot. Should have gone to the tennis tournament but didn't. Emma came to see us. Made me feel homesick. Bought some nasturtiums. New people went in our house. Sunny.*
>
> *3rd: Got up late. Helen had her bath at dinner-time. Went to Diseworth through D. Lane. Made me feel terribly homesick. Wanted Jimmie. Sunny.*

***

But the new house was just grand. 18 Moira Dale: such a posh address! It's hard to believe it now, but in 1938 to live in a council house was a respectable aspiration. Although rents were high and many tenants could scarcely afford the payments, it was a step up in the world for a working-class family. The interiors of the three- or four-bedroomed houses varied, but included a front room, a good-sized kitchen with a pantry and a brick copper in the corner, a bathroom and a toilet. A privet hedge was set at the front and an apple tree planted in the generous garden at the back.[12]

Norah noted in her diary that when the architect came to look round the houses in early 1939, he was impressed. I'll bet he was. The Hodgkinsons were model tenants. Houses on these new 'garden estates' represented a movement not only to clear slums, but to uplift the poor. The tenancy agreement came with strict rules about housework, maintenance, children's behaviour and the keeping of pets. I haven't been able to find an example for Moira Dale, but a letter from the Corporation of Bristol Housing Estates on 15th June 1936, sent to a prospective new tenant making an offer of a new house on Bristol's Knowle West Estate – where, coincidentally, Marsie's younger brother Frank and his new wife Mary were soon to move – reveals the reforming intentions:

> The Housing Committee realise that you have been living under very undesirable conditions, and that in worn out houses it is very difficult to get rid of vermin. But there will be no excuse in your new house. Do not buy secondhand furniture, bedding or pictures unless you are quite sure that the articles are free from vermin. Insects do not like soap and hot water, and they also dislike dusters and polish. So if in the new house you keep your windows open, and keep your bodies and clothing, floors and stairs, furniture and bedding clean; use the duster frequently on all skirting and ledges, you are not likely to be troubled again with vermin. This sounds a lot, but life isn't going to be all work for the housewife. The new house will be easy to keep clean and it will be well worth looking after.[13]

Maybe it is the word 'corporation', or maybe it is just the tone, but I imagine this conveyed over the wireless as the new residents cross the threshold, in the Queen's English of the pre-war BBC.

What will the architect have seen? My mum tells me that it was a proper cottage garden at the front of number 18. The boys – Richard, Frank and Helen's husband-to-be, Joe Twells – had ripped out the privet and replaced it with lilac trees, Marsie's favourite. There was a snowball bush by the gate and flowerbeds set with honesty, stocks, yellow daisies, bought as gifts by Hill Top friends, running either side of the slabbed path up past the lawn to the front door.

'You went in the front door...'

My mum is set on walking me through the house, but I stop her, keen to know the colour of the front door. We laugh. Council house front doors interest us more than they should. For the first fourteen years of my life, we lived with my grandparents in a post-war Nye Bevan beauty of a house on a big corner plot round the corner on Garden Crescent. When the men from the council arrived every few years to re-paint the front door, giving the tenant a choice from one shade each of blue, red, yellow or green, my gran would choose red (for Labour!) and then, in her own small protest at this excess of local authority uniformity, would get her paint-brush out the following week.

'Did she ever just ask them not to paint it?' I ask.

'Oh yes, but they had to. They knew what she'd do. Nobody batted an eyelid when she got that olive green tin out'.

It turns out that the front door at Moira Dale was plain brown wood. On entering, you were greeted by the aspidistra at the foot of the stairs on the right. Above the door to the living room on the left were some stag's antlers that Pop had picked up in Donington Park on his postal round and which the owners had mounted for him:

Fig. 13 Pop's antlers, courtesy of Castle Donington Museum. Photo: A. Twells, 2025.

The front room was a living room and not a parlour. The kitchen wasn't big enough to be a 'living kitchen', but even if it had been, Marsie would not have had a perfectly good room with a big window that got the morning sun and not enjoyed it daily.[14] As you walked in, the gramophone, and later the telly, stood against the front wall. Then, beneath the window, covered with a crocheted throw, was a dark horsehair sofa, replaced in the 1950s by a pink moquette. At the far end, in an alcove, there was a built-in cupboard where Marsie kept the darning wool, the needle box and Sunday evening games: Sorry, draughts and a pack of cards. On the shelves above was her wedding-present Crown Derby and china tea set with the delicate green pattern. On the other side, beyond the black range, a second alcove housed a tall bookcase holding encyclopaedias, book prizes from school and Sunday school and Marsie's Bible. In front of the range were two chairs, the wooden one Pop's, inherited by Birdy when his father died in 1945, and Marsie's, upholstered and without arms (more comfortable for darning and breast-feeding).

'It does sound a bit cluttered', I say, remembering that in my great-grandmother's scheme of things, untidiness, *stuff* and even a bit of dust were not at odds with homeliness.

'And I'm far from finished yet', my mum says. On the wall that ran from the alcove to the kitchen door stood Marsie's piano, above which hung a wall clock and two or three prints of Derbyshire countryside scenes. And then there was the oak sideboard with glass knobs. The wireless sat on the top of it, and arranged underneath, from the late 1940s and 1950s, Norah's multi-coloured collection of high-heeled shoes, a big attraction for her young niece. 'And there was a dining table and chairs in the middle of the room! We all used to sit there to watch the telly'. She pauses. 'I honestly don't know how we fitted in. It was certainly cosy'.

Upstairs, all four bedrooms were in use. Marsie and Pop took the big back room while the boys shared a double bed in the front and the girls had a small room each. Helen, biding her time until her marriage, overlooked the back garden. Norah's box room, bright and sun-drenched all morning, the small-paned window looking out onto the front garden, is the only one I can describe: the single bed covered with the satin eiderdown; the small oak dressing table, with a wooden jewellery box and little pot pourri dish, a clothes brush, hair brush and comb; and an over-the-stairs cupboard that held her clothes and where, I guess, she stashed Jim's and Danny's letters throughout the war.

Into the kitchen, there was a Belfast sink, a long pantry with a meat-safe at the end, a crowd of coats on the wall near to the stair-hole door, a brick copper in the corner and next to it, the door to the much-prized bathroom. A small passage led out past the lavatory and the coal house, into the back garden. My mum remembers the rambler rose, Frank's peach tree, and beyond a small scrappy lawn, vegetable beds and raspberry canes, blackcurrant and gooseberry bushes, plum trees, another lilac, the hen house and a compost heap to the left of the bottom gate. No more tripping up the lane to the allotment for some veg or flowers or hanging out washing in a dusty shared yard, the garden was Marsie's pride and joy.

Norah's next-door neighbour, Irene Marsh, seven years old when her family moved into number 16 that same summer, remembers admiring Marsie's washing from her bedroom window. 'She used to hang it up in order of size', she tells me as we sit in the living room of her Derby bungalow. 'I used to watch her from our upstairs, putting things back in the basket, picking out the right one'. She pegged the shirts with the collars bent taut over the line to hold their shape, towels to create two even loops. 'My mum just used to sling ours over the line, all higgledy-piggledy', she tells me. 'But Mrs Hodgkinson's: it was like a work of art'.

Some summer evenings, the families in the terraced row – the Robeys at number 14, the Peggs, the Hodgkinsons and then more Peggs at number 20 – would sit out on wooden kitchen chairs and planks lined up along the back path that linked the houses. The grown-ups in their pinnies and shirtsleeves dished out boiled new potatoes tossed in butter with fresh peas and mint sauce. Chatting and laughing, they looked out over the gardens until the sun set over Bucknall's orchard beyond.[15]

Fig. 14 (left) Tom and Milly in the front garden at Moira Dale, and Fig. 15 (right) Norah in the back garden, both c. 1940. Private papers of Norah Hodgkinson.

***

A beautiful brand-new council house: they had really gone up in the world. And lovely Arthur had brought them here. Norah would add his name to her list. But before him: she had nearly forgotten Cousin Eric who visited in early May, Uncle Will driving them all – Marsie and Pop, Norah and Eric – to Southwell Minster and Newstead Abbey, Lord Byron's former home. *Adore Eric.* And then there was Woolley, a friend of her brother Frank. His smiles from the school bus had added some spice to her days. *Waved to Woolley all week.*

And next? Bernard Limb from Belton, of course! She hardly gave him a second thought any more but had been so giddy about him in the summer. *Sat with that lovely Grammar boy & like him*, Norah wrote in mid-July. That was the first time they'd talked. *Sat with Bernard*, she wrote each day that week. *I absolutely adore him. Talked to B all the way home.* Did Norah smile at the memory of how her daydreams annoyed her teachers

(*Shellie got on to me about looking ponderous*) and remember how lonely her weekends felt at that time? *Thought about Bernard all day long,* she wrote one Sunday in late July. *Absolutely terribly love-sick for him.*

Even more of a flash in the pan had been *Fishboy,* aka Henry, whom she had eyed up on trips to the village shopping street. It is highly likely that she wouldn't have remembered him at all without flicking through those months. This diary-keeping malarkey: it was grand. Was this the point at which Norah committed to writing a diary forever? A diary could 'anchor the past' as it disappeared behind her. It was 'a message in a bottle', to the future self whom she did not yet know.[16]

Norah was reminded of seeing the Northern Lights in the late January sky and a few weeks later, tasting her first Cadbury's Milky Way. The false news that Hitler had been assassinated, then Eden's resignation and the government crisis that followed. Her minor domestic triumphs: making lemon curd and baking pasties that *even Birdy liked,* skinning a rabbit in record time (*10 minutes*), going to the Park in April, moving house in late June, starting her periods that summer and travelling all alone up to Bamford in Derbyshire – two train rides – to stay with her sixteen-year-old cousin. That was another grand week, her days spent roaming the moors with Jeff the dog before meeting Peggy from work in a Sheffield department store. Two nights running, they went early doors to the pictures, seeing Jane Withers in *Checkers* and Constance Bennet in *Merrily We Live.* She'd shared Peggy's bed and listened to her talking about her own crazes as they drifted off at night.

Other highlights included being chosen for the school hockey and netball teams, as the artist for Burton House, and for the part of Sir Andrew in *Twelfth Night.* There were some disasters too. She maybe smiled as she read her blasé account of the marble cakes she and Kathleen *burnt to pieces. Bad luck.* Her crowd of friends had the usual fallings out. *I'm back on Agnes,* she wrote. *Kathleen and Enid snubbed me all day.* But they were giddy, often helplessly so – *couldn't stop laughing all afternoon.* Telling her off for her *rather perverted sense of humour,* a teacher had made her *write out Anaerobic Respiration five times at 4pm.*

In September, Bira was back, racing in the T.T. and Norah was *crazy over him again.* Did her heart skip a beat as she was reminded of her fears when, a few days later, she heard that he had been involved in a crash in Northumberland in which a motorcyclist was killed? She was keen to know that it wasn't his fault (it was) and that it wouldn't stop him from racing (it didn't).

Grave week in politics, Norah had written in late September, as Hitler invaded the Sudetenland and Chamberlain went to Munich. The German racers, Auto Union and Daimler-Benz, set for victory at Donington Park, were back and forth that week. Though she wouldn't know it, they were ordered by the German Embassy to leave for Harwich and instructed to fire the cars if they were stopped on the road.[17]

At school, the Grammar boys came to dig a trench in the grounds. *Dozens! Lovely. We joined in,* Norah wrote delightedly on 28th.

> *29th September: Awful talk of war. Germans back at the Park. Dug trenches in Gym and in English in the afternoon too. Lovely among the boys! Awfully warm. Frank & Den went to pictures. Sunny, warm. Chamberlain went to Munich.*
>
> *30th: Chamberlain came back. Saved us from war. 3 cheers. Took a spade. No need now though. Chamberlain was given a terrific welcome. Everyone went crazy over him. Rained. German Racers Gone. Bad.*

As war loomed and was then averted, Norah enjoyed fratting with the boys. Although the crisis was over, ever hopeful, she had still taken her spade to school.

A few weeks after Chamberlain turned his back on the Czechs, a touring troupe of Germans performed a show at her school. One of them, referred to in her diary as the *Marionette,* was *a lovely handsome young man. We're all crazy over him.*

***

'End it here, with the visiting German!', insists a creative writing tutor and poet. Coinciding as he does with Chamberlain's triumphant return from Munich and his countrymen racing at Donington Park, closing with the marionette has a certain Germanic neatness to it, a focused poetic appeal. But as a historian, I can't leave out a perfectly true part of the story in the interests of literary aesthetics; the final 'craze' which shows us more of Norah. A story needs a shape, I see that, but real life is never that trim.

14th December: Water was turned off about all day. I can walk quite alright now, except for the limp. Listened to Bandwaggon. Saw a picture of Frank Soo. He's a beauty. Crazy over him.

15th: I'm still crazy after Soo. He's a Chinaman & plays for Stoke City.[18] Can walk on my foot now. Wall's house in Eastway set fire. Absolutely burnt to the ground. Made mincemeat.

16th: Made the Christmas puddings. Spent the afternoon looking at his photos (FS). He's grand. Frank taught me how to play Patience. Knitted a lot. Tommy fought Lou Nova (lost). Rained.

17th: Read about Soo in bed. He's stupendous. Derby's playing Everton in the cup & Leicester's playing Stoke City. Hope SC wins. Had the electric fire. Lovely. Uncle Frank (Bris) came. Stoke lost to Arsenal. Derby lost 4.1 to Middlesborough. Leicester lost 6.1 to Grimsby.[19]

And of course if this was a novel, I wouldn't have three men all called Frank in as many diary entries. I'd give them different names, like Bill and Maurice maybe. But Norah had an Uncle Frank, a train driver visiting from Bristol, and a brother, named for him, who taught her card games that week. And now there's Frank Soo, the beauty at Stoke.

There's another thing, again about trimming. Deleting Frank Soo and the superfluous domestic detail loses the everyday texture: the inconvenience of the turned-off water, the warmth of the new electric fire, the fruity aromas of Christmas cooking. And there's the unintended humour. It can't have been much fun for the Wall family, losing their home to a fire, but there's something in Norah's reportage (*absolutely burnt to the ground. Made mincemeat*) that makes me smile.

***

'What was she like?' my mother exclaims again. 'It's 1938 and she's thirteen years old, from a good Christian home! It's only two months since she was describing *Snow White* as the best thing ever'. My mum lapses into dialect, what we call 'broad Donington': 'O wor a bit of a gel, that o wor'.' And then, in a more judgmental tone: 'Maybe this is where it all started. You remember what she was like, even in her seventies'. She is again viewing Norah the schoolgirl through the lens of later life.

Norah always picked up male admirers on her SAGA holidays.

'It took me three months to shake him off', she once told me in an exasperated tone about some retired banker from the plushest road in the poshest part of west Sheffield. Another well-to-do old fella who in his younger days had clearly been used to reeling in the women, he had pursued her since a fateful beverage at Heathrow's Teminal One after a fortnight cruising on the Doura. 'I knew what was coming, as soon as he asked me for a coffee. I thought, "Oh Lor', here we go again."' She was in her early eighties at the time.

> **GENTLEMAN: AGED 77**
> Would like to meet lady for friendship/relationship and days out. Reply to: Derby Telegraph Box No 873, Northcliffe House, Meadow Road, Derby, DE1 2DW.

Fig. 16 'Gentleman seeks lady' ad. Private papers of Norah Hodgkinson. Photo: A.Twells, 2025.

Playing with a box of odds and sods on Norah's coffee table during one of our visits, my younger daughter unearthed a small ad for a local gent seeking a lady friend. Norah was unperturbed by this exposure. 'I don't want another husband' she protested, by way of an explanation. 'But a chap who lives about six miles away, who can take me out on daytrips and come round to knock the odd nail in, that'd be nice'.

***

Once you've spotted this liking for boys and men, they crop up everywhere. I flick back to Norah's first ever entry, made just after Christmas 1937. While the diary proper begins with the printed rectangular window for 1st January 1938, twelve-year-old Norah, keen to get started, created pencil-drawn boxes for the last two days of the outgoing year. *30th December 1937,* she wrote. *King Farouk dismissed his cabinet. Dull, rainy day.*

If we didn't know any better, we might consider this a curious entry for a young girl's diary. But far from parroting *Daily Herald* headlines, or writing what she assumed diaries should contain, we can be confident that Norah will have been inflecting this news item with her own schoolgirl interest in the handsome young Egyptian king.

So it should come as no surprise that when the lady from the Women's Voluntary Service (WVS) visits her school in 1940 to recruit sock knitters for the troops, Norah Hodgkinson jumps at the chance. Or that once the heavy seaboot socks are finished and ready to be sent off to the Royal Navy Comforts Fund, she cheekily slips her name and address inside the package.

II

A quickening of the tempo of the sex-life of young people is about the commonest form of war neurosis. Hurried marriages, friends getting suddenly engaged, boys and girls trying desperately for a good time on the argument that 'next week may be too late' and, above all, men who, being called up, do things in uniform they would not dare do in civilian life, feeling that the uniform will preserve their anonymity, all help to bring about a large change in the sex-life of the country.

— WW2 diarist

War is very erotic. People had love affairs they would not otherwise have had.

— Mary Wesley

4. A Poke in the Eye for Hitler

For the people of Britain, 1940 was the year the war really began.

It is also the year for which Norah's diary is missing. I am planning a class on J. B. Priestley's radio broadcast in May of that year, in which he repackaged the horror and the lies of the Dunkirk evacuation to tell a story of pluck and heroism, the 'little boats' pitching in to aid the rescue attempt coming to represent ordinary English bravery and a national proclivity to create triumph out of despair.[1] Norah, as we know, had enjoyed Priestley's novels. Certain that she would have approved of his politics and his sentiment, I am hopeful that she had commented on this, the first of the famous 'Postscripts' that made him second in popularity with radio audiences only to Churchill himself. 'Listened to JB Priestley on the wireless tonight', she might have written. 'He was grand'.

But when I open the suitcase to pick out the diary, I discover that 1940 is not there. At first, I am puzzled but not unduly alarmed. I empty the case, put 1938 and 1939 to one side, and then carefully stack the remaining diaries in decade-high towers of ten. 1940 is nowhere to be seen. I look under the piles of papers on my desk and in other boxes of documents from Norah's archive. Not there. I return to my stacks and count them again, working backwards: 2009–2000, 1999–1990, 1989–1980, 1979–1970, 1969–1960, 1959–1950, 1949–1941, 1939, 1938.

For a moment, I doubt that there ever was a 1940 diary. But then I remember my mum reporting a fight with her brother Birdy that Norah had recorded. They'd been squabbling over washing up and he had shoved a dirty dishcloth in her mouth.

'She did have a rough time with him', my mum had laughed. 'It was 1940, so he was 19 or 20 and still tormenting her'.

I gradually move my search further afield: the side of the settee, the recycled paper bin into which items from my desk occasionally fall, the

©2025 Alison Twells, CC BY-NC 4.0 https://doi.org/10.11647/OBP.0461.04

garage where I sat drinking tea and transcribing diary entries as I waited for my car to be fixed. But 1940 is nowhere to be found.

By the end of the week, I am waking at 3am, eyes wide and staring, my heart racing, aware that something terrible has happened. It is a feeling reminiscent of the end of a love affair: the fleeting assumption on waking that today is just an ordinary day, then the split-second, pit-of-the-belly realisation, that the world is irrevocably changed. Norah kept her diaries safe for all of those years and then, in the space of a few weeks, I've lost one of them.

I start to obsessively scan the diaries, storing memory sticks in multiple places – at work, at my mum's, in my bedroom. I reason (fully aware that this is the wrong word) that the side of my bed is safer than my office, a tiny box room which adjoins the living room of the upstairs flat next door. The fact that they have a lot of 'comings and goings' – our (very pleasant) neighbour clearly making a bob or two outside of his tenancy agreement – fills me with worry. How careful are they with their cigarette ends? Our downstairs neighbour unwittingly fuels my anxiety: she is indignant that he shouldn't be subletting rooms and if the Housing Association won't intervene in the illegal profiteering, they can at least fit some fire doors. Maybe I should just deposit these diaries in a library, because having them in my house, living in the archive, might send me to an early grave.

There is an accompanying guilt: I have two children in this house and here I am fretting over some old diaries. Indeed, my level of anxiety is on a scale otherwise reserved only for my daughters. Since my first days as a mother, I've worried about them travelling without me, the A1 looming particularly large in my mental map of killer roads. And then there's the out-of-town shopping centre, for a while off limits after a local newsagent told me that its vast basement is stuffed with body bags: 'Waiting for a major incident'. I know how it reads, stark on the page like this. But I am quite secure in the knowledge that other mothers will allow me my maternal neuroses; that they are every mother's prerogative.

My elder daughter texts me from the A14, where she is travelling with her aunt and cousins to visit her nana and grandad in Norwich.

'U will b plzd to knw aunty helen driving at 5 mph', she writes sarcastically. 'In a traffic jam'.

A few minutes later, when my daughter exclaims that a driver pulling off a slip road 'could have killed us all', her aunt tells her gently: 'that's what your mum worries about, the lunatics on the road. It's a mum thing'.

It feels like a mum thing with these diaries too. I am protector of my children's futures and keeper of my family's past. Or maybe it is less healthy than that. Like a guilty bulimic, I try to conceal my diary obsession from my partner. Unsympathetic to my maternal madnesses, he won't take kindly to my new obsession. I binge on them in his absence, dashing upstairs to scan a few more months as he nips to the shop. In a trip to the gym, I can devour two whole years.

The worst of it is, I think I lost 1940 during one of my obsessive manoeuvres. I took them back and forth to my mother's house during those early months after Norah died and wonder now if 1940 fell out of the boot of my car into the February snow. If someone picked it up, even outside her house, they wouldn't know it was ours. The only address is 18 Moira Dale – just round the corner – written on the opening page in Norah's neatly rounded hand.

One afternoon, as we make our way back to my mum's house after a blustery walk with the dog over Daleacre and Eastway fields, we stand outside Number 18, my mum pointing out Norah's sun-filled bedroom above the front door, looking down over what is no longer a cottage garden but a paved car port.

'How times have changed', my mum says, sadly. The once rich red brick fell victim to a cheapskate local authority cladding scheme in the 1980s, just before a sale under 'Right to Buy'.

I make a snap decision. 'Let's see if the diary's been handed in here', I say. I knock and a twenty-something boy answers the door, his arms outstretched against both doorposts and his rangy frame filling the space between. I explain about the diary. It is one of those conversations: do I just launch in with my question, or do I pursue a lengthy but self-conscious preamble, explaining who Norah was, our relationship to the house? I hover painfully between the two. He humours me politely. No, he is sure the diary hasn't turned up there, but yes, he will check and let us know if it has. Trudging back round the corner, we cackle at what he'll report to his family, once the front door is closed and we, a windswept, bedraggled crew, are safely out of earshot.

Fig. 17 Moira Dale, Castle Donington. Number 18 is second from the left. Photo: A. Twells, 2025.

I try to make the best of a bad job. If one has to go, 1940 is *the* diary to lose. 1938 and 1939 give an uninterrupted insight into a schoolgirl's life. 1941 is a crucial log of Norah's early correspondence with Jim the sailor and her first meeting with lover boy Danny. 1940 might mark the start of her sock-knitting career and the year the bombs dropped on Donington, but otherwise, I tell myself, it will be more of the same – school days punctuated by Norah's telegraphic responses to national and local events: 'Sat with Peggy on bus. Coventry bombed. Cathedral destroyed. Terrible' or 'Had biology test. Lousy. Frank joined CD Home Guard'.

***

Sitting in the café at work, at a table of creative writers, I find myself lamenting my carelessness, wondering again if I can write this book without a full run of diaries, without this crucial year.

'You could make up some diary entries for that year', someone suggests, a bit too breezily.

Well no, I'm a historian, we don't do that.

'You can use it as an opportunity', says another. 'Have a creative chapter in amidst all the history…'

But why would I, when I've got a story like this?

'Just to help it along', someone else chips in, 'at a point where the sources don't exist'.

'Make it a memoir', suggests some other clever Dick. 'That gives you artistic license. Writers are doing all sorts of exciting things with memoir these days'.

They don't get the magnitude of it, I think. In fact, they look at me with a hint of pity, as though I'm lacking in imagination.

'It's one thing creating a scene from the evidence', I say. 'But I don't have any here. How would I signal the difference, between what is real and what is not?' I see them glazing over at the mere mention of historical truth. But I know that imagining Norah writing her list of crazes – and many historians would disapprove even of that – is a world apart from diary entries that I've made up. They don't think it matters, but for me, it really does.

While I work it out, I do what all good historians do in a crisis. I visit an archive.

***

I settle down at a microfiche reader in the Local Studies Library with reels of the *Derby Evening Telegraph*. I have come to see for myself the news that Norah would have read in 1940, her missing-diary year.

I have a good idea from her 1939 entries what Norah will have noted and what will have passed her by. The war crept up on her in the end. After Munich, pleased with Chamberlain and his 'peace in our time', she barely noted international affairs. On the few occasions when she made a war-related entry, her scant attention meant she sometimes got the details wrong. *Hitler made a speech,* she wrote on 29th January, when in fact, Hitler's address to the Reichstag on the sixth anniversary of his coming to power – including his chilling prediction that a world war would see the 'annihilation of the Jewish race' in Europe – came a day later. It seems that thirteen-year-old Norah was writing her diary entries a few days at a time, casting her mind back over the week, world events not feeling so urgent as to require a daily report.

Fuss about Hitler again, wrote a blasé Norah in mid-March, four days after German troops marched into Czechoslovakia. While other diarists noted the Czech humiliation – President Edvard Beneš had been excluded from Munich – and lamented that 'the whole European situation looks almost as black as it did last September',[2] Norah's daily entries drifted into distracted juxtapositions. On 7th April, after a hot-cross bun breakfast and a trip to Isley Walton *violeting* with Helen, Norah noted that *Mussolini marched into Albania* and *Derby beat Portsmouth away (2.1).* A fortnight later, Hitler appeared again. *20th April 1939: Nice sunny day. The architect came round to look at the houses. Said ours looked nice. Sunbathed in the back. Hitler's birthday.*

Maybe it was the Hodgkinson family's very 'homey' spring that led Norah to domesticate the German dictator and to largely ignore the build-up to war. Ten months after the move, they were throwing themselves into the new house with gusto. Norah was busy, helping her brothers to paint the kitchen, dig a vegetable patch in the back garden and sow lawns and borders.

She isn't alone in her reticence. Even a more worldly diarist, like twenty-four-year-old Derby schoolteacher May Smith, who records that Hitler had 'marched into Czechoslovakia – the old devil!' – and notes the enforced ARP (Air Raid Precautions) lectures at work, rebukes herself for her lack of interest. A boyfriend took the political situation very seriously, she writes; 'I suppose one ought'. Jean Lucey Pratt, five years older still, mentions 'the persecution of the Jews' in a diary entry of late March but says nothing more about the international crisis until the end of August, when she seems pleased that 'our foreign policy' was now defined and even wonders if conflict might benefit mankind in the way the Great War had 'hastened the emancipation of women, broke down class prejudice and swept away much stupid social etiquette'. These nonchalant young women. It was the mothers of sons of fighting age who lived in dread.[3]

While Norah notes the trial-run of the *black-out over most of England* in early August, she makes no mention of the WAAF receiving Royal Assent, the *Daily Telegraph* campaign to bring Churchill into government, the declaration by Fascist leader Oswald Mosley that Britons should not die in a 'Jews' quarrel', or *Picture Post*'s urgings for peace. She is in tune with the fifteen Margate holiday makers who take part in a snap poll, eight answering 'no' to the question 'Do you think there will be a war?', four 'yes' and three undecided, and when asked 'Do you think Hitler wants war, or is he bluffing?', all fifteen reply with 'No, he's bluffing'. Even as the nation readies itself and re-armed, the hope remains that the longer Hitler was held at bay, the less likely it is that war would happen at all.[4]

Norah is living in this event, the build up to war, not through it. By early August, she is absorbed in preparations for her sister's wedding, with frock fittings at Pearls Bridalwear in Long Eaton and trips to Loughborough Co-op to help Helen choose her green and gold upholstered front room suite. She knits a tea-cosy wedding present and spends long days skinning and re-papering walls in the rented cottage down the hill in Hemington, feeling like a bit of tour guide as relatives and friends arrive with gifts of crockery and kitchenware.

The day before the wedding, she and fellow bridesmaid Mary Twells set out the trestle tables and lay out the cutlery for the wedding reception at Moira Dale, persuading Birdy to *sunshine the wazzy*.[5] The garden is in full bloom: roses, hollyhocks, glads in their gaudy glory, the heavenly honey-like fragrance from the phlox.

> *19th August: Helen's wedding day. Awfully nervous. Fell down steps when coming out of chapel. Had lovely feast. I love Len Dakin. Mary & I went to Derby with H[elen] & J[oe] when they went to Bristol. Sunny. Derby lost to Leicester 4.6. Stoke lost to Wolves 2.0.*

That was the only downside. If only the football had gone according to plan. That and Hitler, of course.

The countdown begins. As family and friends enjoy the wedding feast at number 18, Stalin informs Hitler that his foreign secretary, Molotov, is prepared to receive his German counterpart, Von Ribbentrop, in Moscow for the purpose of signing a deal. 'Crisis again', writes diarist Joan Strange. 'Amazing news of a Berlin-Moscow Pact. Sworn enemies but uniting in a non-aggression pact'.[6] With nothing now in the way of Hitler's threatened invasion, tension mounts: nurses are called up, soldiers are inoculated, Poland advises foreigners to leave.

As Marsie, Pop, Helen and Joe travel to London for Dennis and Nollie's wedding the following week – churches and registry offices seeing 'the greatest flood of marriages ever counted in British statistics' – Parliament passes the Emergency Powers (Defence) Act. Volunteers begin filling sandbags and digging trenches. Schoolteachers prepare for evacuation. Art works are moved from the Imperial War Museum and the Tate.[7] Vivienne Hall, a typist in Putney, writes in her diary: 'New hats, frocks, coats, theatres and even holidays are forgotten and replaced by purchase of tinned foods, black curtains and adhesive tape'. But still some remain unconvinced: 'News very bad but we are hopeful in this household that war will not come', writes Joan Strange. 'Mother hasn't got any extra food in, any black stuff for black-outs or even a gas mask'. Marjorie Gothard, a Huddersfield butcher's wife, catches this mood: '[w]e think in our hearts that peace will prevail'.[8]

It is only now that Norah stops to look upwards and outwards. *Worked*, she writes on 30th August. *Trouble with Hitler. Lovely, sunny.* And the following day: *Hitler trouble. Tea at Helen's.*

And then, in a rush, it all kicks off:

> *1st September: Hitler declared war on Poland. Had to dye curtains. Everyone got wind-up. Ma went to help evacuation kids in. Not many came. Balloon barrage over Derby. Went to Helen's with Pop. Everyone must have dark curtains. Sunny, cold.*

> *2nd: Hitler bombed six Polish citys. Ma went to help with evacuees. Frank had letter from Jean! Chris had fight with Mrs M. in street. Pa went to match. Terrible storm. Four balloons burned down. Derby beat Villa 1.0. Stoke drew 2.2 with Middlesborough.*

> *3rd: Got up latish. England declared war on Germany at eleven o'clock. Terrible. Chamberlain spoke on radio and King at 6. Helen & Joe came up. Stormy morn. Sunny.*

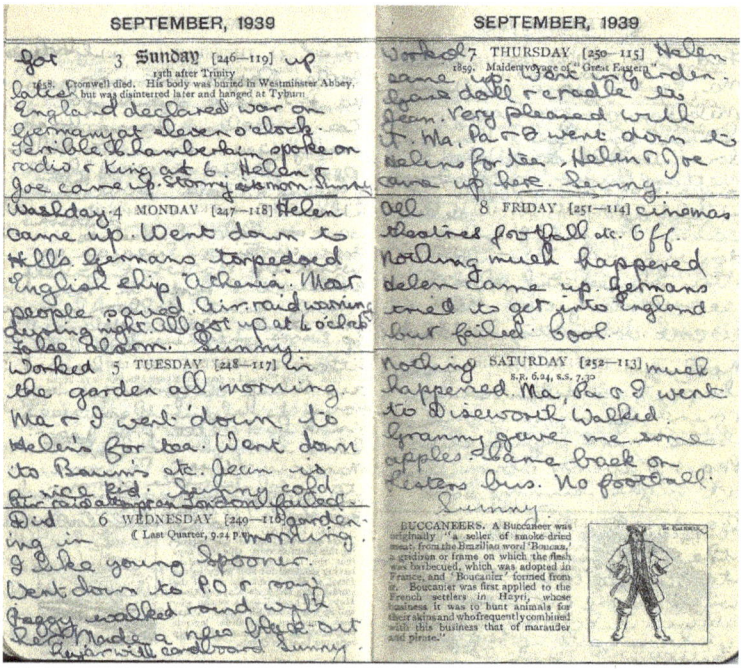

Fig. 18 Norah's diary, early September 1939. Private papers of Norah Hodgkinson. Photo: A. Twells 2025.

As the Government issues gas masks and instructions on what to do in the event of bombing, Norah, like the rest of the nation, expects destruction and chaos. *Germans torpedoed English ship 'Athenia',* she notes on 4th September. *Most people saved. Air raid warning during night.* The following day sees a failed *air raid attempt on London* and on the 6th, Norah and Marsie make new cardboard black-outs for their windows. *8th September: All cinemas, theatres, football etc. off,* Norah writes. *Germans tried to get into England but failed. Cool.* (I read this 'cool' wrongly: Norah is commenting on the autumnal weather and not celebrating, teenage style, the German failure to invade.)

On her return to a new school year in 'Mac's Form', Norah finds the tennis courts lost to air raid shelters. The girls move between classes with their gas masks swinging on their straps. *Had about half a dozen air raid practices,* she writes with a note of irritated exaggeration. *Had to wear outdoor shoes all day.* Her diaries sketch a new wartime topography, as searchlights traverse the sky, aircraft fly low and the colours on the street change to khaki and slate blue. Loughborough town centre has a slightly menacing air. *Nasty,* Norah writes after a lunchtime encounter with a group of soldiers, dismissing as an *ass* the one who takes the liberty of giving her a kiss.

Everyone is ready now.[9] But against this anxious, expectant backdrop of everyday life, *nothing much happened*:

> *9th September: Nothing much happened. Ma, Pa & I went to Diseworth. Walked. Granny gave me some apples. Came back on Lester's bus. No football. Sunny.*
>
> *12th: Nothing much happened. Helen came round. Germans sunk some more English ships. Ma & I went down town at night. Sunny cold.*
>
> *14th: Did some gardening. Helen came up. Nothing much happened. Had some fish from Spooner's. Went down to Hill's.*
>
> *15th: Nothing much happened. Saw Mary. Cleaned my room. Started to read 'John Cornelius' by Hugh Walpole. Sunny warm. Ivy had a daughter.*

While the Germans advance through Poland, the 'Bore War' sets in at home.[10] Norah attends school and does her homework: *finished reading* The Knight of the Burning Pestle *(Thank goodness)*. She gardens, blackberries and listens to *Bandwaggon*, now back on the airwaves. She follows Soo, delighting when he scores for Stoke in a reduced football league. The family enjoys tea parties for Frank's seventeenth birthday and Marsie's fifty-second. Norah knits: a blue jumper, her red and white school scarf, her bolero. Her main concession to wartime seems to be to stay away from the re-opened picture house. She will catch up with *Gone with the Wind* and *The Great Dictator* in 1940.

Christmas – *pheasants for dinner & big tea,* board games and singing at the piano – comes and goes. As they take the decorations down on the 30th, the family relaxes to a music hall turn by Stainless Stephen, a Sheffield comedian. New Year's Eve is so uneventful, it doesn't warrant a diary entry at all.

***

I learn from the *Derby Evening Telegraph* that 1940 began not with a bang but with a freeze, as temperatures plummeted, pipes burst, rivers froze and snow drifts kept thousands of children away from school. In the midst of this chill, the coldest winter for forty-five years, rationing began. As the housewife had to register in advance with her chosen retailer, the *DET* was full of ads: 'Join the Meat Rationing Register Now'.

While Derby picture houses remained open, we can safely assume that Norah stayed away. Neither would she have seen Jack Helyer play at the Art Deco Gaumont Palace in January, nor take the bus into town with Marsie to steal a bargain at Ranby's Winter Sale or be wooed at Whitsuntide by Midland Drapery's promise of 'Unrepeatable offers in Dainty Undies'.

'Battle for Narvik', reports the *DET*: 'RAF swoops on Stavanger and the fjords'. I imagine Norah parroting headlines as the Phoney War came to an end and the German invasion of Norway took Britain by surprise. She will surely have reported in her diary the 'Vote of No Confidence in Chamberlain', that 'Churchill [was] head of the War Cabinet now'. On 10th May, the *Blitzkrieg* began. 'Nazis Through Gap', declared a now-frantic *Telegraph*. Was it a relief? Frances Partridge 'felt calmer than for a long time… as if one had lain for ages on the operating table and at last the surgeon was going to begin'.[11]

'EPIC BATTLE!' screamed the *Telegraph* in late May, 'FEROCIOUS FIGHT AT DUNKIRK! ... EPIC WITHDRAWAL GOES ON!' Within weeks, Italy had entered on the side of the Germans, Paris had surrendered and British cities and seaside towns – all unnamed – were under fire. Norah won't have needed the *Telegraph* to tell her about the explosions in Derby on the night of 25th June, or the string of bombs that dropped on Donington a few weeks later: the small explosion in the vicarage paddock, the full incendiary 'bread basket'' on the playing fields on Station Road and a blast on Bond Gate, the impact of which, one local resident recalled, felt as if 'our house had been lifted up and plonked back down again'.[12] We don't know where the Hodgkinsons dashed for cover when the siren started up: the cellars under the Castle Inn, maybe? The shelter on the waste ground down the road? Or, with everything crossed, the cubby hole under their own stairs?

While the Germans could be after any number of local sites – Stanton Iron Works, Crossley Premier Gas Engines, Toton railway sidings, Chilwell Depot – it was Rolls Royce, nine miles away in Derby, that they really wanted. Royce's had made most of the Allied engines during the Great War. This time, their Merlins powered the Lancaster and Mosquito bombers and the Hawker Hurricane and the Spitfire fighters that were about to come into their own in the Battle of Britain.

Did Norah know that from above, Royce's site on Nightingale Road looked like a residential district, the sheds and stores disguised as houses and roads, the water tower and big glass engine workshop now a church and chapel, all transformed by Derby portrait painter Ernest Townsend into a work of art? Had she heard talk about the 'dummy town' in the fields around the villages, 'starfish sites' with wooden posts and wires that lit up at night, circling the south of the city like a glistening necklace of fire, fooling the Germans that Derby was already ablaze? A 'wizard war', Churchill called it.[13]

If the *Telegraph* was restricted in its coverage of the raids, it threw its weight behind the ARP, naming and shaming torch-flashers, bonfire-lighters and other offenders too free and easy with car headlights and bicycle lamps. These firefighting auxiliaries had done a full days' work before embarking on black-out surveillance, the editor told his complaining readers, who saw them as jumped up, play-acting lackeys of the police. The morale-boosting public services of the WVS also got good copy, their whist drives, mobile canteens and food convoys, complex evacuation successes, coordination of Bundles for Britain, Saucepans for Spitfires, and wool supplies for 'comforts' all duly reported. The Local Defence Volunteers (later the Home Guard) was 500,000 strong by end of June, Birdy and Frank among their number. Fears of Fifth Columnists were met by the internment of 'enemy aliens' and removal of road signs and railway signage as the country imagined German airmen dropping like bats in the dusk sky.[14]

In early September, after months of news censorship, London came into view, as if from the cockpit of a plane emerging from thick cloud. Woolwich Arsenal, Royal Victoria Docks, Surrey Docks, the Elephant and Castle, the East End, even Buckingham Palace, all ablaze and all named, photographs showing St. Paul's miraculously escaping damage against a fire-livid sky. 'Terrific AA Fire: Big Dog Fights', reports the *DET*. 'Tremendous Air Battle: Waves of Nazis over Thames'.

In November, the Luftwaffe turned its attention to another provincial Blitz. For local historian Delia Richards, this night forms her earliest memory: held in her father's arms at their landing window in Castle Donington, he pointed to the distant orange glow that was Coventry on fire. Just down the hill in Hemington, along the road from Norah's pregnant married sister, six-year-old evacuee Geoffrey Abel was woken from his bed and led out into the darkness to stand on the railway bridge and watch the flaming night sky. As ports and industrial cities – some named, some not – came under attack, the nation tried to adjust to a fearful sleep-deprived 'front line life'.[15]

Knitting crops up in unexpected places.

'Almost every time a man was asked if he needed anything, the reply was "we could do with a good pair of socks"', reported Mr Fletcher, secretary of the Derby and Derbyshire Chamber of Commerce and organiser of the Tennant Street Soldier's Rest, present with the Lord Mayor and other notables to greet the first exhausted Dunkirk survivors on 4th June with some cheering words and the proceeds of a whip-round organised by Rolls Royce. 'Considering what they have been through, I think it is the least that we can do to see that this need is met'.

In between escorting customers to their seats, torches in hand, and the final lights-up at the end, usherettes at the Gaumont Palace spent their time knitting. 'I saw Mr Smidmore [the manager] wading about in a welter of wool, needles, Balaclava helmets, scarves, mittens, pullovers and the like', wrote the *Telegraph* reporter, 'and giving advice to would-be knitters as if knitting and not cinema management was his work. But, as he said, we all find ourselves doing queer jobs these days'.[16]

***

Women and girls knitting 'comforts' for men who were not their own kin had been pioneered by the newly-formed Red Cross during the 1899–1902 South African War. By WW1, knitting for troops had become a 'national mania'. The surfeit of woollen goods sent to France saw men using the surplus socks and comforters to clean their rifles and wipe their cups and plates. During WW2, the number of knitting parties grew (to between 6,000 and 7,000 by April 1943) and the Red Cross was joined by the Women's Institute, the WVS and more organisations to distribute wool, collect finished garments and send them to servicemen at home and overseas.[17]

Wartime knitting was viewed as part of a reciprocal relationship: men fighting to protect women and children; women and girls deploying their domestic skills to provide 'comforts' and care. It wasn't altogether fair. Servicewomen had to knit their own woollies. 'One day word went round our camp that the Padre had issued knitted pullovers to some of the Airmen', wrote Eileen Davison for the BBC People's War project, 'but although in many instances we women did the same work as the men, there were no garments for us'. Despite their protest, they were told they were 'quite capable' of working full time and 'knitting their own'.[18]

Popular representations of wartime knitting as exclusively performed by women for men obscure finer details and small subversions. The initial spur for the emergence of 'knitting parties' was levels of anxiety among women; that is, to calm and comfort women themselves. Boys also knitted, at home and school, as did some men. In *Mr Lucky*, a 1943 romance, tough career-gambler Cary Grant allowed an Englishwoman to teach him to knit, his willingness and look of intense concentration endearing him to the female cinema-going public. 'Can you help me?' he asked. 'I dropped my purl. I'm beginning to like it'.[19]

Knitting was also feared as an espionage tool. 'Spies have been known to work code messages into knitting, embroidery, hooked rugs etc.', wrote the authors of *A Guide to Codes and Signals* in 1943. 'Small knots are tied at certain intervals in the threads of yarn. When unravelled, the thread is placed alongside a decoder and the spacing of the knots reveals the letters of the secret message'.[20]

And then we have the schoolgirls. School logbooks reveal that parcels of knitted woollies and other gifts were often shared between prisoners of war, the British Ship Adoption Society and their own adopted ships, and that letters were sent in return. 'Two extremely interesting ones this time', records Radnor Girls' in Cardiff in May 1945. 'Girls should gain considerably from this correspondence and also from the American letters, a second batch of which were received yesterday'. Timetables were suspended as sailors were received as guests.[21]

Of course, what the schools hoped their pupils would gain from these encounters may well have been at odds with the girls' own views. Joan Bakewell describes a fictional school assembly where girls shamelessly scrutinise merchant seamen, becoming helpless with laughter at the headteacher's choice of hymn, 'Jesu Joy of Man's Desiring'. In a similar vein, BBC People's War contributor Edith Wilshaw remembered a ship's captain coming to visit her Nottingham school to thank the girls for their letters and knitted comforts: 'he was gorgeous'.[22]

***

Tracking down a sock-knitter is my aim when, during a moment of purposeful Googling, I stumble across Loughborough High School Old Girls' Association (OGA). In the helpful email exchange that follows, I am invited to write a short piece for the newsletter, describing Norah's diaries and her correspondence with Jim the sailor. I enclose two photographs from Norah's collection, one of three teachers and the other of Norah, her best friend Peggy Stevens and another girl, Betty Garrod, sitting on a bench in the grassy quad. I drop in a few more memory-prompting names, including Norah's crush from the summer of 1938,

Bernard Limb. 'I would love to hear from anybody who remembers digging the trench with the Grammar School boys during the Munich Crisis', I tell them, 'and who maybe' – just maybe – 'was a schoolgirl knitter'.

Mary Belton's reply arrives in my pigeonhole at the end of a busy term.

> Dear Alison,
> I was very interested to read in the recent Loughborough Old Girls' Newsletter your article about LHS during the war years. I was actually there at the same time and in the same form as Norah. I remember all the names on your list and recognise Norah and Peggy in the photograph...
> I too knitted for the war effort and sent sea boot stockings to the navy. I too had a letter from one of the recipients who had been torpedoed and survived but when I replied to his new ship my letter was returned undelivered so I never knew what happened to him. I do remember that I was summoned to Miss Bristol's office to receive the letter and told to be sure to show it to my mother! Miss Bristol was very protective of her 'gairls'.
> We always had to have an emergency ration box with us in case we had to stay long in the air raid shelter. I am afraid that mine was very much depleted when I did need it as the contents were very tempting at lunch and break times.
> If I can help in any way with other memories I would love to hear from you. There can't be many of us left!
> Yours sincerely,
> Mary Belton (Freeman)

Mrs Belton's maiden name rings a bell and after a bit of scrabbling around in Norah's archive, I find that she was one of three girls on a slightly blurred photograph that was taken at the same time as the one I'd sent to the OGA: 'Bettina Hurd, Kathleen Clowes, Mary Freeman, 1941'. She also crops up in Norah's autograph album, her cheekier contribution following verses from Tennyson and Keats by Marsie and Pop, a few worthy entries from teachers and the jokey rhymes of other family and friends. 'Two in a hammock, attempting to kiss', she writes. 'When all of a sudden, they ended like (written upside down) THIS. (Mary Freeman, 26.1.38)'.

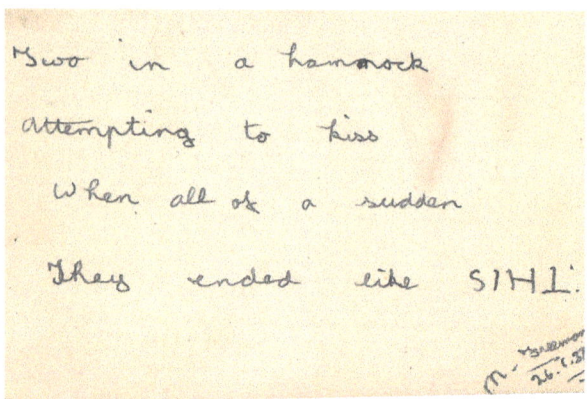

Fig. 19 Mary Belton's autograph, 1938. Private papers of Norah Hodgkinson.

A few weeks later, I am sitting in Mary Belton's front room, examining a scroll-like photograph of her year group at Loughborough Girls High School. It takes us a moment to identify Norah, with her short side-pinned bob and broad smile. Mary, neat and slender, is slightly obscured by the wild blonde mane of the girl in front. All are in their summer dresses, the variety of blue, green, yellow, pink and brown pin-stripes muted to grey and white. The year is 1941 and this is their last term at school.

Mrs Belton had started in the Upper III at Loughborough High School on the same day as Norah, 17th September 1936, after passing the scholarship with an A1. She and Norah were in the same form for all five years, leaving after the Oxford Certificate exams in July 1941. While Norah took a job at the railway office in Derby, Mary began work with the Post Office in Leicester. Put off by the nightshifts in the black-out, she moved to Standard Telephones and Cables. She was relieved to discover that her comptometer training meant she was exempt from the call-up and did her bit by working as an air raid warden and manning the switchboards in Birstall village hall.

I am surprised at how much Mrs Belton reminds me of Norah. It is not so much her appearance, although, like Norah, she could easily be a decade younger than her eighty-six years. Most of all, it is her voice. High School elocution lessons have not erased her flat East Midlands vowels, but just like Norah's, her tone is clear as a bell.

Mrs Belton can't remember the trench-digging operations with the Grammar School boys in September 1938. 'I probably wasn't that active in the digging!' she laughs. 'But we would have been excited at mixing with the boys. We were always under such strict instruction to keep apart. It was the same at home. It was always "it's not ladylike" to do this and that and the other. So when we had the opportunity – well, we did like to have fun'. It was a bus ride with the boys that made going back on Saturday mornings – the punishment for too many 'order marks' – more bearable.

Miss MacKenzie, Mary and Norah's form tutor in 1939, a fierce Scot who taught French and took a party of girls to Paris every year, had lost her fiancé during the Great War. At every Remembrance Day service, the girls would study her face intently, waiting until she cried.

'We were cruel'. Mary's voice betrays amusement as well as remorse. 'And not just to her. A lot of these teachers, they were ready for retirement, but they were brought back, you know, because of the war'. She tells me about the ageing Miss Freer, their form tutor in the Upper V, known for her mass of grey hair and the hand-knitted faun stockings, thick and ribbed, that she wore all year round. 'We all used to laugh at her, poor soul. I remember during a particularly harsh winter, she travelled to school on skis'. The 1940 freeze goes through my mind and I wonder if Norah will have mentioned in her missing diary this minor act of teacherly eccentricity and devotion.

As well as her memory of her empty ration box – the chocolate-covered raisins and caramel wafers from the Home & Colonial proving just too tempting to leave alone – Mrs Belton shares a rich assortment of images of life as a schoolgirl in the Second World War. There was the compulsory gas mask banging against her chest. The beetroot sandwiches (done in vinegar and seasoned with salt and pepper) that by lunchtime had dyed her bread bright pink. The cocoa and Camp coffee, brought in from home, to add to the third-pint of milk (warmed in winter) provided by the school. The siren scuppering home-time and the chilly evenings spent in the air raid shelter beneath the tennis courts.

And the knitting.

Like Norah, Mrs Belton was a proficient knitter, taught by her mother as a young girl of eight or nine. She sounds almost surprised at her expansive range: balaclava helmets, sleeveless pullovers, many scarves in Air Force blue. She tells me about the rib, which ensured the garments held their shape. The thick dark navy wool for the sea boot socks was untreated, oily, with the lanolin still in.

'We knitted these great long socks that would turn over their sea boots. But we had big pins, so they soon grew'. Turning a heel was skilled work and picking up the stitches along the side of a sock took patience and practice.

'You took your knitting with you everywhere', Mary tells me, remembering knitting on the school bus and while sitting on the cloister wall as sportier girls went off to practice tennis. When working on the switchboard, women would knit all day, in between answering calls. 'I even remember going to the cinema at Birstall and knitting in the dark!'

There wasn't much that a young girl could do to help the war effort. The National Service Act (No. 2) of December 1940 had seen women drafted into the services, munitions and work on the land, but did not apply to schoolgirls, of course. But if they were knitters... Friendly letters, your best photo, a hand-knitted balaclava or pair of socks: they all helped servicemen to 'smile through'. 'We felt virtuous', Mary says proudly, 'like we were really doing our bit'.

The sailor who received Mary's socks wrote to her. She remembers her nervousness on being 'sent for' by the head teacher, Miss Bristol, who handed her the letter 'with the strict instruction to make sure that my mother knew about it'. Theirs was a one-off correspondence. 'I can't even remember his name now', she tells me. 'It was a pencil-written letter, very – to us it was almost illiterate, it was just a piece of paper ripped out of an exercise book, thanking me. His ship had been torpedoed and he got the socks when he came back. I wrote back to his new ship – all eager and keen – but it came back "not known" and that was the end of it'.

I tell Mary about Norah's letters from Jim. 'I would guess he came from a similar family to ours', I say; 'not very well off, father in a manual job. There were a lot of children and a number of them passed the scholarship. But not him'. I mention Jim's shocking possessive apostrophes and poor spelling. 'Norah was clearly keen to correspond, but would she have felt...' I search for the right phrase.

'... that he was beneath her?' Matter-of-factly, Mrs Belton finishes my question. 'Maybe. Unless that it made it more exciting. To us, so far from the sea, we knew nothing about sailors at all'.[23]

***

After our chat, it isn't difficult to picture fifteen-year-old Norah standing in the school hall one autumn day in 1940, listening attentively to a bustling woman in green and grey tweed regaling her audience. They weren't half formidable, these WVS types. Impressive, but a bit of a snob-show: Marsie had helped them out at the start of the war, but they weren't her cup of tea. Yet they certainly got things done. They'd done a grand job of finding homes for all those kiddies with their funny Brummie and Yorkshire accents. Now they were branching out, collecting hosiery to send to Coventry, and pots and pans, colanders, meat-covers and heaven knows what else for the 'Saucepans for Spitfires' campaign. 'Up housewives and at 'em!' as Herbert Morrison had said.

It seemed that socks were the next big thing. The lady was braying about how the WVS had been handing out comforts since Dunkirk and was now collecting five tons of knitting a month. Five tons! Soon she was waving a paper pattern in the air, outlining the options: scarves for the less accomplished knitters, and balaclavas and sea-boot socks for those who could shape a neck and turn a heel. 'Come on girls. Get those pins clicking. It'll be a poke in the eye for Hitler'.[24]

That's me, Norah thought. She could do that. She'd been knitting since she was a little girl, when she'd sat on the kitchen table at Hill Top, legs dangling and crossed at the ankles, concentrating through a furrowed brow on her pins, uncomfortably secured in each armpit, to ever-patient Marsie's words: 'in with the needle, round with the wool...' She was so proud of her lovely green cardigan which that last winter, 1939, had taken her less than a month to complete.

Did the imperious lady visitor echo *Woman's Own* and tell the girls to include their names and contact details with their comforts?[25] I think she did – the boys would want to know whom to thank. But she emphasised it should be their school and not their home addresses. You couldn't be too careful, in this day and age.

Norah was keen. This year, she would spring into action. Socks were easy, even those great long sea-boot things. And besides, she quite liked the idea of knitting socks for sailors.

5. Jim Gilbert, Royal Navy Stoker

While Norah was knitting his socks through the winter of 1940, Jim Gilbert was in the North Sea serving aboard HMS *Elgin*, a 'Smokey Joe' minesweeper built at the end of the Great War. The *Elgin* had been moth-balled in Malta and was now back in service as part of the 4th Minesweeping Flotilla, based at Great Yarmouth, sweeping ahead of the convoys that travelled between the Firth of Forth in Scotland and the Thames at Southend.

Was Jim pleased to be back in English waters? It is clear from his letters that he was restricted in what he could say. He'd had plenty of adventures overseas, a life he had no doubt hoped for when he'd travelled along the Sussex coast to the Royal Naval Barracks at Portsmouth in June 1937, to sit the written exam at the Recruiting Office in the morning and – bated breath – pass the physical in the afternoon. His memory was surely etched with his first proud encounters with the naval town. The welcoming lights of the Sailors Rest and shops full of badges and uniforms. The feeling of walking through the dockyard gates as a new recruit, in the footsteps of men who had fought Napoleon at Trafalgar. The sight of officers, ratings and dockyard workers, all busy and purposeful. The tethered destroyers and looming grey warships in dry-dock, all up close.[1]

We don't know how old he was then – Jim never revealed his age to Norah – but as stokers were often more mature than the usual boy entrant, we can guess that he was a young man; twenty-two, perhaps. He completed his training – rifle drill, seamanship and more – and was soon aboard a submarine depot ship, to see two years of action, in Gibraltar, Malta, Yugoslavia, Greece, Alexandria and Tangier, defending routes to India and Suez, keeping an eye on Mussolini's activities in North Africa, then witnessing the unfolding horror of the Spanish Civil War.

By all accounts, it took some getting used to: doing your own washing, keeping clean and smart, the officers belting you with a stonikey for the slightest lapse. But it couldn't have been all bad. On the best days, Jim played with machinery all day long: with engines, turbo generators, dynamos, evaporators and fans. Perhaps he didn't even mind the morning watch with its chilly 4am start, coming off at 8 to clear the mess deck and prepare the midday meal, always meat and potatoes, and fill up the big tea urn in the galley. His off-duty hours were spent in the stokers' mess, reading from the ship's library, writing letters, doing crossword puzzles and even some embroidery, maybe arguing with his fellow ratings, singing bawdy songs and occasionally sneaking a forbidden game of cards. Were they happy ships? Was it like they all said: the companionship was the very best thing?

It was obvious to anyone in the forces that war was coming. The nation was chuffed to bits with Chamberlain at Munich but Jim knew it was only a matter of time. It was Spain that sealed it. He would have seen it firsthand when they were there on patrol duty: starving people fighting for the ship's waste food, civilians desperate to escape the fascist onslaught, some sailors abandoning ship to join the republican forces. But the Germans: was he among the British sailors who had played them at football in Gilbralter and Tangiers? Were they decent-enough lads who seemed alright to him?

And when war was finally declared, was Jim with those who were shipped over to Egypt, to the place they knew fondly as Alex? I'll bet he got really plastered that night.

***

Back in Blighty on the *Elgin* at the end of 1939, it had been straightforward work at first. The sweepers moved slowly in echelon – in parallel, diagonal, ladder-like rows. Each vessel was fitted with a wire to slice through the mooring cable of contact mines, freeing them to be shot at and destroyed, the sweep of the one in front protecting (in theory) the one behind. They often got the buggers straightaway, although sometimes the bullets just bounced off the steel sphere, like dried peas from a schoolboy's blowpipe.

This image, and many of those that follow, come from Paul Lund and Harry Ludlam's *Out Sweeps! The Exploits of the Minesweepers in WWII*. I'm no military historian. Immersion in the details of battles, tactics and leadership, or innovations in guns, aircraft or minesweepers, does not come naturally to me. But like Hitler in 1939, this book was full of surprises. Compiled from the diaries, reports and verbal accounts of dozens of men, the vividness of the images grabbed me. The Thames estuary as 'a gigantic graveyard of wrecked ships', victims of the magnetic mine which took out fifteen merchant ships and two destroyers in five days in November 1939. From Harwich, you looked out at the *Simon Bolivar*, masts and two big funnels standing above the water, spookily half-sunk and abandoned. Then there was the puzzle as to how the mines got there, sitting in the middle of swept channels, like they came up through the seabed and bred overnight. It was only after a mine was recovered from the marshes at low tide that the Admiralty knew what they were dealing with, that the unmarked aircraft that came under cover of darkness were in fact enemy planes.

The ships were fitted with the newly-developed 'LL' ('Long Leg') sweep, two heavy electrified cables, one long and one short, towed astern by small boats, the current creating a field in which mines were set off at a safe distance behind them. The minesweeper itself was protected by the 'degaussing cable' fitted around the hull to reduce the ship's magnetic field. For a man who loved machinery as much as Jim, this must have been thrilling stuff. Maybe his favourite was the raft sent ahead of a flotilla, so magnetised that a spanner would jump out of a man's pocket and his watch hairsprings reduce to a tangled knot. A Jules Verne-like creation, he'd love the idea of that.

The flotillas themselves, with their columns of rising black smoke, gave the appearance of a small settlement on fire. They had to take it easy at night; too speedy and they'd be visible from all over, the funnel gushing sparks like a Roman candle. Up close, it was all about muck and heat. The huge, filthy decks were inches thick in coal dust. It got everywhere. The crew had Welsh anthracite for breakfast, dinner and tea. Sailors reported that life aboard could feel like being sealed off from the outside world for weeks on end, like the Derbyshire village hit by the plague.

Occasionally, Jim would have seen other bits of the war. Sweeping eastward in early 1940 as Hitler invaded the Low Countries, the *Elgin* had met hundreds of boats of all descriptions bringing Dutch and Belgians to England as refugees. Some seamen, those who'd joined after the call-up, saw their first dead bodies then, floating by like debris.

A few weeks later, they were off to Dunkirk. The work was almost sedate at first, transporting men to cruisers. But then the Germans stepped up their air attack and the Navy was soon steaming back to Margate loaded up with thousands of men, British and French, depositing them and turning on their heels for another treacherous cross-channel trip. Eight days they were, without washing, shaving or changing boilersuits and hardly any sleep. The RAF was nowhere to be seen. They were all sore about that.

Did Jim have a grandstand view of some of that summer's more fantastic sights? Like when Hitler granted Mussolini permission to lead an attack on London and the men were wide-eyed at the wooden Italian bombers which, when shot down, looked like grand pianos dropping from the sky? Or was he always below the waterline, working as part of the engine room 'black gang', stoking up the coal-fired boilers and keeping the carbon off the sprayers, while men on the deck were pointing their guns at the swooping enemy above? He would be able to hear the twelve-pounder going off, the roar of an aircraft diving and swooping overhead, and the blunt thud of bombs exploding in the sea. He will have been at the ready to block holes with hammocks and tarpaulin, to join a bucket brigade in the event of a hit.

If a ship couldn't stay up, if it set ablaze and then started the sudden lurch downwards, there was nowhere to escape, just the freezing grey deep. If the sister ships couldn't get to you, you were done for. Jim and his fellow ratings thanked God for the *Gossamer*, who took the *Elgin* in tow when she was damaged by an acoustic mine, while the *Niger* and *Speedwell* covered behind. In turn, the *Elgin* had rescued survivors from HMS *Dunoon* when she hit a mine off Yarmouth at Smith's Knoll. Twenty-three ratings and three officers were lost that day.

You heard terrible things from other ships. The damage a 'tin fish' could do. The rating who almost had his neck severed by a massive shard of wood, men with limbs blown clean off. Swilling out bits of bodies in buckets of water after an engine-room hit. The cries of men left flailing in the sea. Sometimes survivors got ill with nerves and were unable to return to duty as one unit. Cracking up under enemy stress, the medics called it. It was all kept hush hush, of course. Civilians knew nothing about it.

But even for those who didn't lose the plot, it could be hard to keep your spirits up. Sometimes even the women in port couldn't do the job. Had a night on the town been Jim's half-plan, back on the Thames in February 1941, the day Norah's socks arrived? During the freezing tedium of weeks at sea, had he craved the lustre and bustle of London, with its snug pubs and welcoming women?

When the parcels from the Comforts Fund were doled out that afternoon, when Jim slipped his fingers inside a sock, stretching the stiff navy wool and maybe imagining the hands of the woman who had cared enough to knit for him, his knuckles had brushed against sharp-edged brittleness. He plucked out a snip of paper, turning it over to reveal a girl's name and address written in a gently rounded hand:

> Norah Hodgkinson,
>
> Upper III,
>
> The High School,
>
> Loughborough,
>
> Leics.

Did that bring a smile to his face? His socks had not been knitted by a middle-aged matron, but by a young woman, a schoolgirl! 'Whooah! Look here! I've got a girl's address!' No doubt the usual lewdness followed.

But that evening, in the Crown and Anchor maybe, a short distance from where his ship was docked, did Jim find himself suddenly wearied by the empty banter between his fellow ratings and the town girls? Did he want to write to her, to Norah, straight away? When he was finally settled into his hammock, struggling to prop himself up on one elbow to keep his right hand steady, maybe he took more care with his writing and paid greater attention to his spelling than he had done in a while. Norah was a grammar-school girl, after all.

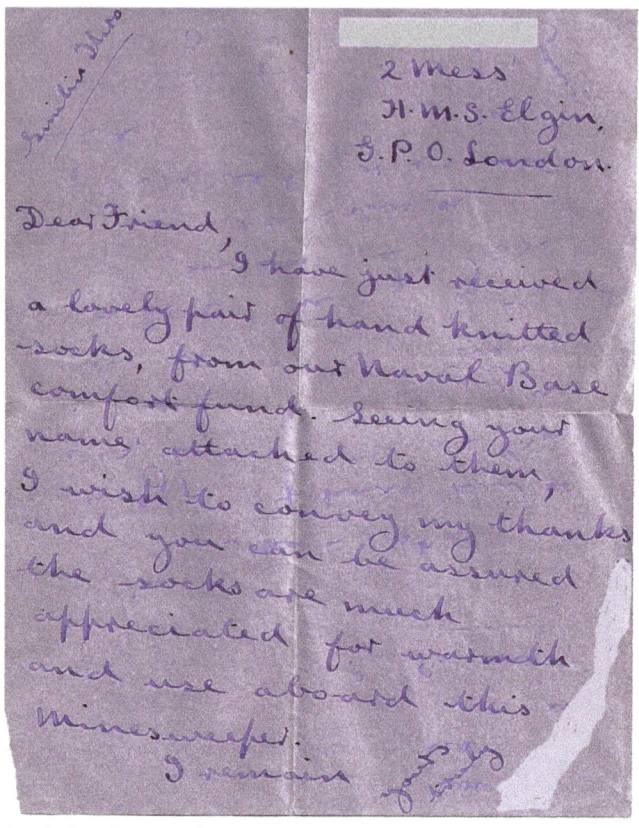

Fig. 20 Jim's first letter, February 1941. Private papers of Norah Hodgkinson. Photo: A. Twells, 2025.

6. Dearest Dimples

'Dear Norah', Jim writes on 5th March, 'your letter has reached me at a time when things seem dull and uninteresting, but thanks to you for raising my spirits from the depths of the sea to the heights of the heavens above'. After filling her in on his naval career to date, Jim tells Norah about his family life. Four of his five brothers are in the Services, he reports, one in the RAF, the others in the Army, Armoured Corps and Air Force Cadets, while the youngest is still at school. Their father is a locomotive shed chargeman, an air raid warden and in the Home Guard. 'We are a loving family', he writes, 'and we keep in constant touch with one another'. (Jim also has two sisters and a mother. Why they fail to get a mention here, I have no idea.)

Is Jim hoping to ascertain how posh she is, when he asks whether Norah had won a scholarship, like his little brother? 'I think you must have swell times at those kinds of schools', he writes, lamenting his own focus on sport and subsequent status as 'the poorest scholar in my family'. Hence, he is a Royal Navy stoker while two of his brothers, on account of their education, had become corporals in just one year. But Jim isn't daft. 'Every time I come in contact with my grammar school brother he gets me on a spelling B', he writes. 'This was his last one: "It is painful to witness the embarrassment of a harassed pedlar gauging the symmetry of a peeled potato." I made one mistake, put one m in symmetry'.

We can hear Norah's questions in Jim's replies. Romances are his preferred read, he tells her, citing as his favourites Rider Haggard's *She* and *King Solomon's Mines* and a trio of novels by Warwick Deeping. Jim has 'also' seen the film *Balalaika*, and his favourite stars are Alice Fay, Gloria Jean, Deanna Durbin, Jean Muir, Madge Evans and Paulette Goddard. He likes listening to Vera Lynn, Evelyn Dall and Kitty Masters, but is 'no lover of swing or dance jazz'. We hear too

Norah's expressions of admiration. 'Our job is nothing', Jim writes, 'and we are happy when tossing about the ocean just hoping there will be a fan mail when we return to harbour'. He tells her about the *Elgin* being mined, and that their rescue of survivors from the *Dunoon* had resulted in medals for the captain and the coxswain; 'but it is all in our day's work'.

'I see you have the Arsenal's colours, red and white', Jim says, in reference to her school scarf and hat ribbon. The north London club is his team; with his claim never to have heard of Derby County, he edges gently into banter. In April, five letters in, Jim tells Norah that he tries to picture her, 'Blonde about 5' 6".' He will 'sleep with her in his thoughts', he says, signing off 'Cheerio Blondie?' She must have put him right, as he opens his next letter with a half-hearted apology: 'I am sorry about the blonde and brunette affair, but being candid, the brunette is preferred'. He asks what her family have to say about their correspondence; she must get her leg pulled. He steps it up: 'We are just leaving port for an unknown destination but it does not stop me corresponding to my —?'

'Dearest Norah', Jim writes, his 'cheerio' now accompanied by 'lots of love'. Norah confides to her diary that he has sent *two beautiful snaps of him & one of brother Danny in RAF* and asked to see a photo in return. Just as Jim's photos of himself and his family – of sentimental value – are to be admired and then returned, Norah can trust him with her snap.

But Norah really has only one photo to send him: her bridesmaid snap from Helen's wedding, taken in the garden at Moira Dale before the little group made their way to the Baptist Chapel in the village. She liked the photo very much, just as she had loved everything about that day. But as she had stood in front of the man brandishing the Box Brownie in August 1939, her concerns were no doubt very different from those in 1941. Not to catch the peach net over-dress on the rose thorns. That her nose was well powdered and her hair, set to curl the night before, still bobbed neatly. That as the shutter clicked, she wasn't caught in the sunlight, squinting like a bag of nails. Wind forward twenty months, to Norah a little uneasy that she looked too young in this photo, too childish, to send it to Jim.

Fig. 21 Norah as bridesmaid at her sister Helen's wedding, August 1939. Private papers of Norah Hodgkinson.

She needn't have worried.

'Dearest Dimples', Jim opens his next letter of 12th April: 'We have just returned off night patrol, and half an hour afterwards your nice letter was handed to me. Gee! I think you are very attractive and pretty'. He now asks for a snap to keep, 'for my writing box looks rather bare without a girl's photo'. He likes it that she ended her last letter 'with love' and imagines walking with her down a country lane. 'I thought of you 5.30pm Good Friday when your favourite song came through on the ship's wireless, Smoke Gets in Your Eyes'. *14th April 1941: Received a rather romantic letter from Jim. Called me 'dearest dimples'.*

Folded inside the envelope with Jim's next letter is *a lovely 'Royal Navy' handkerchief*:

Fig. 22 Royal Navy silk handkerchief. Private papers etc. of Norah Hodgkinson. Photo: A. Twells, 2025.

A beautiful piece of handiwork, delicate lace framing a silk centrepiece of the most unexpectedly glorious purple, it had quite possibly been sewn by Jim himself.[1] Norah is delighted: *it is terribly sweet of him*.

Within a few short weeks she is 'my darling', my 'dream girl'. Jim tells her that he hopes one day 'to collect the four kisses' she had placed with her signature. 'Do you mind my intimate feelings towards you?', he asks. He would like a lock of her hair: 'it is a common thing in our ship and I would like to be in fashion'. He is still careful: 'Norah if you do not approve of some of my saucy remarks tell me where to get off, but please don't. I shall let smiling through play its part if your Prince Charming comes along ... Tons of love and xxxxx xxxxx', he writes, ending with a suggestive 'P.S. The best things in life are free but very hard to get.'

As Jim steps up the intimacy, we do not know if Norah finds him a little too bold. If she has any qualms, she pushes them to one side. He is aboard a minesweeper, in the freezing North Sea, and if her letters and photo make him 'the happiest person afloat', as he claims, then that is good enough for her. And his chat is just within the acceptable parameters of banter which, growing up with three brothers and their friends, she will know well enough. Just sixteen, about to take her exams and leave school that summer, she is enjoying this introduction to a new grown-up world of flirtation and romance.

28th April 1941: No letter. Terribly disappointed. When Jim's letters fail to arrive at the end of April, Norah's disappointment soon spirals into anxiety. *29th: Still no letter. ON 6 & 9 NEWS THAT H.M.S ELGIN HAD BROUGHT DOWN HEINKEL III. OH JIM! Went about in a trance. Heard cuckoo.* We see here another kind of 'diary time': a day split between the postman's fleeting failure to deliver the longed-for letter that morning and the six o'clock news; a day in which birdsong is the only other event of note.

Norah will have heard about ships around Britain that had been bombed, blown up or sunk. As well as the Luftwaffe's heavy blows on the ports at Bristol, Merseyside and the Clyde, the three months between late February and late May 1941 had seen 142 merchant ships sunk by U-boats and a further 179 in air attacks. In mid-April, Churchill had ordered the Ministry of Information to stop publishing the weekly shipping losses, fearing their usefulness to the Germans and their impact on morale at home. In that week alone, one ship in a convoy near Cromer went down, as did an anti-aircraft vessel off the Tyne. HMS *Raleigh* took a direct hit at Portsmouth, forty-two dead and thirteen injured. A minesweeper off Milford Haven was sunk with 'all hands lost'.[2]

Did Norah imagine the range of feelings that accompanied the signal from the skipper that enemy planes were approaching? Fifty miles off, then twenty-five, ten, five. An initial excitement maybe: it could be so dull on board, a bit of a scrap was a welcome change. Then the first sighting of the tiny black dots in the sky and hearts skipping beats. Fear giving way to purposefulness as men jump to their duties, pointing their guns. Resignation as bombs rain down, just missing them, dropping into the sea or hitting other ships full of boys and men just like them, which go up – and then down – in seconds. But the *Elgin* on that April night not only survived with no casualties but brought down an enemy plane. Petty Officer Archie Snook and Able Seaman Robert White were decorated after the war.

Norah knows none of this and yet she seems to know it all.

> *30th April: Returned to school. Still no news so had a good old weep. Mock Oxford on May 8th & Practical Domestic Science on May 26th.*
>
> *1st May: Had Hygiene instead of Music Appreciation. Oh, Jim where have you got to?*
>
> *2nd: Rolled tennis court. 48,000 British troops evacuated from Greece. Wonder whether Jim is there. If he doesn't write soon I'll go mad. Had clothes inspection.*
>
> *3rd: Still no news. Bought blue shoes from Wyles. Churchill made speech.*

Norah's use of parataxis, the juxtaposition of unrelated daily events, is at its comical best in these entries. The high drama of the war at sea and the first cuckoo of spring. Churchill's speech and her new blue shoes.[3] Her sense of melodrama too, expressed in her tears, dramatic trance and capitalised expressions of worry. I imagine giddy breaktimes in the High School 'quad' (remember Bernard Limb?) as Norah and her friends make their correspondents the focus of their days. There may well have been girls amongst her friends who were in a similar boat. While Mary Belton's exchange with a seaman extended to only a couple of letters, did Kathleen, Doreen or Agnes enjoy an ongoing correspondence with a romantic sailor boy?

Central to their excitement, no doubt, was the question of where it might lead. 'Marriage is one of the few things the war has not knocked sideways', wrote Leonora Eyles in *Woman's Own*. 'It flourishes in wartime.' In 1940, 534,000 weddings took place, 40,000 more than in 1939 and an increase of 125,000 on 1938. Granted, these were mainly weddings between couples who had met before the war, many shortening their courtships due to the call-up, others catapulted by heightened emotion into hastily-arranged matches. Weddings between people who met because of the war – like all the local girls whose affairs with soldiers and airmen billeted in Castle Donington Norah will note in her future diaries – would come in a few years' time. But their courtships were starting now, at dances up and down the country, maybe even through letter-writing and sock-knitting... As Lord Castlemane had said, if a girl ended up not married after the war, then she simply was not trying hard enough.[4]

I am reminded of Millicent King, the main character in Margaret Forster's *Diary of an Ordinary Woman*, who is shocked by the obsession with marriage among the young women with whom she shares a hut as a WAAF. 'In our hut at night, the talk is endlessly about men and marriage, it's absolutely incessant [...] The girl in the next bed to me is at this moment describing how she will have dark red roses at her wedding and the bridesmaids will be in blue and silver, yet she hasn't even a boyfriend'.[5]

Indeed, it is hard to overestimate the prominence of love and romance in the lives of girls of Norah's generation. The 1920s had been a watershed decade as the booming mass market of consumer capitalism and new focus on leisure and pleasure promised young women lives that were vastly different from those of their mothers. Romance was at the heart of it, replacing the pragmatic approach to courtship of past generations: finding a spouse who was capable and reliable, who could earn a family wage or budget and keep a clean house. Hair bobbed, noses powdered and skirts shortened, young women devoured the new magazines, full of the pleasures and perils of men. They flocked to the cinema, often multiple times a week, and at dance halls, they cast off chaperones and old notions of propriety to foxtrot and flirt.[6] 'God is love' became 'love is God' in these decades, writes philosopher Simon May, as romance, tasked with filling the gap left by the retreat of religion, became the 'ultimate source of meaning and happiness'.[7]

As Norah and her friends began their High School careers in the mid-1930s, young women were immersed in a new world of feminine beauty, glamour and romance. These were the years when J. B. Priestley described lipsticked factory girls as 'looking like actresses' and George Orwell noted the mass production of clothes that allowed women to dream of being Greta Garbo.[8] A film-star style, achievable by all. Norah decorated her Latin exam paper in 1941 with doodles of glamorous Hollywood stars; her copy-cat bolero knitting project was inspired by teenage actress Deanna Durbin. While her 'crazes' for 1938 included celebrity sportsmen rather than film stars, her list captures perfectly the giddying search for romance that was an essential part of being a modern girl.[9]

For some among the older generation, young women's devotion to romance was cause for concern. A particular worry were girls of the working class, especially those with a bit of hard-earned cash, characterised in one memorable description by by their 'emphasized erotic attitude, [...] their love of dancing and cinema, their loud shrieks of laughter in the streets'. In her studies of girls' leisure in the 1940s, Pearl Jephcott emphasised young women's 'unrealistic expectations and unsuitable values', including an unhealthy preoccupation with the opposite sex, nurtured by romance magazines. 'It boils down to this', she wrote: while girls knew that the world presented in such magazines is 'quite unlike the real world', they nonetheless hoped that some glamour may come their way: 'It is just possible that the boss's son may ask them to marry him, or a pilot-officer may invite them to his father's country mansion next week-end'.[10]

The focus on romance and sex appeal was amplified during the Second World War. Young women were tasked by films, magazines and government propaganda with keeping up men's morale through gentle flirtation and looking good. Yardley's No Surrender range promoted 'the subtle bond between good looks and good morale... Never must we consider careful grooming a quisling gesture. PUT YOUR BEST FACE FORWARD'. Readers of *Picture Post* were advised at the start of the war to 'invest in a warm dressing gown with large pockets to keep your air raid beauty make up in...' while Ursula Bloom in *Woman's Own* recommended beauty preparations for 'His' leave: 'the right make-up for your kind of face helps you to look radiantly lovely for a very special occasion'. Despite shortages, make-up was protected during the war years in 'one of the most complicated of the controls over manufacture and supply that had been evolved within the Board of Trade'.[11]

Men in the forces were encouraged to share this expectation. The Navy circulated pictures of pin-up girls and 'bathing belles', to keep the sailors happy, while the Army used the same to teach map reading and camouflage techniques to new recruits. The British forces' newspaper, *Union Jack*, reprinted *The Daily Mirror*'s popular cartoon strip, 'Jane', which famously featured a scatty and glamorous young woman, previously a socialite and now variously a land girl or munitions worker, with a hallmark ability to accidentally lose her clothes and bare her breasts. As one member of the wartime Admirality recalled, none of his colleagues 'ever settled down to his day's work until he had looked to see whether the young lady's clothes were on or off. During periods of bad news the editor always kept up morale by keeping her clothes off'. Another serviceman put it rather more wryly: 'Many of us follow her adventures with more interest than the war against Japan'.[12]

***

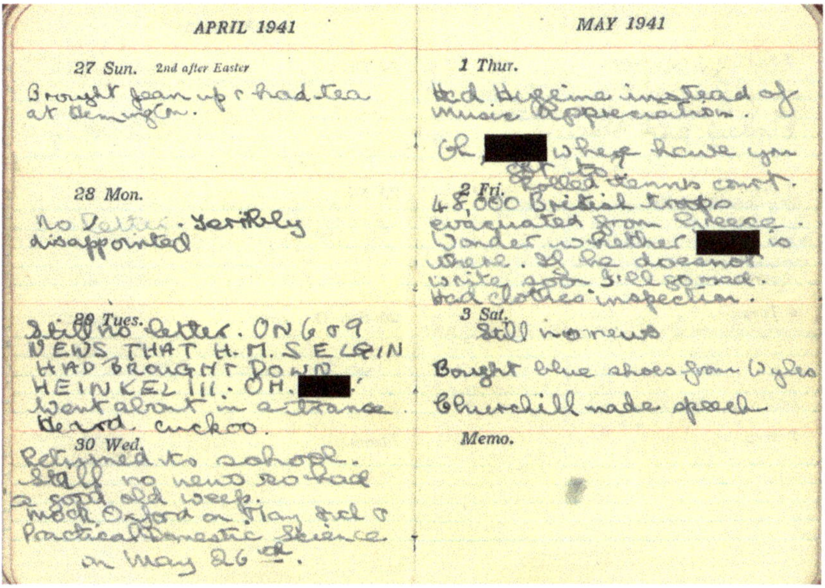
APRIL 1941

27 Sun. 2nd after Easter
Brought Jean up & had tea at [illegible].

28 Mon.
No letter. Terribly disappointed

29 Tues.
Still no letter. ON 6 o 9 NEWS THAT H.M.S ELGIN HAD BROUGHT DOWN HEINKEL III. OH. [redacted]. Went about in a trance. Heard cuckoo.

30 Wed.
Returned to school. Still no news so had a good old weep. Mock Oxford on [illegible] & Practical Domestic Science on May 26th.

MAY 1941

1 Thur.
Had Higgins instead of Music Appreciation.
Oh, [redacted] where have you got to
Rolled tennis court.

2 Fri.
48,000 British troops evacuated from Greece. Wonder whether [redacted] is there. If he doesn't write soon I'll go mad. Had clothes inspection.

3 Sat.
Still no news
Bought blue shoes from Wyles
Churchill made speech

Memo.

Fig. 23 Extract from Norah's diary, April 1941. Jim's real name has been obscured in these entries. Private papers of Norah Hodgkinson. Photo: A. Twells, 2025.

When finally he writes, Jim is bound by confidentiality and restricted by the censor to keep his wartime duties strictly under wraps. 'We have had a busy and exciting time so I have been unable to write to my good-looking friend', he tells Norah. He is full of banter: 'It is impossible to wrap up one of your dimples so what else can I cadge off you? ... What are Arsenal's chances in the cup, I bet you a kiss [...] Have you found a photo for me, of course I prefer you in person, but there is a war on'. His cheek and fun make Norah laugh: *10th May: Replied to Jim. Arsenal & Preston drew in Cup Final* (1-1). *So my fate is not sealed yet!!!*

When Jim again fails to reply to her letters a few weeks later, Norah picks up his wartime catchphrase, popularised that year by Vera Lynn. *My last letter to Jim returned saying 'No Trace'. Wonder what has happened. Must keep 'Smilin Thro''*. Her resolve doesn't last: *If Jim never writes again,*

I'm sure I'll go crazy. On 5th June, as Castle Donington raises £83,000 for War Weapons Week and Preston beat Arsenal 3-2 in the Cup Final replay, Jim replies: *At last HE has written to me,* Norah writes. While Norah is genuinely worried for Jim's safety, she is a modern girl, her diaries revealing the new set of grown-up romantic emotions that she is trying on for size. *Oh, Jim!*[13]

'Dear Norah, you cannot imagine how happy your letter made me today'. Jim skips back and forth between war news and poorly punctuated flirtation. Did she know they had brought a Heinkel down? His brother is at Derby for a Parachute Jump Instructor course. 'Darling! what about a snap, honestly I regard you a dream lover (may I?). Do you show your mother all your letters. What about a love letter from you "shy"'. He signs off: 'Cheerio sweetheart, all my love xxxxxxxxxx Jim. Always thinking of you'.

What do Norah's letters really mean to Jim? Is she, as he claims, his only girl correspondent, holding a special place in his affections? Or are her letters trophies among his fellow sailors, read out in the mess to bawdy comments, her photograph passed round like a tin of sweets?

7. I Believe You and I Have a Few Things in Common

Was Jim like Arthur Ford, a Dorset ploughboy, who blamed his decision to join the Navy on his restless desire to travel and his abiding interest in sex? 'I got fed up with just walking up and seeing one hedge and walking back and looking at the other hedge all day long', Ford told an oral history interviewer. How else could a poor and uneducated man see the world? Plus: he knew that it gave him 'a better chance of mixing with — well, of course, you hear these things, don't you?' Sex was 'the predominating thing' in the Navy, he said in a later reflection. The stuff of daily life at sea, 'sailors talked about it all the time'.

Many men found the exposure to sexual knowledge and experiences of intimacy that accompanied life in the armed forces to be exhilarating. For others, the unrelenting focus on sex could bring unwelcome pressures. Bill Batters felt secretly ashamed of his sexual initiation as a teenage recruit with a young prostitute in Argostoli, Kefalonia in 1937. He did not let on to his shipmates, of course, who had pushed him into the encounter and greeted him on return 'like a young lion'. Another ex-sailor confessed to being so embarrassed by his youthful ignorance that he ordered a sex manual through the post, relishing his mess-mates' delighted surprise at his medical lingo and technical know-how. It made him part of the gang.[1]

Some inevitably got up to no good. Dennis Maxted, a new recruit on the training ship HMS *Collingwood*, was shocked at the public dressing down given to four young sailors. One night at about 5pm, after instructions to 'clear lower deck', a group of 'matlows', all from Scotland, were arranged in line. The guard – mounted, with gages and rifles – and the Chief Petty Officer were also present. The charge? Sending 'obscene literature through His Majesty's post'. They had been corresponding with a girl in Glasgow 'and telling her all the things they were going to do with her and to her, sexually of course, and her father found 'em and reported 'em to the Commanding Officer', Maxted said. 'They all got 90 days cells, but of course there was "off caps, off collars", they took their collars off and their silks off and they marched 'em away under guard [...]But the drama that was in that, seeing three ranks, and you looked at that and you said "no way am I going into be getting myself into trouble" [...] Real drama I thought that was, very well staged too'. How much the Navy hierarchy was concerned for the girl, or whether the outrage was directed at the threat to their own reputation (or the abuse of His Majesty's postal system, as Maxted suggests), is hard to tell from his account.[2]

We can hazard a guess that peer pressure led these Scottish lads to write letters they wouldn't have composed alone. A key feature of 'scribal culture' in the armed services is that letters were often shared; in some cases, replies were jointly authored. The sailor's 'ditty box', where personal letters were kept, apparently private, was also for public display and discussion, an ambiguous space in which masculinity was performed for other men on the lower deck.[3]

***

In his first letter to Mollie Baker, a married mother of two and a mover and shaker in the Maidenhead Comforts Fund, Bill Stewart thanked her for her woollen 'comforts', sought to direct her future knitting efforts ('sock's seem to be the chief worry of men') and gave her advance warning of 'the boys' on his ship. As skipper of the requisitioned trawler-now-minesweeper HMT *John Stephen*, Stewart told Mollie he had seventeen men on board, fifteen of whom 'can drink any pub dry'. One of his seamen was a keen letter writer who 'writes the most passionate letter's to every dame who gives him encouragement'. After receiving Mollie's reply later that month, Bill told her: 'I let my boy's have a read of it, so if you should get some very affectionate letter's just don't blame me'.

Sam Gibbs lived up to Bill Stewart's mock warning from the off: 'You asked if we would like to be adopted', he wrote in his first letter to Mollie on 8th September 1940. 'I'll say we would then we could say that John Stephen has a few sweethearts'. 'Don't forget I've a good pen', he tells her. 'I can write any kind of letter from Love to blackmail Love letters are my speciality ask Bill he'll tell you'. 'Well hows the gang going', he asks Mollie a few weeks later. 'I hope there all OK give them my love, how old is your youngest member, if she's single drop me her address I'll write her a letter that'll make her think she's engaged to be married'.

A married father of five and a North Sea fisherman from Grimsby, Sam Gibbs sends his letters from a trawler base in North Shields. 'Dear Mollie and the Knitting squad', he writes. 'You keep the needles going and we'll do our best to keep you in food by keeping the seas clear for the Gallant merchant men'. A few letters in, Sam switches from addressing Mollie as Mrs Baker: 'I hope you'll excuse me calling you by your christian name but if we're going to be pals, that's how it will have to be'. Acknowledging the Maidenhead women's lack of experience in making some of the more complex garments, Sam was happy to guide their knitting practice. They all want socks, he tells Mollie, suggesting she works to a size 9. He later asks for a sweater which, when it arrives, is perfect except that the arms are too long. The helmets fall over their faces; can they have woollen hats instead? He shares with Mollie a cheaper way to make mittens and says that as they wear short wellingtons, the boot stockings don't need to be quite so long; she can save a third of her wool. He is also perfectly at home with some gentle ribbing: 'I had to smile when I saw the stocking without heels but one cannot look a gift horse in the mouth'.

Sam tells Mollie about an ATS girl called Joan with whom he has been corresponding for some months. They had not met – she was based in Nottingham – but they had exchanged photographs ('she looks a peach'). He elaborates at a later date, telling Mollie that Joan had been moved near to Newcastle: '[I]f we can meet half way we can have a afternoon and evening together and I'll mind my P&Qs'. He continues: 'This girl friend hasn't got a boy and she is over 20, I always write to her as a sweetheart, just to let her feel someone thinks a bit about her. I wrote her some lovely love letters but she knows I'm married and that doesn't worry her she has more sence than take any serious so we're just 2 good war pals'. Sam was not looking for a lover: 'I've a good sweetheart waiting at home', he tells Mollie. 'We have been sweethearts now 23 years. We started courting while we were at school and I never had no other girl....' For him, flirtatious letters and the occasional date, whether with a married mother of two or a young, single woman, were part of keeping up spirits during the war. 'Give my regards to all our Girl friends', he writes to Mollie, 'also your husband, and my love to the kiddies. CHINS UP'.

There is much care in this correspondence. Sam thinks of Mollie during the raids and offers reassurance: 'keep the chin up, were a long way from being licked and all the lads are ready for anything'. They exchange photographs of their families and he asks after her husband, in the Horse Guards, and children, Buffy and John. After Gibbs shares his excitement about his first Christmas at home in twenty years ('three sweeps' away, he writes on 13th December; his wife already has the tree 'all rigged up'), she sends toys for his children and a box of apples for them all. He doesn't know how to thank her: 'I know you will know how I feel so I'll say no more'.

Sam loves writing. He can write more than he could ever talk if he met her, he tells Mollie; although he can adapt himself to any company, he is 'on the shy side'. But 'I love writing to someone who can appreciate a letter', he says. 'I think letter writing is my favourite sport'. Writing to a class of woman with whom he was unlikely to have been in contact during peacetime opened up a new world of self-representation; he knows she'll know nothing about his work, fishing on deep-water ships around Iceland, Greenland, Bear Island, Sea Horse Island, the Russian coast. He tells her about his days, the different jobs on board, the speed of travel (11 mph), the trawls themselves – shooting the traps, hauling the fish onto the deck, gutting – then the welcome dry clothes and bottle of rum, the journey back with over 4000 boxes (the fish stiff as boards), each weighing six stone, the dangers of icebergs, the cold and the blinding snowstorms, the men washed away. Once near to home, they get shaved and polished up. They might have a night at a show, the fish is sold the next day and then they're away again: 'sometimes we might get an extra day in the dock but its always the same, you leave the wife with a tear in her eye and God speed and that goes on until your too old or the sea claims you'.[4]

I will confess: I am a little bit in love with Sam Gibbs and even more with Bill Stewart, his gentle, fun-poking skipper. When Sam ranges beyond ordinary letters to include his two pieces of life writing, Bill expresses his sense of awe: 'What a gift', he writes to Mollie, 'to be able to sit down and write a nine page letter'. With a nod to his own deficiencies as a writer (though, we could say, while revealing a decidedly literary ear) he continues: 'My wife reckon's it's a shame to waste a stamp on the letters I send her but one cannot tell about his undying love all the time and if I write and tell her about my kidney's she sends back a Pithy letter about drinking. The hardest letter a man can write is to his wife', he concludes, 'a Prophet gets no honour in his own home'.

What a treat Sam's and Bill's letters must have been for the Maidenhead women. I imagine them taking breaks from their knitting to enjoy Mollie's readings, laughing uproariously at their fun, desperately keen to write back, worrying for their safety in the weeks in between. 'Sam reckons if you read it [the nine-page letter] to the B knitters there will be no knitting that day', writes Bill. 'I reckon Sam is a bit of a Fifth columnist because he is stopping production at the knitting B'.[5]

Rather than simply pressing on with Norah's story, I include Sam and Bill here – their letters to Mollie and 'our Girl friends in the knitting squad', those 'B[lessed] knitters' who 'done there bit just the same as my gang', the banter between them, the way the language of romance is part of the morale-boosting package of care – because their contrast with Jim helps us to see him more clearly.

Sometimes we need more than the story itself to know what it might mean.

***

We don't know from Jim's letters how he got on with the men in Mess 2. His early request for a lock of Norah's hair, 'to be in fashion', suggests he wanted to be one of the lads. He had already told Norah that he spent his shore leave on his own. Whether he was a bit of a loner or merely trying to distance himself from stereotypes of sailors, we can't know. He must have been well aware that he had some work to do there. But maybe it was simply love and romance that he wanted: the adventure and the intense emotion, the idealisation of another, the masculine reassurance that a bit of chivalry could bring, feelings of being cherished in return.

He wouldn't be alone in that. Romantic overtures are very evident in the collection of letters written by servicemen to Doris Dockrill, a tobacco factory worker from Wandsworth, South London and a teenage knitter. Doris produced socks, gloves, scarves and balaclavas for British servicemen all over the globe. Most of the letters she received were one-off notes of thanks. Some contain a brief reference to the author's far-flungness and loneliness, their discomfort or boredom. Quite a few go further with an offer to repay Doris's kindness and hard work 'by taking you out somewhere and giving you a good time… what do you think of the idea?' 'Don't think I am being forward…' continues Ron Cotter, a driver in a Royal Artillery Anti-Tank Regiment. 'Perhaps we could go to a show over the West End eh, still you think it over & let me know. If you say yes, could you send a photo of yourself if you have one'. Cotter confided that he had been engaged but the girl had found someone new 'in Civvy Street […] so you can see that I have been let down very bad'.

Ron kept Doris's photo in his wallet. He wrongly assumed her age to be 24-25 years when, in fact, she was 14 in 1941. 'I hope I haven't given you a shock', he wrote, telling her that he was thirty-one. 'I don't think age counts do you, if a couple likes each other, & both have a pleasant nature, that I think goes a long way towards a nice friendship, you think it over Doris & let me know as soon as possible'. Thirty-year-old Eric Bowring was similarly 'surprised' in 1943, to find that Doris was only sixteen. 'I expected you to be a little older. Nevertheless, I expect you are much older in experience and ideas. You know the saying about a woman being as old as she looks and a man being as old as he feels. I would still like to meet you anyhow. You say you look older than sixteen so there is not many years between. We can always be friends anyhow. You can see for yourself when we meet, that is if you agree to. I shall be very disappointed if you don't'.

Other men were keen to ascertain Doris's marital status. 'Dear — Doris Dockrill', wrote S. E. Ridge, a sailor serving on HMS *Ganges*. 'Sorry I can not write much to you, as I do not know weather you are a miss or a mrs which makes a lot of difference in letter writing as you must know'. Peter O'Dwyer, given to reminiscing about nights at the Locarno and nostalgic for 'a walk along the high road and a stroll round Tooting Bec', was similarly pulled up short: 'PS It has just occurred to me that you might have become engaged since you made the comforts or perhaps you are an elderly woman, if so disregard my letter and accept my deepest thanks for what you sent you may be assured they are appreciated'.

Some letters very quickly read like dating profiles. 'Doris I believe you and I have a few things in common, such as we both like films, but to give you an idea of my character I will endeavour to tell you what I do and do not do', wrote Pete Hunt. He does not dance much, he tells her, nor go in for drinking but 'unfortunately' is a heavy smoker. Errol Flynn, Anne Sheridan and Ingrid Bergman are among his favourite actors and for music, he likes the Glenn Miller Band and Bing Crosby. He hopes to meet her on his next leave and would like a photo. 'You might be surprised to hear that I am approximately 6 ft tall, so I do hope you are not too small, although I shall not worry about that... Yours, Peter xxx'.

Writing in response to Doris's reply, Peter 'was very pleased to hear that we are some what similar in our doings, such as dancing and film stars', though he was 'very sorry to say I do not indulge in reading books very much', confessing that he had only read six books in his life. He had enjoyed *Jamaica Inn* and *No Orchids for Miss Blandish*, but supposed 'the latter is not in your line'. As a crime novel with controversially explicit scenes of sex and violence, about the kidnap and rape of a young woman, searched for by her father who wanted her back but with the proviso 'better dead than deflowered', I feel confident that this admission would not have endeared him to Doris or her parents, who kept a close eye on her epistolary affairs.[6]

***

Historians have written a great deal about letters between servicemen and their mothers, wives and girlfriends, showing the correspondence to be a crucial means by which men gained emotional sustenance and stayed in touch with their pre-war selves.[7] Here, however, we have something different. The letters that many men sent via the comforts funds in WW2 were written in a romantic register to unknown women and girls. While not quite love letters, they were an attempt to create intimacy and explore new romantic possibilities, sent to the girlfriends of their fantasies and, very possibly, by 'the selves of their imaginations' too.[8]

We know nothing more about Doris Dockrill and her pen-friendships. She appears not to have met any of the men, despite their requests. Although she gave Pete Hunt directions to her house, he later wrote to apologise for not turning up: his long-term girlfriend had arrived in town.⁹

Should we be concerned for her? Maybe not. While some men were perhaps a tad too bold, requests for photographs and gentle flirtation were part of the now-usual exchange between knitters and their correspondents.

And Norah? The sheer excitement of a budding romance overrode any concerns she may have had that anything could possibly go wrong.

8. Where Is That Photo? A Summer of Snaps and Studio Portraits

'Darling', Jim writes to Norah in mid-June, 'I am longing for your photo so I can have it on view when writing to you'. Jim has been pressing for weeks now for a photograph 'for keeps'. He continues to nudge over the coming weeks: 'How are the snap's of you looking. I will have time to study them now I am home'. But Norah has nothing to give him, not yet. She is short on snaps in 1941. As revealed by Jim's 'dearest dimples' address, she had sent him her most recent portrait, her bridesmaid photo from August 1939.

But suddenly, that summer, it was snaps all round. In the lead up to her final exams, Norah borrows a camera (from whom, we don't know) to take photographs of schoolteachers and friends on the bench in the grassy 'quad'. That same week, Jim sends her more *lovely photos of Danny*, his younger brother who was on a training course in Derby.

These snaps are surely among those in Norah's suitcase and which I now have laid out on my desk. I dearly wish I could show them to you but for now, at least, ethical considerations must prevail. You'll have to take my word for it that they are two good-looking boys. Jim, sailor-suited and in his Royal Navy cap, is shorter and stockier than his brother, his features – broad, full lips, straight nose, hazel eyes – pleasant and even. On another photo, sent to Norah at a later date, his handsome appearance is ever so slightly spoiled by the sense that his mouth is crowded with too many teeth.

Danny was suave. One pre-war snap shows him lounging in a park, cool and casual in an open-necked polo shirt. In another, he wears a camel coat and cashmere scarf as he leans against a tree trunk in a studio in Westward Ho! Then we see him besuited, Brylcreem-ed and oozing prospects, standing at a gate on a street of modern houses. Two wartime snaps show a smart and chisel-boned officer cadet in the shiny modern RAF. He is most handsome on the second of these, dated 1944. His smile makes the difference, tautening the skin across his cheekbones and adding a twinkle to his eyes.

Jim reveals in this June letter that he has asked Danny to meet Norah and sincerely hopes she 'will not be offended' by this request. Is this introduction a way of building familiarity and trust, drawing her more securely into his life? Or is it borne of an anxiety, suggested by his questions about schooling and dormitories, a hope that his brother will confirm that Norah is not a too-posh grammar school girl, out of his reach? *20th June: Received a letter from my sweety. He's going home. Hope he's not ill because I've got it pretty bad on him. Says Danny will try to meet me.*

Norah is not offended, not in the slightest. But when, on 5th July, Danny does *not turn up*, she is unperturbed. She has plenty else to think about. After her *last Scripture, Gym & Art lessons ever!*, followed by her *last Tutorial, French test, Arithmetic & Biology lessons* the following week, Norah is headlong into her Oxford School Certificate exams – some *ghastly*, one *lousy*, a few *not bad*. She continues to follow the war, noting the Syrian Armistice and the pact of allegiance between Britain and the USSR. She worries about Jim, who is out of touch again. *Where on earth has Jim got to? Where is my Jim?* As she leaves school forever, a letter arrives from Danny. At an airbase in Wiltshire, he is due to go home for a week's leave (*on a motorbike,* Norah writes). It seems that *he too has not heard from Jim for a very long time.* He encloses *a lovely photo of him for keeps.*

These airmen: they had allure. The 1930s had seen the RAF transformed from a rudimentary fleet – biplanes with open cockpits, wooden propellers and engines of no more than 650 horsepower – to the most modern and technologically advanced of the armed services; a 'new class of warriors'. And if the nation had been ambivalent about their youthful, carefree swagger, everything had changed the previous summer. While the Army was so far away in the Med and North Africa, the men of Fighter Command, Churchill's glorious few, were dog-fighting in British skies, and the 'bomber boys' in the great four-engined machines – the Lancasters, Stirlings and Halifaxes – risking it all with their nightly German raids.[1]

'I can't describe the effect wings have on a WAAF', wrote Joan Wyndham, referring to the pilot's badge above the left breast. Quite how much airmen should cash in on their erotic appeal was a subject of disagreement in the RAF. Many among the top brass thought it best crew members steered clear of women, lest they were distracted from the job at hand. But as Nevil Shute wrote in his 1944 novel. *Pastoral*: for 'everybody at Hartley aerodrome [...] love was as essential a commodity as petrol, and much more interesting'.[2]

8. Where Is That Photo? A Summer of Snaps and Studio Portraits

But for now, at least, Norah is perfectly happy with her sailor. *Where is my beloved?* she writes, as Jim falls silent again.

***

Norah was displeased with her first attempt to get a decent photograph of herself. Taken in Derby by a 'Mr. B.', it was *horrid. Absolutely lousy*. She couldn't possibly send it to Jim. She and Marsie made another trip, this time to the well-established studio of W. W. Winter on Midland Road.

In these years just before camera prices dropped and ordinary families began taking their own snaps, a trip to a photographic studio was quite an event. Not cheap, involving anticipation and forward planning, such portraits often marked a moment of transition: an engagement, a new baby, the entry into adulthood with a first job, an imminent death.[3] They were a rarity for the Hodgkinson family. We have photos of Marsie and Pop on their engagement (although, oddly, not their wedding day), some portraits of propped-up chubby babes and growing children, then – none at all. We can only assume it was the lack of funds that prohibited a series of 'pop as paterfamilias' portraits that Norah's paternal grandparents had enjoyed in later life.

This trip to Winter's: what would Norah tell me, if I was able to sit with her and talk about her studio photo, as historian Penny Tinkler has done with her interviewees?[4] Would she remember anything of how she felt that morning as she ironed her best frock and darkened her newly shaped brows? Would she remember snatches of her conversation with Marsie – about not wearing too much make-up, maybe, or which bus they should catch into town? Once at Winter's, she will have given her dark hair one last brush, checking her deep parting, re-gripping, hoping perhaps that her lighter brown roots would not be too noticeable in the sepia-toned image. Did she feel relaxed as she listened to the photographer's instructions: how to stand, hold her arms, perch against the bench?

I'd ask her about her dress. It must have been a special one as we found the pattern among her possessions when she died. I assume that it was made by Marsie in 1940, the year of the missing diary. It is not 'Utility': buttons, size of collar, gathered yoke and plentiful knife pleats to the skirt place it at the start of the war.[5] The colour? If only because Norah records in her diary that she bought blue and then green dress fabric in 1941, my guess is russet red or milk chocolate brown.

Fig. 24 Norah, W. W. Winter, Derby, 1941. Private papers of Norah Hodgkinson.

I'd quiz her too about the range of 'looks' on offer. While the studio style had become more relaxed, the question still stands of how much control the sitter could exert over her depiction. There would be a small number of options, including the one that Norah chose: informal but not too casual, half-sitting on a bench, with a backdrop of plain 'domestic' walls. What were the possibilities that she rejected? Too stiff and stuffy, perhaps? Too sultry? Without her Victorian-born mother watching on, might she have been more exploratory, made a different choice?[6]

And how do we see her, you the reader, and me, her great-niece? In *Camera Lucida*, his extraordinary study of photography and grief on the death of his mother, Roland Barthes proposes the idea of the *punctum*, the element of a photographic image that unexpectedly moves the viewer. The word is from the Latin, meaning to prick or to wound, and refers to an unexpected but arresting detail that affects us on an emotional level, unintended by both photographer and sitter and not necessarily noticed by other viewers. It is often something small, even banal, that bursts through the planned elements of the image – the set, the careful pose – to catch us off guard, to elicit a response, to feel, in Barthes' words, a laceration or 'tiny jubilations … buried in myself.'[7]

Barthes' *punctum* requires no prior knowledge of a photograph or its setting; its purest impact is on a viewer coming to it fresh. But my sense of Norah's later life shapes the power of her image. I am struck most of all by the contrast with her later portrait from 1945, the one that graces my mantelpiece (see Fig. 28). Her adopted movie-star gaze – elegantly impassive, eyes resting on the middle distance – is far removed from the immediacy of this earlier photo, where Norah smiles directly at the camera, her symmetrical features innocent, youthful and open.

I have known this portrait of Norah forever and yet it is only now, in the context of the adventure that was her life in 1941, that I can see its essence; the meaning that lies outside of the frame. At sixteen, with a sailor boyfriend and an impending first job in Derby, nine miles in the opposite direction from her school, her world is opening up, unfurling before her like rolling green meadows on a fresh summer's day. She is on the cusp of a new life, anticipating happiness, poised to seize the day.

And what was it that Jim had said? That her bridesmaid snap had kept his spirits high. Norah hoped this pic would do the same trick. And more besides, perhaps.[8]

Three weeks, Winter's said. When the photo arrived, she'd send a copy straight to Jim.

9. I'm in Love with Him and I Don't Care a Scrap

No sooner has he introduced Norah to Danny, than this still non-existent snap, the photo that lies in Winter's developing room, becomes the focus of Jim's jitters. His fear? That she has already sent a copy to his brother. In a strange letter singing Danny's praises and urging Norah to meet him, Jim requests that she saves 'an evening during this winter when I will endeavour to see you. Patience, I have got', he says, 'and can wait until 194.... for a photo. I bet Danny has got one (sorry)'.

There is no evidence at all that Norah had a romantic interest in Danny. Despite his lovely photos, his friendly overtures, it was Jim's letters that she waited for, Jim whom she worried about and had giddied over with friends. But again: 'You must have many admirers (why change your subjects) (sorry) …Yours Devoted, ~~Danny~~ Jim'. Jim signs as his brother before striking through. Is he bowing out? I can't help but wonder if he has lost out to Danny, his attractive, younger brother all through his life.

Norah seems not to notice, not at first.

> 19th August: Received a simply marvellous letter from my Jim. I adore him. Enclosed cutting about P[icture] P[ost] adopting 100 Abs [Able Seamen] & two naughty cartoons. Also a lovely letter from Danny. He is to be made a pilot. How awful.

But the following day, after a wry recounting of a visit to a local farmer she believed was sweet on Marsie, Norah ponders the dynamic between herself and these two men:

> 20th: Ma & I went up to Mr Sharman's. Gave Ma a lettuce like a cabbage, a white rose bud 'The Bride' & a grape each from bunch worth 15/ per lb. It seems to be a fight between Jim & Danny.

Fig. 25 'Between two fires' cartoon, 1941, enclosed in Jim's letter postmarked 17 August 1941. Private papers of Norah Hodgkinson. Photo: A. Twells, 2025.

'Fight' is an interesting choice of word, of course. Why not 'choice'? It was Norah who was doing the choosing after all. But 'fight' performs different work, positioning her as the object of desire. It is Norah who is between two fires.

'My Dream Girl', Jim gushes in early September, as his letters come thick and fast. 'I hope you ignore the saying about sailors because this one do care. I expect my loving brother's letters are more interesting only my schooling was neglected'. He tells Norah that a friend of his is getting on well in the boxing world – 'Freddie Mills, have you heard of him, a future champion, he is in the RAF'. Jim is not yet on the ropes.

> *1st September: Oxford results: I've passed. Received letter & photo from my sweetheart. I'm absolutely crazy about him. Also one from Danny, who says he too is fond of me. I like him a lot.*
>
> *2nd: Received letter from Station. Auntie Mabel & Uncle Roadley came. I'm still in love with —*
>
> *3rd: Replied to Danny.*

But three weeks into September, Jim blows it. In a letter with 'I LOVE YOU' written in kisses across the top, he engages in some general chitchat – congrats on her exam success, another request for a photo – and then asks, should his ship visit Grimsby, whether Norah 'would or could see me secretly for an hour or two'. He hopes that she will 'understand this unusual procedure on a first meeting... As I have said before I am casual and different but I will not promise to refrain from kissing if you give me an opportunity'.

Norah is affronted. It is an *awful letter* [...] *I'm terribly upset & disappointed*. What sort of girl meets a man in secret? And secretly from whom? Does Jim mean his brother, with whom Norah is now acquainted?

> *13th September: Received letter from Danny. Says he's coming today. Went to Derby to meet him but missed him. Came home and found him here. He's absolutely spiffing. Went down with Helen in dark. He gave me some wings and all stayed up til 12. Danny is absolutely lovely, marvellous, wonderful.*
>
> *14th: Danny & I went down to Hemington to phone & see Helen. Went to see him off at Derby. He kissed me on the station and I liked it. He'll reach Filey at 7.33pm.*
>
> *15th: Talked of no-one but Danny. Went down town with H & J.*
>
> *16th: Received short note from Jim who has not heard from me yet. Shah of Iran abdicated.*
>
> *18th: Ma received lovely letter from Danny. Replied at night. Replied to Jim.*

***

The *lovely letter* sent to Ma is the only one from Danny that seems to have survived. And what a letter it is.

RAF Filey
16th September 1941

Dear Mr and Mrs Hodgkinson,
   I wish to tender my sincere thanks to you all for the wonderful hospitality that you bestowed upon me. It was exceedingly fine and

> nice of you to welcome me to your home like you did, seeing I am quite a stranger, although you made me feel as though I was a son, and I appreciated it very much indeed.

Marsie would have been more than happy to open her home to him that weekend. It went without saying. 'Be not forgetful to entertain strangers: for thereby some have entertained angels unawares'.[1]

> It was a grand though short week end and the welcome I received will live in my mind forever, and I enjoyed myself exceedingly and I left Castle Donington with a hang in my heart.
> The journey was a tedious and tiring one seeing it was between 9.30 to 10 pm when I arrived at camp but I never cared how long it took for I had the lovely memories of you all especially Norah.

He was an impressive young man: charming, polite, well educated, conversing so easily with them all and, it now transpired, quite the letter writer. (Unavoidable: the contrast with his brother.)

And Norah? How did she read this letter from Danny? (Danny who writes her name four times!)

> When I left Norah at the station I sincerely hope the dear girl arrived home quite safely, it was very sweet of her to accompany me to the station, seeing it's such a distance from home. I shall never forget our parting, it really made me sad to see Norah waving to me as the train was pulling out.

No mention of the kiss, of course.

After his description of the slow journey back to Filey and his arrival at his very basic – *no lights, no comfort* – hut, his two days of note-taking (on the Thompson Machine Gun, and then on revolvers), she crops up again:

> Norah was vastly different to what I imagined, in fact she was far above my already high estimation of her. I think she is a fine, well-mannered and sweet young lady, and a daughter to be proud of. Also she has the sense of a much older person, and I couldn't help but take to her the first time we met.

He signs off:

> Well dear friends there is very little to write about at the moment so I will have to draw to a close. Please convey my very best regards to Frank, Richard, your eldest daughter and little Jean, and not forgetting Norah, give her my very best, and my sincere wishes to yourselves. Hoping this

finds you all enjoying the very best of health. Hoping to see you all again very soon.

Thanking you from the bottom of my Heart.
I am
Yours sincerely,
Danny

***

> *19th September: Received sweet letter from Danny. Enclosed beautiful photo and cutting called 'sweetheart'. I'm in love with him & I don't care a scrap. Went to Derby. Bought blue dress material & fed swans in river gardens.*

Did this next *sweet letter*, addressed just to her and to her alone, drop through the letterbox as Norah enjoyed her first cup of tea of the day, sitting at the table in a living room ablaze with autumnal morning sun? Its arrival will have put a spring in her step, as she prepared to leave the house for the bus. I picture her throwing her coat over her shoulders, kissing Marsie on the cheek, casually rebuffing some caustic remark thrown her way by Birdy, and reporting that she'll be back after lunch – or dinner, as we didn't call it lunch back then.

The ten-minute walk to the bus station is mostly downhill, the gradient adding momentum to Norah's jaunty stride. The birds sing. She flutters past neighbours and acquaintances and flashes them a smile with her sing-song 'hello'.

Forty minutes later, does Norah head straight to Midland Drapery, dithering over a flowery cotton fabric before dismissing it as too summery, settling instead on a vivid blue? As the haberdashery assistant measures two yards, snips with scissors and then tears through, does she imagine herself in the finished dress, walking out with Danny, holding his hand, in his arms? Not yet ready to catch the bus home, maybe she nips into the Market Hall for a white cob and, after a brief inward tussle, buys a celebratory bar of Cadbury's chocolate from the sweet stall (yes, chocolate was available during the war). Leaving by the Guildhall exit, she walks the hundred or so yards to the River Gardens. Good manners force her to head for the nearest available bench, but she feels too animated and eats half of the cob standing up, not registering her usual feeling of boredom, without even wishing for potted meat mixed with a thick spread of butter against the doughy bread.

Perhaps, true to form, Norah is eager to move onto dessert as she edges to the banks of the river and breaks the remaining bread into pieces. She stands there, slender and bright eyed, the breeze catching her dark hair and the skirt of her dress. Two swans glide towards her as she scatters the bread on the water, trying to make sure they get the same sized handful but half-noticing that one of them swiftly moves in on every last crumb.

Norah is sixteen and a half. Everything in her life has been moving towards this day. She'd had a momentary creeping doubt that summer, a worry that it wouldn't work out; that she'd become pot-bound when all she wanted was to burst into bloom, like Marsie's single agapanthus, chic and shimmering under a cloudless blue sky. But then, it all fell into place. The exam at the LMS Railway HQ. Her Oxford results – a respectable clutch of credits (Art, Domestic Science, English Language and French), passes (Arithmetic, Biology and Geography) and just the one fail (Shakespeare). An invitation to interview and her clerical position confirmed. And then, beyond her wildest dreams, this handsome airman walks up from the bus station and into her life.

I'm in love with him and I don't care a scrap.

Why should she care a scrap? Maybe she was harbouring a nagging concern about allowing herself to be kissed by a boy – indeed, a grown man – whom she had only just met. Danny, ready to board the train at Derby station, had turned and kissed her full on the mouth, lingering just long enough for her to move beyond the awkwardness and feel an unholy desire.

Did anyone see? What if some busy-body reported the scene to Marsie that morning as she queued at the Co-op meat-counter? Norah could not imagine her mother behaving that way when she was courted by Tom in 1908. But things were different back then. Now, romance and glamour were the order of the day and Norah wanted both as she headed for married life. As she stands on the edge of the Derwent throwing bread to the swans, does she wonder if she will walk up the aisle at the Baptist Chapel to meet Danny at the altar, sometime after this blessed war is over?

Or is the not caring a scrap a bid to suppress a sense of guilt about Jim? *My minesweeper*, now passed over in favour of his swish younger brother. Lovely, marvellous, wonderful Danny. Danny with his wings, and looking spiffing in Air Force blue. Danny, at ease with all the family, so sweet with baby Jean, so charming with her mother, chatting with Birdy, Frank and Pop, as they all stayed up until 12. Danny who kissed her like she'd never been kissed before, sparking feelings she didn't know she even possessed, leaving her utterly transformed.

Norah wondered if Jim would make a fuss. But it *was* he who had put her in touch with his brother. And he *was* a sailor. And he'd said he was casual. It must have been now, in the autumn of 1941 that she copied the following words into the back of her diary:

> *Some men would make a terrible scene, but my experience of sea going men tells me that they have a sound knowledge of human nature. They know that girls change their minds: that people fall in & out of love, that one has to accept what comes as one has to accept storms at sea. They are usually broad minded and philosophical.*

I wonder where it came from. A women's magazine, maybe? I try various searches, with no success.

A few days later, when Norah's photograph comes through the post, she clean forgets her promise to Jim. *20th September 1941: Photos from Winter's arrived. Sent D. one.*

10. The Erotics of War

27th September 1941: Danny wrote me a beautiful letter. I think he loves me, anyhow I love him very much.

And all from a pair of socks!

Most civilian girls met their servicemen lovers at dances in 1941. In the words of social researcher Pearl Jephcott, dancing was

> one of the recognized ways in which to meet and look over men, with an eye to selecting a husband. The dance-hall and relatively few other institutions, now that churchgoing has so declined, provide that range of young masculinity which the girls very properly desire to explore. To say that you will go dancing implies that you are going man-hunting, in a perfectly reputable sort of way.[1]

'Oh it was so exciting!' Kath Jones tells me one afternoon as we sit in her first-floor flat, drinking tea and talking about the war. Castle Donington was 'over-run with billeted soldiers' in 1941 and Kath, a few years older than Norah, was a regular at the dances put on for the Army units stationed at the Hall. The stately home in Donington Park had been requisitioned as a subsidiary of Chilwell Transport Depot, where Kath worked in the offices. Her workmates often came for the dances. 'There could be four of them', she told me, 'they used to love to come over, all staying at our house… The friendship was different somehow, during the war, you could talk to people and make friends'.

Kath's main dancing companion was Mary Twells, my great-aunt and Norah's fellow bridesmaid at the wedding of my grandparents, Norah's sister, Helen, and Joe Twells, Mary's brother, in August 1939. Mary and Norah had enjoyed a brief flurry of friendship that summer but soon went their separate ways. Fifteen months older, Mary was already working at the local factory known fondly as Sammy White's. She lived for fashionable clothes and nights out. Even on her walk back

©2025 Alison Twells, CC BY-NC 4.0   https://doi.org/10.11647/OBP.0461.10

from work, Kath recalled, she'd be at the heart of a raucous gaggle of laughing girls and dressed to the nines.

The dance venue, the dining room at the council school on Dovecote, had a wooden floor and chairs lining the walls and a stage for the military band. Cups of tea were served, not alcohol, leading some of the girls to start their night in one of the village pubs. But not Kath and Mary ('Ooh no!').

If the dancers had looked up at the high windows, they would have seen a huddle of younger girls peering in from their perch on the top of a coal heap outside. 'I was mesmerised', Norah's neighbour, Irene Marsh, told me. 'The uniforms! The elegance! The glamour!'

Kath met her own soldier husband when he plucked up the courage to ask her to dance one Friday night. Ron Jones was a big, gentle Welshman who had been at Dunkirk. After a spell in hospital, he was billeted at the farm on Apiary Gate that is now the village museum and had first spied Kath in her cap and gown, when he joined the largely female church choir.

'I see we've got a full choir today', the vicar welcomed them drily, as Ron's regiment turned out in force.

After the RAF arrived, a second dance started up at the aerodrome on the edge of the village. This is where Mary Twells met her husband, John Davison, on his first night at the airfield in 1944. The girls were not supposed to be there. On account of the short-cut home across a desolate wasteland, Kath's father had insisted they stay away. The girls ignored him, of course, assisted by the silence of Kath's mother.

'I told her it was better up there, with the RAF', Kath chuckles, 'not so rough. And we *were* invited'.

She remembers one journey home through the fields: 'I was wearing a pair of nylons that Ron had sent me from Germany, and I fell. Mary called out, "Oooh I hope that's not Kath in her nylons!"' I hear my Aunt Mary's voice as Kath speaks, her exclamation a mixture of fun and anxiety.

Tripping in the field on another occasion, Kath muddied up her new coat – green, full length, with a half-studded belt, bought at Ranby's in Derby for thirteen guineas.

'I knew my dad'd kill me if he saw it. He'd know where we'd been'.

She went home with Mary, and between them, in the Twells' kitchen, they made a bad job of removing the top layer of mud. Arriving back at the house attached to her father's decorating business on Borough Street, Kath pushed the shop door ajar a couple of inches, reaching up to muffle the bell as she slid in. Her plan to make an anxious dash past the living room door to her bedroom was thwarted as her dad called out drolly, 'I've 'eard yer'. Quick as a flash, she turned the coat inside out and left it on the stairs before greeting her parents with the least guilty expression she could muster. On her way to bed, she removed the coat to her wardrobe where it would hang to dry before being stiff-brushed clean.[2]

***

As far as oral histories go, my interview with Kath is not the best. The failings are all mine. Although I was as prepared as an any other historian would be, my blindspot about the excitement of weddings is plain to see.

'We went to Leicester, my mum and me', Kath told me, 'and bought a green silk outfit with a plain skirt and a top with a tie bow. It needed shortening. I said "well I'm being married on Wednesday" and they said "we'll get it to you"'.

It was such a rush. Ron had a seven-day pass before being deployed as part of an advance party to Normandy. There was no time to plan. Kath borrowed a fabric orchid from an aunt ('she kept telling me, "I do want it back, you know"'), a pair of shoes from a girl at work and a little brown fly-way hat from Mary's elder sister, my Aunt May. ('It had a lovely band of silk tied on and a flare. I didn't want to part with it'.)

'Your Aunt Mary, she kept saying to me, "Why don't you borrow our May's wedding dress?" But I said no, I didn't like to ask her. But I regret it now, not having a white dress, I feel like I missed out'.

For a historian exploring romance in WW2 – and at that, one who sat and admired the lovely photos of Ron in his uniform, of Kath, lips reddened, dark hair waved and set, slim and elegant in her green silk dress – to fail to follow this up is a poor show. A good oral historian would go further still, not only asking what would have felt different about the white dress, but trying to explore how this feeling had changed over time, to ascertain if this post-war lament was born of the later twentieth-century boom in the white wedding.[3] As Penny Summerfield writes, the oral historian needs to hear 'not only the voice that speaks for itself, but also the voices that speak to it', that is, the ideas in the culture at large since 1945, from which personal stories are shaped. When did the absence of a fairytale dress come to trump the feeling that a modest and hasty wedding was exactly right in 1944?[4]

My second major failing that afternoon is that I was inhibited by mine and Kath's long family acquaintance to ask her questions about sex. Some historians are impressively good at this, engaging in full and frank discussions with elderly interviewees about contraception, technique and pleasure.[5] I, it turns out, am not one of them. Indeed, my mum was perched on my shoulder as I imagined Kath's son, wide-eyed and furious, meeting her in the street: 'You will not believe what your daughter asked my mother!'

So in terms of oral history, this interview was a missed opportunity. There has been so little in the way of exploration of these wartime affairs[6] that would otherwise not have happened. But Kath's memories and the laughing, delighted tone in which she recounted them – the fun of friendships, the excitement of dances, the thrill of romance – corroborates other studies, from Denmark, Germany, Australia, which suggest that young women began to embrace a new way of loving during the war, the promise of a different future.

And sometimes a memory, or even a single image, can be just as powerful as historical analysis. Kath's nylons story, for example, revealing that the girls still went to the dances and enjoyed chaste flirtations with other men, even when they had boyfriends overseas. Of course, the lads were also out dancing, wherever they were stationed. For the rest of his life, through forty-plus years of marriage, Ron Jones kept a photograph of a Dutch girl.

'There were many times I meant to ask him about her', Kath mused. 'But I just didn't get round to it, somehow'.

***

I pay a visit to my Aunt Mary and Uncle John in their former council house over-looking the chip shop, four doors down from my mum. As always, I let myself in, and find my aunt in the armchair next to the gas fire and my uncle at the far end of the settee, his feet resting on a pouffe. He wears an unreadable expression and glances first at me and then, with one eyebrow raised, inviting a question, at a photograph of a soldier on the mantelpiece. I do as I am bidden. 'Who's he?' I ask, not very respectfully.

'It's Peter Pritchard', he replies. His voice is faster and at a slightly higher pitch than usual, emphasising his Liverpudlian twang. He notes my blank look. 'You mean you don't know Peter Pritchard?'

There is more than humour driving this question. I sense exasperation.

'Peter Pritchard, my first boyfriend'. My Aunt Mary has a slightly dreamy quality to her voice. 'I met him at the dances at the aerodrome. He was a lovely boy'. She smiles warmly and I give her a kiss, but I am not sure she knows who I am. She looks thinner and more frail than ever. Dementia doesn't make you very thoughtful regarding other peoples' feelings, including – or especially – those of your husband of sixty-five years, even if you were that way inclined to begin with.

'What's he doing up there?' I ask, unable to contain a smile.

'Your Aunt Mary fetched him out. All she wants to talk about. Peter bloody Pritchard'. He mouths the swearword to me, but she catches it.

'Now John'.

I make a pot of tea and then, wondering if he'll welcome a distraction from Peter's intrusion in his day, bring him up-to-date on our diary saga. 'Mum's been reading 1945', I say. 'You're in it'.

'I am, am I?' He is interested, wary. 'What does she say?'

'22nd September 1945: Mary Twells married John, her airman.'

He laughs. 'So that's who I am, is it? Her airman?' He isn't used to being anybody's anything, my uncle John. He's somebody in his own right. Tailor and shopkeeper, long retired. Liverpudlian, Blue not Red. Catholic parishioner, former Labour Party councillor, Rotarian, joker, and heart and soul of our family for sixty-five years. When he's better, I tell myself, I'll ask him about those dances in 1944.

I fill him in on Norah's passionate affair with Danny the airman.

'Passion isn't a quality I associate with Norah', he remarks.

I perk up and set down my tea. 'What do you mean?'

'She was cool and aloof'. He considers for a moment. 'Aloof and attractive'. I give him a look, try to embarrass him, draw him out further, but he shoots it straight back. He's having none of it.

'She was a lovely looking girl', Aunty Mary chips in, missing the passion bit.

My uncle's comment reminds me again that people in the village sometimes thought Norah a bit stand-offish. I realise also that he didn't meet her until late in the war, when he started courting his future wife. I think of the difference between the two wartime photographs. By 1945, Norah had adopted her movie-star gaze and calm and unruffled persona. But the first, the one we've seen, taken at W. W. Winter's in the autumn of 1941, shows her open-faced and smiling, looking directly at the camera. She was a lovely looking girl. And she was passionate.

Sadly, my Uncle John died the following year. Apart from everything else that I miss about him, I was looking forward to him reading this book as I wrote it. He had some misgivings, but I was confident I could talk him round. I also knew that he would give me a sense of the excitement of the dances from a serviceman's perspective and, if I dared push beyond his initial disapproval, an insider's 'gen' on sex and the RAF.

His daughter found some letters from his friend Bob Evans, written in 1944. I knew about Bob. A year or two before he died, my uncle had asked me to find out where his old friend was buried. They'd joined the RAF together in Liverpool, but Bob, on 'ops' from RAF Scampton at Lincoln, was shot down over Duisburg a few months before the war ended. I had located him easily via the Commonwealth War Graves Commission and then found my way to a website about Venray Cemetery, just over the border with Holland, where he is commemorated. The digital memorial bears his name but no further details. I clicked on 'contact' and emailed through: 'Please can you add the following?' I had written, wondering who was this American who managed a website devoted to honouring our war dead. 'Sergeant Robert Evans, date of birth 24th February 1923. Much loved son of Charles and Ada Gertrude Evans of Liverpool'.[7]

'I went to see them when I got back after the war', my uncle told me when I gave him the printed sheet. 'But he was their only son. They didn't want to know'.

***

Bob's letters are great; lovely, actually. There was lots he couldn't say, about activities at the base. But occasionally he wrote about the daily dangers that he – they all – faced:

> Bugger me if we didn't 'prang' in a crash drome called Carnaby, about a mile outside Bridlington. The flaps and undercart wouldn't come down, so I radioed base, and they diverted us to Carnaby. And there, to make things worse, the starboard outer went for a burton and so we landed on three engines at 140 mph! I had my right arm crushed a bit and the navigator got cuts in the head... I wasn't going to mention it at home [...]

And the losses:

> These Halifaxes go up within ten seconds of hitting the deck, you know; they reek of petrol from nose to tail. I lost thirteen pals that night, John, and when you've been laughing and joking with them in the briefing room a few hours before, it shakes you, believe me.

He wrote about how much he was looking forward to finishing his stint at Scampton:

> We are all in house again here, the same as at Finningley, one crew to a house. Believe it or not, our house is number '26', my lucky number! Anyway, I hope it keeps lucky for me until I leave this station. The day I do leave Scampton, I'm going straight to Lincoln and nipping sharpish on a train to Derby, where I intend to get the two of us (you and I) so 'canned' it will make those 'boozy do's' we used to have at New Brighton seem like child's play!!

But most of all, Bob wrote about women. There was his main girl, Nell L., back home in Liverpool, and another Nell (Little Nell), whom he had met at a dance when he was stationed in Hereford. Then there was Dot, who had an eye for John. And Joan, whom Bob considered 'very do-able'. There were the WAAFs, about whom he had some reservations.

> I told Nell (L.) I went to see you in Derby that time; always best to tell the truth, you know. Of course I forgot to tell her that I had Little Nell with me as well [...]

> (Little) Nell writes every day, which means I always get two letters from her on Monday, and she sends a parcel every couple of weeks, which includes biscuits, tins of spam, cake she makes herself etc. This week she sent me 200 players too, so you can see she's worth knowing! All I got from the other Nell in three years was a 2/6 book of stamps [...]

And he poked gentle fun at his old mate John who, while known for his craic, was a good Catholic boy and a hopeless romantic.

I can't understand how you have such bad luck with the women when you're freelancing at home. Even the guys here from Canada reckon they're about the easiest in the country and I guess they aren't far out at that. And as for that crack of yours, I don't think there's much I can teach you about the finer arts of twentieth century seduction! Of course I could leave you alone with Nell for half an hour (Little Nell, I mean), there's nothing worth mentioning that she couldn't impress on you! What a woman – sexy from head to toes. Wizzer. By the way, I agree that she isn't as nice in disposition as Nell L although her inclinations more than make up the balance.[8]

'Uncle John. Interested in character as well as looks', my mum says fondly, later that night. We are pondering the thrill of the war as girls like Kath and Mary and Norah suddenly had greater scope for meeting potential romantic partners from outside of the village. The gene pool in Castle Donington had remained relatively unchallenged for some time. While in the post-war years the development of transport links to Derby, Loughborough and Nottingham saw an exponential growth in population, there were few influxes in earlier decades. 'The local lads must have had their noses put out of joint', my mother says. 'Apart from those who were billeted elsewhere, causing a stir in some other village'.

Norah seems to have gone dancing a few times only, all at the beginning of 1941. *Frank & I went to dance,* she wrote in late January. We think there's a good chance she and Frank felt out of place. She didn't mix so well in the village. Kath had said as much. Like John, she found Norah a bit aloof. ('A lot of people did', my mum said. 'It was that school'.) Maybe the whole evening – the girls who rolled in from the pub, that most had gone to the council school bar her and Frank, that they were working and earning and she was not, the absence of lads who they might know from Hill Top – meant it wasn't quite their cup of tea.

But not going to dances didn't stop her. *4th April 1941: Broke up for Easter. Peggy & I stayed in Loughborough to see 'someone'. Went in Bolesworth's for a snack on 1/6. Three soldiers made eyes at us all the time!* And then there was the aerodrome, with its steady supply of flirtatious airmen. *15th July 1941: Man at the aerodrome gave me a super kiss.* Next came Jim and now there was Danny, whom she loved so very much.

This whole wartime kit and caboodle of meeting men who you wouldn't normally clap eyes on: it was so exciting. 'War is very erotic', writes Mary Wesley, author of *The Camomile Lawn*. 'People had love affairs they would not otherwise have had'.[9]

11. Poor Jim?

Despite his strange letters in which he pretty much conceded her to his brother, Jim had no intention of giving Norah up without a fight. In a letter of late September, he tried to put right his earlier gaff, explaining that his shyness was the real reason that he wanted to meet her privately. 'I hope to collect the kisses on the end of your letters soon', he continued. 'I am longing for your photo and hope the dimple's will not be missing. Did you enjoy Richard Tauber on the wireless? If I ever hear "Rose Marie" you are her in my thoughts'. He writes the words 'I LOVE' in kisses and 'you' in his normal hand.

By the time Jim penned his next letter, he had received Danny's unwelcome news. 'Danny seems rather struck on you and your family', he wrote curtly. 'Please read carefully, do you like Danny more than a pen-friend. If I visited you I am positive now that someone will be awfully disappointed… Please write by return all what you think of our affair'. He then switched to a more conciliatory tone: 'I like you and Danny very much and it is okay with me if Danny introduces you to me "one fine day" … I want to make things easier for you so it is a true friendship all round'. Jim *wants to clear up the puzzle of whom I love & wants to make it easier all round & enclosed D's letter to him,* Norah wrote on October 2nd. *It's terribly sweet of him.*

Poor Jim. Norah does want to behave well, to let him down nicely, but it's as if Danny's kiss and then his letters have left her sideswiped, propelled her into a strange new world where she momentarily loses her moorings. *4th October: Received a letter from Danny. He seems to want to clear things up a little. I think I am in love with Danny but I think Jim really cares for me & he is very sweet.*

In fact, it isn't just Danny. Two weeks after their first meeting, Norah started work as a clerical officer at the LMS (London, Midland, Scotland) Coal Office in Derby. Her job was the kind of position for which Loughborough High School had been turning out girls since the transformation of office work at the end of the previous century. By 1931, the 'white blouse revolution' saw that women accounted for 45% of the hugely expanded clerical workforce. By 1951: 58.6%. It was attractive work: clean, respectable, secure, and despite operating different scales for women and men, relatively well paid.[1]

From her first day in early October to the end of 1941, Norah wrote nothing at all in her diary about her actual work. For her, a job was a job, a means to an end: nice clothes, seaside holidays, evenings at the pictures and dance hall, her bottom drawer; an interlude between school and marriage. Her focus was her chats and lunchtime dates with Connie and Jean, two older girls who had boyfriends in the forces, and the mysterious Mrs Harris, who would lose her son in Germany in 1943. Norah notes also Marsie's regular spur-of-the-moment trips into town, often inspired by the arrival of a second-post letter from Danny or Jim, their lunches at Midland Drapery usually topped off with a browse in the shops.

Most of all, Norah wrote about men:

> *6th October 1941: Started work at LMS. Frank was passed grade II in medical exams. Is going in RAF. Radiolocation. Posted my Danny's letter.*
>
> *8th: Jean didn't go to the Institute. New soldiers arrived.*
>
> *9th: Poured with rain all day. Colin Brier came on leave & said it was all around his camp that I worked at Derby.*
>
> *10th: Ma came to Derby, so had lunch together at Boots. Saw Naval Officer like Danny.*
>
> *11th: Missed train at dinner time by going down town, so arrived home at about 2 o'clock. Terribly disappointed because my Danny didn't write.*
>
> *14th: Posted letter to Kathleen. No letter from my Danny Boy. Hundreds of WAAF on Platform 1. Made friends with boys in Night Office. Very foggy.*

That's five days out of her six-day week: the new soldiers at the Park, Frank's friend Colin and the lads at his camp, a naval officer who reminded her of Danny, and Danny himself, cropping up here and elsewhere with letters received, replied to and longed for. The following week, Norah meets the boys in the Night Office. Norman takes a shine to her: *My nice office boy gave me some more chocolate and asked for date. Turned him down.*

It seems Jim was right: Norah did have admirers. And the realisation was giddying. Sixteen years old, straight out of a girls' school, her days were suddenly alive with this new charge of energy, even among young men she'd known half her life. She was like a diver on a coral reef, slipping beneath the sea's calm surface to find this new world, intense and vibrant; a world which had been there all the time but of which she had previously had no more than an inkling. And in it, she had currency. As women were encouraged to define their social value through their capacity for romantic love, Norah was coming to know her worth.[2]

'Now we come to your letter, I think you have got me all wrong', Jim writes in mid-October. 'Although you may not be inclined to be serious with Danny and me, we are with you. I have loved you from the first letter but you are the one to decide [...] The reason I said my visit will be not certain, is you. I am in love with your photo so you know what position Danny and I are placed in. Please write and what is your verdict. "I love you"'.

In the absence of interest from Norah, whose diary entries are all about Danny, Jim's letters become shorter and more mundane. 'Remember I am still your mystery boy', he writes. 'I hope you approve of my photo, it is just as I am. Please write soon'. 'Dear Norah, I am still awaiting an answer to my last letter which contained a photo', he writes again. 'I hope you received it'. At the end of the month, Jim proposes a date, hoping that Norah would spend an evening with him, walking and talking. 'I hope you will reply by return, a love letter this time, or is it Danny?'

'He's trying very hard to appear casual, isn't he?' I muse to Mark, my then-partner and children's father, and a psychologist. 'Norah has dropped him for Danny, who hasn't got the balls to write to his brother. Jim's even asking her to nudge Danny into sending him a letter. I can't help but feel he is terribly hurt'.

'He's been betrayed', Mark replies, matter-of-factly.

'But by whom?' I am interested in who he thinks Jim sees as letting him down the most. His brother has gone off with his love interest after all.

'Norah, of course'.

***

Poor Jim, you're probably thinking. But I have an apology to make. I haven't been completely honest about Jim the sailor. Just this once, I've done that novelist's thing, choosing what to tell and when, delaying a small snippet that might have raised a question mark in your mind, as it did in mine. I've done this not to present some big reveal, but simply to show Jim as Norah saw him.

Almost from the outset of their correspondence, Jim presented himself as 'unusual'. 'Girls have never interested me', he wrote to Norah in early April 1941, 'and I have always had males for company'. Whilst he is 'the greatest of friends with most of the ship's company', he is a loner, he tells her, spending shore leave on his own.

I doubt that a virginal school girl knew in detail what naval ratings got up to on shore leave. But just in case, Jim deliberately represents himself as different from the sailor of popular stereotype. The possibility that he is gay also crosses my mind. 'My friend and I are very attached, and write regular', he wrote in one of his earliest letters. Despite the all-male shows, the beauty contests and cross dressing, life in the Navy for a secretly-gay sailor would be no walk in the park. But the final sentence in this same letter blows this lazy speculation: 'Have you a photo of yourself in school uniform', Jim asks, 'or are you shy?'

While I took particular notice of this request, Norah doesn't bat an eyelid. Her attentions are on the enclosed photograph of Nelson, Jim's best friend. *13th April: Received a rather romantic letter from Jim. Called me 'dearest dimples'. Asked for correspondent for Nelson.* So I force my reservations to one side. I am open to the possibility that I have got this wrong; that I might be projecting our contemporary fears about predatory men and grooming onto a moment in history when this exchange might have been viewed through another lens. It might simply be the case that school snaps were more readily available; that he was more likely to get one 'for keeps'. And much of what Jim writes is a little bit risqué, after all. He wants a love letter from Norah, whom he calls his 'dream lover', but he doesn't expect she'll comply ('shy'). Even when he asks her whether she shows her mother all of his letters, it is pefectly possible that he is winding her up.

When Jim makes another request for 'school snaps' a few weeks later, I am not so blasé. This is the letter where he tells Norah he has asked

Danny to try to see her: 'I would like to see you in your school outfit', he writes. 'I understand (shy). I wonder if you will send some school snaps, I will return them'. He signs off 'Yours more than imagination'. Again, Norah was unperturbed. In fact, she didn't seem to notice. *20th June: Received a letter from my sweety. He's going home. Hope he's not ill because I've got it pretty bad on him. Says Danny will try to meet me.*

It is perfectly plausible that this would pass Norah by. Before feminism, before the UN Convention on the Rights of the Child, there was no clear way of talking about predatory men. Norah knew that there were dodgy men around, men who could not be trusted, who could ruin you forever, even if she was not quite sure how that happened or what it entailed.

She will have had a fair acquaintance with the language of 'moral danger', used to refer to girls who were unmarried and pregnant, who were lured into prostitution or who were just plain 'flighty' and led men on. None of these applied to her, of course.

Sixteen-year-old Norah would also know from the newspapers that in cases where terrible things happened to girls, it was assumed that they were to blame.[3] She would be aware, from reticence and disapproval at school and at home, that it was best not to know too much, that sexual knowledge itself was seen as a corrupting influence, somehow dirtying and immoral.[4]

She'd hear the sexual slurs heaped on servicewomen – that the Women's Land Army had their 'Backs to the land', the ATS was the 'Groundsheet of the Army', and that men were 'Up with the lark and to bed with a Wren'. She'd no doubt note the endless discussions of their uniforms, whether they were too masculine, or too glamorous and slutty. She might have an opinion on make-up, may even have agreed with the army officer who, in a letter to service girls published in *Girls' Own Paper* in 1945, declared it 'quite out of place to smear yourselves with rouge and paint when you're on duty'. He hadn't much against 'using cosmetics in moderation, but when ATS girls in uniform appear with lips looking like over-ripe tomatoes, you ought to hear the men's remarks'.[5]

Those all-important, worth-defining *men's remarks*.

Might she hear counters to these, such as from those servicewomen who were forced to develop strategies to manage unwanted sexual attention and resorted to carrying hatpins to fend men off? Or from those who, like the censors in the WRNS, shared knowledge gleaned from a serviceman's letters to his would-be girlfriends to show that he was a bad lot? Did purer-than-pure Joyce Grenfell go public at the time she was serving with ENSA (Entertainments National Service Association) in the Middle East and found that her uniform 'stood for "the easy to get"'? (Of course she didn't, though she 'resent[ed] it deeply'.) Did anybody in Norah's circle echo Zelma Katin, a wartime transport worker in Sheffield, who wrote of conductors positioning themselves at the foot of the tram stairs to look up the skirts of ascending women, and a (male) general public, whose 'inhibitions vanish before the sight of a uniform', emboldened by the belief that girls in public places could be 'singled out for a special blackening of character'?[6]

The sullied reputation: Norah would know well enough that it was a fine line to tread. The waters might well have been muddied by her inkling that times were changing, by the tension between the old-fashioned propriety and a popular culture full of sexual charge. To be more worldly about sex was to be modern. But whether she would have any sense of the possible meaning of Jim's schoolgirl snap request, any means of identiying an unhealthy sexual interest in a man – I'm guessing not.

Indeed, she might even believe, like Home Defence volunteer Dorothy Williams, that it was only the Germans who did bad things.

> My father said that if the Germans did land, there'd be pillage, rape and he wouldn't *ever* allow us to be subjected to anything. Having said pillage and rape, he did not exactly use those words, because one did not in those days talk about rape... But I knew that it was something that he would never allow us to be submitted to. And if they ever landed he would *kill* us all rather than us ever fall into their hands. That frightened us a little bit, too. We didn't know which was going to be the worse of the two (*laughter*).[7]

And Jim: am I doing him a grave injustice? Did he want the photo simply to put name and face together, to imagine his correspondent whilst writing his letters? Or for his personal gratification – a furtive wank in his bunk, perhaps? Or maybe as part of a dare? Perhaps his messmates were bad lads, like those whom Dennis Maxted encountered at HMS *Collingwood*, egging each other on to extract what they could from unknowing girls?

It could be something or nothing. It is one step forward in the salaciousness quotient, that much is true. But it's not evidence of anything more untoward. Maybe the request was just an extension of the flirtation Jim was already engaged in. Perhaps for him it was all about the letters and photos; that he left the seduction to Danny, his smooth talking brother, who didn't mind putting in the work, chatting up the parents, turning on the charm.

But we don't know. At the very least, Jim's requests for schoolgirl snaps should alert us to the possibility that this might not be a straightforwardly reciprocal exchange. We would be happier, surely, if Norah had more knowledge about men and what they got up to. What we know and Norah doesn't is that it is perfectly plausible that Jim could be up to no good behind the scenes. As we've seen, it was not this request but his perceived slight to her respectability that offended her.

I will confess that after reading Jim's requests for snaps, when Norah switched her attentions to Danny that early autumn of 1941, I was mightily relieved. But included with that same letter from Jim was a small, rectangular, orange card which appears to have come from a seafront fortune-telling machine:

Fig. 26 Jack of Spades. Private papers of Norah Hodgkinson. Photo: A. Twells, 2025.

A Jack of Spades, it is, it states, 'a not over-lucky card to draw, as it indicates a reverse in love or contact with the law'; a card 'much used by fortune-tellers to signify a dark, deceitful friend of the male sex. You are on the road to marry a deceitful partner, and you are not always eager to tell the truth yourself. This is followed by a life of worry'. Whose future is being predicted, however, is unclear. Does Jim fear he is being deceived, or is he trying to give Norah a warning that things with Danny aren't quite what they seem?

Again, Norah makes no note of it. Why should she? She was already head over heels. Danny was spiffing and this new romantic grown-up life was grand. And he and his brother, an airman and a sailor, protecting women and children and our way of life: why would she worry? They were our heroes after all.

12. Went over Daleacre: The Likely and the Plausible

11th April 1942: Received a letter from my Danny. He's definitely coming today. Danny came about 8 o'clock & I fell all over again. Stayed up til 1 o'clock. Kissed me goodnight beautifully.

12th: Danny & I went over Daleacre in morning & down to the Trent at night. Mum told him all my secrets. He said he'd kiss me every time I said 'yes' & carried it out about 8 times. I love the way he kisses & him too.

13th: Danny went by bus to Birmingham just after nine. He says he hasn't so much confidence now but I hope he'll soon recover it. Received letter from Jim & let Danny read it.

I was hopeful in the early days that we might find Danny's letters in one of the piles of documents we salvaged from Norah's bungalow. But after a few months of sifting and sorting, we had to accept that they were gone forever. As her letters to him are also missing (of course), we are left to piece together their developing relationship from her diaries alone.

Received a letter from my Danny, Norah notes in her diary twice, three times, four times a month. He writes frequently, but in terms of the content of what he has to say, she gives little away. *Received a lovely letter from my Danny with a beautiful photo of him & his flight… Danny arrived in Isle of Man… He's passed his course… Danny went on battle exercise… Received a beautiful letter from my dearest sweetheart.*

It is hard to know how established a relationship this was. With Danny at such a distance – in Wiltshire, then London, followed by a longer stint on the Isle of Man, then Worcester in late February 1942 – they were hardly an item. But the lovely letters that he wrote to her, the beautiful Christmas telegram *from my love*, the Greetings Telegram that arrived on her seventeenth birthday, all suggest that the relationship was *on*, that they were well on their way to becoming a couple.

The most fulsome set of diary entries about Danny concern his visit at Easter 1942. This was only their second meeting. If Norah had any worries that over the months she'd romanticised him beyond all recognition, or that he wouldn't still be attracted to her, she doesn't say. But in those hours between 8pm and 1am, she *fell all over again*.

How did the evening pan out? Danny arrived after dinner – which, I am guessing, would have been about 6pm. With everybody working out of the village, the Hodgkinsons will have made the switch from dinner at noon to a cooked evening meal. I doubt, with men to feed, that they delayed. Maybe Marsie kept a plateful of food warm for Danny or Norah rustled up a quick snack on his arrival, a ham sandwich perhaps, and a welcome cup of tea to wash it down.

We can only guess at their conversation, of course. There would be family news. Danny was polite enough to enquire. He will have known from Norah's letters that Helen had been ill with pleurisy, that Dennis, Norah's eldest brother, was already in the Army, somewhere in North Wales, and Frank's papers were due any time soon. Birdy was still hoping his epilepsy would see him exempt, but I doubt he'd crow about that in a room with a serving airman and a Boer War vet, and Norah and Marsie would refrain from the ribbing they dished out on a normal day.

They surely talked about the progress of the war. Maybe they caught the 9 o'clock news. At this point, early 1942, it was hard to be upbeat. The public, annoyed by the 'soft-pedalling of bad tidings', could read between the lines. The Blitz was stepping up again, though Churchill's promise to unleash 'shattering strokes of retributive justice' on German industrial regions was still a few weeks away.[1] Pop will have had plenty to say about recent catastrophes: the disastrous fall of Singapore, the surrender in Java and the Japanese entry into Rangoon, the wolf-packs of U-boats in the Atlantic which meant the war at sea was going badly. No doubt he agreed with public demands to help the Russians and was disappointed by Churchill's focus on the mess at Tobruk and the 33,000 men now captive there.

Marsie and Norah tried to keep it light (no easy feat with Pop and Birdy in the room). The man needed a break, after all. Did they chat about the ingenious ways they dealt with rationing, now extended to absolutely everything: canned meat, fish, veg, dried fruit, canned fruit, tapioca, sago, condensed milk, tomatoes and soap? What with Joe being a butcher, they didn't do badly for fresh meat (shhh). They no doubt joked about the impact on Norah of plans to include syrup, treacle and biscuits in the next roll out, with a 'personal points' scheme for chocolate and sweets coming in soon.[2] Danny knew all about Norah's sweet tooth. She will have mentioned in a letter the lovely Victoria sponge she had made for her birthday (but probably omitted reference to the gifts from Norman and the boys in the Night Office: *all the lovely choc*).

Birdy may well have teased her about her successes at bartering clothing coupons, taking on his household jobs in return for a new pair of shoes. Perhaps Norah had a brief moan about the upcoming Utility Wear that was just plain ugly, with pleats, seams and buttonholes, decent hems and collars, all things of the past. Still, 'Make Do and Mend' was nothing new, had long been a way of life for women like her. You just had to smile through.

Are there too many maybes in this story? Historians don't like too much uncertainty. 'Though astute, the author is sometimes too dependent on speculation', writes a reviewer of *The Five*, Hallie Rubenhold's excellent study of Jack the Ripper's victims. 'There are many conditionals – and in search of nuance she makes some assumptions which, in the absence of a firm historical record, are impossible to check and have to be left to the domain of the likely and the possible'.[3]

The many 'would haves', 'perhapses' and 'maybes' is the basis of James Buchan's criticism of Natalie Zemon Davis' *Trickster Travels* (2007), her study of al-Hasan al-Wazan, the man known to history as Leo Africanus, traveller and author of the first geography of Africa published in Europe in 1550. It is, Buchan writes, 'not history but a sort of romance laden with footnotes, a novel dragging an academic ball and chain'.[4]

But what do we do when more than fragmentary sources elude us? Do we just not tell those stories, confine our knowledge of the past to the well documented, the already told? We are back to the lives of Great Men that way. In his positive review of the same book by Davis, Jonathan Berkey writes that while 'the reader cannot help but notice how frequently terms like "might have" and "probably" or "possibly" pepper the text', it is, for him, 'not an obstacle'. Davis poses questions, draws on comparable evidence, makes plausible comparisons.[5]

Comparing silence and absence in history with the phenomenon of the black hole, Hannu Salmi suggests that as astrophysicists can determine features about such holes on the basis of their environment, so historians can draw inferences about the past even when it provides no direct evidence. 'In a situation in which history is a black hole', Salmi writes, '... we can imagine nothing about the core of the hole that would contradict the information provided by the surrounding cosmos'.[6] But we know it exists. Much of history comprises an 'unknowable territory', in Frank Ankersmit's words. 'Saying true things about the past is easy', he writes, 'anybody can do that'. It is the 'dogged effort' to explore unknowable borders that is most compelling.[7] As Davis explains in her introduction to her earlier study, *The Return of Martin Guerre* (1983): 'When I could not find my individual man or woman in Hendaye, in Artigat, in Sajas, or in Burgos, then I did my best through other sources from the period and place to discover the world they would have seen and the reactions they might have had. What I offer you here is in part my invention, but held tightly in check by the voices of the past'.[8]

The detail of Norah's courtship with Danny is my 'unknowable territory', my black hole. All we know for certain about that night is that at getting on for 1am, the family disappeared up to bed, leaving Norah and Danny alone. *Kissed me goodnight beautifully.*

***

There is a trio of men in these three diary entries: Danny, Jim and Norman, the boy from the Night Office, who had been wooing Norah with chocolate since her arrival at the LMS in October 1941. She had turned down his first few requests for a date, but he was persistent and, when they finally went to see John Wayne in *The Citadel of Crime* in mid-February, he wrote her a (love?) letter the next day. A fortnight later, they saw *Ice Capades*, a slow-moving American comedy and again, he followed up with a letter.

But beyond friendship, Norah was not interested. Her diary entry after their third date betrays her lack of excitement. *19th March: Went to pictures with Norman. Saw Nelson Eddy & Rise Stevens in 'Chocolate Soldier'. Rotten.* Her disinterest is even more palpable when she hears that Danny has a cold and wishes she could nurse him back to health, while poor old Norman is off work with *mumps or something*. A week later, he sends her a *shirty letter* and accuses her of having *led him up the garden path*.

Norman almost gets his revenge during Danny's Easter visit, when Marsie reveals the dates her daughter would rather keep under wraps. *Mum told him all my secrets,* Norah writes. She seems unperturbed, nonetheless: while she no doubt enjoyed Norman's attention, she'd been careful to not give him the wrong idea. Her sights were set on Danny alone.

Norah's confidence is surely borne of her and Danny's shared intimacy, including reading together the letter from Jim which arrived during Danny's visit after a month-long silence. Jim explains why, despite his promises, he'd failed to meet Norah in Derby a few weeks before.

HMS *Elgin*, GPO London
[Postmark: Aberdeen 10 Apr 1942]

Dear Norah,

I expect you think me rather odd and fail to understand my attitude towards you. When we first corresponded it was my sole intention to start an intimate friendship. Since Danny has come in the picture you can see why my letters are not frequent and my visit to Derby has not taken place. When I got your photo I naturally fell for you the same as Danny. I had the pleasure of seeing Danny just recently and he described you and said you are swell which I don't doubt. It makes me happy to know you and Danny are such good friends. We may meet one day but I would never make a special visit to see you. Would you tell me if in your way do you love Danny? I can assure you he does. I want you to know I am not put out or jealous because Danny is a swell brother and he spoke on fair terms concerning you so we are settled over you. Please do not imagine we are taking things for granted but if you love Danny he is yours.

Please write and tell me your thoughts.
Cheerio,
Love Jim

Norah will have expressed her upset that Jim had declined to meet her and seemed no longer inclined to write. And Danny? That final sentence is the crucial one: *if you love Danny he is yours.* We can presume that he did not demur.

***

And then there are their walks. *Down to the Trent* could refer to any number of locations (Cavendish Bridge? King's Mills?), whereas *over Daleacre* is specific: the high grassy ridge connecting two neighbouring villages, a half a mile or so from Norah's home. With their thatched cottages and pretty streams, Hemington and Lockington are as chocolate-boxy and quaint as any Derbyshire village even if the plains of the Trent Valley are far removed from the undulating charms of the Dales, and Daleacre itself (pronounced Daliger, with a hard 'g'), in the scheme of things, is nothing special.

Except it is, to us. Like Norah, I love this landscape. There is nowhere that I feel more strongly the sedimented layers of history, the intimate connectedness between time and space.[9] Daleacre was Marsie's picnicking site with her children and grandchildren over five decades before I was born. More distant ancestral presences exist on the Twells side, the fields still bearing the imprint of medieval strip-farming and the generations of labourer ancestors who have lived and toiled in these villages since before the church records began.

Daleacre has been the site of teenage dog walks, intimate ambles with lovers and friends and in more recent years, the mid-September blackberrying spot for my young daughters and me. Leaving grandma's house on Barroon, we'd follow the same route that Norah took with Danny, passing the grand old houses and smaller cottages, then the cemetery, where Norah and three of her siblings are now buried, the allotments and Cherry Orchard now bereft of cherries. We'd enter the grassy slopes of Lady's Close through the kissing gate, leaving by the same at the bottom of the field. Crossing the road, passing beneath the ruined church reputed to have been used for canon practice by Cromwell's men, we'd head up through the overhanging boughs of Church Lane and Dark Lane, looping round through the red-brick farm houses and cottages of Lockington, taking a path through another kissing gate into an open field and, keeping an eye out for cows, start the climb up onto Daleacre ridge.

The gradient makes blackberrying a precarious business, the slightest over-reach tipping the picker forward until they threaten to topple into the prickly beds below. Bags and tupperwares full, younger daughter snagged and juice-stained, we made our way down towards Hemington, where a modern form of enclosure has seen the ruined church absorbed into the garden of a plush house in a new gated community. Grandma and Bessie dog on look-out duty, my daughters and I enjoyed the thrill of the illicit clamber up the stone wall to the damson tree, shaking the sturdy trunk and branches, straining to catch the black fruit before it dropped into the cowpats below.

A few weeks later and we'd be back again, Daleacre now forming the course of our Sunday morning walk after a night at Donington Wakes, an age-old annual fair which sees the main shopping street lined with stalls and fairground rides. The walk over Daleacre was as essential as the hook-a-duck stall or, as my girls grew, the Cyclone ride in the Turk's Head yard. It was as much part and parcel of the weekend as our late-night open chips, eaten as we perched on the low cold concrete of Mrs Kinsella's council-bungalow wall, in that final hour before the lights went out, the rides were dismantled and the main street litter-strewn and dulled, like the underside of a rug. The following morning, after younger daughter had scuppered all hope of a lie-in, we walked up through the now golden autumnal lanes, stopping for a teacake on the bench on the top of the hill. It was there, in the years after her death, that my thoughts would turn to Norah, here on her dates with Danny in 1942, when *walked over Daleacre* was code for romance.

***

Walking alongside another has been developed as a life story research method, a way of enabling interpersonal understanding. If I walked with Norah now, sharing a rhythm, the same views, checking out together whether the bull was safely gated in a neighbouring field, and I asked her about other walks over Daleacre she had made in her lifetime, what would she tell me? My guess is that she might chat about Marsie and their picnics and warm autumn afternoons spent blackberrying. But those most embodied, most sensual of walks with Danny? She'd remember, and feel, in silence.

Instead, I mobilise my possibles and probables and walk in her footsteps. I stand before the gate and look across 'into the unattainable past on the other side' and try, in the words of biographer Richard Holmes, to bring it alive 'by other sorts of skills and crafts and sensible magic'.[10]

Norah and Danny, walking out together on this their first meeting since his visit seven months before. Norah wearing one of her new dresses, either the blue or the green, Danny in his RAF uniform, exuding that ashy blue flyboy glamour. Do these well-trodden paths now feel unfamiliar underfoot, as she links her arm in his, trying to keep in rhythm with his stride? Do encounters with people she has known since childhood feel just as strange, like she is an interloper in her old life? Maybe she wonders if any of them have felt as she feels now, this hidden but utterly transforming swell of passion. Do the kisses start on the kissing-gated grassy slopes of Lady's Close, or maybe as they reach the leafy seclusion of Church Lane, the green hedgerows alive with birdsong, arm-in-arm becomes arm-around-her-waist and Danny pulls her in, pausing to kiss her every time she says 'yes'?

On our imaginary walk over Daleacre, is this what Norah would remember? Her and Danny disentangling as they enter Lockington village, then once onto Daleacre's slopes, she is heady again with the day's wild sweetness as they reach the series of small hillocks that give good cover for a canoodling couple as well as a vantage point over the path below. She would surely remember how Danny seemed to know what she herself didn't know, that she had a 'hidden self' to be discovered, by his mouth, his hands, his sometimes gentle, sometimes fevered attentions. How her own body now told her what she'd had no inkling of before: that 'the world was matter, not words'.[11]

The smell of his aftershave (fruity, flowery, bitter?), the burning look in his eyes, the confidence of his kisses.

13. If You Love Danny He Is Yours

Jim's Easter letter niggles me, but I can't put my finger on what it is that feels not quite right.

At the beginning of 1942, Jim had changed tack, his letters to Norah coming to focus on her relationship with his brother. 'Danny thinks you're the sweetest girl he has ever known' he wrote in mid-January. 'Please don't tell him I am giving his secrets away'. 'Danny has passed the writing part of his course. I think you will be proud of him', he told Norah the following month. 'I guess you are both longing to see each other again, his latest letter is all about Norah. If ever you want to ask anything concerning Danny, don't be shy to ask me'.

Although Jim seemed straightforward enough in his promises to visit Derby during his upcoming leave, informing Norah of his lodgings in town, he failed to turn up to their planned meeting. His Easter letter, the one that arrived during Danny's visit, offered an explanation for his absence. Here Jim reveals his disappointment, confessing that it had been his 'sole intention' to start an 'intimate friendship' with Norah, but insisting again that his own hopes for romance came second to brotherly love. But the 'fair terms' he mentions puzzle me. If Jim admitted to his brother that he was keen on Norah, why did Danny not offer to back off?

I hear Mark descending the stairs and call him into the front room.

'I just don't get this', I confess. 'Why is Jim claiming he is happy to offer a helping hand in Norah's relationship with his brother, yet that same brother has stolen her from under his nose?'

Mark protests that he hasn't got time, but I know that if I can keep him long enough to hear one choice extract from Jim's letters, he'll be hooked. Mark is a psychologist. A bit of male angst and concealed emotion is right up his street. I read him the lines where Jim explains why he has not visited. I can see from his face that I've reeled him in.

'What do *you* think is going on?' His half-amused expression suggests that he expects me to have no idea. He knows from bitter experience that men are a mystery to me.

'Well, Jim seems quite reasonable', I start tentatively. 'He had set his sights on Norah , but when it became apparent she was into Danny, he seems to have set himself up as a sort of go-between'.

Mark looks at me with a quizzical expression. 'No', he says flatly. 'Jim's fishing. He wants Norah to say something definite, that she really wants to see him, or that Danny is the special one now, so he knows where he stands'. He pauses. 'He says he won't come to Derby, but do you think if Norah said she really wanted to meet him, he wouldn't make that visit?'

'He'd be there like a shot?' I venture, the words at odds with my voice as it tails into uncertainty.

'Of course he would. He wants to see her reaction to him saying he wouldn't visit. He feels jilted. He knows he can't be bitter and angry, he'd lose her completely. He's doesn't want to be disloyal to his brother, but he wants to win her on his own terms'.

He points me to the phrase 'since Danny has come in the picture'. 'He's an angry man', Mark says. '"I had the pleasure of seeing Danny just recently." Can't you hear it? "We may meet one day but I would never make a special visit to see you." This is strong stuff!'

I can see it is a fine line for Jim. He is working hard at being gracious, in the hope that she'll decide he's 'the one' after all.

'When Jim says he and Danny "spoke on fair terms" about Norah, that they are "settled" over her: what's that about?' I tell Mark my theory that Jim had revealed to his brother the extent of his interest in Norah, in the hope that Danny would step aside.

'That's just not how it works'. Mark looks at me with an almost pitying expression. 'Jim will have played down to his brother how much he wants Norah because he suspected she had an interest in Danny'.

'But how do you know it worked that way, with these men, then, more than half a century ago?' I ask. 'It was a different time. People's emotional lives, feelings of hurt and pride, are not unchanging, throughout history'.

Mark ignores my question. If I'm a doubting kind of gal, he is a very certain kind of man. And psychologists aren't generally interested in the historical nuances of fraternal relationships, masculinity and emotion. I find it helpful to think about Jim's behaviour in terms of questions posed by modern psychology, but only so far. It might ring true, but that's surely because it makes sense to us now. It is no substitute for history.

I realise too that these letters are at the heart of this book; they are my 'exceptional normal'. For a sailor to write sexually explicit letters to a schoolgirl sock-knitter was unusual, if not unknown, as we've seen. As has been said to me many times, it is not typical behaviour. The implication, I think, is that I cannot draw conclusions about actions that are not representative, are not the norm. But I am not suggesting that all men behaved this way (#notallmen, of course. Although always, without fail, a man). I am well aware that servicemen were a thoroughly mixed bag; that very many would find Jim's behaviour abhorrent, then as now. It remains the case, nonetheless, that when properly investigated, Jim's letters burst open a world of usually concealed interaction, revealing more about courtship dynamics in the 1940s than would a more commonplace exchange.[1]

***

Mark and I agree that the arrival of his letter during Danny's visit did Jim no favours. Norah showing it to Danny offered scope for intimacy. 'They could talk about emotion', Mark says. 'Jim's, Norah's upset about his lack of visit, Danny's'. He pauses briefly. 'What happened next?'

As I unfold Jim's next letter, a small slip of lined paper falls out. I catch it and hold it behind the page as I begin to read:

Dear Norah,
I have just received a letter from Danny and your name is mentioned quite a lot. He had a marvellous time with you and your family. I think he is crazy over you. Why should my last letter upset you? I would not hurt your feelings for anything. You know Norah to be candid I would not fit in so well as Danny, remember I am a sailor and my words and ways are different. The life in the navy is reverse to that of the RAF. We are rough. I may be a little different to the average but I am still a sailor. I know definitely you are the swellest girlfriend I have and hope you will always remain so. Norah, is Danny taking you too serious? If you want me to tell him indirectly anything special, you can depend on me to make things right. I do want you to realise I am not put out in any way because when Danny is happy, I am. My brothers are more to me than anything else, especially Danny. I hope you will write me a letter and tell me all

your secrets. Well darling, I close, wishing you and all at 18 Moira Dale all the best.

Your greatest friend,
Jim

'So Norah told him she was upset by his decision not to visit', Mark says, 'but she didn't beg him to change his mind'.

I turn my attention to the small torn-off scrap of paper. It seems to be an extract of a letter sent by Danny to his brother, describing his stay at Norah's home. I start to read:

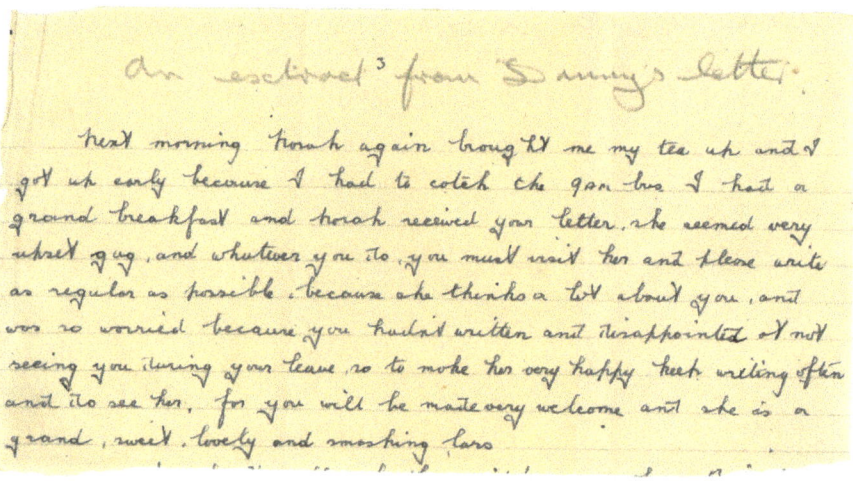

Fig. 27 Snippet from Danny's letter, April 1942. Private papers of Norah Hodgkinson. Photo: A. Twells, 2025.

Next morning Norah again bought me my tea up and I got up early because I had to catch the 9am bus. I had a grand breakfast and Norah received your letter. She seemed very upset, and whatever you do, you must visit her and please write as regular as possible, because she thinks a lot about you and was so worried because you hadn't written and disappointed at not seeing you during your leave, so to make her very happy keep writing often and do see her, for you will be made very welcome, and she is a grand, sweet, lovely and smashing lass.

'A bit odd?' I say. Norah took it at face value. *23rd April: Received a lovely letter from Jim & sent a grand bit out of Danny's letter to him. They're a grand couple.* A few days later, she met Danny at the station as he passed through Derby on his way up north to a Tank Course. *I'm absolutely crazy about him & it was grand to see him.*

But Mark is looking very dubious. 'I just don't believe this', he says. 'I don't believe that's how Danny would describe Norah to his brother'. He pauses. 'Think back to your Uncle John and his mate from Liverpool. What do you think Danny would have said, in the real letter?'

'Oh, you know, some RAF news, maybe some horror that he wanted to share, a near-miss at the base, some lads who had failed to return. He would talk about their family in Eastbourne. And he'd definitely mention his visit to Norah'.

'But *what* about Norah?' he presses. 'The thoroughly wholesome Norah of this description? They will talk about women, boast to each other. Danny won't choose modesty over his own satisfaction at his sexual successes'.

I sift through the stash of letters from Jim, shuffling into date order those postmarked May-July 1942. I know that Mark won't stick around long enough to hear me read them all, so I flick through the next few, picking out eye-catching passages.

> 'I wish I knew you really and truly loved him. Soon you will be telling me off for being so nosy. Anytime you have any problems concerning Danny please let me help you.'

> 'My kiss will be cancelled until I am best man.'

> 'To be candid, I know I should be jealous of Danny so perhaps that is one reason I don't come and see you. Danny is the greatest pal I ever had and please grant him my kisses that will make me just as happy...'

> 'Norah if you want Danny don't be afraid to let your feelings go or are you shy. I wish you would tell what you and Danny do when he stays with you, or don't you get the opportunity, meaning being alone. Have you had more than a parting kiss?'

> 'Norah perhaps I have no right in butting in your private affairs, but you can depend on me and I will do anything to help you. I wish also you would ask me a million questions. Next letter then I will expect a real —? Have you any young snaps of yourself?'

'Oh God', I say. '"Young snaps" again. And now he is encouraging Norah to – presumably he means to have sex with his brother?' I move on to Jim's next letter, sent from Great Yarmouth in early June. After telling her she is the 'swellest friend' he could have, and 'no wonder Danny is crazy over [her]', he then launches into his love life pre-war. 'I was a proper pansy', I read:

> and only ate dainty foods and always bought myself Rowntree's blackcurrant pastilles, and with experience girls enjoyed my kisses much better than with fellows who smoked a lot. I used to like to tease girls and get them all unnecessary, which I guess Danny did with you, 'did he'. I am no angel but my motto has always been 'have fun and be good' because five minutes pleasure is not worth a life's worry. When two lovers have known each other for a considerable time and say they are engaged they become more intimate, it is true if the boy is decent and respects his loved one he will never ask too much from her. I have known cases where the girl loves too much and would not refuse, so darling whatever happiness don't forget to marry in white. I don't expect you have any confessions have you.

Mark snorts. 'A "proper pansy"? He's not making it easy to take him seriously'.

Norah does, though. She describes this as a *grand letter*. Boys being considerate, the desirability of the white wedding, not scuppering that by acting in passionate haste, and his signing off: 'Your future brother-in-law'.

On the envelope of his next letter, Jim has scrawled an epitaph: 'In precious memory of our beloved daughter Barbara Forrester, passed away August 29th 1936, aged 16 years. "Gone from us but not forgotten/ Never shall thy memory fade/ Sweetest thoughts shall ever linger/ Round the spot where thou are laid"'. Inside, he explains:

> In an early letter I told you my favourite song was 'Smilin Through' and I would like to tell why it is. At the time the picture was showing in Eastbourne my pal and I were friendly with two girlfriends who to this day we both class the best we ever had. Their parents were rather strict and forbade them associating with boys so it was only by scheming and strategy that we saw them and I believe that just several minutes was worth hours to us. Now this is where Smilin Thru comes in and still plays its part, all four of us saw the picture and if you have seen the picture you will see the meaning of my story. Now for the tragedy. My friend caught typhoid fever which caused her death. It was not until a week after her burial did I even know she was ill. My pal and I visited her grave and found her flowers were buried with the coffin so the wreath we placed on her grave was the only one. I selected the words and wrote them on a plain

white card and ended it from friends Nelson and Jim. She was the only daughter and I learned that she was all her mother and father lived for, incidentally her father was a director of a tea plantation in Assam, India. Several months later we visited her grave again and the words on her stone were the ones I had written on the wreath. I expect you can read them on the snap. I know you will understand. I have also enclosed her photo.

What Jim wants to achieve with these letters isn't clear to me.

'The point of this one is to show Norah that he has had girlfriends from good families', Mark replies. 'That he is respectable enough for her. What does she say?'

'18th June', I read. '*Received grand letter from Jim containing a lovely photo of a grand girl called Barbara Forrester*'. So it worked.

I wonder if this is even a true story, whether he had heard a version of it in the mess.

Jim then reverts to his usual chat, declaring that his 'nerve will not allow me to ask those intimate questions because you may look on the rude side and may not wish to correspond again ... Norah what actually is the meaning of a white wedding? ('shy')', he asks. 'If you loved a boy and was engaged to him would you give way a little to satisfy yours and his feelings?'

'I am glad you wangled the time and place to make love to Danny', Jim writes, telling her how Danny had always been popular with girls:

> I can remember when he used to play cricket and several girls hung around until the game was over, but he never was interested in girls and so his kisses must have been stored just for you. I expect you know all the answers, especially if you are great pals with your married sister. Passionate kisses are marvellous when both involved respond to each other's. Please tell me how and where you and Danny were alone because the way he wrote to me seemed that all his time with you was always in company with your family. In his first letter, after his visit to your home he told me he plucked up courage and kissed you on the station platform, and he was worrying if he had offended you. I have not heard from Danny but he did say he was looking forward to seeing you when he passed through Derby. Was Danny the first to make real love to you if so what effect did it have on you? –

I am aghast. 'What the hell..?'

'Hang on', Mark cuts in. 'I thought you said Norah and Danny hadn't had sex?'

'They haven't. Mum's read later diaries, there are times when Danny is trying to persuade her to do it, "give in" is the term he uses. Her diaries make it really clear they hadn't'.

'But that sentence – "Was Danny the first ..." It's hardly ambiguous, is it?'

'But they hadn't', I insist. 'It is a fact. And the phrase "making love" meant something different in the 1940s. It covered a lot of things. He could easily be referring to the canoodling over Daleacre'.[2]

Mark looks dubious. He never believes what I say without hard evidence in front of him. 'Keep going'.

'Do you mind me asking you intimate questions?' Jim continues:

> I wish you would ask me some only I don't want to offend my best friend but if you start first it will make it hundred times easier for me. When I look at your photo, to just kiss your hair I would be thrilled. I could ask you lots, but may I? ... I have read your letter several times and it is the kind I like and the promised kiss will mean a sure visit. What can I bet that I can outpace you. Not smoking plays a great part, and it is better for the girl. That is the thing I study, negative onions etc., unusual am I not? I am very fussy over my teeth. Darling this is being written in a great hurry, only I want to write by return of post. I know you will, and make it extra special, and remember Danny will never know and it will never be against him because we both adore (love) him. Cheerio dearest and I will write a longer one next time if you will (help)... Jim X when we meet. Write tonight beautiful.

I am barely finished hooting at the negative onions before I am plunged into maternal mode, horrified by Jim's candid request for Norah to ask him intimate questions. 'Oh my God!'

'Danny's obviously told Jim that he and Norah have done more than they have, if what you say is right', Mark says. 'Jim is trying to ascertain whether Norah is the girl Danny is telling him she is, or whether she is who he sees in her letters. Norah comes across as shy and modest to him. That doesn't match Danny's description'.

I am pondering all of this when suddenly, alarmingly, Mark breaks into song. '"We made out, under the dock". Think of Danny Zuko in *Grease* when he is telling his mates about his summer affair. Remember the one who asks – "Tell me more, tell me more, did you get very far?" Danny – Norah's Danny – is exaggerating for his brother. "Met a girl crazy for me, met a boy cute as can be." That's the dynamic. Norah is Sandy, interested in love and romance and hand-holding and kisses, but there he is, telling his mates: "Well she was good, you know what I mean!"'

But there is a puzzle here. Danny seems to be lying to Jim about his escapades with Norah, telling him stories of an intimacy far in advance of what had actually taken place. Jim is downplaying his own feelings to both Norah and his brother: he is deeply jealous and pretty angry and still wants Norah for himself. But Jim is also sending Norah scraps of letters supposedly written by his brother, in which Danny describes her as 'a grand, sweet, lovely and smashing lass'. And Mark is insistent that these are not the words Danny would have used. He thinks Jim has made it up, maybe even persuaded a fellow bored sailor to write it for him.

But the thing is, I have Danny's letter to Marsie and Pop in front of me, the polite 'thank you' letter he sent in September 1941. It is definitely Danny's hand-writing on that snippet that Jim sent on to Norah. But if Mark is right in his insistence that Danny would have used a far fruitier, more boastful language in his letter to his brother – and I have to admit, he is pretty persuasive – what was the purpose of a scrap of paper describing a sweet and smashing Norah bringing him tea in bed? Are Danny and Jim simply in cahoots, trying to hasten her seduction with words she would like to hear?

It seems Norah objected to his line of questioning. 'Why did you take my letter the wrong way, it was not intended to hurt or corrupt', Jim protested. *Received a spiffing letter from my love,* Norah wrote on 9th July. *He's splintered his finger. Had a little apologetic letter and pc from Jim.*

Jim's letters to Norah make for confusing reading. The blackcurrant pastilles and negative onions: the man's a comedian. The schoolgirl photo: a paedophile? He seems to be trying to establish an intimacy with Norah through the only route left open to him: a 1940s equivalent of sexting his brother's girlfriend. His own claims to sexual experience seem to be an attempt to shock Norah, to gain more of a sense of her from her reaction. Maybe he wants her to write the same, to give him some copy to read in the mess, boost his credentials with his fellow ratings.

I can't help but wonder if it is closer to the truth that Jim has had little experience with women and that the endless focus in the mess on sex – the talk, the songs, the bragging – was at times too much for him. That his encounters with prostitutes in port towns were more tentative, that it was as much the kindness of the good women of Chatham that he needed. Maybe Jim found the petty discipline hard to stomach, didn't enjoy the hyper-masculinity, the much-vaunted brotherhood they all claim to miss once they've disembarked for civilian life.

But I don't know. There really are too many maybes here. And here's another: maybe it had always been this way and Danny, eighteen months Jim's junior, had pipped him to the post: more handsome, a better scholar, the star cricketer, more popular, better prospects all round. Maybe Jim had long played second fiddle and girls had always vaulted over him in their bid to get to Danny. Maybe he had believed that this time it would be different. Norah had knitted the socks for him, after all. But here he is, playing matchmaker in order to keep in touch with Norah, travelling in Danny's slipstream yet again.

Jim's letters in the summer of 1942 are a scattergun of comedy moments, morality tales, sexual impropriety, prying questions and self-revelation. One of these bullets should hit the spot, he hopes, and make Norah declare herself. But none of it works. Norah, reading *Danny* by Walter Brierley, doesn't give him what he wants. After his letter of 18th July, Jim retreats, beaten. It will be a full year before he writes to her again.

14. Glorious Letters from My Sweetheart

In the 'Monthly Accounts' section at the back of her diary, Norah listed *Letters Received*, with ticks in a second column denoting her reply. While in June and July 1942, she received letters from Jim and Norman as well as from Danny, by August through to the end of the year, Danny was her sole correspondent.

'Seems like poor old Norman got the message'. My mum looks down-hearted. 'But what happened to Danny's letters?'

My mum remembers dusting Norah's room as a ten- or eleven-year-old in the early 1950s and picking a letter from the front of a dressing table drawer that was slightly ajar. She slid it from its envelope, unfolded the thin paper, noted Danny's signature and hurriedly put it back. There was a whole stash of them. At some point, Norah clearly felt that the time had come to remove the letters from their prime position in her life, a daily reminder of what might have been. We agree that she must have destroyed them, but we are no closer to knowing why or when.

And of course, Norah's letters to Danny are missing too. What did she tell him during that summer of 1942? We can't know for certain, of course, but her diaries allow us to make a pretty good guess. Norah will have certainly told Danny about joining the WJACs, the Castle Donington branch of the Women's Junior Air Corps, formed in May 1942. Known as the Jacks, they had existed at the national level since 1939 and, like the Girls Training Corps (1941) and Girls Nautical Training Corps (1942), aimed to prepare young women for the services, in this case, the WAAF. Meeting twice weekly at the Church School, the Donington group varied their activities between games of rounders, country dancing and war-related classes: aircraft recognition, squad drill, first aid and morse code, which saw a local lad, known as Billy Blob on account of his

©2025 Alison Twells, CC BY-NC 4.0   https://doi.org/10.11647/OBP.0461.14

rotund shape, come into his own. Norah, a corporal within a few weeks, seems slightly bemused by the earnestness: *Had inspection by top knob in Jacks.* But she liked the uniform: the grey blouse and black tie, grey forage cap and blue-grey skirt, which she *remodelled* to give a better fit.[1]

Norah will have told Danny about the bombs that dropped on Rolls Royce on 27th July, leaving twenty dead. It was the talk of the village. Daisy Warren, a land girl at Powdrill's market garden in Hemington, just down the hill, was cycling to work early that morning when she heard a hum-hum-hum overhead. Minutes later, a grey plane with swastika markings passed directly in front of her, flying so low that she got a good view of the pilot and crew as they followed the railway line to Derby, keeping down to miss the barrage balloons. Mr Powdrill had been watching from the gate. 'I wish I'd got my gun', he was telling everybody. 'I wouldn't have missed at that height. I'd have had a pop at him, the ruddy Gerry'.[2] *27th July 1942: Germans bombed Royces. Syd Higgins among the dead.*

There were plenty of life-goes-on-as-normal events to report, such as Norah's walks over Daleacre with Marsie; they'd keep Danny's romantic memories alive. There was her summer reading. Did she tell him that she had lapped up Hugh Walpole's *Jeremy* over sunny lunchtimes in the River Gardens during the early June heatwave? She might have told him that her shorthand at Kemp's Commercial College was coming on nicely, and that she and Jean from work were thinking of joining a dancing class, and that she was looking forward to showing him her steps after the war.

Did Norah mention to her airman boyfriend her anxieties about his pilot training? I doubt it very much. She knew the rules of letter-writing: light, loving and up-beat. 'Set down for him the gay happenings about you, bright little anecdotes, not invented, necessarily, but attractively embellished', wrote Dorothy Parker. 'Do not bedevil him with the pinings of your faithful heart because he is your husband, your man, your love. For you are writing to none of these. You are writing to a soldier'.[3]

She will surely have mentioned Connie's trunk call from her soldier boyfriend Frank in Bognor Regis, summonsing her down for a next-day marriage, and the cake and port they enjoyed on her return. But it is unlikely that Norah shared her interest in the progress of the affairs of local girls and their servicemen boyfriends as they headed towards engagement. That would presume too much. Neither would she have let on her pleasure on hearing from Frank in Oldham that there were *enquiries about me in his gang*. But maybe she dropped in the odd snippet of news about Norman ('my friend at work is in the Navy now'), just to keep Danny on his toes.

***

Very occasionally, Norah's diaries report that Danny was a bit of a let-down, sending scrappy, short, perfunctory postcards and letters, the sort you might expect from a casual acquaintance and not the object of your heart's desire. Love letters demand intimacy, their sole purpose to bind the lovers over time and space, to provide proof that love and desire are enduring, despite separation. What scholars call an 'epistolary pact' lays out unspoken but recognisable expectations about letters: their frequency and length, the amount of space given to answering questions and addressing daily concerns, the sharing of sentimental memories and dreams for the future.[4]

When Danny failed to play the game, when his letters failed to seduce Norah, to make her feel that she had *fallen all over again*, she is not merely disappointed, she is furious. *Received terribly disappointing letter from Danny*, she wrote in May 1942. *Felt awfully mad but sent fairly decent letter back*. Again in mid-October: *Received a lousy letter from Danny & tore it up. I think I hate him.* I am taken aback by the fierceness of seventeen-year-old Norah's responses. Danny's letters clearly fail to express the ardour and affection that she believed befitted their affair.

5th September 1942: Received a letter from my Danny & a grand photo of him. Went into raptures about it. But always, even after a shocker of a letter or a promised visit that didn't happen, Danny comes up trumps. *31st October 1942: Received a glorious letter from my sweetheart, he's been home to Jim, I love him terribly. He wants to know what age I want to marry.* And with that, he is back in her good books. Because of course Norah wanted to marry. But before then, before the wedding, before she, the glamorous modern girl, could welcome her hero-lover home from the war, she wanted romance in the form of passionate letters. 'Romantic love was not only the basis for marriage in the 1940s', writes Marilyn Lake, 'but for women it was meant to supply the meaning of life'.[5]

***

We – here, now – tend to see romantic love as natural, timeless, universal, spanning cultures (and even species). Progressive, liberated, it marks us apart from places in which it is outlawed or discouraged, where couples are denied the intensity of connection which – we believe – should be the basis of their future together.

Here, now: these are a historian's qualifiers. Evolutionary psychologists tend to suggest that romantic love is humanity's evolutionary destiny, a 'panhuman emotion' that first evolved over four million years ago to enable human reproduction and that can now be found in almost every culture around the world. Biological anthropologists compare romantic love to substance addiction: the craving, euphoria, obsessive thinking, yearning for emotional union and the signs of withdrawal if all goes wrong. Historians beg to differ, pointing out that while that longing for human connection seems to exist as an intrinsic emotional state, cultures of intimacy change over time. Compare courtly love in twelfth-century France, for example, with the changes in courtship in early industrial Europe or the shift in focus from the spiritual to the erotic in the twentieth-century USA.[6]

Norah's introduction to romance coincided with romantic love taking the Western world by storm. The 1920s and 1930s, in Eva Illouz's nifty phrase, saw the 'romanticization of commodities' and the 'commodification of romance'. Cinema, dance music, romantic fiction, fashion and beauty products all promised romance, as romantic love, sexual desire and ideas about marriage became tightly interwoven in mid-century Britain.[7]

True to her time, Norah believed in love and its essential component, the romantic couple. At no point in her life would she have had truck with feminist critiques of romance as conservative or oppressive. For her, romantic love should be expansive, transformative, transcendental, the key to happiness and fulfilment.[8]

With his twinkly eyes, nice manners, passionate kisses and loving letters, Danny fitted the bill.

When he chose to.

15. Danny Told Me a Thing or Two

In mid-January 1943, Norah booked tickets for the pantomime (*6/1 in Orchestra Stalls*) and then heard that Danny was *ill in bed again with flu. I do wish I could get down to look after him*. He reassured her: he would *try & come next weekend*.

> *20th January: The office gang went to the panto. British Army is 40 miles to Tripoli.*
>
> *23rd: My sweet did arrive last night & rang me up from Hemington. I dashed home & went to meet him. He's adorable. Went to the pantomime & it was grand. Had a really wicked night kiss. Left me a terrible 'love mark' etc.*

Norah doesn't mention her theatre-going companions, but she will surely have been chaperoned by Marsie, Birdy and maybe Helen and Jeannie, who at twenty-two months was perhaps still a bit too young to enjoy the slapstick fun. In any case, Norah would have been less concerned with introducing her little niece to the ribald joys of the panto than with the pleasure of being out with Danny: the cosiness of the stalls, the secret hand-holding, the surreptitious pressing together of knees. Sharing laughter and innuendo, she would have felt like they were a proper courting couple.

> *24th January: Danny told me a thing or two about 'things' such as …? He's going to ask me when I will marry him when I'm eighteen. He went back on the 6pm to London.*
>
> *25th: I've never been so miserable in all my life now my love has gone away. Told Mrs Harris something that shocked the office.*

©2025 Alison Twells, CC BY-NC 4.0   https://doi.org/10.11647/OBP.0461.15

Was it some snippet of sexual knowledge which stopped the office that Monday afternoon? Did she divulge to Mrs Harris the reasons for her high-necked blouse? Was she trying out a new persona, keen to cast off the innocent school leaver and emerge, butterfly-like, as a worldly young woman?

Danny, now stationed at Skeabrae in the Orkneys, was back again at Easter.

> *12th April: Received letter from my love to say he was coming tonight. He turned up about 7 o'clock. Went to Helen's to see Jeannie bathed. Had another glorious night and retired about twelve.*

The trip to Helen's in Hemington would be less about seeing little Jean frolicking in her bath water than providing a useful cover for the courting couple. After the walk down Lady's Close, squeezing through the kissing gates at each end of the field, Norah and Danny will have checked the time – an hour until sunset – most likely deciding against the left turn into Main Street and the direct, two-minute walk to Helen's cottage, choosing instead the longer route: Church Lane, Dark Lane, a deserted Daleacre at dusk. After some brief fun seeing Jeannie splashing around, the walk home would be a similarly dilatory stroll up Lady's Close in the moonlight.

13th April: Danny hadn't to go back until 10.30 so I asked the Boss for time off. Did Norah travel into Derby station that morning, waving him off before ambling into the office for a late-morning start? I imagine her fluttering to the very end of the platform as the train pulled out, waving her smiling, sad goodbyes.

The day after Danny's departure, Marsie took the bus into Derby to bring Norah another letter bearing the news that he was coming again on Saturday. This was some trip, five hundred and ninety-four miles from the Orkneys to the English Midlands, twice in one week. These visits were surely about more than the bleakness and boredom of the island base. Danny was keen.

Marsie was enjoying her daughter's romance, as well as the opportunity for some of the pleasures of town life; the life she'd wanted when she married Tom, thirty years before. She could see how Norah was totally bowled over. She might even have thought it a blessing that it couldn't be a new, modern courtship, that Norah was sending him copies of *Punch* and parcels of tobacco, giving him love and care rather than pining for flimsy tokens of romance and other fleeting things.

> 17th April: My love came. Went up Daleacre in the moonlight and had a glorious time.
>
> 18th: Had a marvellous time up Daleacre with Danny in afternoon. He had to return at 8.50pm.

Marvellous. Glorious. Beautiful. Norah feels the sweet rush of longing. It is the wonder of sexual desire as well as the starry-eyed charm of romance that makes her feel alive.

***

Oh, but it was hard.

I've taught women's history for very many years and am shocked every time – every teaching year, every fresh lecture crafted, every new piece of reading – by the historical horrors of women and sex.

In Victorian England, it was alleged – by medical authority – that women wished only to be wives and mothers and suffered sex purely to that end. Dr William Acton was 'ready to maintain' that 'as a general rule, a modest woman seldom desires any sexual gratification for herself. She submits to her husband's embraces, but principally to gratify him: and were it not for the desire of maternity, would far rather be relieved of his attentions'. Any hint of sexual desire and a woman was at risk of condemnation: a nymphomaniac, a whore, unnatural, unsexed.[1]

The people who challenged this unscientific claptrap were the early feminists. Society had been moulded on this 'false assertion', wrote Dr Elizabeth Blackwell, the first woman to receive a medical degree (in the United States, because she couldn't study for one in the UK). But in actual fact, women were put off sexual relations by fear of conception or damage from childbirth or 'brutal or awkward conjugal approaches'. The crux of the matter was this: women had 'been taught sexual passion as lust and as sin – a sin which it would be a shame for a pure woman to feel, and which she would die rather than confess'.[2]

Although romance had arrived with great fanfare by the time Norah was growing up, an essential ingredient in the modern world, it remained a fine line. Being marriageable was still everything. Anything too libidinal in a woman could jeopardise that. And even in marriage, supposedly revolutionised by Marie Stopes' emphasis on mutual fulfilment in her best-selling *Married Love* (1918), a wife didn't initiate but responded to advances. 'It's nice, for a woman to enjoy sex', said one of Kate Fisher's interviewees, 'because a man likes you to enjoy it doesn't 'e?'[3]

But not too much. A study of working-class marriage conducted in 1943 by Moya Woodside and Eliot Slater revealed that men considered sex their conjugal right and neither expected nor particularly welcomed responsiveness in a woman. Both men and women believed that 'for a woman to feel lustful would be an unseemly thing'. 'Men and women have very different attitudes towards sex in marriage', Woodside wrote in 1946. 'The pattern is of habit and duty, of "rights" and submission. Men are satisfied; women are bored or indifferent, or mention active dislike'.[4] Raised in ignorance, loaded with guilt and unfocused feelings of shame and fear, denied the possibility that a physical relationship might be a source of pleasure, many women put up with sex, to keep their husbands happy, to stop them from wandering, to anchor them at home.

How babies were made (and born) was unknown to many young women in the 1940s. They saw their mother's bodies ruined through endless childbearing. They grew up hearing terrifying tales of pregnant unmarried girls drowned with their babies in the dead of night, or rolled in carpets and suffocated, or just cast out of their families in shame. They 'knew' that men had urges that once set in train, could not be stopped; that they needed vigilance, to take utmost care.[5]

Indeed, many girls colluded in their ignorance, carefully avoiding exposure to sexual information, their innocence an essential component of their respectability. Thus Richard Hoggart, in his widely acclaimed study of changes in working-class culture in the face of new forms of mass entertainment, described as 'wonderful' how many working-class girls 'can walk through the howling valley of sex-approaches from the local lads and probably of sex-talk at work' and yet 'retain both an ignorance of the facts of sex and an air of inviolability towards its whole atmosphere that would not have been unbecoming in a mid-nineteenth-century young lady of the middle-classes'.[6] Wonderful, indeed.

While books on the mechanics of sex and contraception were becoming more readily available in the 1930s and more risqué topics appeared in newspapers and magazines, there was very little in the new mass-market magazines for young women beyond her depiction as a 'sweet untaught girl'.[7] Their mothers, young women in late-Victorian Britain, are unlikely to have broached the subject. If morality was insinuated by pursed-lipped silence at home, school provided nothing more than the most basic of biological and physiological facts, with a likely dose of scaremongering about pregnancy or venereal disease. The National Union of Teachers specifically stated in 1933 that the provision of 'class sex instruction' was 'undesirable', even when head teachers were keen. Their worry? That they would be charged with 'low morals' and exciting 'undue interest' among their pupils.[8] *Had domestic science until break,* Norah had written in her diary in 1939. *Miss Martin told us about the boy & his –. Had craft until dinner.* (*The boy & his –*, and above, *Danny told me a thing or two about 'things' such as ...?*: we should note the self-censorship in Norah's diary, her concealment of sexual knowledge.)

Even decades later, when relaying their memories of courtship, sex and marriage, women distanced themselves from a too-active sexuality. Their focus was respectability and restraint, with little reference to romance and passion. As young women, they had known too well that the ease with which they gave in to sexual advances would be used by men to test their wifely suitability; that they risked being labelled 'loose' and 'easy'. It was down to them to police these boundaries, to play 'hard to get'. In the words of a factory worker born in 1923, who rejected her future husband's advances: 'well if I let 'im 'ave his own way, he'll think what sort of a person is she, yer know, so that's why I never encouraged him at all'. There was so much at stake.[9]

Some women worried about their own feelings. 'I heard talk on the wireless lately, that if you marry simply because you are violently in love, your marriage may fail', a young woman opined to *Woman's Own* in 1945. 'My boyfriend and I are passionately in love, and now I feel worried in case we are making a mistake...' But mostly, their concern was how to manage sexual pressure. 'Coping' was the term women used to denote staving off a randy man: 'I *like* Bill and he *is* a Squadron Leader and all that', wrote a Mass Observation respondent, 'but I simply can't face the coping I have to do every evening'. As another young woman wrote to *Woman's Own,* 'Is love real? [...] I am engaged to a boy who is very passionate and, although he has never tried to do anything wrong, his life seems to be one long fight against temptation. Are all men like this? It makes me feel that love is nothing but desire'.[10]

Indeed, in the world of most women's magazines, especially those read by Norah, the jury was not even out. 'It's not romantic. It's not grand and unusual and altogether up to date. It's not even kind to the man', Rosita Forbes had written in *Woman's Own* in 1940. 'You can love him with all your heart and yet have sufficient courage to wait. Of course it's hard. You do agree, don't you, it's up to you to give him the best. So give him faith and honesty and courage. Give him love that is going to last, that he can look forward to, and that he can trust for the rest of his life'. As another agony aunt replied to a letter in 1942: 'If you do such things to keep another's love, you will lose it and your self-respect with it'.[11]

But change was afoot. The stats suggest that attitudes to sex were liberalising. While 36% of women born between 1904-1914 engaged in pre-marital sexual activity, this rose to 39% and 43% of those born between 1914-1924 and 1924-1934, Norah's generation. Alongside a general approval of marital virginity, petting – an American term for various non-coital physical expressions of desire – was promoted in sex manuals from the 1940s. For women as well as men, there was a growing acceptance that testing the water was not so bad an idea.[12]

As novels from the time suggest, the war sped up this change. 'Girls like me were brought up to be respectable', says Polly, a character in Mary Wesley's *The Camomile Lawn*. 'The atmosphere of the war shook that [...] There were dozens of girls who went on being virtuous, but we broke out'. There was an intensity to daily life, an openness to connection and experience; meeting a glance straight on and holding it, instead of averting the eyes. 'Walls went down', wrote Elizabeth Bowen, 'and we felt, if not knew, each other. We all lived in a state of lucid abnormality'. Even a pair of heels tapping in the black-out could sound suggestive, like 'an illicit semaphore' in the night. 'War [...] was sex', muses Prudence, a character in Henry Green's *Caught*, written at the time of the author's own affairs during the London Blitz.[13]

But, for women, as Katherine Angel writes, desire can be 'most difficult to tell'.[14] While many women shared Birmingham diary writer Lillian Rogers' wartime delight in 'flying her kite', an over-focus on sudden sexual 'liberation' is too simple. It took time to cast off what Norah's contemporary Jean Lucey Pratt describes as '[r]eason, upbringing and fear all preaching caution', to gather up whatever it took to go with the 'impulse and instinct urging you violently to take the plunge'. But plunge Jean did – and before long, it was the times without a lover when she felt like 'an unlit lamp'. 'Felt very pleased with immediate life and our bodies', young London civil servant Olivia Cockett wrote in her Mass Observation diary. 'Man and I have thoroughly enjoyed our three nights together. Abandon and experiment have brought us into closer and closer tenderness'.[15]

Doreen Bates was another young woman who moved gradually towards sexual exploration. She was a twenty-seven-year-old civil servant when she began an affair in 1933 with 'E', an older married man with whom she shared an office in Paddington. She describes how she 'lost the fear of sex that I must have had even 18 months ago and dug up at least some of the repressions I had, and that before I was too old to wake up and find that everything had passed; this is entirely due to E – his consideration and understanding and restraint and honesty; this is a priceless gift which he has given me'. 'I was unafraid and unashamed' she wrote on another occasion. And later still: 'It was one of the quickest and loveliest fucks we have ever had, so easy and light-hearted and gorgeous'.[16]

An expert on romance, Norah is short on sexual knowledge. She wants passion, but still we sense her careful negotiations: desire battling it out with self-consciousness, ignorance, the terrible fear of pregnancy, the dire warnings about being thought too easy by a man who, in that moment, you truly believed could never think badly of you and would never let you down. Could she trust him? Was he genuine? If in these years 'men began to focus on how far a woman would let them go', the dilemma for women was 'how to tell if his feelings were sincere'.[17]

Norah's diary entries make clear the full extent of her sexual ignorance. In July 1943, when she welcomed her period with the customary tick in her diary, she wrote the words *Thank God*. Usually a clockwork twenty-eight days, she was six days late. She had not seen Danny for three months, had had two periods since, but clearly believed that she might still be pregnant. And they hadn't even 'done it'. I'm reminded of Marion Paul, a young woman from a small village near Doncaster, who received her sex education on entering the ATS: 'I'd led a very sheltered life. I used to sit on my bed and my ears were like tureens, listening to all this conversation, half of which I didn't understand, and half of which

I never knew. I mean I thought you could get a baby from a lavatory seat...'[18] Norah clearly worried that kissing and canoodling on Daleacre might leave her in the family way.

14th April 1943: Jean, Connie and I went a walk at dinner-time. Back at work after Danny's visit, Norah enjoyed a stroll with the office girls. Jean's Cyril was in the Army, as was Frank, whom Connie had married the previous autumn on a forty-eight-hour pass. The three of them were to spend a lot of time together that spring and summer, sharing lunchtimes at Pingpongs and Pierpont and evenings out to see 'The Gondoliers' and 'The Gentle Sex'. On this April day, Connie and Jean will have been keen to hear about Danny. And in telling them, Norah surely revealed all that she didn't know. *26th May 1943: Con bought two Birth Control books so I had one. Oh boy, what a book!!! What diagrams!!!*

She was a good friend, was Connie Cooper.

16. Unconditional Surrender?

Norah was cross with Danny again in early May 1943. His visits to Castle Donington that Easter had been so special (*marvellous, glorious, beautiful*), and then, would you believe it, he sent a *lousy little postcard from Eastbourne, which I promptly tore up. Please God what have I done to Danny to make him like this,* she wrote the following day, *and please bring him safely back to me.* Two days later *a rotten little letter from Danny* arrived in the post. *Replied to him [...] It ought to shake him up a bit.*

What does Norah tell Danny, to make him buck up his ideas? Does she mention the *little airman* with whom she chats on the bus home from work? Or poor strung-along Norman, whose occasional hopeful letters have started up again? And then there's Alan, another young man who helped her in the street with some unspecified problem in February 1943 and, after sending her a *mystery Valentine (post-marked Ambergate)*, pursued her through that spring and summer? She'd had no plans to respond to his letters requesting a date – *had another letter from Alan, which I didn't welcome* – but if Danny was going to treat her so shabbily... Whatever she says to him, she soon regrets her haste. *12th May: I love my Danny terribly and I am sorry I sent that letter. Please God let him take it the right way and come back to me.*

One reason Norah feels so guilty is because she has a sense of the magnitude of all that she doesn't know. Danny was night flying from Orkney, for heaven's sake! That meant escorting convoys, providing fighter cover for merchant ships travelling between Scapa Flow and Murmansk. He got low, miserable, and was it any wonder? And Skeabrae was a dreary place. Beyond a cinema at the base, there was nothing there. Who could blame him for the occasional scrappy letter?

Norah didn't see what the women on the stations saw, of course. WAAFs like Joan Wyndham, who waved the flyers off, awaited their return, debriefed them after ops. Who kept a close eye on them as the sorties progressed and noted the general air of irritability and restlessness around the base, the sweaty palms, nervous tics, upset stomachs and other aches and pains as their fear crept 'closer and closer, like a cat stalking a sparrow'. They saved for her the stuff that couldn't be shared with other men. The brief distraction of sex, then sleeplessness, weeping in her arms, confessing that going 'back on ops, tomorrow' left them 'scared witless'.[1]

Norah didn't see this, but she knew: the horrifying deaths, the lives ruined by missing limbs or disfigurement through fire, the futures suspended. Acts of love and everyday care were the essential commodity in this war, not shirty letters. It would be her own selfish fault if she'd blown it. On a walk over Daleacre with Marsie, she fought back the tears as she remembered the lovely time she'd spent there with Danny only a few short weeks before. Tucked into her diary for that week are horoscopes that she had cut out from the newspaper. Along with all Pisceans, Norah could face 'storms ... with difficulties coming to a head on Wednesday', but improvements were expected before the end of the week. Danny's stars – Scorpio – suggest he'd feel let down 'in connection with social life' and warned against any 'experiments'.

Finally, she received *a beautiful and unexpected letter from Danny who asked forgiveness etc. The happiest day of my life.* She brought a book titled 'France', packed it up for him and posted it. A few days later, another *beautiful letter* asked for *forgiveness. I love him dearly.* Yet another *beautiful letter* arrived the following week. *He is ill and has pains in his stomach.*

After that upset, Norah's relationship with Danny enters a new, settled phase in which she vows to give him comfort and care and not get worked up over some absent silly romantic words; to be more like a wife in wartime. The victories were coming in thick and fast now: the North African campaign finished in May, and in June the war in the Atlantic was turned around, by Danny in the air and Jim at sea. It could all be over any day soon, and marriage would then be on the cards.

Eighteen-year-old Norah starts collecting Crown Derby and Wedgewood for her bottom drawer. She borrows a library book on Eastbourne, Danny's home town, where he has the promise of a sports master's job after the war. She spruces up her housewifery skills. *13th June 1943: I cooked all the dinner: roast lamb, new potatoes, cabbage, mint sauce and gooseberry pie.* Her *flaky pastry that wasn't too flaky* was soon improved and she managed some nice cheese straws into the bargain, soon extending her repertoire to include rock cakes, chocolate cakes, mutton pies, dumplings and suet puddings. She'd spoil him rotten when he came home.

Danny's *beautiful, loving letters* continue to arrive throughout June and July. He calls Norah his *little passion flower,* sends her a parcel *containing 1lb of lovely farm butter,* asks her *to go away with him on his leave.* He is her *cherub,* her *love, mon cher,* the man she was going to marry. *I love you so very much, mon ange. Je vous aime beaucoup.*

She buys *lovely blue material for some pyjamas* and a gold quilting for a dressing gown and is thrilled to find a matching golden girdle (2/11). Mary Twells compares her to Deanna Durbin, the star of *The Amazing Mrs Holliday*, which Norah saw that summer. I Google the popular actress: Norah was indeed a homelier version of the girl-next-door Hollywood star. It is easy to imagine Miss Durbin perched elegantly at a dressing table in an English guesthouse, Norah's golden gown falling open from her pretty shoulders, brushing out her glossy chestnut hair, while Danny waits in bed. *22nd July 1943: Saw a beautiful engagement ring in Smith's (£50).* (Actually, it might be £30. The 5 (or 3) has bled into an illegible sterling smudge.)

This plan to go away together... Norah swayed gradually towards sex that summer. Before the weekend away could be arranged, Danny was moved from Warmwell in Dorset, to Lincoln, and came to stay.

> *4th September: Danny came. He's adorable.*
>
> *5th: Things got hot with Danny in bed in the morning. He had to go back on 6.55 bus to Nottingham.*
>
> *6th: Mum and I went to Nottingham and bought 2 stockings 6/4 each. Posted letter to my cherub. I do miss him so.*
>
> *7th: Wrote to my love again. Received letter from Doreen. Helen made me mad about Danny and me getting engaged.*

We don't know what Helen said that riled Norah. Maybe she took the moral high-ground, suggesting that an engagement should precede the cheeky weekend. Or maybe she implied that Danny was dragging his feet, that Norah should be careful. Perhaps she was just plain jealous. The war had come too late for her. She had dawdled into her marriage in 1939 and was now resigned to a lifetime with butcher Joe Twells, reserved in nature and occupation. Was she already weighed down with worry and, without Marsie's patience or her faith, grudgingly accepting the drudgery of housework, the drag of childcare and the never-ending struggle to make ends meet?

'She always thought Norah had it so easy', my mum says, 'the High School education that she waltzed into, the white-collar wage, the nice clothes…' and now this smooth and courteous airman with his bright eyes and ready smile.

My mother is shocked by all this bedroom activity, nonetheless.

'Where was Marsie when all that was going on? She wouldn't have allowed a carry-on like that in her house!'

'Norah just did what we've all done', I say. 'Waited 'til the coast was clear, then jumped into bed with him. They probably had an hour while Marsie went to the Co-op'.

She glances at me suspiciously. 'Do you think she's making it up?'

'No', I laugh. 'The diaries are too small. There isn't room for a fantasy sex life'.

She looks me in the eye and stifles a giggle, dropping to a whisper as a child drifts into earshot: 'What a bugger she was!'

> 8th September: Returned to work. Received lovely letter from my sweetheart. Replied to my dearest and to Doreen. Italy capitulated with unconditional surrender.
>
> 9th: Posted letter to my love. Ma and Pa went to Bristol.
>
> 10th: Rumour that 7th Army has invaded France. Received lovely affectionate letter from my darling.
>
> 11th: My dearest one came. Had beautiful time.
>
> 12th: Had a beautiful time in bed with my cherub. Went a walk in the afternoon. I do love him so dearly.

Of course, this again begs the question of what precisely Danny and Norah *did*. We know from her diaries that despite the kisses, the love bites, the late period and the *hot* and *beautiful* times, Norah and Danny might have come very close to it, but they hadn't done the deed.

But, just like Italy in Norah's diary entry of 8th September, was an unconditional surrender on the cards?

Was she making it up? I don't believe she was. If Philippe Lejeune is right, while diarists can tell lies if they so wish, they rarely do. When writing for herself, in such a tiny space: why would she? But we should hold Norah to the same scrutiny as the men and their letters. There is no doubt that the rendition of the self in a diary can be a similarly performative act, even if just for the author. Do we see it here in the language of love that Norah chooses: *my cherub*? Despite the concealment in her reportage that *things got hot* (what *things*, precisely?), she distils an undoubtedly more complex experience – fumbling, uncertainty, lack of confidence, desire? – into this (idealised? knowing? grown up?) sexual encounter. Or maybe not. Maybe it was just as she says it; that *things got hot*.

Totally unexpectedly, Jim gets back in touch, penning a short letter on 24th August which, through some postal system mishap, Norah does not receive until the end of September. 'Dear Norah', he writes, 'At last I am introducing pen to paper, "about time" says you. Danny usually kept me informed of your health and activities, because I had neglected my pen duties do not think you were dismissed from my thoughts. Have you ever regretted knitting socks for sailors? I am rather cheeky and full of cracks tonight, but you should know me by now, unlike Danny'.

Norah does not pick up on this strange aside. Danny visits again on 2nd October, his third weekend in four at Moira Dale. Again, he and Norah walk over Daleacre and have a marvellous, beautiful time. He returns to Grantham on the 6.50 train the following evening and Norah misses him instantly. He writes three letters the following week, telling her on the 9th that *he would be coming, but he didn't. The staff officers must have stayed there all day. Please God let my Danny stay at Grantham for another course*, she writes the following day, *or I won't be seeing him in a long while*.

But after that letter of 9th October 1943, Danny simply disappears.

17. Please God ... Waiting for Danny

> *11th October 1943: No letter from my cherub, I wonder where he can be?*

At first, Norah assumes that Danny's next letter is merely taking its time to arrive; she is more frustrated than unduly concerned. But after marking his 26th birthday in his absence, the anxiety starts to kick in.

> *27th October: Please God keep my Danny safe & please don't let him be overseas and please let him write soon.*
>
> *1st November: Please God take care of my Danny and let him write very soon.*
>
> *7th: Please God keep my Danny safe always and let him write soon, please don't make him be in the 2nd front. The Russians are 40 miles beyond Kiev.*
>
> *14th: Made another lovely sponge cake. Started my Fair Isle gloves. Please God keep my Danny safe and please let him still be in England.*

When Danny still doesn't write, Norah finds his parents' address in one of Jim's early letters and drops them a line. Does she introduce herself as a friend of their son who is anxious for reassurance about his safety, leaving them to fill in the gaps? Or perhaps she assumes that on one of his visits Danny has told his mother that he has a young sweetheart in Derby, whom he had met, could she believe, via Jim and a pair of socks? Might Norah have taken a leap of faith and said how much she was looking forward to meeting them, once this dreadful war was over and Danny was safely home? *16th November: Posted a letter to Danny's Mother and Father. Please God, let it be alright.*

Apart from the Sword of Stalingrad, a personal gift from King George to the Russians, bejewelled and resplendent and passing through Derby on its triumphal tour, everything is doom and gloom. Norah injures herself falling up some steps at work. She witnesses a dog run over by her bus and sees a girl killed in a traffic accident on Litchurch Street. She comforts Mrs Harris, who breaks down in the office after receiving photographs of the funeral in southern Bohemia of her son John. *26th November: No letter from my love or Eastbourne. Tomorrow, D.V. Please God keep him safe and let him write very soon.*

Norah distracts herself with knitting and reading (*Ivanhoe: just about the best book I ever read*). Marsie gives her a cookery book as an early Christmas present and she makes celery soup, batter pudding and potato cakes for tea. With Doreen, her old school-friend, she attends the annual Carol Service at Loughborough High School (*just grand*). Afterwards, they walk into town, killing time in Bolesworth's Tea Rooms before the early doors showing of *You Were Never Lovelier* with Rita Hayworth and Fred Astaire (*super*). Does Doreen press Norah on the progress of her love affair with Danny? Would Norah confide, or does she brush off too much concern as she perfects the breezy brightness of her later years? *17th December: I wonder if my love is in Corsica? Please God watch over him and bring him home safe again.*

Norah spends Christmas Day with Marsie and Pop, Birdy, Helen, Joe and little Jeannie, now nearly three. The food shortage has kicked in and they have *stringy cockerel* from their own coop. On Boxing Day, Pop and Birdy go off to the Baseball Ground (*Derby beat Forest 2.1*) and Norah, her sister and niece take a walk up to the coppice on the eastern edge of Donington Park. Frank, on Army duty in Newcastle, comes home on the 29th, only to be called back by telegram two days later. *31st December: I wonder if the 2nd Front is going to open soon. Please God take care of my Danny and bring him back safe as soon as possible.*

No Christmas or New Year telegram from Danny.

***

1944 starts as 1943 ended: with life as normal as it gets in wartime. Norah has a perm, knits a skull cap and buys a lacy duchess set for her bottom drawer. She and Mrs Harris sample Kardomah, a posh new coffee lounge, and a new fish and chip shop on Babington Lane. She sees Phyllis Calvert and Stewart Grainger in *Fanny by Gaslight* (*very good*), Noel Coward's *This Happy Breed* (*quite good*) and, with Helen and Jeannie, *Cinderella*. She helps her sister to clean the cold, north-facing cottage that she has taken on the main shopping street in Castle Donington. Now unofficially pregnant with her second child, it will be handy for the Co-op, the school and Marsie. She prays for Danny.

But where the devil is he? Norah wonders if Danny is with the RAF squadrons that have *made a new landing near Rome* to bomb a route ahead of the Army as it threads its way up through Italy, forcing the Germans – now alone, after Mussolini's surrender – further and further north. *I wonder if that is where my love is. Please God keep him safe always.* She follows the anxious progress of the Anzio Bridgehead, where the surprise amphibious assault had resulted in stalemate, our men trapped behind a line of artillery units. *I don't think my love can be at Anzio now,* she writes in late February. *Please God take care of him always & bring him home safely asap.*

The truth of it is, Danny could be anywhere. The Allies are well and truly on the offensive in early 1944 and the RAF, replenished and fortified, is engaged in crucial service in Europe and beyond. Danny could be with Coastal Command, striking at the enemy ships ploughing the North Sea in a desperate bid to beat the blockades. He could be on ops over Berlin, the daylight raids made possible by the new P-51 Mustang, its powerful Merlin engine manufactured at Royce's just down the road. He could be on sorties to other parts of Germany, or dropping supplies to the Yugoslav Partisans, or even further afield, assisting at Imphal and Kohina where our troops were besieged by the Japanese. *22nd March: Helen told us that she is expecting another baby in September. Please God take care of my Danny & please don't let him be fighting the Japs.*

The fact of the matter is that Norah hasn't a clue as to Danny's whereabouts. And despite his opening promise in his next letter, Jim is not about to offer any illumination.

HMS Gazelle
6.2.44

Dear Norah,

Just a line which I hope finds you well. I guess you are somewhat mystified about Danny, well I will enlighten you, he is abroad for an indefinite period and before he left asked me to convey thanks to yourself and your family for swell times spent at your home. No-one's received

news of him yet. Danny said you would understand why he never told you of his departure. My mother apologizes for not replying to your letter so I hope this covers all.
Cheerio,
Your Friend,
Jim

Thanks to yourself and your family? The message relayed by Jim from Danny is oddly formal, not at all what you would expect from the man you are planning to marry. *I hope this covers all? Danny said you would understand?* Norah must have puzzled its contents throughout the day. His mother had received her letter, but had left it to Jim to reply. Norah writes back and, just for good measure, posts another letter to Mrs Gilbert. *8th February: Received strange letter from Jim saying Danny is overseas. Wrote to Jim and his mother.*

Her own mother has lost hope. *9th March 1944: Had nice letter from Norman. My 19th birthday. Mum thinks that Danny won't write again, but please God don't let that be so & please keep him safe.* Marsie will have taken no pleasure in voicing her concerns. On her letter-bearing missions to Derby, she shared in Norah's longing for Danny's news. But now she fears that he is a fly-by-night. She no doubt feels a hollow dread that her youngest daughter is facing her first of life's big let-downs. But when Norah bats her concern away, she doesn't have the heart to press it home.

27th March: Had pleasant surprise when Frank arrived home on leave. Frank thinks it is quite probable that my love is in Yugoslavia. Had Norah followed the British government's U-turn, announced by Churchill in December 1943, as they withdrew their backing for the Chetniks and pledged to support Marshall Tito and his communist Partisans? She committed to 'genning up'. *18th April: Had Yugoslavia book from library. Please God take care of my Danny always and please God bring him home safely as soon as possible.* Did it make her feel closer to him, reading about the places he might pass through, seeing photos of fairy-tale towns and cities and the beautiful Dalmatian Coast, some of the sights he might see? Connie tells Norah about two RAF officers – ordinary airmen and not from the SOE (Special Operations Executive) – just back from Yugoslavia after parachuting into Tito's Split HQ early that year. *We think that my Danny must be there.*

In early May, Norah attends an exhibition on Occupied Europe at the Art Gallery in town. The map alone was terrifying: Nazi control carpeting the continent, from France across to Russia, the top of Finland down to Greece. There were a few neutrals (Ireland, Switzerland, Sweden) and then the Allies: just a growing number of Italians, the Soviets, and us.

In the face of no information – from Danny, Jim or their mother – Norah recasts herself as a waiting woman. England in 1944 was full of women waiting. Mothers and wives worried themselves ill. Small children forgot the details of their fathers' faces. Girlfriends dreamed of forbidden intimacies, homes of their own, the children to follow. Time was suspended, its spooling towards the future interrupted. What more could they do, except hope and pray and post chirpy letters to unknown destinations? *Please God take care of my Danny & bring him home alive & safe & well as soon as possible.*

3rd May 1944: Had nice dinner at Pingpongs. Kath Fowkes was married. I love you so my darling & please God bring him home safely as soon as possible. Even for Kath, one of the lucky ones, the waiting seemed endless. Her new husband, Ron Jones, a Dunkirk survivor, would be in France within the month. (Sometimes the waiting momentarily slipped her mind, Kath told me, and she was too-easily occupied with films and dances, coupons and swapping clothes. 'They were good times', she smiled, remembering a blue silk box-pleat skirt she bought from a girl at work. But as she left her office at Chilwell Depot, she'd be pulled up sharp. 'Then I'd see the soldiers, it was there all the time'.)[1]

Perhaps waiting became part of the romance. 'How many of our greatest love stories depend on suspense, on temporary disappointment and frustration before fulfilment?' *Woman's Own* had asked in 1940. 'Separation only serves to deepen their love, and every letter strengthens it'.[2]

If only he'd write.

Norah's diary that summer traces the gradual rolling back of the German occupation. *New Offensive in Italy started,* Norah writes on 12th May. Once the Anzio Bridgehead was joined up with the rest of Italy, it was only a matter of time before the Allies were able to break *through Kesselring's last line before Rome.* As Rome falls in early June, 150,000 Allied troops finally land on the Normandy beaches. Then onto Bayeaux, Elba, Assisi, Perugia, Cherbourg, Caen: *reports say they are going strong. 19th June 1944: Churchill says the war will probably end this year.*

Connie's brother Bill is killed at Normandy. Audrey's brother, Barbara's brother: both dead. The navigator boyfriend of another girl at work is lost at sea. Norman's ship, HMS *Wishart*, is involved in a skirmish with German U-boats off Gibraltar. Norah makes a phone call to Mr Morley, his boss, to check that he is safe.

Still *going fine in France*, Norah reports throughout August as the Americans *push the Germans back & out of the Brest peninsula*. The Allies make a *second landing, between Nice & Marseilles*, while others *cross the Seine, covering Paris on two sides. Please God*... As Helen gives birth to a baby boy, the French capital *is liberated by the Allies*... *The Rumanians liberate their capital, Bucharest*... *The Bulgarians ask the Allies for Peace Terms.. The Allies* take Verdun and advance into Belgium. *The Czechoslovaks rise ... Please God... Finland breaks... The British enter Holland* and *Brussels falls. The British capture Antwerp & cut off the Germans in Northern France. The Allies ... The British ... All going strong.*

Norah keeps an eye on the Slavic states as, from the east, the vengeful Russians roll through Poland, Romania, Bulgaria, Hungary, and finally, Yugoslavia, where Danny must surely be.

> *7th September: Saw in 'Monitor' that Audrey was married last Saturday. The blackouts to be lifted from the 17th. The Russians contacted Marshall Tito's forces in Yugoslavia. Please God bless my Danny.*
>
> *9th: [in pencil: Danny home? In pen: no]. Read in 'Herald' about Yugoslav girl partisans being trained on Vis Island. I think that must be where my Danny is.*
>
> *24th: Mrs Wall knows an ATS girl who hadn't heard from her now repatriated husband for over a year.*
>
> *26th: Read in paper and heard on wireless about our men who were dropped in Yugoslavia. Please God take care of my Danny and bring him home safely to me as soon as possible, as I love him very dearly.*
>
> *28th: Read some more in paper about our men in Yugoslavia. I am pretty certain my Danny must be there.*
>
> *1st October: Made sponge cake. The Russians liberated 20 Yugoslav towns. It is a year today since I last saw my dearest.*

Norah's diary entries continue to smack of superstition. It is not just the daily exhortation to God, or her plaintive *Danny home?* on September

9th with its disappointing rejoinder: *no*. There's also *Danny home on leave 7/7/44* pencilled in a diary window for October, the July date referring to the summer's day when Norah made the hopeful prediction, although on the basis of what it is impossible to tell. *Danny home 4.25 am on 2/11/44 according to cookery book*, Norah wrote, again in pencil, in the first week of November. Like those airmen who were big on 'magical thinking' – the lucky rabbit's foot, four-leaf clover, a stocking belonging to a girlfriend, their aim to allay anxiety, bring comfort and inject a semblance of control – Norah uses the weights of ingredients like some random opening of the Bible to receive a sign.[3]

In the autumn, Norah's attention shifts southwards. *8th October 1944: Heard on the wireless about our troops who were landed in Greece. I think that must be where my love is.* Was Danny among the Allied forces who had seized the airfield at Araxos? Did he look on as the last German soldiers took down the swastika from the acropolis, enjoying the spectacle of thousands of joyous Greeks ringing bells and waving flags as they jeered the Gerries northwards and home? Was Danny horrified at the state of the country after three and a half years of occupation: the destruction of industries, ports, roads, railways and bridges; the plunder, looting, torching and massacres; the deaths from starvation of 40,000 Athenians alone? Maybe he was surprised at how little they needed to do, as large parts of the mountainous interior were already liberated by the partisans. Or that when fighting did occur, the Allies found themselves teaming up with former collaborators against the Resistance movement itself, now deemed too dangerous on account of its communist wing?[4] *4th November 1944: Danny home 26/9/44 [in pencil]. No [in pen]. Heard that Greece has been absolutely cleared of the Germans, so please God bring my Danny home safely to me as soon as possible because I love him so dearly.*

'It appears your feelings are still for Danny', Jim wrote in a letter of late November, 'and if it will enlighten his are the same towards you. It is his wish to keep you mystified why he has not wrote...' 'Mystified' will be Norah's word: 'I am absolutely mystified as to why I haven't heard from Danny', she might have written. 'We spent all that time together last September and then I've heard nothing from him since, not a word in a whole year'. Norah surely must have wondered why Danny was managing to communicate with Jim, but wasn't writing directly to her, letting her know that he was safe. One thing was certain: with the news from Jim that his family had decamped back to south London, 'where we originally came from', she would not be writing to his mother to find out. Norah focuses not on her own worries for their relationship, nor on Jim's predictable quip ('remember "good looking" no is not an answer if it's love'), but on Danny's safety and his feelings for her. *24th November: Had a beautiful surprise when I received a letter from Jim saying my Danny still loves me and has been in hospital a month and that I can write to him. Thank you so much God. Please take care of him.*

Mary Twells gets engaged to *John, her airman* at her 21st birthday party on Christmas Eve. In Greece, WW2 gives way to civil war. Connie's Frank has his leave cancelled *because of the trouble.* Churchill and Eden impose a government on Athens, the Greek people now wondering what the hell they had been fighting for. *Please God bless my Danny always and take good care of him and send him to me as soon as possible so we can get engaged by my 20th birthday,* she writes on New Year's Eve, *and please God let him be better now.*

***

Norah knits and stitches her way into 1945: a pair of khaki gloves for Frank, some fabric-covered coat hangers for Mrs Harris' birthday, a jacket for herself made from an old black coat belonging to Ma, and a hem-stitched tablecloth and embroidered 'lady' cushion cover in wove, both for her bottom drawer. She reads *All Quiet on the Western Front* (*very good in patches*) and enjoys the high jinx of 'Humpty Dumpty' at the panto with little Jeannie, now nearly four. With Jean from work, she attends an ENSA performance and a 'smoking concert' at the Institute, accompanied by Mr Hearne and Mr Maclean who, despite the lack of first names, are *getting pally*, the latter flirting by trying to teach her jujitsu in the office.

In his first letter of the new year, Jim rattles on a bit too long about his brother Jack, currently stationed at Spitalgate, Lincolnshire and keen to contact Norah. She isn't interested, not in Jack, nor in bomb aimer Bob, yet another brother to whom Jim has given her home address. Jim says he has 'no dope' on Danny and Norah homes in on the details that he does provide. Danny who is out of hospital and on the mend and who may be able to set a date to see her soon. Danny who 'still thinks you are the sweetest girl in the world' ('So do I', Jim adds, though Norah misses – ignores? – that quiet reminder). *22nd January: Wrote to Jim. I love you so much my sweetheart. Please God take care of him. Read in paper of men from Greece who arrived here last night.*

Jim's letters change in tone again and lurch towards sleazy. 'Please remember, I am your best friend so share your secrets', he writes, although he no longer sounds very friendly. He calls Norah an 'iceberg', says he would 'gamble my life that no boy has ever been allowed to put his hand up your knickers', asks her if 'girls ever get the feeling that they want an intercourse? I do hope you will confide in me a little'. He requests schoolgirl snaps, twice more: 'Please send school photos in your next and let me keep one. Have you one about 12-14 years'. He issues low-level threats: 'It would be fatal for both of us if Danny knew of our intimate letters so you can depend on me that I shall never mention anything'. He claims to have been out with 'hundreds of girls, all nationalities'. He has 'never failed to go so far', he writes, 'and believe me never against their will, perhaps a little persuading, but it is generally shyness and embarrassing at times and refusing often offends and who would me (I would say you)'. 'It is possible you will give in to Danny on your next meeting...', he says, before telling her that he collects 'a very rare souvenir' from his girlfriends 'which you would not guess or give.' He asks all the same: 'The only thing I would like is a souvenir... It is a curl from ____. I told you it was an unusual souvenir, but please ignore the rude and embarrassing side of it (please Norah)'. 'Please return and write an intimate letter if you wish. I can be trusted'.

I'm utterly bored with Jim now. Norah is too. When he sends extracts from letters from 'some girls I have been out with', she tells him what she thinks. What is there to lose? 'PLEASE DON'T CONDEMN', he writes in his reply. 'I knew what attitude you would take after reading those girls' letters, please don't blame them entirely, because my unique technique has got me whatever I wanted, and it is plain to see what I usually wanted'.

But Jim is still her only route to Danny. 'I am now writing Danny's letter, so the next time I answer yours I may have some good news'. 'I am still going to keep you in the dark about Danny but he is on his way home and he sends his love to you alone'. 'Would you marry Danny if you had the chance? I could help you with that'. 'Yes Norah, I can play a big part in your love affair with Danny'.

Does Jim think Norah owes him something? Of course he does. He's out in the bloody North Sea, risking his life to keep her safe. It's her job, to send him comforts and photos and romantic letters, to keep him happy. And it was he who found her in the first place. Those socks were his. How is she still waiting for Danny after all this time? She continues to puzzle him. Her letters give him Norah the nice girl whereas what he wants is what his brother seems to have had: Norah the sex object, the girl who can boost his standing among his fellow ratings.

That's a factor, surely: the ship. All of his mates will know about Norah. He will have bragged about her, shown off her picture. He is hardly going to confess that she has gone off with his brother.

Is there more to say about this kind of environment? Australian Defence Corps veteran and sociologist Ben Wadham thinks there is. In his view, this type of attitude to women is not an individual aberration – Jim as a random 'bad egg' – but a style of masculinity seen as 'crucial to making soldiers', and 'a structured and inherent element of institutional masculine culture'. 'Mateship', as he terms it, is forged against a range of 'others', including civilians and the feminine in themselves (which must be obliterated), and sometimes involves sexually abusive practices.[5] The latter are constantly in the news. As I write, the man rather comically known as the First Sea Lord is attempting to defend the way the Royal Navy handles allegations of rape and sexual abuse, while London Fire Brigade, until recently an all-male workplace, is accused of institutional misogyny. Don't even get me started on the Met.[6]

The possibility that Danny and Jim were less than in control of the situation, that what started as a bit of a lark but got out of hand, fits with Wadham's account. It may even have been circumstantial, like Jim might not have been interested in a fifteen-year-old girl until one turned up – in his sock, as it were. But living in the stoker's mess or at a RAF base, men weren't under surveillance like they would have been at home. As one twenty-seven-year-old newspaper reporter recalled, 'Uniforms and postings to places where they were unknown gave our lovers anonymity and a lack of self-consciousness'.[7] It makes me think of internet dating. A man could make himself out to be anyone he wanted, someone completely different to each new woman. And maybe they believed, in the words of George Ryley Scott, that girls and young women were 'prepared to fall in love with any young man wearing a uniform'; that for some, the obsession went to such 'ridiculous lengths' as to rank as 'a fetish'. That the uniform combined with patriotism removed the 'ordinary standards, social and otherwise' by which more discerning judgements would normally be made.[8]

And goaded on by each other… On the ship, a bit of a loner, Jim feels the pressure from the other men. We shouldn't underestimate that.

***

What does Norah make of Jim's behaviour? What I see as part of a continuum of sexist abuse – Jim knows Norah doesn't want the sexual content of his letters but sends it anyway – she sees, I guess, as smut. But she's not really listening to him. It is the possibility of news about Danny that keeps her hooked in.

For her twentieth birthday on 9th March, Norah receives a box of truffles and two handkerchiefs from Mrs Harris and a kiss from Mr Marsh. Jean treats her to a plaice and chip supper at Jimmie's Chip Shop. They see *The Mikado* and discuss their holiday plans – Cornwall or North Wales? – for the summer.

Norah notes that local girl Madge Hudson has married her airman, while Lily Smith's boyfriend has been killed in action.

It could still go either way.

18. Danny

At the end of March 1945, Norah receives the letter she's been waiting for.

> *24th March: Received the most beautiful surprise of my life when I found a letter from my Danny at home. He's in East Lothian in Scotland. Thank you God. I do love him so. Replied to him & posted it. Went to Gift Sale at Council School. The British are across the Rhine.*
>
> *25th: Thank you God for my Danny & for taking care of him for me. I do love him so, I hope he will be able to come home to me for Easter.*

'[T]he joyful Easter promise of a resurrection of life seems startlingly applicable to temporal affairs', writes Mollie Panter Downes on 1st April. 'Every dazzling headline is a promise that the hard, dark years are nearly over and that at any moment now the incredible word of Victory may come'.[1]

'Thank the Lord for that', my mother says, during one of her daily phone bulletins. 'I was getting heartily fed up with all that praying'.

Danny's *beautiful letters* keep coming, but beyond that he is in Scotland and carrying an injury, Norah reveals nothing about the adventure that has kept him away for almost eighteen months.

I am intrigued to know where Danny has been. His service number takes me nowhere. The Ministry of Defence embargo on servicemen's records means his papers are irretrievable to all but next-of-kin. But looking again at his Blair Athol address at the back of Norah's 1945 dairy, I see that it includes a squadron number. A spot of Googling reveals that Squadron 2737 was at Dyce Airfield near Aberdeen for a few weeks that spring, and that before that, for a whole year from 5th February 1944, at Macmerry in East Lothian. So far, it all squares.

It turns out that 2737 was one of the squadrons engaged in an elaborate 'deception plan' known as Operation Fortitude North. This was part of a ploy to trick the German High Command into believing that a huge army was assembled in Scotland, poised to invade Norway. The idea, of course, was to divert German attention – and troops – away from northern France prior to the D-Day landings. Kitted out in mountain gear, snow boots and white camouflage smocks, servicemen were transported in their hundreds from the south of England, returning under the cover of night to make the journey again the next day. As per the plan, the troops were spotted by German planes.[2]

However – and this is where we come unstuck – just because Danny was with 2737 in early 1945 does not mean his whereabouts in 1943 and 1944 can be matched with that squadron's activities. If I have learned anything about the wartime RAF, it is that squadrons merged and were abandoned, reformed and renumbered. Men moved between them, depending on depletion and demand. A single airman might be attached to four or five squadrons during his wartime career.

We know from Norah's diaries that Danny was at Skeabrae Airfield until July 1943. He then had a brief period at Warmwell in Dorset before arriving at Grantham in early September. These places don't tally with the information I have gleaned about 2737 which, formed in March 1943 at Fairlop in Essex, was in Cornwall, East Sussex, Norfolk and Suffolk, before passing through Gibbet Hill in Warwickshire en route to Macmerry. But Danny could have joined 2737 that October and from all of those airfields, he would have been involved in sorties over Europe. Jim's announcement in his letter of late 1944 that Danny had been in hospital but was now on the mend is not out of keeping with this version of events. All we know, however, is that as soon as he was well enough, he was sent to Aberdeen. Where he was in 1943-1944 is anybody's guess.

Danny doesn't come for Easter, as she hoped he would, and Norah worries that he might be sent back overseas. To lose him now...

By early May, the war is drawing to a close. Dresden is razed. The last V-2 rocket drops on Kent. The Allies enter Buchenwald and the Russians and Americans meet at the Elbe. 'The war is shaping up to some vast Wagnerian finale', writes Frances Partridge. 'The Russian army has completely encircled Berlin and is pressing through the suburbs to the heart of it'. In Italy, Mussolini is executed, he and his mistress 'strung up like turkeys' in a Milanese square. Hitler is reported dead.[3] *3rd May:*

Berlin gave in to the Russians... (And of course, Berlin didn't 'give in'. The Russians rampaged through the city, raping and killing at will.)

Danny writes to tell her that he is due to go to Norway to oversee the transition to peace. He has sex on his mind. *7th May: Received beautiful letter from my love who wants me to give in when he comes again. The Germans surrendered unconditionally & tomorrow is to be VE Day. Replied to my love. Please God take care of him always.*

***

That 'giving in' again... I have to pause here, this phrase is central to my story.⁴

It is possible, of course, that Danny means Norah should 'give in' to her own desires. But I think not. I think not because the evidence surrounding this particular black hole points to the contrary. If in the culture at large, sex is something that respectable girls don't do, that they have to be cajoled into, their modesty coaxed to one side... And if this is then combined with a wartime role of patriotic femininity, essential to buoying up men's morale and to serving the nation... Danny's meaning seems clear. What it might mean to Norah, however, secretly, excitedly, slightly ashamedly, is another matter altogether.

I am reminded of a post-coital exchange in H. E. Bates' 1944 novel *Fair Stood the Wind for France* between Franklin, the main character, and Françoise, known as 'the girl', the daughter of the family where he had found protection after his plane had come down in occupied territory.

'Did you mind what happened tonight?' Franklin asked, after they'd had sex.

'No. I wanted it to happen', 'the girl' replied.

She wanted it to happen: all good. But his question: did she *mind*?

'Did she MIND?' asks Jess, a reviewer on Goodreads. For her, Françoise is no more than a plot device. Bates fails to give her a character or even to use her name. From her role in the Resistance, we can assume that 'the girl' is a brave, resourceful young woman, but all we know is that Franklin is attracted to her. As Jess writes, 'Franklin cannot describe any interaction without paying an interminable tribute to her "clear, dark eyes" or "smooth breasts beneath her blouse"'.

I see this. Indeed, my natural sympathies are with this view, if slightly tempered. In a culture in which women cannot express desire, in which desire in a woman is 'unseemly', an acceptable level of enthusiasm might not extend beyond making it easier for a man remove a blouse. But I pause at 'Did you mind?' The fact that even in the act, Franklin hadn't been able to tell... Sex, quite simply, didn't require her participation, or her pleasure.

'This is not sensible', she had said (when Franklin began to undress her).

'You said you would do anything for me'.

'Yes, I will do anything', she said.[5]

'She is living out the double bind in which women exist', writes Katherine Angel of a much more recent encounter. '[T]hat saying no may be difficult, but so too is saying yes'.[6]

Novelist Elizabeth Howard lost her virginity around the same time that Bates' novel is set. She had no idea what to expect. Her later reflection was that it had been 'surprising'. Pete had been loving and gentle, it hadn't hurt much and 'he'd repeatedly told me how lovely I was and how much he'd enjoyed it. Somehow I'd thought I'd enjoyed it too, but nothing was said about that. This, I concluded, was because women – and surely now I was one – did it for love, and if you loved somebody, you must want to please them'.[7]

Giving in. 'Appeals to patriotism could fuel sexual coercion', writes Amanda Littauer. Commentators in wartime America acknowledged the pressures exerted by some servicemen. *The Ladies Home Journal* reported that 'many a teenage girl was told that having intercourse with a soldier ... was a way to contribute to the war effort'. The *Washington Post* quoted a sailor who was overheard telling a young woman, 'Now, we're going overseas in a day or two and this may be your last chance to do a good turn for your country'. Another recalled the sense of sexual obligation: 'If you weren't interested they'd say "that's what we're fighting for," ... and you'd feel guilty for not wanting to go to bed with them'. 'You Can't Say No to a Soldier', declared the popular song.[8]

In his study of the wartime RAF, Martin Francis writes of servicemen who saw the 'pursuit of love' as both 'a welcome release from the alternating boredom and terror of war' and 'a fitting reward for those who had undertaken the obligations of military service'.[9] The problem surely is when the 'release' of sex and romance tips over into practices which are altogether more entitled; the expectation of a 'reward'. When love and romance as part of their support for men in the forces is combined with sexual ignorance and the requirement not to be too keen, girls are made vulnerable. ('You said you'd do anything for me', Franklin cajoled, just before he was due to row down a river in occupied France...)

According to Nesta Wells, a woman police surgeon in Manchester during and after the war, there was a drop in sex crimes the early 1940s because so many men were away and the foreign troops hadn't yet arrived. When assaults did occur, the ignorance of the girls was a major factor. These were often girls who were 'taken advantage of', because, while not willing partners, they didn't know what the man was up to until it was too late.[10] I've heard other accounts that corroborate this, including a story of a local girl raped in a Sheffield hotel room by an American GI she had been dating for a while. She thought she was meeting him for a goodbye kiss and cuddle and didn't know what he had in mind until, her underwear briskly removed, she felt a burning pain inside.[11]

To be clear: 'the girl' Françoise was not raped and passively 'giving in' to a man's advances might be the only acceptable way to say yes. But as Elizabeth Howard suggests, this could make for an ambivalent experience. 'Modernity was constructed as a culture of greater sexual openness that contrasted with "Victorian" prudery', historian Adrian Bingham writes, 'but there were widespread silences about the disparities of power between the sexes that ensured that these greater freedoms would be exploited in profoundly unequal ways'.[12]

***

Norah attends the VE Day party in Borough Street where four-year-old Jeannie and nine-month-old Roger enjoy their Victory Tea. *8th May: Churchill broadcast at 3pm and the King at 9pm. It's so lovely to have it over, thank you God, especially for taking care of my Danny & Frank & everyone. Posted letter to my sweet. I love him so.*

Norah worries about *conflicting reports of whether or not the Germans will fight in Norway*. Even in the final days of war, as the Czechs rose in Prague and the Red Army ransacked Berlin, as high-standing Nazis killed their families and then themselves, Grand Admiral Karl Dönitz, Commander-in-Chief of the German Navy, was pressing to fight on. In the event, when the instrument of surrender was signed on 7th May, the 350,000 German soldiers in Norway gave themselves up peacefully. The weather was more troublesome. Three of the Short Stirlings that flew out of Great Dunmow crashed at Gardermoen aerodrome in heavy rain and fog, killing all on board. With the war over and Europe celebrating, it felt like a terrible injustice that these lads were lost in extra time.

14th May: Received letter from my love saying he is going back to Norway & is probably now on his way. Please God take care of him and bring him safely to me very soon for always. Danny's squadron travelled to Norway with the First Airborne Division, an army unit that had been regrouped after the losses at Arnhem the previous year. Their plan was to remain until the arrival of Force 134, raised in part from the 12,000 young men who had fled over the border to Sweden in 1940. *15th May: Posted letter to my dearest one. Please God watch over him and take care of him and bring him safely to me within two months or so, for always please God, I love him so.*

Christiansand, Norah writes on the 20th. Danny might have described the picturesque old town with its low, white, wooden houses, the rune stones at the ancient parish church, the harbour and cannon-dotted coastline. Was he among the airmen who, marching through Karl Johansgatan, were offered aquavit and mobbed for their autographs by flower-holding girls? Or who saluted the newly-returned King Haakon VII as he travelled to and from the palace on his bike? Did Danny help with the rounding up Gestapo agents? Or with the Russian POWs, all 80,000 of them, hearing their stories of gratitude to local people who left them packages of food in unlikely places, saving them from sure starvation? We can't know. Other than *he is now at Christiansand and has good billets*, that he *hopes to come home on leave in July and be home for keeps in August*, Norah reports little of what Danny had to say.

Winging their way from Castle Donington to Kristiansand during the summer of 1945 are copies of *Punch* and the *Dispatch*, the *Herald, Mirror, Chronicle, News of the World, Empire News, Leader* and *Lilliput*. Norah searches for a dictionary for Danny and posts some election papers, no doubt telling him that she had been to hear Dr Mont Follick, the prospective Labour MP, at a pre-election rally in Castle Donington. (In an otherwise *lovely* later letter from Danny, she is disconcerted to discover that he *seems to favour the Tories*.) She cancels the holiday in Abersoch she has planned for September with her friend Jean, reads

Happy Times in Norway by Nobel prize-winner Sigrid Undset and orders a copy of *The Hero of the World*.

At Midsummer, just a fortnight before the general election which saw Labour's landslide win, Norah's father dies. She had noted in her diary his recent spells in hospital with an enlarged spleen and the fainting episodes that followed, that the doctor had said there was nothing more they could do. She doesn't mention her regret that he didn't live to see Atlee installed as PM. After his funeral, she and Marsie travel by train to London to visit Dennis and his growing family. They have dinner at the Strand Corner House, taking in sights – Westminster Abbey, St. Paul's, Buckingham Palace, Tower Bridge – that have miraculously survived the Blitz. The next day Norah sunbathes in the back garden and chats with a visiting airman friend of her brother before going with Nollie to see 'Arsenic & Old Lace' in the West End.

When she next hears from Danny, Norah writes that he was *a bit upset about me talking to that airman at Dennis's. God bless.* She is comforted by his jealousy; it shows how much he cares. Marsie, however, has other ideas. *4th August: Mum and I had a row, as she thinks my Danny breaks his promises, but I love him so. Please God, let him be alright.*

***

VJ Day has supplied some of the most iconic images of the twentieth century. A sailor kissing a nurse in Times Square. A pirouetting man in a Sydney street. Piccadilly Circus in the sunshine, servicemen, WAAFs and civilian women laughing and dancing while linking arms. Japanese POWs, reflecting on Emperor Hirohito's announcement of surrender, heads bowed low in shame.

Sadly, we haven't been able to locate a single photograph of the street party on Moira Dale.

'I can just remember it', my mum says. She was four-and-a-half years old and sat outside number 18 at a long table piled high with sandwiches. 'They were a rowdy lot!'

Irene Marsh, Norah's next-door neighbour, can remember more, especially the races to the far end of the street and back again that preceded the tea. Aged thirteen and built like a whippet, she won them all. She remembers the bunting fetched out again, the trestle tables, her dad's piano dragged into the street by men in shirtsleeves and the jubilant but weary women, dishing out beef spread sandwiches to small boys in tank-tops and bobbed-haired girls. After the jelly (or junket) and homemade cake – food which had been in such short supply but which materialised quite miraculously from who knows where – the tables were hoisted onto the pavements, the neighbours taking turns on the piano as the dancing began. Heart-felt renditions of popular war songs – 'Keep the home fires burning', 'We'll meet again' – followed the National Anthem and toasts to the King and Queen and all absent friends.

16th August: Jeannie went to our tea party in the street. Jim had his piano out in the street and everyone had a singsong. Had another huge bonfire & a lovely Lantern Parade. Wrote to my love again (12 pages). God bless. Irene and her sisters were not allowed to hold the metal lanterns, hangovers from the blackout, which were suspended on sticks and carried with arms outstretched. The blazing bonfire, built on waste ground down the road, burned through the night and into a new post-war world.

17th August: Mum brought me a letter from my love, he's been very depressed. He is flying to Tromsö and says Group 20 will be out by 31st. Norah's diary entries describe Danny's misery and the delays and uncertainties surrounding his demob date. *23rd: Received a censored letter from my dearest love who says he may be at Tromsö a fortnight but is hoping for leave.* She hears on the one o'clock news that the 1st Airborne Division will be leaving Norway within a fortnight. In the last week of August, Norah sees a new statement on RAF demobilisation: *Group 22 will be out by the end of October.* The next day, the newspaper reports that *all our men will be home from Norway by Christmas. Please God…* I find this confusing, not least because it is impossible to make out whether Danny is in Group 20 or 22 or whether these demobilisations are merely markers on the road to his own return. All we know is that he is delayed, temporarily hospitalised with an injured back. *Danny hopes to be home by the 20th September. DV.*

Norah is reading *Arnhem Lift: Diary of a Glider Pilot*. She might just want a better understanding of what it had been like for him, an airman in this terrible war, so that she can really look after him once she gets him home. Or Danny might have told her that he had been in Holland in September 1944, nowhere near Yugoslavia or Greece after all. The Allies' largest airborne operation had intended to capture the bridges to the south of the Rhine but was disastrously thwarted by fog. I Google the images: the parachutes eerily descending like jellyfish in the daybreak sky. Maybe Danny had landed under the enemy fire so badly underestimated by Allied leaders. Maybe that is where he damaged his back. We can only guess.

From his Tromsö hospital bed in, Danny sends Norah *twelve marvellous snaps*. It is one of these photographs that we found in a transparent wallet tucked inside Norah's last diary, together with a scrap of paper with the phone numbers for two people with the surname Gilbert, both with the Eastbourne area code. Danny poses beside the driver's door of a military car against a background of tall pines and gabled roofs. He is slender, smart, unsmiling, his hands clasped behind his back in that neat folded-up way in which men used to stand.

22nd September 1945: Mary Twells was married to John, her airman. Jeannie was bridesmaid. Two days' later, Norah notes her work-mate Jean's 21st birthday (*no engagement ring forthcoming*). In early October, Connie's Frank is demobbed and she is given eight weeks' leave. Norah hears from a woman in the Night Office that Norman has returned safely and is now engaged. *7th October: Spring cleaned my best clothes in preparation for my Danny, DV.*

Was it a worry too? 'Will your man be changed?' asked *Woman's Own* in April 1945, declaring the following month that 'a reunion can be more frightening than a parting'. For many it was. The men were 'strangers in the house', war-damaged, unknown to their own children, struggling with newly independent wives. In the words of one woman, 'When their war ended, our war began'.[13]

Norah again borrows a book about Eastbourne from Derby Library. As she leafs through the photographs, she surely imagines herself enjoying Saturday morning coffees with Danny in one of the shiny new cafes, matinée shows at the green-domed Winter Gardens and Sunday afternoon strolls along the bright undercliff, arm in arm. She'd love a detached house on one of the many new tree-lined avenues or, if Danny's salary didn't stretch that far, a neat, light, dormer bungalow in a nice part of town.

Norah books in at W. W. Winter's to have her photograph taken. With her dark waves and shaped brows, her almond-shaped eyes gazing dreamily beyond the camera, she looks every inch the wartime glamour girl. She will raise his spirits, and reel him in.

Fig. 28 Norah, W. W. Winter, Derby, 1945. Private papers of Norah Hodgkinson.

In early November, as Norah's youngest brother Frank departs for India with the Royal Engineers, Danny lands in England. He writes to say he is hoping to come to Grantham at the end of the month. Norah phones him from the telephone box in Hemington, but – oh! the frustration! – the line is so crackly she can hardly make him out. More letters arrive, including snaps of Tromsö in the midnight sun. After two false alarms, Norah has a *glorious surprise when my love rang me up from Derby. He's here 'til Thursday.*

19. Our Night of Love

Had Marsie decided against any great fanfare to celebrate Danny's return that Tuesday night in November 1945? It is surely inevitable that Norah's mother faced an internal battle as she tried to tally the well-mannered young man of his visits and letters with her sense that there was something not quite right. She couldn't ignore the fact that Danny didn't always come when he said he would; that he let Norah down. And that disappearance… She knew he'd been injured, in hospital, that terrible things could have happened to him. It was true that there were soldiers and airmen who had been out of touch for months, even years. But even so…

I imagine Norah interrupting her mother's thoughts, clattering down the stairs and flying through the front room to appear at the kitchen door, flushed and smiling, more bright-eyed than Milly had seen her in months. How did she look? Marsie wouldn't need to force a smile as she complimented her daughter – wearing her newly made-up red skirt and red and white polka dot blouse, maybe, the colour so striking against her dark hair. I picture her, Norah, clasping her hands together in a bid to contain her excitement, spinning round and skipping through the front room and back upstairs. Oh how Milly hoped he would turn up! She couldn't bear to see her lovely girl disappointed again.

In the absence of evidence, I can only imagine my great-grandmother's fears. At first, welcoming Danny into her home, she had been guided by basic humanity – he was another mother's son – and her faith, that a stranger might be an 'angel unawares'. But now, as much as she wanted to trust – 'Wait on the Lord: be of good courage, and he shall strengthen thine heart' – the word that was going through her mind was not 'wait' but 'watch'. Watch out for deceivers. Watch out for the wolf in sheep's clothing. See that no-one does her wrong or leads her astray.

You heard such shocking stories. There was a girl from Ripley who'd had quads by an American airman, married of course. And just around the corner in Castle Donington, there was a girl of Norah's age who'd had a baby boy to a Canadian pilot and then discovered he had a wife at home. That poor little boy. But how did you stop a girl like Norah, so headstrong and full of ardour?

This is the scene as I imagine it. Milly rests her spoon in the bowl and, wiping her hands on her apron, makes her way through to the front room to stand in front of Birdy who, just in from work, is reading the paper in his father's wooden chair.

'Richard love, I need to ask you something'.

He looks up and smiles eagerly.

'Will you stay up tonight, keep an eye on Norah?' He raises an eyebrow, looks ready to speak, but she forces a bit more authority into her voice, competing now with the kettle which is building up to a shrill whistle in the adjoining kitchen. 'I just don't want her down here alone with him'. And then more gently, 'Will you do that, love?'

Birdy nods, half-smiling.

> *21st November. Had lovely time in bed with my love. Stayed in all day. Dynamos beat Arsenal 4.3. Terribly foggy. Birdy stayed downstairs so couldn't have our night of love.*

Birdy, on sentry-duty, succeeded in preventing Norah's 'giving in', but not the lovers' snatched hour in the morning between his departure for work and Marsie's return from the Co-op. *22nd: Had smashing, hectic time in bed with Danny. Went to Hemington to ring up about trains. My love had to return on the 2.40 train. Had tooth filled. I'm lonely without my love.*

'Hectic' seems a strange choice of word to describe an erotic encounter. I am relieved to see the preceding word is 'smashing', but I wonder about it, all the same. Was Danny more insistent than Norah was comfortable with? Had it started out beautifully, tenderly, but become a bit of a battle to hold him off?

> *23rd November. Returned to work. Rang my love but he sounded a bit mad, he didn't get in until 11am.*
>
> *24th: Posted letter to my love, please God let him love me again and please let him come next weekend.*
>
> *26th: No letter from my love. Please God let him still be loving me.*

> *27th: Still no letter, so rang Danny from the* [*Sailors and Soldiers'*] *Club, but the man said 'he is not on the station tonight'. Please God let him have written for tomorrow.*
>
> *28th: Posted letter to my Danny. I'm getting fed up, and I'm not going to write again until I hear from him.*
>
> *29th: Received letter from my love. He is going to try and come at the weekend.*
>
> *1st December. Received three letters from Frank, he should have reached Bombay last Saturday. Danny did not come and mum was very mad and wants me to pack him up. Please God make him good.*

Norah wrote to Danny three times the following week and continued praying to God. *No letter from Danny* appears daily in her diary, alongside feint little notes in pencil, written months earlier, predictions based on who knows what. *D & me engaged* is the only one I can clearly read.

And that was it. No engagement. No glorious family Christmas with her love.

'So what happened to him?' I ask my mum on the phone.

'I've absolutely no idea. That was it. He didn't visit again'. She sounds weary. She has been diarying all afternoon.

'Poor Norah'. I feel so sorry for her. 'All that waiting. All that expectation'.

We fall silent for a few seconds. Norah had indeed spent the entire war thinking he'd come back and marry her. My mum suggests that Norah was too keen, had scared him off. Or he maybe had more than one girl on the go, and the other one won out, in the end.

'She was a silly girl though', my mum replies. 'He didn't get in touch for months on end and she thought he was coming back. Marsie clearly knew something was amiss. She and Norah even rowed about it and I can't imagine Marsie rowing with anybody'.

'But men did disappear for months on end', I say defensively. 'There was a war on'.

'The odd thing is', my mum continues, 'apart from when she burned his letters, Norah never mentioned Danny in her diary again. Not that I've seen, anyway, and I'm up to 1955. I don't think he's going to make a re-appearance now'.

And that was it. Norah never heard from Danny again. Not directly, anyway.

***

This is where Norah's diary lets us down. In those lonely, disappointed days after Danny's last visit, she clearly felt far more than is conveyed by the words that appear on the page. It is not that the daily windows are too small; she's squeezed emotion into those spaces before. Here, her minimal wordage is a choice. From all-consuming waiting and worrying, from daily prayers for Danny's safety, she turns to an almost total silence. It is as if she is practising for a New Year's resolution. She *will* get a grip of herself. She *will* stop wasting her life waiting for Danny. She *won't* use those little squares to confess her heartbreak. Into the new year, her blue Railway Clerical Workers' Union diary for 1946 becomes a means of self-discipline, to keep thoughts of Danny at bay.

'Every woman who has ever kept a diary knows that women write in diaries because things are not going right', writes Mary Helen Washington.[1] But not Norah. Norah wrote her early diaries because things *were* going right. Because there she was at grammar school, on her ascent. She wrote not to be published, or to be read by others, not to rebel nor to practice for a life as a writer, not to document the war, a journey or any other significant event, but in the simple belief that her ordinary life, her *life on the up*, was worth it. She captured her days, for future reference, for her future self. But now, after Danny's last visit and disappearance: silence.

No doubt in her angrier moments, Norah felt he wasn't even worth twenty words a day. Maybe she felt foolish too. Marsie had an inkling a long time ago that all was not well. And then there were her brothers and Helen, her school friends and the folk at work: had they seen through the excuses she'd made? She had worn her heart on her sleeve when maybe it had been clear to them all that Danny was leading her a merry dance. She will have noted a comment made by her brother Frank, in a letter sent just as he departed for India with the Royal Engineers: 'Is Danny with you all? Surely he should have had leave by now'. He had let her down too many times. She had allowed him to take her for a besotted fool.

I find myself comparing Norah's silence about her wartime experience with Annie Ernaux's account of her formative sexual encounter documented in her memoir, *A Girl's Story*. In the summer of 1958, aged eighteen and working as a *monitrice* in a *colonie de vacances* in a town in northern France, Ernaux became infatuated with H., a fellow *moniteur*, who reminded her of Marlon Brando and whom she termed 'the Archangel', and in whose bed she spent two nights before he rejected her. She then hooked up with a series of other boys, her 'promiscuity' becoming the subject of bullying and mockery by her peers. Much later in life, Ernaux remembers 'a tissue of chaotic feelings, sensations, motivations, and desires as well as a distinct anaesthetization, an (emotional) vacating of the self...' Like Norah, she had an 'absolute ignorance and anticipation of what is considered the most unknown and wondrous thing in life – the secret of secrets'. Both girls were ill-equipped, had recourse to no interpretation beyond romantic fantasy (of H. as Ernaux's lover, of Danny's certain return).[2]

Should we see Norah's silence as evidence of trauma? (I have my mum on my shoulder again: 'For God's sake', she mutters. 'What is it with your generation? Everybody in the world gets their heart broken'.) An 'ordinary trauma' perhaps?[3] At the very least, it is (what Ernaux describes as) an 'inassimilable experience', which she links to her subsequent eating disorder, the cessation of her periods and to her later development as a writer, even if the legacy of shame means it was many years before she could confront the experience head on. Turning a traumatic event into a story might be a way to confront it, to get a handle on it, to control it, enforce a distance between the event and oneself; a way of forgiving oneself.

But Norah's diary is mute. She couldn't write of her abandonment by Danny. While we wouldn't expect her to tell the story in her pocket diary, her silence is surely significant. The traumatic ending to Norah's sexual awakening 'disturbs the emerging "I" ... and renders the subject voiceless, at least for a time'.[4]

The January silence is momentarily detonated by the arrival of more news from Frank in Bombay: 'I hope Danny is out of the RAF now', he writes, and no doubt 'feeling a bit strange after seven years in blue'. He hopes they enjoyed their Christmas dinner – 'with champagne. I hope it wasn't too strong. You didn't say whether Danny was staying at CD or not'.

Ah. So Norah had bought a bottle of bubbly with which to celebrate Danny's safe return and, she will have hoped, their engagement.

'I'll write to Frank', Marsie may have said gently, adding a PS to her next letter: 'It looks like it is all off with Danny. He visited just after you left, but we haven't heard from him since early last month. Norah is bearing up'.

But we can only assume that Norah was bearing up, as her diary gives nothing away. How often did she have to summon her resolve, to put him out of her mind again, to try her utmost to banish those nights pricked with sadness and regret? What were her feelings on the day in mid-January when she received *two letters I sent to Danny at Folkingham, marked 'unknown'*?

There will have been other reminders, of course. All those nosy questions from neighbours and colleagues. Was she still courting? Had her nice young man got his demob yet? Engagements and wedding announcements were coming thick and fast in 1946. Even her walks over Daleacre and down to the River Trent brought him to mind, as winter turned into spring.

And what if this was it, if how she had felt about Danny when she was with him was her one and only chance? Did she worry that no-one else would kindle such passion, that she'd never feel that way again? How could she settle for any other life? And even if she felt up to looking for someone new, how would she ever meet him? Any man worth having was spoken for now.

'She's missed the boat'', my mum says.

'That's ridiculous', I say. 'She's twenty years old'. I am wary of my mother's belief that Norah's affair with Danny shaped the rest of her life. But waiting so long for him to return meant that Norah had arrived late on the dating scene.

'It's 1946', she replies. 'Everybody was engaged by the time they were Norah's age. And then in the Fifties, it was even younger. That was your sole aim in life'. She pauses. 'Mind you, it certainly explains Eddy. She was desperate not to be left on the shelf when she met him'.

Norah mentions Danny once more that year, at Christmas, when Frank was home from Egypt and they were all together again. *25th December 1946: Had turkey for dinner, and Danny's champagne.*

20. A Terrific Surprise

In the early summer of 1947, Norah and her mother accepted an invitation from Marsie's brother, (another) Frank, to join him and Mary and their nine-year old daughter, (another) Jean, on a holiday in – of all places – Eastbourne. Norah's diary reports that they had booked into a guest house a few streets back from the front and enjoyed long *boiling hot* days on the beach and evening walks along the prom.

Eastbourne: Danny's home town. Norah must surely have imagined a chance encounter. Is that why she agreed to the trip? Did she choose her holiday wardrobe with him in mind? Was she looking out for him on every corner, seeing his family members in random people in the street? Did she plot his home address and her hotel on a map, maybe finding some time alone to wander in his direction?

She'd had a few little flirtations in 1947. The year had kicked off with a string of dates with a good-looking lad called Alan who had just started work in her office and with whom she had a *smashing time*. But a few weeks in, after Norah missed the last bus home and he abandoned her rather than miss his own, she turned down his next invitation (though was a bit put out when he was spotted with a new girlfriend in less than a month and was engaged before the summer's end). Then there was 'P' at work, who invited her to go with him to Bakewell Show and offered her some clothing coupons (*AT A PRICE*). And George, who told her he had a crush on her. While Norah didn't believe he had finished with Beryl, she was flattered all the same.

At the time of her Eastbourne holiday, Norah was enjoying a flirtation with 'Blondie', a driver on the Trent bus. He was *a smasher*, a bit of a hero who had steered his passengers to safety when the river burst its banks. Renamed 'Ginger' by a sarcastic Birdy, in the hot early summer he had an ice cream waiting for her on the 5.40 bus home. *5th June 1947: Blondie called me glamour girl and threw me kisses.* Norah did her homework, discovered that his name was Jack and he lived in Aston-on-Trent, suddenly a new destination for evening bike rides with Peggy (*Aston is lovely*). The potential for romance was abruptly curtailed, however, when Norah discovered that what she had assumed was Jack's bachelor boy's motorbike was actually *a motor-bike and side-car!!* Some days later, she *saw Ginger's wife on the 10pm bus. She didn't look very thrilling.*

Everyone was getting engaged, married or having babies that year, from Princess Elizabeth to Irene next door. Both were younger than Norah. *15th September 1947: meet HIM 15/5*. This diary entry is written in pencil, a horoscope prediction from a magazine that she had read around the time of her Eastbourne trip in May.

In the meantime, she was perfectly busy. With Sadie, the replacement for Connie who hadn't returned to work after Frank's demob, she lunched at Pingpongs, tried out new cafés and signed up for classes at Derby's Progressive School of Dancing, learning to tango, quickstep and waltz. She knitted and sewed and slowly replenished her wardrobe, which wasn't easy with rationing still in force. She picked up her shorthand again and she read, this year a number of classics, including *Persuasion* (*the best book I've ever read*) and *Jane Eyre* (*lovely*). She made many, many trips to the cinema and went with Birdy and Frank to the Baseball Ground on Saturday afternoons (*Derby knocked out the cup by Liverpool. 1.0. Heartbroken*). She attended lectures by a local vicar on contemporary social issues: reconstruction, German history, the Soviet Union and more. She read the Labour Party's *The Way of Recovery* (*wonderful*) and ordered the *Economic Survey for 1947*, the controversial White Paper on the need for a planned economy. She became a paid-up party member later that year.

The following month, out of the blue, days after Norah remembered Danny's *30th* (*?*) *birthday* (the question mark surely denoting her suspicion that Danny hadn't told the truth about his age?), a letter arrived from Jim:

> 27 October 1947,
> HMS *Challenger*

Dear Norah,

Undoubtedly you will be somewhat mystified at my letter, so please read on and I will endeavour to enlighten. Before mentioning any further, I sincerely hope these few lines won't offend or cause any ill feeling towards anyone. Naturally a sailor does the most crazy things

and introducing my brother to you was one of them. Little did I realise that a close friendship was to be established which Danny and myself knew could not materialise. We are of a poor family although a happy one and Danny knew it would not be fair to you or your loving family to have gone any further than just a friend. Many times during and after the war we have talked about you and the terrible and most ungrateful way we treated you and we both apologise and wish you all the happiness in the world.
Jim

31st October 1947: Had a terrific surprise when Mum bought me a letter from Jim. He says Danny packed up because his family were poor. Could she possibly have believed Jim's explanation, when Danny had spent weekends at 18 Moira Dale? He knew about the council house, the blue-collar jobs, the scholarship successes. But maybe it was the apology that mattered; the bit about them treating her dreadfully and ungratefully; that they were sorry.

I wish Jim had left it at that. His next letter is harmless enough, written in early December from Aden where he is aboard HMS *Challenger* on his way to the Persian Gulf. There is 'trouble ashore with the Jews and Arabs', he writes. 'I thought when the war ended I might get a bit of shore time, but they mean to get a good twelve years out of me'. He replies to Norah's news that she has been to Eastbourne on holiday ('a grand place') and sends his congratulations on Derby beating Arsenal. 'I bet you have many admirers now you are grown up', he writes, 'or would you rather take Danny a cup of morning tea and a kiss (blushing). Did he tell you I knew, "well we are brothers". I suppose you say "the same old Jim"'. He asks her for a photo. Norah takes the compliment. *12th December: Received lovely letter from Jim, he's based in the Gulf of Persia. Tells me to always stay as nice as Danny says I am.* I note the conversation between the brothers and wonder about the tag-team correspondence between the two men and my young great-aunt.

23rd December 1947: Had lovely trifle, fruit jelly, sponge cake, rock cakes, mince pies, biscuits, tangerines, apples, nuts, cider and parsnip wine. As Norah enjoys her office Christmas party, a truly post-war feast, Jim writes again. 'Oh boy aren't you pretty', he says, though Norah's photograph seems to catalyse his need to launch into his 'wide experience with girls all over the world' and his quibble with English women, 'so cold and narrow minded'. 'Did Danny want more than your friendship', Jim writes at the end of March. 'If he did I know love would never get a yes from you'. Norah notes the arrival of his letters but that is all. She takes weeks to reply.

In a letter sent in April from Port Said, Jim takes 'a chance in writing my views on sex', asking her if she has 'ever felt that you have wanted to relieve your feelings', and why it is that 'girls always get the impression that only the boy gains'. For me, as a historian, Jim's challenge to the buttoned-up 1940s and his questions about female desire are interesting. As we know, even during the war, it was far from acceptable to have an *appetite*, to be seen as a libidinous woman. But as Norah's great-niece and a mother of daughters, I'd rather he didn't grapple with these questions in his letters to her. He tells her that Danny is working in civil aviation before snidely signing off: 'I bet you will marry in white (nasty Jim again). Fancy Danny failing'. This comment gives me pause. Was that it? A bet that Danny could seduce Norah, get her to 'give in'? Or is that just Jim's take, as the jealous and rejected older brother?

In his final letter, dated 15th May 1948, Jim continues in much the same vein. He is disappointed that Norah didn't reveal her secrets, he says. He thinks he'd have 'gained a yes' if he'd been in Danny's shoes. He tells her again that boys go elsewhere if they don't get what they want. And that is it. Norah can't even be bothered to reply, let alone complain. In fact, apart from a passing reference in the early 1980s, she doesn't mention Jim again until 2008, the year before she died. *30th September: Found some letters from Jim Gilbert. He was a silly, empty person.*

***

It is not quite the end for me, however. I feel compelled to find out what happened to the brothers – whether they married and had families, lived to be old men.

It is a warm August day and I am sitting at home in my small study at the front of the house. The sun, lighting up the park across the road, has not yet moved round to slant through the wooden blinds. The dog is lying at my feet, having taken to shooting up the forbidden stairs as soon as her lord and master leaves for work.

I have logged into Ancestry.co.uk., the family history website. I decide to start with Jim and type in his surname, which is not Gilbert (you'll soon see why), and then his forenames (which did not include Jim), which were written out in full on the back of the envelope which contained his first letter to Norah. There are results, I am informed, but they can only be read if I join. I do so; membership is free for a fortnight.

I write a reminder in my diary to cancel before I get stung for a year's subscription. I am aware that I am delaying.

I type in Jim's name again and there he is, in an instant: birth, marriage and death records listed down the the right hand of the screen. According to Ancestry, he was born in London in 1912. He died in the late 1970s, aged sixty-six. There appear to be two marriage records for him. One in 1948, in Sussex, and another in London, in 1951. He must have married as soon as he left the Navy. I wonder if his need for 'relief' got the better of him as it seems to have been a hasty affair which didn't work out. There is no sign of a divorce but I know I am not using this website very proficiently. I quickly compute the dates. Jim was nearly thirty when he began writing his mucky letters to schoolgirl Norah in 1941.

Danny. It is time. I take a deep breath before typing in his real names and, giving him the benefit of doubt, the birth date he gave to Norah: 26th October 1917. Then, true to her suspicions, I select the option for 'plus/minus 5 years'.

Again, the results flood in.

Danny did indeed lie about his age. He was born in 1914. He died in Eastbourne in 1996, an old man of eighty-two.

A public member tree pops up on the screen. I click on it. A shiver goes down my spine.

'I've found him'. I phone my mum that instant. I am pacing up and down the landing, unable to sit still at my desk.

'Who?' she asks, puzzled.

'Danny boy. I'm on Ancestry'.

'Oooh', she says in a low tone. 'And?'

'It says he got married in early 1940. His wife's name was Evelyn. She was 20'.

'1940?' I can hear her working it out. 'He met Norah in 1941. He was already a married man?' Silence.

'That's not all', I continue. 'You remember that September when he stayed at Moira Dale on three different weekends? When Norah was looking at engagement rings and making her golden dressing gown?' My mum is silent, waiting. 'Well, it looks like Donington was a break in his journey to and from Eastbourne. That's when his first baby was born'.

My mum takes a sharp in-breath. 'Do you think Norah ever knew?'

'No', I say, 'she can't have done. She'd have mentioned it in the diaries'.

A pause. An outward breath. 'The swine'.

III

Some attachments are elemental and beyond our choosing, and for that very reason they come spiced with pain and regret and need and hollowness.

– Colm Tóibín

Over time, the memory cools, until it is just like a snapshot one might carry in a purse but the cut is still there and eventually she finds that her whole being has grown around it like a tree that has been struck by lightning and survived.

– Annie Ernaux

21. Son of Danny

I want to know more about these two men and their post-war lives: Danny's marriage, if he stayed with his wife, whether Jim was ever hauled up on an indecency charge…

I return to the family history website, Ancestry. Via some poking about and playing around with the 'search' facility – typing in parents' details, nosing at a Public Member's Tree – I discover that Danny and Evelyn had three children over as many decades, including a son, a change-baby no doubt, who is a contemporary of mine. The daughters have first names popular in those years and, both married, surnames that are not uncommon. They would be difficult to chase down. But that last-born son…

What I didn't realise is that when you nosy at someone's profile on LinkedIn, the fact of you being there is recorded, passed on. For those as unaware as I was, I should explain. LinkedIn – linked in, not linkideln, as I was mispronouncing to myself until I twigged that the second 'l' was in fact a capital 'I' – is a professional networking site on the internet. You type in your details, your work, and put yourself out there. So when I discovered that Danny's son is a member, I signed up to the service to get a better look. I had no idea that he was informed that I'd been snooping, not until this email dropped into my inbox:

> Dear Alison,
> You have been looking at my profile on LinkedIn. Please feel free to get in touch.
> Regards,
> Rob Gilbert

Lordy! I froze in my seat as my heart began beating fast. I was unsure whether this was an automated message, generated by any visit to

Rob Gilbert's LinkedIn site, or whether he really knew that I had been looking and had sent it, knowingly, specifically, for me.

If the latter, it is worse than he imagines, because I have learned quite a lot about him in recent weeks. Not only do I know that he is a former local government officer now working for a charity (that's the LinkedIn info), but going by family photographs on his daughter's facebook site (oh yes, I'm afraid so, the teenage girl with the same surname living in Bexhill is one of his three daughters), he has been married more than once. This daughter's profile leads me seamlessly to her sister's wedding, Rob giving her away. He is the image of Danny, his dad.

It would be so easy. My fingers would run away with me. I'd tell him that I had an aunt who died and left me her diaries spanning seventy-one years, and a bundle of letters and photographs, mostly of Danny and Jim Gilbert. I'd say that she got to know them through knitting socks for the Royal Navy Comforts Fund as a schoolgirl and that there was a romantic entanglement. I'd make it clear that I am a historian by training and that I am writing a book. Obviously I'd tell him that I have disguised the names. And I'd drop it in that I plan to use some of the photographs, of Jim in his sailor's uniform and of a very dapper Danny as a young airman. I wouldn't ask his permission, just see what unfolds.

And then there is the hard bit: at what point would I tell him that neither Danny nor Jim comes out of this little affair very well? When would I offer the reassurance that I didn't set out to discredit them? That to the contrary, I have read lots about the experience of being a pilot in WW2, to understand more about the emotional impact of those night flights and bombing raids. That I would love to hear more about what Danny did, how the war affected him, what he was like as a husband and a dad (and, of course, where he went in 1943-44...). I get ahead of myself. Due a trip to Brighton to see friends, I am already in the Pavilion Gardens café on a sunny summer's afternoon, enjoying a cup of tea with Danny's son.

But I don't pursue. I feel a vague sense of unease, a nagging self-doubt, and decide to sit on it for a while. When eventually I mention the possibility of contacting Rob Gilbert to colleagues, the strength of feeling, the polarised responses, leave me startled.

Writers are generally very keen.

'Holy shit!' they exclaim, or words to that effect. 'What a chapter!'

Historians, to a woman, are dead against. 'You're surely not serious?' two very professional oral historians looked aghast as I told them the story over a beer in a Sheffield pub. Everything goes through an ethics committee with them. It was like I had gone down ten notches in their estimation for even entertaining the idea.

I told them what a shock it was, receiving the message.

'I think what's more shocking is you stalking this poor guy on social media', one said reproachfully. 'You know his whole life story! And looking at his daughters' facebook profiles…' She laughed, deadly serious, and sipped her drink. 'What are you, a historian or a tabloid journalist?'

I'm less troubled than some by the social media voyeurism. Facebook has privacy settings afterall. But when I tell Mark later that night, he agrees with them.

'But he's *our age*'. I am emphatic. 'Surely people know odd things happened during the war? Could it really be so devastating to find your father had an unconsummated love affair years before you were born? He stayed with his mother after all'.

'You just don't know what you'd be raking up', Mark says. 'You could unravel his story of his life'. He pauses. 'Ok. I'll put myself in his shoes… A woman gets in touch to talk about an affair my dad had before I was born. My dad and mum are both dead. I have good memories of a happy childhood. My dad was hard working and attentive, he might have had a bit of a roving eye, but he was devoted to my mum, who loved him dearly. Then this woman turns up out the blue. She wants to pull that rug from under my feet, to give me a different view of my dad, of my whole childhood, all because she wants good copy for her book. What possible benefit to me is this piece of information? How dare she intrude on my life in this way..?

I find it so hard to believe this, but some anxiety about my ability to judge what is right and proper holds me back.

***

How do we respect the living when we write about the dead? (How do we respect the dead when we write about their lives?) What are the limits of the historian's right to know, especially in an age of digital traceability, when so little is out of bounds?

People are vulnerable in death. Perhaps I should care more that Danny can't respond to my allegations that Norah was groomed by him and his brother; innocent until proven guilty, and all that. But he is isn't my worry here. Abusers and their victims are not equal before the law. The evidence is clear. How else can it be read?

My concern is Danny's living children who, I don't doubt, can well do without my posthumous revelations. I tend to agree with Thomas Couser as he urges lifewriters to always undertake a 'conscientious and scrupulous consideration of who might be hurt by life writing and how';[1] to do no harm.

But. (There is always a 'but' for me, often more than one...) The question of which takes precedence, the story, or a subject's privacy, is never as clear cut as that. How can anything ever be written, when 'my' story, Norah's story, is also 'theirs'?

And: we can't possibly know what their reactions will be. We can *guess*, of course, but is it really a foregone conclusion that harm would be done? I know nothing about Danny's children and their relationships with their father and their uncle Jim (though I can't help but note that Danny's granddaughters are not friends with Jim's children on Facebook...). 'A family without secrets is rare indeed', Annette Kuhn has written, and those secrets 'haunt our memory-stories, giving them pattern and shape'.[2] What if my revelations confirm long-held suspicions; spark some kind of closure they'd sought for years?

(Indeed, might we even say that there are other ethical considerations – like recovering the lives of women in history, for example, and telling long-concealed stories, about sex and secrets, about the abuse of power and the wrongs done to girls...?)

But... the thing that holds me back is my knowledge that I have a tendency to be rash. The email to arrange that cup of tea with Rob Gilbert in Brighton Pavillion Gardens? It wouldn't be the first time in my adult life that my enjoyment of uncertainty, of the unknown, overrode consideration of unintended consequences. What if I stopped to really interrogate my own motivations, to delve into my heart and mind, as life writers suggest I should?[3] I suspect I would find that as much as my need to know the whys and wherefores of Danny's war, it is the sheer pleasure of stories spooling forward in unexpected ways, the fresh perspectives on Danny's wartime affair with Norah, the new topics, emotions, theatres of war that I can then explore, that I find so very compelling and that spur me on.

There's the legal stuff as well, of course: invasion of privacy, defamation, libel, slander. Scary words. I don't go there, despite Mark's best efforts ('And what if he tries to stop you from publishing your book. It might only take a phone call to the university…'). I began this project so long ago that it falls outside of the university's ethics process, whereby any project that involves human research must obtain ethics approval prior to commencement. I'd already commenced, undertaken some interviews, delved into Ancestry. I'm more interested in personal moralities than policy and the law. But I know the gist: to change names and identifying characteristics, to decline from using photographs. I want to balance honesty, the book's integrity, with empathy for Danny's living children. And also: I'm too long in the tooth now for feelings of regret.

***

Without a conversation with Danny's son, there is no way of knowing for certain why Danny disappeared from Norah's life between October 1943 and March 1945. Whether he flew out of English skies one autumn day into some European horror that prevented him from visiting or writing to Norah for eighteen months. (Remember that 'Norway again' in one of Norah's diary entries for May 1945.) Or if the sight of his baby daughter nestling in her mother's arms was just so heart-wrenching that he vowed to bring an end to his wayward days? I can't know without asking what war stories Danny's children grew up with: his near misses on night flights from Skeabrae, maybe? his back injury at Arnhem? the remarkable double agent 'Garbo', who was crucial to Operation Fortitude and its success? his repeated tellings of (or his silences about) small heroic acts that would show more of him?

I realised too very late in the day that it has taken me so long to write this book that the MoD policy of releasing information to no-one but the next of kin for twenty-five years after an airman's death no longer applies. But – by then I was reconciled. Because: to what end? This story was Norah's all along.

22. Men's Regrets

Although we have exhausted the diaries and letters, and have ruled out other ways forward, I find myself replaying certain scenes in my head. These incidents, about which I can find out nothing more, are to my mind pivotal to the whole affair. My proposition is this: that based on my now intimate acquaintance with the characters in this story, an imagined vignette will take me closer to the truth.. Some historians will hate it, of course, but I'm prepared to take the chance. Let's try it once and then call it a day.

The first letter in that final post-war spate of correspondence from Jim plays on my mind. This is the one in which he describes introducing Norah to his brother as a 'crazy' idea, where he claims it was his family's poverty that was the barrier to their romance before apologising for his and Danny's 'terrible and most ungrateful' behaviour. This letter surely emerged from a conversation between the two men in which they talked about their treatment of Norah and decided to write to her, to make them feel better about the sorry affair.

I know it's neither here nor there that in my mind this letter takes shape in an Eastbourne pub, or that Danny has initiated the 'talk' while Jim is less than keen. I picture Jim tapping a Senior Service cigarette on the packet and bringing it to his lips, taking his time to light it, drawing and then catching his brother's eye as he exhales. Why should he do Danny's dirty work for him? He never made himself out to be anything he wasn't. It was Danny the married man, pretending to be foot-loose and fancy-free, who was to blame.

Jim was fed up to the back teeth with it all. He was still in the Navy with nearly a year to go. He was hacked off with the RAF. Already, the war barely over, and they were the true heroes, the boys in bloody blue. It hadn't exactly been a cruise for him, on board a minesweeper, knowing he could be torpedoed at any minute, nothing around but the night sky and dark sea, miles in width and depth. Hearing the boat behind you in the convoy taking a hit, the deck buckling, lads screaming as they fought for their last breath in boiling oil. Danny the hero. Danny who had Evelyn at home, worrying about him, waiting to look after him. And it's not as if he hadn't tried to warn Norah. He'd sent that fortune-telling card, right at the start. Later on, he'd tried to tell her she didn't know Danny like she thought she did, but all to no avail.

But Danny saw the whole caper as Jim's idea. It is true, his brother had himself in mind when he asked Danny to check Norah out. He hadn't exactly jumped at it, had cancelled their first date. But then her letters had been so friendly and when he met her and she was so pretty and so open to him; he was flattered, he supposed. The kiss at Derby station; he hadn't planned it.

She wasn't the only one, of course. Norah had questioned him about a photo with WAAFs. He'd slipped up when he sent that. But with the women at the base and the others: it was just a bit of fun. Lots of men were in the same boat, marrying hastily as they joined up, then thrown together with the opposite sex.

Norah was so trusting, so innocent. And her family... Her father was an odd ball, a bit of an old Bolshevik, but the way her mother welcomed him into their home... He could tell, that last time, after Norway, that she knew he was a fraud. It seemed unreal now, how easily he had stepped into a new life, like a character actor in a film. He'd behaved as if he would marry her. And he'd believed it himself, somehow. It was like he'd been two separate people. He couldn't explain it. Had he needed the anxiety and excitement of the bombing raids to be matched in his personal life? Being a pilot was thrilling as well as terrifying. It stirred up a restless energy. Coming home had not been the comfort he'd expected. There had been times when he felt he wouldn't be able to go back to Evelyn, to settle into that life. He considered leaving her in 1942. But staying with Norah's family either side of his leave to see his newborn daughter... Did he really do that?

His daughter. Not only had the sight of his baby nestling in her mother's arms led him to vow to bring an end to his wayward days, but I'll bet my bottom dollar that she was a factor in that apologetic letter. She was nearly four now and Danny loved her dearly. It was seeing her grow that brought it home. In no time at all she'd be the same age as

Norah had been when he first met her. If any man treated her like that, he'd break his legs.

Does this ring true? I could make Danny more self-congratulatory, more pleased with himself for his wartime conquests. And maybe he was, at other times. But on this occasion, he genuinely feels a degree of remorse. Maybe I shouldn't allow him to redeem himself. Never mind Jim and his 'young snaps', his grooming behaviour and souvenir curl: Danny was just as unpleasant. Was he really only interested in persuading Norah to have sex with him? Remember those sulks on the phone after he arrived back at camp? She was a young girl of seventeen, trying to find a path through respectability and desire. He had schemed, had as good as promised marriage. He'd even written letters to her gentle, trusting mother.

With a story as rich as this, I don't need to make things up. But even if my version of events doesn't tally with yours, it takes us to the heart of the story, to a kernel of truth that helps us to work things out. Like the emotion squeezed between the lines in a letter, the feeling in your bones, like intution and faith, truth can lie somewhere other than with visible evidence, with what is written on the page.

Like Danny, men had regrets, some far greater than his and Jim's. We're back to that odd juxtaposition. On the one hand, the mild and gentle serviceman, kindly, good tempered, homely, brave when he needed to be, with a sense of decency and fair play; a kind of uniformed boy-next-door.[1] And then, the lies, the deceit, the abandoned mothers, 'unwanted intimacies'. And that's just at home, not even in theatres of war, where violence against women was 'standard operating procedure', an 'authorised transgression' which officers expected of their men and for which they would cover up. Where sexual violence served different functions: as entertainment, a male bonding activity, a bribe to induce men to fight, a means to enforce women's compliance in camps. We know this despite the silencing of evidence by sexual and moral norms, and neglect by historians.[2]

Not that we 'remember' any of this, of course. Since the last quarter of the twentieth century, Britain has undergone a very selective 'memory boom' about the Second World War, all invocations of 'Blitz spirit' and punchy slogans – Keep Calm and Carry On – that were little more than propaganda tools at the time. According to the French historian

Peirre Nora, in times of rapid social change and lost bearings, it is commonplace to become attached to a historical 'memory' which gives us a sense of stability and calm, but which may well be a world apart from what actually happened. The myths we live by: this is powerful stuff, shaping memories and various national 'forgettings': the wrongs done to 'enemy aliens', for example, or that the Brits didn't 'stand alone' in 1940 but had help from colonial subjects all over the globe, or the curious re-prioritisation of events which sees street parties on the 75th anniversary of VE Day and VJ Day all but ignored.[3]

And the ways in which women are collateral in wartime; there's so little discussion of this. In our rush towards easy myths and banal hyperbole, we idealise as heroes men who were perhaps just brave, preferring to set them up like one-dimensional icons for 'a form of ancestor worship', rather than seeing the messy complexity of lives.[4]

Some years ago, a student on a women's history course told me that when she tried to ask her grandfather about his wartime experience as a British serviceman in Italy, he broke down and cried. She sensed, somehow, from other choked-up silences, that sex and violence were involved, and that the sight of her, his raven-haired flesh and blood, the twenty-year-old grandaughter who loved him, made him weep with shame.

Danny's regrets about Norah, they were small-fry compared to that.

23. Still Part of Me

I thought about opening this book with Norah's silent diary for 1946, where the absence of any mention of Danny surely reflects her desolation at his disappearance after their scuppered night of love. The narrative would move backwards in time, like Sarah Waters' Booker Prize-listed novel *The Night Watch* (2006), which tells four interconnected stories from 1947 to 1941. Kay, a former ambulance driver, is in and out of relationships with women, looking for love. Helen, Kay's ex, lives with her losing-interest lover, Julia, a crime novelist, and works in a lonely-hearts agency with the glamorous Viv, who is involved with a married ex-serviceman she met during the war. Duncan, Viv's brother, works in a candle factory and lives with an elderly man whom he describes as his 'uncle' after spending some years in prison. The book's main story, in the words of Philip Hensher, is 'the slow revelation of why people have become as they are'.[1]

This backwards movement ought to feel confining, as if potential futures are being closed down, yet it has the opposite effect, revealing life stories that might have developed in any number of directions. In presenting her characters and their relationships with one another prior to revealing the events that shaped them – love, desire, disappointment, loss – Waters echoes the many historical studies that focus on the lack of measurable change in women's lives, despite the common myths about the war as a herald of liberation. Kay, in her element on the Home Front, now receives sniggers at her man's suit ('Don't you know the war's over?') and is sneeringly called 'Colonel Barker'. Explaining to her friend Mickey her tendency to watch films in two halves, the second half first, Kay says 'I almost prefer them that way – people's pasts, you know, being so much more interesting than their futures'. Referring to their work in the Blitz, Kay says: 'I've got lost in my rubble, Mickey. I can't seem to find my way across it. I don't think I *want* to cross it, that's the thing. The rubble has all my life in it still –'.[2]

©2025 Alison Twells, CC BY-NC 4.0   https://doi.org/10.11647/OBP.0461.23

To read Norah's life backwards in this way would not work, as her past, while full of promise, hadn't quite happened. The war was all hope for her. But Norah too had got lost in her rubble. Her future had come tumbling down with Danny's disappearances in October 1943, in December 1945, in January 1946 when her letters were returned 'unknown', and even that next Christmas, when the family polished off his champagne. It wasn't that Norah didn't want to move forward. But like Nehemiah rebuilding the walls of Jerusalem, how would she pick through the charred rubble and build a new life? And at each hard-won step forward, what did it mean that Danny, his memory, kept turning up, like a stone in her shoe?

***

Fig. 29 Norah, 1948. Private papers of Norah Hodgkinson.

Danny is there when Norah ends her first post-war love affair – with Vic, a man she met at work. Their first date, in May 1948, just as Jim's final letters fizzled out, was a trip to the cricket: *Derbyshire v Warwickshire. We lost*. A host of nice times followed: more cricket, then football, midweek films at the Regal and the Gaumont, weekend nights at the Hippodrome, Thursday evening tea with his mother and holidays in London and Devon. By December, informally engaged, they were spending their lunchtimes perusing houses on Derby's new estates, saving hard.[3]

But it never felt quite right. It doesn't take much reading between the lines to see that after Danny, with his school master prospects and sophisticated ways, Vic was a bit of a come-down. *Am I falling in love???* Norah asked herself hopefully, on 12th June. *Vic wants me to be his girl, thinks I'm a smasher, think he loves me. Please God make things be allright.* She confessed to her diary that she felt *a bit downhearted about V and me. But I suppose there are other things in life besides social standing.* Norah knew full well that a woman didn't just marry a man, she married a life. 'The status of a woman is primarily determined by the status of her husband', wrote Ferdynand Zweig in his study of women's lives in 1952. 'It is a reflected, not an autonomous, status… Marriage, not work or study, is the main door of escape from class membership'.[4]

Vic's lack of prospects aside: she just didn't *feel* it. All her *my angels, my precious, my dearest ones* feel forced. She complains to her diary, wishing that Vic was more demonstrative, made more effort, both in company and when they were alone; that he was less moody and jealous when she spoke to other men (unavoidable in her office) and less pushy, sexually (*had a row because I wouldn't let him give me a French kiss*). An outburst by Marsie sealed it, on a picnic over Daleacre. *13th May 1950: Ma dislikes Vic very much and hopes I won't marry him. She says he's ill mannered, uncouth and ignorant. She wishes I could get Danny back. I wish I could too!*

When the break-up came, Norah felt giddy, free, and very soon, despondent.

'She's on the shelf', my mum says again. 'Waiting for Danny, then wasting over two years with Vic. She's high and dry'. A pause. 'Who was next? The one who died?'

'There was a non-event with a handsome policeman named Freddie before him', I say. As it tells us something of Norah, and post-war romance, I dig out the diary and launch in:

> 6th January 1951: Mum says I must marry Freddie.
>
> 13th: Birdy says Freddie doesn't talk much. Please God let me find my husband soon.
>
> 25th: 'Taffy' says I ought to be thinking about getting married soon!

My mum remembers 'Taffy', a Welshman (of course) who came to Donington during the war and who on this occasion helped pick Norah up when she slipped on ice on Borough Street. It seems everybody's got an opinion on Norah needing to be married.

> *27th January: Peggy said that Jean finished with her Charles in December, she'll be 26 in September.*
>
> *28th: Frank says Freddie sometimes goes to dances!*
>
> *18th February: Mum says she saw Freddie when she went down for her bus about 2.45pm.*
>
> *23rd Had a terrific thrill at night when I met Freddie in Borough Street. He really is the most handsome man I've ever seen. Please God.*
>
> *24th: Freddie you gorgeous beast! I can't get him out of my mind and I don't want to!*

[Laughter.]

> *28th: Shanklin looks a beautiful place, especially for a honeymoon.*

[More laughter.]

> *9th March: My 26th birthday. I'm getting old! ... Saw Freddie's muddy triumph outside his house at night.*
>
> *14th: Helen thinks I should marry Freddie, then I'd have a nice house built for me. I wish he thought so too.*
>
> *15th: The Bailey Bridge is to be repaired over the next eight nights and the police have to be there to hold up traffic. My poor Freddie!*
>
> *22nd: It's nine days since I saw Freddie, I must rectify this as soon as possible.*
>
> *7th April: Saw Freddie at the Moira with two other policemen.*
>
> *14th: My Freddie came cycling round Moira Dale in the afternoon. Please God let him do it for me.*
>
> *24th: Was thrilled to see my Freddie in grubby civvies tonight outside his digs. Gosh isn't he bald! He wears a ring on his right hand. Smiled sweetly at him.*

It seems that she can't actually speak to him.

'Oooh no, that would be far too forward', my mum says. 'This is 1951'.

> *6th May: I'm completely and thoroughly fed up with life. Please please God let something come up soon.*

Then, showing us perhaps that diaries are not just words, that they can include all sorts of extra-textual matter – photos of film stars, horoscopes, news about a would-be love of your life – there's this scrap of paper stuck in a late-May day:

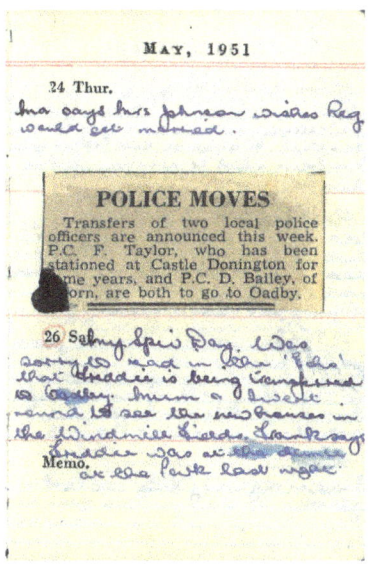

Fig. 30 Freddie, Norah's 1951 diary. Private papers of Norah Hodgkinson. Photo: A. Twells, 2025.

My mum is helpless with laughing. 'Oh no! Poor Norah!'

> 27th May: Helen and I went to the Wesleyan sermons tonight. Freddie was there. He smiled and looked grand. I've been a fool to miss him, feel as though disaster has overtaken me.
>
> 28th: Mum says Doris Moody told her that Freddie comes from Burton, is sorry to be leaving Donington and is an exceptionally well mannered and cultured man, never swears etc. Oh God, what have I missed?
>
> 29th: I'm broken hearted.

While my mum thinks Norah was a drama queen, I feel more sympathy. Marriage was everywhere in the 1950s: universal, ever younger. After all the damage done by the war – the evacuations, separations, adultery and illegitimate births – the Fifties, in Lorna Sage's words, saw a 'postwar moral rearmament, with everyone conscripted to normality and standing to attention'. Novels, films, women's magazines, even the new welfare state were all awash with the new family life, the breadwinner husband and his dependent wife.[5]

Peggy and Kathleen, Norah's friends from school, and Sadie and Gwen, from work, were all married one week in May 1951. Florence and Enid walked up the aisle on the same October day. Norman popped into the office with his little girl, a three-and-half-year-old named Ann. *Please God help me too.*

In theory, there were plenty of available men for Norah's generation. This wasn't the 1920s, afterall. But as we've seen, most had been snapped up well before she joined the market. Norah knew lots of men at work: all married. Or like Vic: a waste of space. She knew men in Donington, although they were mostly blue collar and she had set her sights above that now (that school, etc.) Where on earth would she find him? A few decades later, we'd say it was a case of waiting for the divorcees, but there were not too many of those in England in 1951.

Fig. 31 Jean (my mum), Milly and Norah, Breedon-on-the-Hill, 1952. Private papers of Norah Hodgkinson.

Hot on the heels of the disappointment with Freddie, Norah went on the office outing to Dublin in early June. After a slap-up breakfast at the Wicklow Hotel, she spent the day sunning herself on the buttercup-strewn cliff-tops on the north side of Dublin Bay. The night crossing home from Dùn Laoghaire was rough, enlivened further by Mrs Harris being caught at Customs. On board the Irish Mail from Holyhead to Crewe, Norah dozed on Gerry Harland's shoulder. Transferring to the Derby train at 3am, to stand in the station until the 6.50 departure, they found a secluded carriage:

> 3rd June 1951: 'Slept' with Gerry, he loved and kissed me. Sheer ecstasy. Arrived home 11am. Went to bed at 6pm.
>
> 4th: Returned to work. Gerry told me he meant all he did yesterday. Held my hand. Kissed me beautifully and told me he has loved me for three years. Geoff Duke won the Junior TT in record time.

There was just the one problem: Gerry Harland was married. Unhappily so, he told Norah. He and his wife had talked about separation and she was willing to give him a divorce. Norah felt bad, *wicked, poor Mrs Harland*. But if the marriage was on the rocks anyway, was already on its way out… Gerry felt guilty too, but more for Norah than his wife. She deserved *a proper courtship with a decent chap*. They settled into a regular routine of lunchtime loving: Darley Park, Alvaston Park, Allestree Park, Allenton allotments, Markeaton Park, *our wood in Sinfin, our lane*.

Once news got round at work, they were shunned. Marsie only knew what she guessed at, but was none too impressed. *Adultery is second only to murder*, she told Norah, *in God's eyes*. This opinion was not uncommon. A Mass Observation study conducted in 1949 found that 63% of its sample disapproved of extra-marital sex. A survey by the anthropologist Geoffrey Gorer in 1955, based upon detailed questionnaire responses received from over 10,000 readers of *The People* newspaper, heralded similar results. At the same time, beneath a general feeling in favour of marriage, both surveys revealed considerable dissatisfaction with marital sex: men who complained their wives were cold and disinterested and women who resented being used 'like a chamber pot'.[6]

Single women involved with married men received a special opprobrium. Opinion was consistent with that expressed by Leonora

Eyles during the war that such women were 'shockingly dishonourable'. The *Woman's Own* problem page, by the 1950s presided over by Mary Grant, was dominated by letters relating to extra-marital affairs. The adultery stories presented on just one day in August 1955 included a woman in love with and pregnant by her brother-in-law, a wife who wanted to adopt the child which her husband had fathered through an affair, a woman who suspected her brother-in-law of having an affair, a wife who suspected the same of her husband, and an eighteen-year-old involved in an affair with a forty-five-year-old married man. Mary Grant's advice to the latter was unequivocal: 'He is talking nonsense about divorcing her. Stop seeing him'.[7]

But Norah had fallen. *I can't possibly give him up now*, she wrote in her diary, some weeks in. She *would die if they had to part.* Their lovemaking was *sheer ecstasy*. Both did regular 'overtime': *loved in the office til 7pm.* They saw Derby County (away, of course), made day trips to Cheltenham and Liverpool, spent a weekend in London and had a glorious time at Kew. Gerry gave her a blue Lloyd Loom ottoman (from the Co-op, 48/), a wristwatch, a powder compact, a purse. Norah bought him a sports jacket and knitted him a pullover. A few weeks later, Norah received a letter from Mrs Harland, begging her to leave her husband alone. The following week, his angry wife set to work unravelling Norah's jumper.

Norah trusted Gerry to do the right thing and it was now, ten months in, in April 1952, that she incinerated Danny's letters. They sat there, the whole stash of them, at the front of her dressing table drawer, still occupying a poll position in her life, a daily reminder of what might have been. She could destroy them now, in 1952, because the future finally looked bright.

> *13th April: Gloriously hot. Re-read and then scrapped a lot of Danny's letters. I think he did love me once!*
>
> *19th: Lovely & hot for most of the day, but thundered, lightened and rained about tea time. G & I stayed in the office til 12.30 pm. Had a simply wonderful time. Please God, let it all come right for us sometime soon, we love each other much too dearly to lose each other now. Other news: Ma went to Frat. at Derby, Birdy went to Silverstone. Set the chimney*

> *on fire when burning Danny's letters! Was terrified. A voice from the grave??!!*

I'm surprised at her query as to whether Danny was dead and wonder if that's what she told herself, to manage the mystery of his disappearance and rejection. She'd clearly stopped analysing it in any depth. Unlike when Danny crops up in Norah's diaries sporadically throughout her later life, it is a positive entry, forward-looking, anxious but happy.

But Gerry was a let-down. He didn't get a divorce, and he and Norah staggered on until 1955, when she was despondent.

> *5th March 1955: I really must finish this business and look for someone for keeps.*
>
> *1st April: The fun's gone out of it.*
>
> *3rd May. Says I'm heartless and never could have cared.*
>
> *4th: I'm so miserable.*
>
> *5th: Friends again, but it's the end. Thanked me for lovely times, made me so unhappy.*
>
> *6th: Hope's my husband will be worthy of me.*

So there she was, thirty and single, in 1955.

How did you meet a man in 1955? Norah was friendly and sociable, never loud or over-bearing. She danced, liked films, and could talk football and cricket with the best of them. She certainly looked the part. Sometimes it took a bit of effort to gather up her confidence, like when she bought her New Look coat after the war and it was a good few days before she could brave it out there in the world. But that mix of a glamorous, cultivated allure and sweet and simple girl-next-door, the classy, unshowy chic of 1950s 'fairytale fashion', suited her down to the ground. She had been compared to Deanna Durbin as a young woman; soon it would be Grace Kelly.[8]

But it was such a game. As a woman, to arrive at this sanctified marital status, this pinnacle of achievement, you had to be chosen. Jill Tweedie remembered that to appeal to men, 'you had to become the Incredible Shrinking Woman. You had to make yourself smaller than them in every way possible: small ego, small brain, small voice, small talk'.⁹ Once you had attracted the attention of your prince, you waited, modest, submissive and (seemingly) composed, until he made a move. Norah could do no more than just be there in the street when Freddie the policeman passed by on his bike, plant the idea of her in his mind; *smiled sweetly at him*.

And when you'd done everything right, you'd put yourself out there, ripe for the picking, had been much admired but were still 'on the shelf' – it was almost shameful. In Fifties Britain, a single woman was no longer seen as an independent, fun-loving 'bachelor girl', but as a spinster: fussy, frustrated, eccentric, obsessive, sour. While there were other options – career-woman, mistress, staying single – marriage and motherhood were relentlessly promoted as the only route to a fulfilled life. 'We shall never have any other lovers, because the past was so perfect', two 'not-so-young women' whose boyfriends had been killed in action wrote to *Woman's Own*. 'But is it true that unmarried women get peculiar, and may suffer in health?'¹⁰

I stumble across a late-Fifties letter in Norah's archive, written to Marsie from her nephew, Eric Leadbetter, now settled in Canada:

> We were pleased with the picture of the wedding group. You all look very well. I could pick out your side of the family allright. You don't look any older than last time we saw you before we left England. Frank and his bride are a handsome couple. Give our best wishes for a happy married life. Norah is a fine looking girl, I thought she would have been married by now but if she is happy as a single girl that is the main thing.

***

There is a tragic addendum to Gerry's story. In 1956, he took a job on the Rhodesian railways, leaving Derby with his wife and two children for Bulawayo and a fresh start. Three letters to Norah from late 1961 and early 1962 (saved in the blue ottoman he bought for her) are full of plans for his first trip home. 'It's been a long time my dear since I heard your voice or saw those flashing eyes', he wrote, tenderly. He wanted her to know that he was a changed man, had learned that problems must be faced up to, not shelved. He suspected she knew he had become a Christian: 'some folks are deft at reading between the lines'. He signed off: 'Cheerio, goodbye and God bless and watch over you until March'.

But there was no watching over him, poor man.

> 24th February: Received a letter from Gerry. They are flying home on March 4th.
>
> 4th March: G & family will be flying to Lisbon today.
>
> 5th: Was horrified to hear on 6pm news that a plane from Laurenço Marques to Lisbon has crashed in Cameroons, all dead. Oh please God, don't let it be.

Gerry, his wife and son – his daughter didn't travel – all perished. Whether they were among the twenty-three identifiable bodies, I don't know. I peruse Norah's collection of paper cuttings:

Fig. 32 Newspaper cuttings. Private papers of Norah Hodgkinson. Photo: A. Twells, 2025.

'Horror in the "Green Hell"' – 'Big Crash Mystery' – 'The Honeymooners' – 'Grandmother Weeps for Aircrash Baby' – '111 Die in World's Worst Single Air Disaster'. *Oh God, this is like a living death,* she wrote. *Poor, poor Gerry. Oh how I grieve for him.*

My mum is stunned. 'It's very odd', she says. 'I was nearly 21 and I spent lots of time with Norah. She kept this all to herself'.

But in that spring of 1962, Norah had other secrets. She was planning a future with Eddy.

***

When Norah next mentions Danny in 1978, twenty years into her relationship with Eddy, he is part of a different exercise – a looking back, taking stock, at a time of regret.

Norah met Eddy in the summer of 1958. Apart from a passionate encounter on holiday in Rome in 1955, there had been no men in her life since Gerry. It was a full life, nonetheless. Norah danced and swam, knitted and sewed, gardened, read novels and saw films. She joined a woodwork class at nightschool, making herself a stool, spending weeks planing the frame, sandpapering and rounding off the legs, beautifully embroidering the upholstered seat. (I have it in my bedroom. When it isn't piled with clothes, it is a lovely piece of work.) Over the next two years, she and her sister Helen made a bookcase (on my landing), a round side table (in my mum's front room), a television table (the one with the too-long legs) and then, would you believe, a wardrobe. After woodwork, she signed up for A-level French. She made visits to cousin Peggy, her husband and two boys, who now lived in Larne, and enjoyed trips to Silverstone with schoolfriend Peggy and her husband Bert and days out with Birdy on his brand new Norton motorbike – to Kenilworth, Chatsworth, Ashbourne, and to Kirby Mallory to meet his motorbiking friends.

'No helmets', my mum tuts. 'She just clambered on and off they shot. No headgear at all'.

'Blimey', Mark says. 'I bet Birdy's mates were pleased when he turned up with her'.

Fig. 33 Norah, Birdy (left) and friends, Kirby Mallory, 1958. Private papers of Norah Hodgkinson.

She took her first foreign holidays, to Switzerland in 1953, Rome and Venice two years later (*simply out of this world, the loveliest place I've ever seen*), and Yugoslavia in 1958. Doreen was her first companion, and then 'Lambie', a friend from work, but when they were late to commit, despite Marsie's protestations, Norah, so keen to see the world, was perfectly prepared to holiday alone.

Buoyed by her overseas trips, Norah joined the International Friendship League, with the aim, she once told me, of sprucing up her French.[11] At a 'Hungarian Night', she found herself chatting with Jorge, from Zagreb, and Edward, a German. *14th July: We're going for supper together on Monday night*, she wrote, after Edward drove her to her bus stop. *God! Wonder what the future holds?*

Supper: not her word, surely? Edward was from a different world. Handsome in a fair-haired, square-jawed Germanic kind of way, he was older than Norah by eleven years. He drove a car, knew all the restaurants and had a sister living in Bourdeaux. He had moved to Derby before the war, following the woman who was to be his first wife after a holiday romance in Germany, taking a job with her father, a manufacturer of chamois leather. Her sudden death in 1956 left him alone with their young daughter. *They are so much above us:* Norah's comment, made in her diary after walking past his big Victorian house, suggests that she felt out of her depth. *Please God don't let us disappoint each other.* He was a gentle and passionate lover.

Three months into their affair, Edward said something strange. *He says he can give me his heart but nothing more,* Norah wrote in her diary. *That I mustn't let him stand in the way of finding my husband. Please God, what does it all mean?* Norah thought he must be referring to some condition about remarriage attached to his late wife's will. A week later, he spilled the beans. *Oh God. Edward is married.* He had hastily married his wife's best friend not long after her death, presumably to help him raise the child. It had failed from the start, from a disastrous wedding night.[12] *Says he loves me from the top of my head to the tip of my toes,* Norah writes. *Belonged completely to him tonight.*

After all the disapproval, adultery seemed suddenly in fashion in the late 1950s. Writing to Mass Observation, a librarian of Norah's age said that she had 'heard on the radio that 80% of people commit adultery. When I first did, I wrote to close friends crowing about it, and they wrote back saying that they too were having affairs… Coming home after weekends, by train, everyone seemed to be wearing a Mona Lisa smile…'[13] But Norah felt *lousy, awful*. She couldn't possibly go through this married man thing again. She wasn't looking for a sexual adventure, but for someone to love, for keeps. She cut him off, but Eddy was persistent, calling her office, eventually winning her round. *5th November: Lovely to be with him. I do love him, truly.*

And that was it. Lots of films, meals out, passionate sex. *Saw mein engelein. Did. Marvellous,* she wrote, many times. *My love and I went to see 'Whirlwind'. Dashed out and did.* And a week later: *Met my love at 5pm. Went out to Stenson and did. She was in town so had to be careful.* On a spring weekend in the Cotswolds: *Oh god it was so wonderful. Did twice!* In July 1959, they had a *lovely holiday* in Biarritz, San Sebastian, Lourdes and Bourdeaux, where she met his sister, Elisabeth, who told her she *looked like Grace Kelly!!!* She arrived home just *in time to see Marsie and the Twellies off to Colwyn Bay.*

A glamorous new life, perhaps, but not all plain-sailing. It is hard to deduce quite what was wrong, however, as after her A-level success that summer, Norah's diaries for 1959, 1960 and half of 1961 are written in French. Lots of *Did. Marvellieux. Je t'adore, mon cher.* But he was also a *cruel homme.* He seems to have been angry a lot of the time: *colère, fâche, froid. 18th May 1960: Nous sommes chez lui et il continue d'être fâché avec moi. La vie avec lui sera très très difficile.* ['We are at his house and he continues to be angry with me. Life with him will be very, very difficult.'] But she cut him slack. He had a terrible war story: wounded at Leningrad, in Egypt as a POW, starving and stranded in Germany in 1946, then to post-war Derby, where life as a former enemy alien was far from a piece of cake. *7th Sept 1962: Went to the art gallery to see exhibition of Bohemian glass. Had row, then kissed and made up at night.*

Eddy's daughter, Dinah, cooked for her dad and Norah each Tuesday evening and remembers Norah at their kitchen table, upright, elegant, her hair pulled back in a bun, smiling, but not friendly.

'She came, she sat down, she ate what was put in front of her. There was no friendly feeling. She was just *there*, polite but distant. She was almost without personality, cold. I didn't have a relationship with her at all'. After the meal, while Dinah did her homework, Norah and Eddy would watch television before he drove her home.[14]

I find this so sad and puzzling, this lack of interest in wooing her new love's teenage daughter, in being friendly to a motherless girl. Did Norah resent Dinah's presence, wanting Eddy all to herself? Did she know Dinah was close to the second wife and was frightened of giving too much away? Did she have complicated feelings about wanting children of her own? (It was around this time that Eddy told her he thought she was too old to conceive. Unmarried, she didn't pursue it.) We'll never know. But it is an uncomfortable image and makes me wonder about that vital, lively, good natured girl, how she became so lacking in warmth.

In 1966, after Marsie's final illness and then my mother's pregnancy kept Norah at Moira Dale, she and Eddy saw a solicitor, the aptly named Mr Loving. *Explained everything to us, and said that his advice is that we should live together. Says I'm a good proposition! Felt relieved somehow. Please God help us.* When Norah had first broached the subject of divorce, Eddy had told her he was *a coward and wants love and comfort from me, not more worries.* She was not impressed: *I've never heard anything so selfish in all my life.* Now she learned that the legal dissolution of a marriage required that one party (the 'petitioner') be found to be legally 'innocent' and the other (the 'respondent') legally 'guilty' of a 'matrimonial offence'. The petition would have to come from Eddy's second wife, who had no desire to grant him an easy way out.

Wanting to *get straightened out, for keeps*, Norah cleared out Moira Dale, saying her last goodbyes to the house and garden. Concerned that her new postman should not learn that she was Miss Hodgkinson and not Mrs Cook, she arranged for her mail to be delivered to Birdy's new address. She stored her old diaries and wartime letters and photographs in a suitcase in his spare room.

The shame of 'living in sin' aside, Norah soon settled into what was, to all intents and purposes, a married life. She gardened, decorated, ran the house. In the summer of 1968, she orchestrated a move to a beautiful bungalow at Makeney, north of Derby. They ate out, saw films, enjoyed holidays in Bingen am Rhein every other year, and Ireland, Jerusalem, Crete, cruises to Athens via Tangier, to Palermo and Barcelona, in between. They bickered and fell out and the sexual passion soon dimmed, but he was *my love*. Life – a middle-aged, unwed, married life – rolled on.

Fig. 34 Norah and Eddy on a cruise, 1964. Private papers of Norah Hodgkinson.

Fig. 35 Norah and Eddy, Crete, 1971. Private papers of Norah Hodgkinson.

***

So what made Norah think of Danny in 1978, twelve years after moving in with Eddy and twenty-six years after the mishap with the fired chimney in 1952? Perhaps it was a chance remembering – a radio news reader, maybe, reminding her that the date was 26th October: *Danny would be 61 today – at least!!!* (That query over his age again.)

Flicking back through her diary for that year, I find this entry at the end of July: *It's twenty years ago about today that I made the biggest long-term mistake of my life. He's unbearable and is driving me mad.* A lack of reflection, as we know, is one of the downsides of Norah's diaries. Apart from regular grumbles about Eddy's temper and a couple of references to her *predicament*, few clues exist. Her short daily entries give no sense of Norah working out her options, but the disatisfaction is palpably there.

And what was her predicament? It was simply that she had no rights. Even after the arrival of the 'no fault divorce' in 1969, with consent no longer required after five years of irretrievable breakdown, Eddy still wouldn't petition. Norah told my gran that as he was a Roman Catholic and marriage a sacrament, he could not divorce. The upshot for her remained the same; that despite all those years of working and earning, all that home-building, if she left him, as a 'common-law wife', she would go with nothing.[15]

Three years later, in 1981, Danny settled in her thoughts once more.

> *17th March: In library looking for the Leicester addresses. Found Danny's number and address in Eastbourne. A voice from the dead.*
>
> *18th: It seems eerie to think of Danny living down there in Eastbourne and I'm up here in Derby. I wonder what he's like, it's like a voice from another world.*

Of course, you don't just find East Sussex addresses while looking at the Leicester directory. You have to search them out, go to S rather than L, lift the heavy book off the shelf, lay it flat on the table top, flick through to G, Gi – too far – Gilbraith, Gilbride – gliding your finger up the list – Gilberto, Gilbert.

That autumn, Norah and Eddy visited his daughter and her family, who now lived not far from Danny:

> *13th September: Forty years ago, Danny at Moira Dale. Today, me in Bexhill and him just down the road. I feel so sad.*

Two months later, she thought of him again:

> *18th November: Full house at yoga, really enjoyed it. Worked up gradually to a perfect cobra. A filthy wet day all day so couldn't do any gardening. While looking for information in my old diaries, re-read some of Jim's letters. He said there was never any hope for Danny and me because they were such a poor family. Had quite forgotten that. Made me feel very sad for what might have been.*

Unlikely as it seems, she hadn't dismissed Jim's far-fetched explanation in his letter of apology of 1947. Or maybe, amidst all the hurt, all of his stories, she had forgotten this detail.

> *21st November: A dull, but dry and mild day. Got the washing dry. Rang the Assembly Rooms – the 'Sounds like Christmas' concert is on Sat 19th and Tues 22nd. Rang Helen, they prefer 19th, so must try and book on Monday. I still feel sad about Danny, still feel that we must surely meet again one day, he's still part of me.*

23. Still Part of Me

How was he *still part of* her, so many years after he disappeared? And why now?

I'm sure that Norah would be the first to say that she didn't have a bad life. Recently retired, she gardened, walked, swam and attended weekly classes in yoga and car maintenance. She and Eddy continued to visit Germany most summers and enjoyed holidays further afield – Thailand, Mexico, Morocco. But there was little companionship, no sympathy of feeling, no intimacy, just endless days when he was *in a lousy mood* and she couldn't *do or say anything right*. *I do get SICK, SICK, SICK*, she wrote on 12th January 1981, and the following day,

> *13th January: He's the bloody KING OF PIGS sometimes. I'm so upset. Why can't we be happy together? Life is such a disappointment.*
>
> *11th February: Eddy took exception to something I said, so had a war of silence!*
>
> *20th March: Where the bloody hell are we going? This is no way for the so-called twilight of our lives.*

Norah's diary entries for 1981 reveal a lonely woman of fifty-six, living with a foul-tempered man and feeling like her chance for the life she'd hoped for was slipping away. Very soon, it would be too late to live in the world any other way.

It was hope, in the shape of Danny, that was *still part of me*. A hope for love and passion, or just for a more companionate life. Hope deferred maketh the heart sick, as Marsie used to say.

***

It actually makes my heart ache to see Norah like this. While our visits were always awkward – Norah on edge, Eddy waiting to pounce – we didn't know that when we weren't there to provoke him, he continued to be a miserable sod.

In 1981, the year that she wrote about Danny, I 'interviewed' Eddy for an O-level history project on Russia in the Second World War.

> *24th May: Al wants to come and see Eddy about Leningrad for her O Level. She says she might stay on for A levels and will do English Lit and History. I'm really glad.*

It is a good little interview, though I say it myself. I've still got it, in a box in the loft. He talked cagily about the rise of Hitler, why so many Germans were in dire straits after WW1. He claimed to know nothing about the Holocaust. After a stint in Czechoslovakia at the start of the war, he had marched through Poland, then Latvia, Lithuania, where people lined the streets, welcoming their liberation from the Russians. He talked about the bitter cold at Leningrad in 1941, how they had arrived in summer and were never given winter uniforms, that their wives sent small Christmas trees through the post, not knowing where they were or that they were surrounded by snow-covered spruces. Norah was pleased with us. He was helpful and I was compliant (*Al seems nice and sensible now*).

It didn't last, sadly. The following year, 1982, I was banned from the house. I'd joined CND and been to Greenham Common and he was incensed. But the row was about racism. Moira Stewart was reading the news and he started shouting about 'Africans' not being civilised, having no history or culture before Europeans gave it to them, almost exploding with bile. I was a fearless sixteen-year-old, a bit of a know-all. I'd just read Walter Rodney's *How Europe Underdeveloped Africa* for my Sociology A-level and had heckled at a National Front meeting in the village earlier that year. But standing up and shouting back at the man of the house... He ordered me out, told me never to return.

I still saw Norah occasionally, when she visited my mum and gran, or at family gatherings when Dennis made his annual trip up the M1 and down memory lane. We would journey between the run-down lock houses at Stenson and Aston-on-Trent, where their grand-parents discussed socialism and read Whitman, nipping over to Loughborough's tree-lined Burton Walks, home to both grammar schools (now private). When they were still fit enough, we'd trek up to Hill Top, returning down Diseworth Lane to Moira Dale, to stand outside number 18 like pilgrims congregating at a sacred place. We'd meet, and we'd talk, and we'd laugh, but Norah was always distant. When she drove off, poised and waving, Dennis would interrogate my mum and my gran: was she really happy, living with that man? They'd shrug. What did they know?

'It's all your fault, with your Nazi hunting', he'd say, his twinkling eyes somehow managing to convey a whole lot of mischief, concern for Norah and sympathy for me.

And then, all of a sudden, I saw Norah at a rash of family funerals as, in less than a decade, Frank died, then my gran, Birdy and then Dennis. And then Eddy. I was thankful to be in Spain that Easter of 1996, relieved that I didn't have to fake my respects, or stifle a laugh at the revelation of his full name – Edouard Adolf Koch – as his coffin was wheeled through the crem.

We don't know for certain why Norah stayed.

'Well she's not alone in that', my mum says. 'How many people do you know, women especially, who stay in miserable marriages? It's just too much upheaval to do anything about it. And how did she know she'd be any happier, on her own?'

Of course, it is also quite possible – in a total turnaround from 1946 – that Norah only wrote the bad stuff in her diaries. That she didn't dwell on their contented days, when she enjoyed caring for him and they rubbed along together well enough. But I doubt it.

'She'd have to have gone into a council flat', my mum continued. 'Can you imagine that? And admit to the world that the relationship had failed? Which we all knew it would'. A pause. 'Women didn't live their lives then like they do today'.

Today, most mid-life separations are instigated by women who, with their own money, can opt out of years of cleaning, caring, listening to the same old stories, and the dull, dutiful sex.

Norah had enjoyed a flirtation in the late 1970s, just before she retired, but it came to nothing. (That was one way out, of course: find another man.) Stuck with Eddy, she immersed herself in a new project, becoming a mean family historian, tracing the Hodgkinsons to a sixteenth-century Derbyshire hamlet, and the Leadbetters, to Staffordshire via the canals. Eddy was jealous, of course, but my mum remembers the defiant pleasure with which Norah brought out her notes and scrolls, reporting on field visits with other researchers, including her new-found Australian 'cousins'. Family history: it was challenging, absorbing, anchoring, the past providing warmth in the present.[16]

8th May 1995: VE Day plus fifty years. Enjoyed the various shows and observed the 2 minutes' silence. Made me feel really sad. If I had asked Kath Jones about her feelings at VE Day commemorations, I doubt that sadness would have been her dominant emotion. We can assume that her 'happy ending' – meeting Ron at the dances, their long marriage

– shaped her memories of the war itself. But Norah, abandoned by Danny and unlucky in love ever after: what was her war story, if not absence and loss? Like when elderly women cry at weddings, Norah's VE Day sadness came from the memory of hope, before life had failed to fulfil its promises, before love had let her down.

Norah's final mention of Danny came in 2009, near the end of her life, when she found herself sifting through her suitcase of diaries and letters, stored next to (? on top of? inside?) the wardrobe in her spare room. The following morning, catching her usual bus into town, she called in at the library and *checked the Eastbourne phone directory. Only two Gilberts: RA, could that be Bob? Also an Ian. Is that a grandchild? Where are Jim, Danny, Jack? Dead? Rained quite heavily once or twice.*

Danny had received passing mentions in her diaries in the 1990s and early 2000s. *Danny is (? would have been?) 80 today,* she wrote on his birthday in 1997, extending the question beyond that of his truthful age to wonder whether he was dead or alive. *26th October 2003: Danny would have been 86 today.*

What did it mean, to remember him this way? Was it anything more than her noting of other birthdays, deathdays – Helen, Frank, Birdy, Dennis, Pop. *7th May 2006: Today is 42 years since Marsie died, feels like a 100 lives ago.* Eddy too, of course, and Gerry (*what if..?*).

The late 1990s, after Eddy's death, were lonely and aimless years. Norah had met her grief head on, starting with holidays, making tentative trips to Durham (castles) and Kent (gardens) in the months after he died. She soon spread her wings, finding her confidence for a solo German river cruise, a week on Lake Garda, then trips to Bucharest, Budapest, St Petersburg, Prague, Vienna. She toured central Spain and Provence and the French Alps and saw Boston in the Fall. They could be hit and miss, these trips, with exhausting schedules, so-so food, too-needy fellow travellers (*Rex is beginning to get on my nerves... Roll on Sunday*). But Norah rekindled her love for adventure. Christmas 2005 saw her contemplating a SAGA world cruise.

At home, she joined a club of widows who held weekly coffee mornings, walked together and shared birthday lunches and days out. She hosted guests – her step-daughter and her neice, a week most summers – and my mum, me and the girls, her favourite step-granddaughter (handsome Italian boyfriend duly noted) all dropping in at different times. She was still an active gardener, confounding me with her persistence in unearthing and then replanting her bulbs every autumn, digging up three tree roots at seventy-nine. She took herself off in the car on spins through ancestral Derbyshire villages and more than once, on a train to London to see a show. She kept up with family history, sharing findings with Hodgkinsons and Leadbetters all around the world, still hosting Aussies and Canadians on the heritage trail. She was always up for the new, treating herself to novel little delicacies (*Bought some kangaroo sausages for lunch – ok*) and enrolling for a course in computing (*Had an awful day with cut and paste*).

But when responsibility for all the good things that happen in your life falls to you and to you alone... And when the problems all come at once: a pulled leg muscle, a prang in the car, a battle with a cocky builder over the leaky roof valley... Norah being Norah, we didn't know how often the sense of overwhelm sent her spiralling down. Even the run-of-the-mill *do-nothing* days, the *dead-and-alive Sundays*, when her friends were cosied up with grandchildren, could leave her feeling empty and alone.

> *2nd March 2007: Went early to Sainsbury's. Bought a pot of lillies for Alison. Had lovely trout for lunch. Felt so weary in the pm so had a nap on the bed. Dreamed of Eddy and woke up realising how lonely I am and how empty my life is. Yesterday was granny and grandad's wedding anniversary (1885) and there were just a few bits of greenery in the hedges.*[17]

I didn't realise at the time how much we mattered:

> *28th October 2008: Jean and the girls arrived just after 2pm. They are two little smashers. Played hangman. Lovely having them and very lonely after they had gone. Started to read the book that Alison gave me on Georgiana.*

I've learned a thing or two about loneliness from reading Norah's diaries. How hard it can be as an elderly, childless, single woman, building relationships in which you feel like you matter, and about which, in turn, you care enough. It strikes me that Norah put down few new roots in her adult life. She'd worked full time but had little interest in a career, had no community of mothers forged via a school gate, not even a long-term staying-put in one village. I wonder how skilled she was at making friendships with women. Her life had been all about men. Finding one took long enough, then there was the process of settling down, the years spent doing for and looking after. The shame of their secret non-marriage deterred her from getting close to anybody not in the know, and Eddy's wearying bad-temperedness curtailed an independent life.

And in the end, the years of cruises and coffee club jaunts were a brief interlude before her friends began to pass away: first Joan, in 2004, then one by one, Mary, Joyce, Maisie, Lucy. By 2007, Norah had decided to call time on her foreign holidays. In 2009, at the age of eighty-four, she'd gone back on that, joining a flood-frustrated cruise on the Seine in April. But October found her struggling to throw off what she thought was a nasty bug (but which, in retrospect, was her heart giving up) and she regretfully cancelled her planned autumn trip on the Danube from Budapest to Vienna. *I shall never go again, ever.* It was a watershed moment, her horizons drawing in like a night tide.

I MUST GET BACK TO DONINGTON, Norah wrote, after a *lovely, lovely day* with my mother, touring old haunts and admiring the new estate (*some lovely bungalows*). It was Norah's very human need for rootedness and belonging that brought Castle Donington back into the picture.[18] She had left the village for a bigger canvas on which to paint her life. It had been a gamble, and in those exciting early years with Eddy, it had worked. But ultimately, latterly, maybe for a long time, she was lonely. On that mid-summer day in 2009, Norah clearly felt that Donington offered her an umbilical cord, could be more than a nostalgic memory. My mum kept an eye out for bungalows for sale and we pictured Norah settling into the new estate, joining the church congregation, volunteering at the museum.

***

Was Norah preparing for this move when she began to clear out her papers at the end of September 2009? While pleased with her ruthlessness, she would be keenly aware that throwing out old gas bills was the easy part. I imagine her, laying the grey cardboard suitcase flat on the bed, flicking the locks. It had been years since she'd clapped eyes on her diaries, but here they were, all packed neatly in rows, the coloured spines of her life, now dulled.

Tucked in a corner was the stash of Jim's letters and beneath them, a handful of photographs of him and Danny, both looking sharp and so young in their military uniforms. These letters from Jim: why had she kept them all these years? Maybe it was pure chance. While Danny's letters were in her dressing table drawer, Jim's were in the loft at Moira Dale with the rest of her High School memorabilia, and then, retrieved from Birdy's flat on his death and shoved in her own roofspace, away from Eddy's prying eyes, they were just part of the nostalgia she felt for that time.

We might ask the same of her diaries: what had compelled her to keep them over so many years? At first, it was surely their role in easing her into the new world she was entering via grammar school and young womanhood. Soon, she saw how easily events slipped from memory, how her diary brought them back. At times, they were outlets for complaint; a confidante when life disappointed. Writing was simply a habit; how she tidied up her days.[19] Maybe at a certain point, their longevity had become self-fulfilling (she'd kept them for X number of years, why stop now?).

I imagine Norah tidying her diaries, shuffling the letters, attempting to neaten the piles, finding herself unable to resist opening one – an envelope postmarked Yarmouth, the date illegible – and unfolding the thin paper:

> Dear Norah,
> I received your letter while anchored at sea last night 9.30pm. At time of writing we are just finishing a job which has taken several days. We are doing a tremendous amount of sea time, so please forgive my delay in my letters. Honestly Norah I love writing to you and receiving your letters, especially like the one I had last. It would be worth coming to Derby just to collect a kiss from you. I rather fancy they are only for special people. To be candid I know I should be jealous of Danny so perhaps that is one reason I don't come and see you...

She scanned down to his cheery 'Cheerio darling' signing off: 'Your future brother-in-law, Jim'.

It was tempting to keep on reading, but she knew the afternoon would be lost if she did. She was faintly aware of her mood starting to dip, a spreading sadness. How could they still have this effect, fifty years on? Maybe she should forget the sorting and just burn the lot.

By the following morning, something had changed and Norah found herself in Derby Library, jotting down numbers from the Eastbourne phone book. That evening, she returned to the suitcase and picked out the transparent wallet containing a snap Danny had sent from Tromsö in 1945. The photo was black and white, but the burst of Air Force blue that had brightened up the drabness of those years now burned through the decades like a tiny pulsar of light.[20] It felt like a thousand lifetimes ago and yesterday, both at once.

Danny. How proud she had felt as her sixteen-year-old self, walking out with this handsome airman. One minute she was a chubby schoolgirl with high hopes for her life, and then, well, she felt like a film star. And the odd thing was, despite that sense of being a stranger to herself, of not being quite in her own body, she knew she'd always been moving towards this point. When, all of a sudden, it arrived, it had seemed so certain, like it was meant to be. And yet, like a bluebird over water, it was gone in a flash.

Gone in a flash and yet it came back in waves. This must be why first love leaves such an impression, the way it draws out feelings you didn't know you possessed, shows you that you can love, be loved. Her time with Danny was like the foundation of her life, the template against which the rest had been measured. Its vividness had dimmed, but she recalled it more clearly than anything that had followed.[21] Every new time since had been a faint echo of those afternoons lying on his rough jacket on the hard ground on Daleacre hill, every inch of her lapping him up, the smell of him, the thrill of his hands on her body, the heat in his eyes.

What might have been. Jim had said that it was her reserve that had driven Danny away. An iceberg, he'd called her. But she hadn't been cold. She'd been pretty darn passionate, if truth be told. And imagine if she *had* given in and he'd still done his disappearing act. She had known nothing of sex then, except that which her own body told her, so much at odds with what was allowed. If word got round, that would be it, her reputation would be shot. She might even have got pregnant and the course of her whole life would have been changed. Poor Marsie: it would have finished her off, or so Norah had thought at the time. She knew better now. Marsie wouldn't have allowed talk of adoption, couldn't care less what the neighbours thought, would help to raise the child and love it just the same. There would have been no Vic, no Gerry, certainly no Eddy. But something, someone, would have come along.

Was it now that Norah slid the Gilbert phone numbers into the wallet, back-to-back with the photo? Did she wonder why she was tucking them away, creating more stuff to be sifted through on yet another day? She was supposed to be be getting shot of it all: keep or chuck! But if memory was life's load-bearer, would destroying these now take some vital pillar away?

Maybe she should just grasp the nettle and ring the numbers. But what if she made the phone call and found she hadn't held the same place in Danny's affections as he had in hers? What if he didn't even remember her? Surely that couldn't be the case. For all she knew, he could have had girlfriends near air bases all over the country. Would she ask him what had happened, where he'd gone at he end of 1945, or would she be content just to know that he had thought of her now and then, down the years?

How strange it was to know nothing at all of his life, yet hers had taken its shape from him. That sense she'd had when she was with him: that she was becoming the woman she was destined to be. But then he disappeared and she never fulfilled that promise; had yearned for her lost self ever after. And what could they do now anyway? She kept forgetting that small fact: that there was no planning now for new times, for new (old) flames.

The chances were, of course, that Danny was long dead, especially if he was older than he'd led her to believe. What would she say to the son or grandson who answered the phone? *I was a girlfriend of your (grand)father's during the war.* Would he think she was a sad case, looking up a lost love from so long ago?

And was she? Maybe she was a silly old fool. Was this something that happened with the passage of time, you stopped looking to the future, had no energy for it, and harked back to the past instead? But Norah sometimes felt like she'd had this separate life running in tandem, that he had always been with her. The paths not taken, the 'what might have beens', that sense of lost futures. It was such a hopeful time, so full of expectation. She just wanted to tie things up, neaten her memories, close the circle. It would be nice to know that she'd been loved. There was surely nothing wrong with that.

She pondered her opening gambit.

'Hello. I wonder if you can help me. I'm looking for a Mr Danny Gilbert, of Eastbourne. We knew each other a long time ago. I wonder if you might be related and could tell me anything about him. I do hope I'm not too late'.

And if Danny himself came to the phone?

'Hello Danny', she would say. 'It's Norah, Norah Hodgkinson as was, from Castle Donington. I've just stumbled across some letters from the war and I thought I'd look you up. I know it's a bit of a bolt out of the blue'.

***

But Norah didn't make a call to Eastbourne that October night, or any night of the following seven weeks of her life. She would have said so in her diary if she had.

What her dreams and fancies were, we simply do not know. She might have had a vague thought about holidaying there in 2010, ringing from a phone box on the prom one sunny afternoon between day trips to castles and gardens. Or she might have abandoned the idea entirely, plumping instead for that French river cruise, the prospect of which she couldn't quite let go.

We can't know, however, because in late November 2009, Norah died. And I guess that, in the end, this is how it is; how history is. Norah, Danny and Jim were real people, with every right to keep some secrets from us. 'Secrets are there to be found', writes Arlette Farge, but 'are sometimes impossibly out of reach'.[22]

There is no timely epiphany supplied by Norah's later years, no redemptive arc, just her extraordinary, ordinary life, untidy, unstoriable, an 'anti-novel'.[23]

'Your gran always thought Norah had it easy', my mum says. 'She swanned into that school. By the time Norah passed the scholarship, what with her and Birdy working, and Dennis sending money home as well, no doubt, they could afford to send her, even with Frank at the Grammar. It set her up for life. All those lovely clothes and shoes, bungalows in Duffield, holidays all over the world...' My mum pauses, then makes up another family story on the hoof. 'This is why she left us the diaries', she says. 'She knew what we thought. She wanted us to know about those years with Eddy, that her life wasn't all sweetness and light'.

Sociologist Carol Smart talks of the families we 'live with' – our real families, which may be riddled with secrets and tensions – and the families we 'live by', the idealised families of popular culture. To reveal a family secret, Smart suggests, might be an attempt to talk honestly about family life, to acknowledge our distance from the image, to bring the ideal down a peg or two, to rid ourselves of shame. This can be insensitive, ethically dubious, when the teller is not the only one who has to live with repercussions. It can also be freeing.[24]

But Norah was not revealing our family secrets to the world. She was showing her life to us, her closest family members. My mum's explanation rings true. Leaving her diaries to me was only partly about my interest in women's history. More than that, it was Norah's final refusal to pretend.

IV

The dead are dead, and it makes no difference to them whether I pay homage to their deeds. But for us, the living, it does mean something. Memory is of no use to the remembered, only to those who remember. We build ourselves with memory and console ourselves with memory.

– Laurent Binet

*Silence can be a plan
rigorously executed*

the blueprint to a life

*It is a presence
it has a history a form*

*Do not confuse it
with any kind of absence*

– Adrienne Rich

24. A Mum's Book?

A strange coincidence struck me as I sat in the garden one Sunday afternoon, pondering the impact of Danny on Norah's life. My younger daughter was tanning herself in the unexpectedly strong April sun whilst revising for her French GCSE. Her elder sister, home from university, was reading in the shade, next to her dozing grandma, an erstwhile sun-worshipper now unexpectedly sensitive to UV light. It will sound contrived, but it is absolutely true.

It has taken me a long time to finish this book, and my girls, aged six and nine when Norah died, eleven and fourteen when I began to write, are now a lot older. The youngest, sixteen that particular week, was exactly the age that Norah was when she began corresponding with Jim.

We've long laughed about the likeness between the two of them.

'Look at you two, peas in a pod!' we'd say, as Maddy the toddler clambered onto Norah's lap or, as a little girl, sat drawing at her feet, while her great-great-aunt stroked her hair.

'Poor little thing!' Norah would reply, clearly pleased. The dimples and the easy smile. The deceptive hint of shyness in their blue eyes. And now, the love of glamour and fashion. (The dimples. A recent chat-up on Snapchat from a boy at school: Hey dimples.)

The coincidence is this: at Easter 1941, just as Norah turned sixteen, Marsie was fifty-three, the same age as me, almost to the day. Had she known what would happen, she wouldn't have welcomed Danny into her home and her daughter's life. But when he came to Donington rather than meeting Norah in town, she didn't think twice about offering him a bed for the night. He was another mother's son, a brave airman and a Biblical stranger – and a lovely young man, handsome and polite.

Marsie enjoyed Norah's burgeoning affair. She was keen to see her daughter make a good match. Marriage and children were everything and a man who would treat his wife well and provide for his family was the only route to a comfortable and happy life. Danny seemed to fit the bill. But she wanted Norah to take it more steadily and especially to not *have to get married*, to not be in the family way when she walked down that aisle, to have more choices in life than that would allow. And she could see already that it would be a battle. Norah was so passionate and headstrong, so swayed by romantic gestures and that awful Hollywood glamour, so set on throwing herself headlong into being 'modern'. Romance: Marsie distrusted it, found it so infantile. But the young, they pursued it like it was a new religion, the very foundation of life. How could she rein her in?

I'm interested in what Marsie could have done, so that Norah was less vulnerable to the kind of men that Danny and Jim turned out to be, but when I start to vocalise my thoughts, the girls quickly complain. Write your own book, they say, we've got revision to do/our own stuff to read.

Instead, my mum chips in. She thinks Norah should have known. Danny disappeared for months on end; clearly he was leading her a merry dance. Maybe she chose not to see what was going on. He was a man with prospects and she was so set on moving up in life ('that school' etc.). 'And it seems like she never got over him, let him affect the rest of her life'. A pause. 'Everybody has their heart broken some time. The rest of us bounce back, just get on with it. But not Norah, oh no'. It sometimes seems that my mum responds to Norah's love affair with Danny in the light of her later-life relationship with the aunt who seemed to have it all: elegant clothes, exotic holidays, a modern bungalow in the posh part of town, a husband who looked down on us. It is as if Norah has been posthumously brought down a peg or two.

One daughter bites. 'But it wasn't just a heartbreak, grandma. It was so messed up. If you think about what they did, it was totally deceitful. It was literally grooming. Jim wrote letters trying to persuade Norah to have sex with Danny – who wasn't who he said he was because he was actually a married man with no intention of having a proper relationship with her. That's not just a broken heart'.

'Catfishing', the other pipes up. 'When someone creates a false identity, to lure someone else into a relationship'.

'You don't think those terms are a bit anachronistic?' I ask. 'Too twenty-first century? Weren't they just two lads, having a bit of a laugh that then got out of hand? Or two servicemen, under a lot of stress?' I don't really believe this but I'm interested to hear their response.

'Just because there wasn't a word for it then, doesn't mean it didn't happen. It might have been a laugh to them, but for her it was almost worse than it would be today. They were so cruel. They knew a girl's reputation could be ruined. There was so much at stake'.

'And she was so young and easy to manipulate', says the other. 'Danny could get away with his promises of marriage, because she was so innocent. I mean, would she even have known that people could behave so badly? And when it went wrong, she must have felt so humiliated. She couldn't confide in her family or friends'. She's big on humiliation, this one.

It turns into a good discussion. About Norah as a sunny schoolgirl, a young woman hungry for love and life. How she had bought into a dream: life on the up and romance as part of it. How the relationship with Danny developed in his absence; in her head at least, she could make it make mean whatever she wanted it to be. And he could, too. We wonder whether Danny's letters created her dreams and expectations, if they set the bar high before letting her down, and how much wartime culture played a part: men as heroes, beyond reproach, women keeping their spirits up through letters and sock-knitting and looking pretty.

I want to push them on this grooming thing. Jim's penultimate round of letters trying to persuade Norah to have sex with Danny were written in 1945. She was twenty by then, not the schoolgirl of earlier exchanges.

But again: the certainty of youth. 'They knew what they were doing. They started when she was fifteen! They had a worldly experience that Norah didn't have. They were hiding the fact of Danny's marriage and were manipulating her into sleeping with him. That's why they felt guilty after the war'.

At the very least, I think they have nailed Norah's experience and I like that they have placed her centre stage rather than trying too hard to understand what it might have meant to the men.[1]

'All that iceberg stuff', my elder daughter says. 'She's bound to have blamed herself, wondered what she did wrong. She'd grown up thinking Danny loved her. She saw herself as lovable, desirable. But then, when he disappeared, and it seemed like he'd lied to her, and sex was all he was really after, and that was all so loaded... well, she must have felt like she was worth a lot less. It was as if she was playing by the rules, doing it all exactly right, and then he pulled the rug out from under her feet'.

The girls conclude that more was at stake than Norah missing the boat, never making up lost time. True, all the decent men were taken by the time she came on the scene. But she could have fallen lucky and met a man like Freddie the policeman or our own Uncle John. She could have had the life she'd imagined with Danny: got married, had children of her own maybe, been part of his family and he part of hers.

The bigger issue, they insist, is the deception. It would not have crossed Norah's mind that two men – two servicemen, both fighting to keep women and chidren safe from the Nazis, for heaven's sake – would behave in such a way. The shame and confusion of Danny's abandonment dented her confidence, made her doubt her own judgement, her ability to tell what was real, made her question her capacity to be loved.

I take this opportunity to get my question in. 'What could her mother have done?'

Talked about sex and relationships, they say.

'Not going to happen', I reply. 'This is working-class England in 1940. Milly is a deeply religious woman. She is fearful of so much about the modern world. She is well aware that marriage is a woman's only chance of having a decent life. Even for Norah's generation, on a clerk's wage, you couldn't support yourself. For a woman to be independent, she'd have to come from money. And in terms of social attitudes, it was probably harder to be a single woman in the 1940s and '50s. You were seen as a failure, without a man. A girl had to get married, and for that, she needed to be marriageable'.

I'm secretly pleased at their response, nonetheless. Norah's story has sharpened my parenting, especially my attitude to romance and sex. It is not enough, I realise, for sex education to be all about warnings – pregnancy, STDs, coercion, consent. My daughters may fake annoyance, but they secretly appreciate my railing against 'modesty' and confining femininity, against the be-all and end-all that is romantic love with its coy and sexist traditions, against porn-soaked representations of female sexuality and the centre stage given to male desire.

I'm backed up by a shed-load of literature, gems from which I occasionally fling their way. (It's horrifying, this stuff, for a parent who thinks they know their teenagers' worlds.) The gist is this: we live in a culture, in the West, where young women are empowered to have sex but not to enjoy it. Where the pressure to conform to a pornified adolescence sees widespread shame, self-harm, depression, even identification out of girlhood. Where, in the places where boys get their sex education, girls get anal but no cunnilingus. The 'pleasure gap', a seemingly natural state of affairs, sets the bar set so very low that many young women describe as successful a sexual encounter that does not involve humiliation or pain. The awful, passive, contractual language of 'consent' – young women as granter or refuser – has little to say about their pleasure, or desire.[2]

'Giving in', I say, 'consenting to have sex done to you, for his pleasure. You weren't expected to participate, to even enjoy it. In fact, it was considered a bit unnatural if you did. There was no real counter-narrative to all of this'. Then, knowing it will raise a laugh: 'No 1940s *Dirty Dancing*'.

I looked for a long time for a film (for anything, actually) that might assist me in my then-tentative, perfectly futile quest to give my girls as much of 'an untamed beginning' as might be possible in a culture that encourages them to be prematurely sexual and simultaneously to feel such shame.[3] I knew it would be an uphill battle. But then my younger daughter handed it to me with her repeated viewings of the film *Dirty Dancing*, about Frances 'Baby' Housman (Jennifer Grey), a teenage girl on holiday in the Catskills with her doctor father, housewife mother and conformist, girly sister, in 1963. While sheltered and middle class, Baby is bright, opinionated, ambitious and, on being taught to dance by resort-worker Johnny Castle (Patrick Swayzee), up for sexual adventure. The film is an unexpected feminist masterpiece. Baby seeks out Johnny, initates sex. He, an older, experienced man, is responsive, considerate and the object of the gaze. There is no declaration of love, no gesture towards marriage; no regrets, just respect and pleasure.[4]

In *City of Girls*, her novel set in America during the Second World War, Elizabeth Gilbert wanted to write about 'girls whose lives are not destroyed by their sexual desires'. Her main character, Vivian Morris, has been kicked out of Vassar and taken on by her aunt Peg as a costume maker in the down-at-heel vaudeville theatre that she owns in Manhattan. Vivian, for whom it is more important 'to feel free than safe', is soon bucking an age-old literary trend. 'Not even in fiction', Gilbert writes, 'is a woman allowed to seek out sexual pleasure without ending up under the wheels of a train'.[5]

Yet such girls did exist, in real life if rarely in novels or films. 'The 1920s and 1930s were a bit of watershed', I say to my daughters. 'Girls of Norah's generation, they wanted the adventure of sex and romance'. They look at me like this is no news. So I tell them about the Melbourne 'Yank Hunters', the American 'Victory Girls', the young Danes who roamed the streets of Esbjerg looking for German men and the 'good-time girls' of Bristol with their GI lovers, resisting attempts to fence them in. We all enjoy the stories, although I note that the most uproarious laughter hails from my mother.

***

They are keen to know this stuff, young women. I recently persuaded one of my daughters to come with me to a lecture on women's cycling in the nineteenth century. It's my interest, and she was bored. Driving home, she asked why women rode side saddle.

'I don't know for certain', I said, 'but I'll hazard a guess. Having your legs apart wasn't considered ladylike. That leather seat might rub against you in an unseemly way. And there's the worry that spreading your legs and the vigour of cycling might tear your hymen. No wedding night deflowering, no proof you were a virgin. And ta da! the end of civilisation as we know it'.

She snorted, sat upright, perked up. 'Why didn't she tell us that? I'm interested now'.

In her book *The Body Project*, historian Joan Jacobs Brumberg explores the gradual shift from good works and character to appearance as the priority in American girls' lives. Girls in the nineteenth century 'rarely mentioned their bodies in terms of strategies for self-improvement or struggles for personal identity', Brumberg writes. 'Becoming a better person meant paying *less* attention to the self…' By the twentieth century, American girls were increasingly focused on their bodies. She found it to be a struggle at first to nudge her students on from naïve claims about how much better things were for American women, now they had shed corsets and could enjoy sexual freedom, to think more critically about how being 'seen, admired and "asked out"' had emerged as the central goal in young women's lives.

And of course – back to my question about what Marsie could have done – it is bigger than individual girls and their mothers; much more than a mother's work. The ideals of feminine glamour and beauty, promoted in films, newspapers and magazines in the years of Norah's childhood, were part of a wider encouragement to shape bodies and sex-appeal through affordable fashion and cosmetics. 'Instead of supporting our early-maturing girls', Brumberg writes, instead of protecting them from the 'unrelenting self-scrutiny that the marketplace and modern media both thrive on, contemporary culture exacerbates normal adolescent self-consciousness and encourages precocious sexuality', treating women's bodies in 'a sexually brutal and commercially rapacious way'.[6]

'How could she have prepared me for this?' asks Melissa Febos, the 'she' being her own mother. In her powerful memoir, *Girlhood*, Febos reflects on the sudden, shocking, overwhelming difference between her twelve-year-old body as experienced at home and as newly received in the world, by men. 'You cannot win against an ocean. There is no good strategy in a rigged game. There are only new ways to lose'. And girls' compliance with this? As Annie Ernaux wrote in *A Girl's Story*, 'we need to push on, define the terrain – social, familial, and sexual – which fostered that desire, seek the reasons for the pride and the sources of the dream'.[7]

Can history help with this? Might Norah's story speak to us now? Historians want our work to do some good in the world but how can it happen if, as academics, we only write for each other? I'm no fan of trite statements about 'learning from history', but might intergenerational conversations about past lives, another kind of 'history from the inside', allow us to feel differently engaged with both past and present?[8]

My conversations about Norah with a PSHE (Personal and Social Health Education) Advisor in Derbyshire schools led us to write a sex education resource for younger secondary age pupils. On reading Jim's letters, she had identified the hallmarks of grooming: the compliments and continual stress on how special their relationship was; his pushing at boundaries, as with the schoolgirl photos and then the 'curl'; his encouragement of secrets, that he could then use against her. Norah's story enabled good discussions of issues that otherwise might have felt too close for comfort or clarity. The students themselves made the links:

comparisons between letters from an anonymous Jim and online stuff today. They talked about the peer-pressure that might have shaped his behaviour, as well as the age difference and Norah's innocence. And we were forced to consider the widespread victim-blaming assumptions that the kids brought to the classroom: whether or not Norah's flirtations – with Norman, mainly – made her blameworthy, 'asking for it'.[9]

History can move us beyond the individualised concern of much sex education, taking us past the language so beloved of psychologists – of Norah made 'resilient' because of her solid family life, her friendships and interests, and Jim as an individual bad egg. History forces us to look at the wider cultural factors that made Norah vulnerable – ideas about male and female sexuality, their intersection with commercial culture. History invites us to ask questions about how these play out in the world today, as, in the wake of #MeToo and the subsequent backlash, we attempt to process and transform individual experiences into a social movement, to create a philosophy of 'intimate justice', a sexual ethics, and stem the rising anti-feminist (and meninist) tide against attempts to centre female desire, autonomy and consent.

***

Historian John Demos tells a story of a student who had enjoyed his study of Eunice Williams, a Puritan girl from Deerfield, Massachusetts, abducted as a seven-year-old in 1704, during the French and Indian Wars, and who chose to remain with her adoptive Kahnawake family rather than return to her birth-family fold. *The Unredeemed Captive*, his student had commented, was 'a dad's book'. This was not so much a reference to the fact that in the absence of evidence from Eunice herself, Demos had relied on her father's narrative of her kidnap and later life. It was a more personal insight. As Demos confessed, the book was researched and written as his own children were flying the nest, embarking on lives as yet unknown, and different from his own.[10]

This, I suspect, is a mum's book. I read Norah's diaries not only as a historian, but as a mother too. When I first encountered the vital, feisty adolescent Norah of 1938, I had the strongest sense of how well she would fit into our family, an older sister to my girls. It is a very strange sensation, feeling maternal towards your late great-aunt's childhood self, but I wished she was mine. And I want to know what I could have done, as a mother, to protect her; what I can do for my own daughters, now.

It has always been a fine line for feminists to tread, between danger and exploitation and agency and desire. How, on the one hand, in stressing our vulnerability, the full extent of the violence against us, we might paradoxically victimise ourselves. In *Unwanted Advances*, her polemic about what she terms 'sexual paranoia' on university campuses, Laura Kipnis makes a similar point. Consent guidelines, she writes, are 'restoring the most fettered versions of traditional femininity through the backdoor', representing women as undesiring and non-sexual. I agree with her, and with Mithu Sanyal when she says that in ensuring that so many women 'live in constant fear', we are almost doing the Patriarchy's work for them. Ann Snitow sums up the challenge: 'We're trying to clarify that violence against women is unacceptable, trying to make it visible without terrifying ourselves. Tough trick'.[11]

Is this a tenuous connection to Norah's story? To me, it isn't. It's absolutely at the heart of it. And my daughters get it. When one was going off on her first overseas adventure, a close family member suggested she watch a film about the abduction, rape and murder of a young woman traveller, just so she knew what could happen, if she did something as outrageously risky as take a train through France. And Norah? We could choose to see only the danger: Jim's dodgy letters, Danny's (now) obvious lies, her foolhardiness in her plans to go away with him that weekend. We could seek to rein her in for her own safety, and when she doesn't listen, blame her, tell her she is a silly, naïve, girl; that she brought it on herself.

'Feminism must insist that women are sexual subjects, sexual actors, sexual agents', writes Carole Vance; 'that sexual pleasure without the threat of danger is a fundamental right'. Yet while so many women found aspects of life in wartime sexually liberating, it was not without risk. As Katherine Angel so eloquently argues, we discover our sexuality in relation to others. 'To be met in one's desire, and to be surprised in one's desire, is an exercise in mutual trust and negotiation of fear. When it works, it can feel miraculous; a magical collusion…'[12] Yet in England in the 1930s and 1940s, where girls were taught that sex equated to shame and fear, where they were to have their sexual feelings awakened by a man on their wedding night, or in our twenty-first-century world, where so many girls have contextless, pleasureless sex: tough bloody trick indeed.

'Imagine a world where girls are brought up to see their first love affair as a kind of debut', I say to my daughters. 'Where they aren't "losing" anything, but gaining entry into an adult life with all manner of other adventures in store. Where they can enjoy their bodies but not be reduced to them. Where their own desires are centre-stage in their own lives, their self-worth is not dependent on pleasing men...' I'm starting to get on a roll, but I sense them drifting away.

'Alright mum', they say, picking up their phones. And then that cruel parting shot: 'You do know that Aunty Norah wouldn't approve of this discussion, don't you?'

25. Writing Norah's Story

My daughter's comment nags at me: *Would* Norah approve? It seems entirely plausible that she would take a dim view of some parts of this book, akin perhaps to the objections of my mother, who is less than thrilled with its final shape.

My mum would prefer a story entirely about Norah and her diaries. Beyond a bit of wartime context, she has zero interest in the other stuff – the historical debates, the questions of method, the politics, philosophising and clever-clog interest in life's imponderables of which I am so fond. When reading the manuscript, she homed in on Norah and skipped the rest. Norah's diary accounts of growing up in wartime Castle Donington: that's all the book needs.

I do love this sense of enough-ness, this rock-solid belief, in the face of all messages to the contrary, that ordinary lives are enough. Norah would feel the same. She would heartily approve of the story of a girl with a postman father and a mother who'd been in service, a girl who loved Derby County, Donington Park, playing cricket with the neighbourhood boys, who read *Picturegoer* while sunbathing in the orchard, killed piglets on Webb's farm, went bluebelling after school. A story set in a council house; she'd like that. An avid visitor to stately homes, Norah would agree that the homes of the poor and the lives of the men and women who lived in them are history too.

But Norah would have no truck with my analysing and agonising over social class, this business of working up, moving away, and the question of what goes with you when you do, whether it has a place and value in your new home, how it resonates down the years. It's an interest of mine, not hers: this plucking out and setting on another course – the struggle for self in this new environment – and our tendency to reduce it to the trivial: the wrongful assumption that the nation enjoys salad cream with its lettuce, maybe, or a lack of familiarity with courgettes.

I catch every nuance of class, including the apparent absence of any sense of culture clash in her encounter with 'that school'. Other girls from her background felt the stretch, many dropped out, but Norah had none of their discomfort. For her, being a scholarship girl was uncomplicated, a benign good, part of progress and being modern. As her boxes of High School memorabilia suggest, it was key to her story of her life.

What Norah saw in straightforward terms – families becoming better off over time, kids getting into the grammar, the next generation going to university – I see with a social historian's eye. While her generation believed they were the start of a sea change that would result in the end of class inequality, their mobility had little impact on the social structure as a whole.[1] Maybe it wasn't meant to. She'd laugh at that. She'd think that for one so educated, I was unfathomably daft. Why would anybody want to stop children getting on in life? For Norah, it was all individual. She had good parents and she was bright enough. She could've worked harder and the white-collar job that followed was a bit of a let-down, but... end of.

Norah would also disapprove of my interest in the bigger picture as regards sex and love: how our lived experience feels so deeply personal yet is shaped by wider cultural trends. I imagine putting to her a compelling case – Eva Illouz's stance, maybe, that the interwar years saw happiness and success increasingly defined in terms of romantic love and erotic bonds, a new development that was intimately tied to consumer capitalism[2] – and picture her looking at me askance, like I'm a bit of a sad case, or have too much time on my hands. While she would no doubt agree that romantic love was the be-all and end-all, in the 1940s and after, she would consider that it just didn't need saying, was common sense, a natural fact of being human.

'That's just how it is', she'd say, vaguely exasperated. There was no point in analysing it, getting too clever.

And then there's Carolyn Heilbrun's claim in her classic book *Writing a Woman's Life*, that while the biographies of men focus on their worldly quests, often with scant reference to their domestic affairs, women are judged relationally, made someone by a husband or children. Only during courtship, the period of women's lives most constantly and most vividly present in films, novels, magazines and advertising, are women truly, briefly, active and agent, in the limelight of their own lives. But,

Heilbrun says, it is little more than an illusion: the young woman 'must entrap the man to ensure herself a center for her life'. And then her killer line: 'The rest is aging and regret'.[3] I wouldn't dare hit her up with this one, but for the years of Norah's girlhood and young womanhood, I am with Heilbrun all the same.

We can be sure, nonetheless, that Norah would love being reacquainted with her teenage self, with the girl who wrote her list of crushes in her *Letts's School-girl's Diary* in 1938, who knitted socks for a sailor at the start of the war and fell in love with Danny the airman. She would no doubt feel wistful for the glamorous young woman in the New Look coat, who went off to Rome, Switzerland, Yugoslavia, learned French and then German at night school, who made bookcases and flower gardens, who swam and danced and flirted with men. We think that she wouldn't object to the discussions of her love life; she liked being desired and didn't mind who knew it.

And Norah would surely agree that the ignorance about sex in which girls were kept was nothing short of an outrage. That the guilt and shame they were encouraged to feel made such an unnecessary misery of it. But beyond this, she wouldn't venture. There are points of real fury in Norah's diaries: those everlasting men at work and their back-patting promotions, the car maintenance night class teacher who told her that women weren't allowed to progress to the next level. But Norah was no feminist. She was happy enough with the mid-century roles allotted to women and men. She believed men needed to be played, that it was best to pander to their egos, to flatter them, baby them a bit.

'Men don't like to be told anything, don't like women to lead the way', she said on witnessing some domestic altercation in the early 2000s. 'You have to let him think it's his idea'. When I assured her I absolutely could not be bothered with that, she looked at me with pity in her eyes.

The 'return' for all of this was the stuff that she valued: a bit of chivalry, being wooed, feeling feminine. (This is *in theory* at least, because in practice, as we've seen, nobody looked after her and Norah could do everything, from decorating to joinery to mending the car. I didn't say it wasn't contradictory.) The absence of romance made her unhappy, whether in the form of Danny's scrappier letters, Vic's lack of attentiveness, her laments about her humdrum existence with Eddy or her old-age wish for a more cossetted life. She just needed men to keep their side of the bargain. She was unlucky with that. The ones she chose never did.

And Eddy? I have tried my best here, really I have. Norah's diary descriptions of him are a very mixed bag. I have been faithful to the passion and excitement of their early dates, his offer of a different life; to Norah and her Grace Kelly look, the years when she was a princess who had captured her prince. But it was complicated, not only by his existing wife, but because he was a deeply (war-?) damaged man. And because before long, passion all spent, she was weighed down with drudgery, tending to his every need, wondering if there shouldn't be more to life than this. But – again, lots of 'buts' – the relationship gave her a role, made her matter. *Happy Birthday Norah,* Eddy wrote in a flowery card that she kept, *with all my love from your very thankful Duck.* And another: *lots of love from your dependent Eddy/Duck.* So he did appreciate all she did for him. At least one day a year. ('Duck': a private joke, a shared send-up of an East Midlands term of endearment.)

So Eddy would be a real sticking point. To Norah, he was the way he was because he'd had such a bad war (poor chap) and women put up with much worse. But to my mum and me, her niece and great-niece, he was a brute. She lived in an unmarried trap, hemmed in by respectablility, secrecy and shame (Miss Hodgkinson still) and a legal status which decreed that if she left, she'd go empty-handed. But: I have said less than I could have here. Norah would want to protect him. Let's leave it at that.

What would she say about Danny and Jim? That Jim was a bad egg, that both had done her wrong, but – I don't doubt – that boys will be boys, men will be men. On a minesweeper in the North Sea, or a series of air raids over Europe, they didn't know if they were going to live or die. You had to make allowances, forgive some bad behaviour. It was just her bad luck (again!) to have fallen prey to them. Hopefully, after the war was over, they made good husbands and fathers, lived decent and honest lives.[4]

Did they groom her? To me, it's as clear as day. But I am well aware that Norah and I would operate in different frames. She was born too early for the confessional, 'expressive revolution' of the 1960s or for feminist analyses of sex.[5] How would she see it? The excitement of wartime romance, the thrill of desire. But disappointment and sadness too, I'm sure of that.

***

I tell you about my imagined disagreements with Norah because I am uneasy with the power I have, as the writer of her story, to make my interpretation stick. There is no doubt that I knew her as well as anybody did, and a good deal better than most. Our lives were bound, as great-aunt and great-niece, god-mother and god-daughter, two women born forty years apart who grew up on the same street. We shared an umbilical attachment to a place, a village where our family – or mine, the Twells side – has centuries of history, but where neither of us wound up living. But who am I to coax Norah's dreams and desires from her daily accounts? To write an intimate story that gives the final shape to her life? How do I stitch it up in a way that doesn't nip and tuck, smooth out all the pleats and folds, that keeps some frayed edges and wayward threads and resists a seamless untruth?

I have a colleague who makes life history recordings with cancer patients in palliative care. Sometimes, after telling their stories, for themselves, and for their families, once they've gone, they panic. 'We can erase', my colleague reassures. 'You can take bits out before you pass it on'. And wipe they do, a grumble cut here, an affair or two shaved there, a greater homing in on the joys of a marriage, a contentment with family life. We don't arrive easily at 'narrative closure', that place of 'psychic equilibrium' when, the pieces laid out, loose strands tied up, we reach a feeling of composure, a satisfying end.[6]

Even without a sense of audience or such looming finality, we reshape our lives. Sometimes it is the culture at large that gives us permission to change our tune. Eddy's daughter, Dinah, tells me about her childhood self in the years following her mother's early death. 'The idea that a child had an emotional life, it was unthinkable then', she says, but the cultural shift that saw the appearance of shelves of memoirs about unhappy childhoods in WH Smith has made hers more than a personal pain. Something similar has happened with veterans who've been quiet for decades about the less heroic aspects of their wartime pasts, now given a voice by recent discussions about military service and PTSD. How does

Norah's experience look in the context of #MeToo? Is it anachronistic, to use a current reckoning as a lens through which to look at the past? Or does it throw a new light, provide a new entry point, a clearer perception? Is it only now that we can really see the grooming that went on in 1941, even though without a language born of feminism or the UN Convention on the Rights of the Child, it happened all the same?[7]

Our slippery, shape-shifting lives, so tricky to catch and fix in place. I think of Virginia Woolf's *Orlando* and the many selves 'built up, one on top of the other, as plates are piled on a waiter's hand'.[8] Do they change, decade by decade, relationship by relationship, year by year, child by (no) child? Do we make our own main stories or, like those wooden sorter toys for toddlers, are we slotted into pre-existing shapes at different points in history and in our own lives?

So: all of this. But mostly, I want to feel that I have behaved honourably towards Norah, that I've done justice to her memory, let her speak for herself. That, as Alain Corbin writes in his history of an unknown man in nineteenth-century France, she would 'forgive me' for the various ways in which a reader may imagine the girl and woman she was, because of my account.[9] That my words allow the reader to see her as she saw herself.

But there is always a conflict. Life story writing 'always means you are playing with another person's life', writes Ken Plummer. It involves 'accurately yet imaginatively' picking up on their understandings of their place in the world, analysing their expressions, presenting them in convincing ways, and 'being critically aware of the immense difficulties such tasks bring'.[10] But *their understandings* and *your analysis* often do not match and the latter – academic analyses at least – can feel very far removed from the experience of living.

Sharing this project with my mother has helped no end here. 'Knowing with' her, rather than simply 'knowing from' her, has shaken up my understanding of Norah's life.[11] In our little authorial collective of two, my voice is decentred, some of my 'tendencies' toned down. Yet still I can't resist asking questions in which Norah and my mother (would) have no interest. I try to suppress them, but they return, time and again.

I can only be honest here, wear my commitments openly, insist again that the histories we write come from somewhere, even those we persist in telling in the third person, in the detached and impersonal academic style. Who we are, our place in the world, what we care about: all shape the questions we ask and the stories we tell about the past. 'Writing cannot be done in a state of desirelessness', as Janet Malcolm states. We might try to conceal the autobiographical 'I', to dismiss it as self-indulgent, solipsistic or lacking in rigour. But it seeps through, in the quiet way perhaps that Laurel Thatcher Ulrich's *A Midwife's Tale* is shaped by the life of her pioneer grandmother, an Idaho homesteader and a mother of twelve. Or like Jill Lepore, oblivious to the many 'interlacings' with her own childhood at the time of writing, but suddenly aware that her account of Jane Franklin's life was 'a book about my mother'.[12]

'Transference is an occupational hazard for historians', Carolyn Steedman writes, 'but I do not see how we would ever get going on anything, were it not available as a device for disinterring our historical subjects'.[13] But after we have 'got going', after we have acknowledged the researcher's life as the basis for how other lives are viewed, we surely must strive to move beyond a too-easy resonance and relatability, to enter the 'different country' that is history, puzzling at and then seeing more clearly the constraints and opportunities of a life lived in another time. As well as hoping that the reader might see Norah as she saw herself, it was my wish that through writing her life, I might too.

26. A Place of Dreams

The idea that romantic love should, for women, 'supply the meaning of life' feels troubling to me. Likewise, the assumption that women's social value, our sense of success in life *as women*, is defined through our capacity for romance and erotic bonds, to the exclusion of all else. At the very least, this suggests that the modern world was not so modern. 'Eve's problems are still your problems for all your modernity', announced the editor of *Miss Modern* in 1930. 'You have not lost that romance and womanliness which is ever your most precious heritage'.[1]

It might be argued (I could argue) that 'patriotic femininity' – the focus on maintaining men's morale through the provision of 'comforts', letters and sex-appeal – offered young women a narrow and decorative role. And yet, to so many, it didn't *feel* confining. As evidence from Britain and around the world suggests, many women found room for manoeuvre within this 'heightened sense of heterosexuality'.[2] Patriotic femininity, it seems, was not merely concerned with women serving – the nation, or men, or both – but a means of imagining themselves as potent and powerful, as independent and with agency in their lives. To varying degrees, their enthusiastic adoption of this wartime role allowed their participation in the war effort and a new-found sense of confidence and self-esteem. It enabled the throwing off of convention, the rejection of ignorance and shame, a new sense of themselves as sexual rather than merely sexualised, ushering in a revolutionary change.

Young women in the 1930s and 1940s were choosing a life that was a world apart from their mothers' experience of worn-out bodies and domestic drudgery. They hoped that they were stepping into an enduring adventure, the fun of courtship leading to a companionate marriage. From this perspective, the post-war ascendancy of domesticity was not a conservative retreat, a return to the past, but rather, in Marilyn Lake's words, a 'triumph of modern femininity', as women sought 'to live as female sexual subjects and explore the possibilities of sexual pleasure'.[3]

But this was the '40s and by the 1950s, the old order had closed in again, ushering in a new, princess-like passivity (*smiled sweetly at Freddie*). As Hélène Cixous writes in her attack on the myths of Sleeping Beauty-like passive femininity which have pervaded Western culture, the woman's value was dependent on her allure as she was aroused to waking by the man's kiss, opening her eyes to see only him. There was 'so little room', Cixous writes, 'for her [own] desire'.[4]

To claim such desire, women must be less Sleeping Beauty and more the Dancing Princesses of another fairy tale, the one in which a spy, employed by their father, the king, to explain the worn-out shoes that caused him such consternation, sees the girls escape the locked palace via a trap door each night, to enter the forest and dance. 'Walking, dancing, travelling', the princesses take pleasure 'in the transgressive act of expressing bodily desire', delighting in the forbidden.[5]

Danish girls roaming the streets of Esbjerg, on the look-out for German men. American women straying from the confines of their family homes. Young Australians on the prowl, Yank-hunting. Bristol girls ripping down fences, besieging the camps that hold their GI lovers. Don't. Fence. Me. In.

Norah does not go so far. She does not, as Cixous suggests we should, write her way into the new.[6] Her girlhood diaries conceal so much, her feelings and desires often no more than half-articulated, even to herself, shut down by respectability and an accompanying shame. But in her list of crazes in 1938, her early romantic hopes for her correspondence with Jim, her *hot times* in bed with Danny and their glorious lovemaking over Daleacre, and her at first tentative then certain sway towards the romantic weekend away: they are there all the same. In these fleeting moments, a different future can be glimpsed.

***

When we found her last diary – under the coffee table in the living room and not in her suitcase archive (of course) – we were anxious to know what Norah had written on the night she died. Had she had a good day? Did she feel ill? Was she in pain? Her very last entry reveals that she'd sent off for the letting agent's brochure for 18 Moira Dale. Like so many ex-council homes, our house, sold under Right to Buy, was in the hands of a private landlord, exactly the people the early reformers had aimed to cut out. *26th November 2009: Received details of 18 Moira Dale. It's grand now.*

But it was grand back then, in 1938, 1939, throughout the 1940s and '50s and into the '60s, and she knew it. Nothing that had followed had been any better. Materially, yes, suburban bungalows are better than council houses, aren't they? The life that went with them – holidays, nice clothes, mod cons – was all good. But what is the indefinable something, the intangible thing that is lost? Maybe it is no more than nostalgia – for childhood, an era long-gone, for a geographical place left behind, but with that (equally nebulous) complicating layer of 'class travel'.

We don't understand much about the emotional dimensions of social mobility, what it does to attachment and love. All childhoods are elemental, their loss like threads of knotted wool tugging in your breast. But a working-class childhood: does it linger, as Annette Kuhn suggests it does, like 'something beneath your clothes, under your skin, in your reflexes, in your psyche, at the very core of your being'? Or in the words of Jackson and Marsden, authors of a famous study of the grammar school generation, is it 'something in the blood, in the very fibre of a man or woman: a way of growing, feeling, judging, taken out of the resources of generations gone before'?[7]

And does the contrast between the now and then leave a different quality of longing, a deeper shade of regret running through your veins? How you never knew quite how poor you were, or how much promise you had, or how fleeting that time of possibility would turn out to be? Life had indeed been full of promises and Danny was there as they bloomed. But had some of them turned out to be empty, in the end?

18 Moira Dale, my family's ancestral home. I thought about this house and another very like it, the council house around the corner on Garden Crescent to where Helen and Joe moved in 1951, and where my mum and I lived until I was thirteen, when I read Penelope Lively's *A House Unlocked*, a delightful account of artefacts in her grandmother's Edwardian country house and the histories they evoke. Her discussions of the range of heirlooms and imperial booty, even her chapter headings – 'The Knife Rests, The Grape Scissors and the Bon-Bon Dish' – are a laughable impossibility in writing about working-class homes (although, I'd suggest, 'Pop's Antlers' might just hold their own).[8]

But our houses come with their own stories. 'The Bathroom and the Four Good Bedrooms' might suffice to evoke a life without the daily struggle with the squalor of poverty. 'Marsie's Bible, the Encyclopaedias and the Rag Rugs' or 'The Lilacs, the Peach Tree and the Chicken Coop' would express my great-grandmother's faith, her resourcefulness, creativity and sense of beauty. 'The High Heels Under the Dresser' nods to the greater affluence of the 1950s, as well as a new style of femininity embraced by Norah, contrasting nicely with 'The Mangle in the Wash-House' at Garden Crescent, where my grandmother fought a battle every Monday with my grandfather's blood-stained butchering slops.

What about 'The Cupboard Over the Stairs' in Norah's box bedroom, where she stored her diaries and her letters from Jim? Or 'The Council House Front Door', which she opened to welcome Danny in, and pulled shut behind them as they headed for Daleacre, her arm through his? And the 'Spare Bedroom Overlooking the Garden', where Danny slept when he came to stay, where those glorious, snatched mornings while Marsie was out shopping were so utterly transformative?

When she died, Norah, like her brother Dennis – after forty, fifty years away – could only be buried in one place: Castle Donington cemetery, around the corner from number 18. She lies there, a few feet up from Marsie and Pop and three of her siblings – Birdy, Dennis and Nollie, Helen and Joe, and Roger, their son – their gravestones and cremation pots all looking down Hemington Hill, past the allotments and Cherry Orchard, Lady's Close and the kissing gates, and up Diseworth Lane to the airport fence, sharp right to the Nag's Head and the Hill Top cottage, long gone, and the racetrack beyond, up and down, over hill and dale, through the passage of the years.

'The archive is [...] a place of dreams', writes Carolyn Steedman, her focus the historian's dreams, her hope of rescuing people in the past, finding meaning in their lives, writing them back into being.[9] But it is also the place of the subject's dreams, of Norah's dreams.

The half-curated archive that is Norah's grey cardboard suitcase, with Jim's letters, his and Danny's photos and the seventy-one pocket diaries of her life, is like a magic box, the inside of which can never fully be glimpsed, the memories and emotions contained there far more expansive, joyous, ambiguous, painful, than its material dimensions appear to allow. In it, in her wartime diaries, Norah takes centre-stage – giddy, excited, so full of hope, as she waits for her life to unfold.

Endnotes

1. Norah's Suitcase

1   Suzannah Lessard, *The Architect of Desire: Beauty and Danger in the Stanford White Family* (New York: Delta, 1997), p. 5; Anne-Marie Kramer, 'Kinship, Affinity and Connectedness: Exploring the Role of Genealogy in Personal Lives', *Sociology*, 45:3 (2011), 379-395; Paul Basu, *Highland Homecomings: Genealogy and Heritage Tourism in the Scottish Diaspora* (London: Routledge, 2007).

2   See Kirsten Harris, *Walt Whitman and British Socialism: The Love of Comrades* (London: Routledge, 2016).

3   Liz Gloyn, Vicky Crewe, Laura King and Anna Woodham, 'The Ties that Bind: Materiality, Identity, and the Life Course in the "Things" Families Keep', *Journal of Family History*, 43:2 (2018), 164-165.

4   Jane Robinson, *In the Family Way: Illegitimacy Between the Great War and the Swinging Sixties* (London: Viking, 2015).

5   Orhan Pamuk, 'My Father's Suitcase', Nobel lecture, *The New Yorker*, 17 December 2006, p. 7.

6   Virginia Woolf, *A Room of One's Own* (Herts: Granada, 1983), pp. 72-73.

7   Carolyn Heilbrun, *The Last Gift of Time: Life Beyond Sixty* (New York: Random House, 1998), p. 138.

2. Norah's Story: Writing History from the Inside

1   Paul Fussell, *Wartime: Understanding and Behaviour in the Second World War* (Oxford: Oxford University Press, 1989), p. 42; Norman Longmate, cited in Philomena Goodman, *Women, Sexuality and War* (Basingstoke: Palgrave, 2001), p. 130.

2   Goodman, *Women, Sexuality and War*; Sonya O. Rose, *Which People's War? National Identity and Citizenship in Britain 1939-1945* (Oxford: Oxford University Press, 2003)

3   Marilyn Lake, 'Female Desires: The Meaning of World War II', in Gordon Martel (ed.), *The World War Two Reader* (London: Routledge, 2004 [1990]), pp. 359-376, 360-361, 366-368; 'The Desire for a Yank: Sexual Relations between Australian Women and American Servicemen during World War 2', *Journal of the History of Sexuality*, 2:4 (1992), 621-633, pp. 623, 627.

4   Lulu Anne Hansen, '"Youth off the rails": Teenage Girls and German Soldiers – A Case Study in Occupied Denmark, 1940-1945', in Dagmar Herzog (ed.), *Brutality and Desire: War and Sexuality in Europe's Twentieth Century* (Basingstoke: Palgrave, 2011 [2009]), pp. 135-167, 136, 142-143, 145.

5   Raffael Scheck, *Love Between Enemies: Western Prisoners of War and German Women in World War II* (Cambridge: Cambridge University Press, 2021), p. 108; Cornelie Usborne, 'Female Sexual Desire and Male Honour: German Women's Illicit Love Affairs with Prisoners of War during the Second World War', *Journal of the History of Sexuality*, Special Issue: Transgressive Sex, Love, and Violence in World War II Germany and Britain, 26:3 (2017), 454-488.

6   Goodman, *Women, Sexuality and War*, p. 132; Rose, *Which Peoples' War?*, p. 91.

7   Hansen, 'Youth off the Rails', p. 144; Marilyn E. Hegarty, *Victory Girls, Khaki-Wackies, and Patriotutes: The Regulation of Female Sexuality during World War II* (New York: New York University Press, 2008), p. 13.

8   Amanda H. Littauer, *Bad Girls: Young Women, Sex, and Rebellion Before the Sixties* (Chapel Hill: University of North Carolina Press, 2015), p. 21.

9   Lake, 'Female Desires'; Littauer, *Bad Girls*, pp. 39, 2; Hansen, 'Youth off the Rails', pp. 136, 161.

10 Exceptions include Margaretta Jolly (ed.), *Dear Laughing Motorbyke: Letters from Women Welders in the Second World War* (London: Scarlet Press, 1997); Jenna Bailey (ed.), *Can Any Mother Help Me?* (London: Faber, 2007). For oral histories of women and girls in interwar Britain, see Claire Langhamer, *Women's Leisure in England, 1920-1960* (Manchester: Manchester University Press, 2000); Elizabeth Roberts, *A Woman's Place: An Oral History of Working-Class Women, 1890-1940* (London: John Wiley and Sons, 1995); Judy Giles, *Women, Identity, and Private Life in Britain, 1900-1950* (Basingstoke: Macmillan, 1995); Jackie Stacey, *Star Gazing: Hollywood*

Cinema and Female Spectatorship (London: Routledge, 1994); Simon Szreter and Kate Fisher, *Sex Before the Sexual Revolution: Intimate Life in England 1918-1963* (Cambridge: Cambridge University Press, 2010); Selina Todd, *Young Women, Work, and the Family in England, 1918-1950* (Oxford: Oxford University Press, 2005); Pamela Cox, *Bad Girls in Britain: Gender, Justice and Welfare, 1900-1950* (Basingstoke: Palgrave, 2003); Carol Dyhouse, *Girl Trouble: Panic and Progress in the History of Young Women* (London: Bloomsbury, 2014).

11   Mass Observation (MO) was formed in 1937 to record everyday life in Britain. Around five hundred volunteers were recruited to keep diaries or respond to questionnaires or to anonymously record conversations and behaviour in various public places, including at sports and religious events. See https://massobs.org.uk/the-archive-collections. For MO generally: James Hinton, *The Mass Observers: A History, 1937-1949* (Oxford: Oxford University Press, 2013). MO women writers include: Richard Broad and Suzie Fleming (eds), *Nella Last's War: The Second World War Diaries of 'Housewife, 49'* (London: Profile Books, 2006); Robert Malcolmson (ed.), *Love & War in London: The Mass Observation Diary of Olivia Cockett* (Stroud: The History Press, 2009 [2005]); Jean Lucey Pratt, *A Notable Woman: The Romantic Journals of Jean Lucey Pratt* (London: Canongate, 2016); Doreen Bates, *Diary of a Wartime Affair: The True Story of a Surprisingly Modern Romance* (Harmondsworth: Penguin, 2016); Dorothy Sheridan (ed.), *Among You Taking Notes: The Wartime Diary of Naomi Mitchison* (London: Gollancz, 2000 [1985]).

12   Molly McCarthy, *The Accidental Diarist: A History of the Daily Planner in America* (Chicago: University of Chicago Press, 2013); Stuart Sherman, *Telling Time: Clocks, Diaries, and English Diurnal Form, 1660-1785* (Chicago: University of Chicago, 1996).

13   Melanie Tebbutt, *Being Boys: Youth, Leisure and Identity in the Inter-war Years* (Manchester: Manchester University Press, 2012) uses pocket diaries.

14   Sally Alexander, 'Women, Class and Sexual Differences in the 1830s and 1840s: Some Reflections on Writing Feminist History', *History Workshop Journal*, 17:1 (1984), 125-149, p. 127.

15   Laurel Thatcher Ulrich, *A Midwife's Tale: The Life of Martha Ballard based on her Diary, 1785–1812* (New York: Alfred A. Knopf, 1990), pp. 8-9, p. 33; Patricia Cline Cohen et al., 'Dialogue. Paradigm Shift Books: *A Midwife's Tale* by Laurel Thatcher Ulrich', *Journal of Women's History*, 14:3 (2002), 133-161, p. 140; Philippe Lejeune, 'The "Journal de Jeune Fille" in Nineteenth-Century France', in Suzanne Bunkers and Cynthia A. Huff

(eds), *Inscribing the Daily: Critical Essays on Women's Diaries* (Amherst: University of Massachusetts Press, 1996), pp. 107-122, 120.

16 Jennifer Sinor: *The Extraordinary Work of Ordinary Writing: Annie Ray's Diary* (Iowa City: University of Iowa, 2002); Sinor, 'Reading the Ordinary Diary', *Rhetoric Review*, 21:2 (2002), 123-149, p. 123.

17 Laurel Thatcher Ulrich, 'The Significance of Trivia', *Journal of Mormon History*, 19:1 (1993), 52-66, pp. 55, 66; Jacques Revel, 'Scale and Discontinuity in History', in Sebastian Jobs and Alf Lüdtke (eds), *Unsettling History: Archiving and Narrating in Historiography* (Frankfurt: Campus Verlag, 2010), p. 50.

18 For the 'exceptional normal' (sometimes the 'normal exception'): Carlo Ginzburg and Carlo Poni, 'The Name and the Game: Unequal Exchange and the Historiographic Marketplace', in Edward Moore and Guido Ruggiero (eds), *Microhistory and the Lost Peoples of Europe* (Baltimore: John Hopkins University, 1991), p. 8; Sigurður Gylfi Magnússon and István M. Szijártó, *What is Microhistory? Theory and Practice* (London: Routledge, 2013).

19 Natalie Zemon Davis, *The Return of Martin Guerre* (Cambridge: Harvard University Press, 1983); John Demos, *The Unredeemed Captive: A Family Story from Early America* (London: Macmillan, 1996 [1994]); Ann Little, *The Many Captivities of Esther Wheelwright* (New Haven and London: Yale University Press, 2016).

20 Thomas Mallon, *A Book of One's Own: People and their Diaries* (New York: Ticknor & Fields, 1984), p. xvii.

21 Lynn Z. Bloom, '"I Write for Myself and Strangers": Private Diaries as Public Documents', in Bunkers and Huff (eds), *Inscribing the Daily*, p. 23; Elizabeth Hampsten, *'Read this Only to Yourself': The Private Writings of Midwestern Women, 1880-1910* (Bloomington: Indiana University Press, 1982). See also: Suzanne L. Bunkers and Cynthia A. Huff, 'Issues in Studying Women's Diaries: A Theoretical and Critical Introduction', in Bunkers and Huff (eds), *Inscribing the Daily*, pp. 1-20; Cynthia A. Huff, 'Reading as Re-vision: Approaches to Reading Manuscript Diaries', *Biography*, 23:3 (2000), 504-523; Suzanne L. Bunkers, *Diaries of Girls and Women: A Midwestern American Sampler* (Madison: University of Wisconsin Press, 2001).

22 Rebecca Hogan, 'Engendered Autobiographies: The Diary as a Feminine Form', *Prose Studies*, 14.2 (1991), 95-107, 103.

23   Hampsten, *'Read this Only to Yourself'*, p. 4. For sparse diaries, see also Marilyn Ferris Motz, 'Folk Expression of Time and Place: 19th-Century Midwestern Rural Diaries', *The Journal of American Folklore*, 100:396 (1987), 131-147; Kathryn Carter, 'An Economy of Words: Emma Chadwick Stretch's Account Book Diary, 1859-1860', *Acadiensis*, 29:1 (1999), 43-56.

24   Lydia Flem, *The Final Reminder: How I Emptied my Parent's House*, trans. Elfreda Powell (London: Souvenir Press, 2005).

25   See Lucy Noakes and Juliette Pattinson (eds), *British Cultural Memory and the Second World War* (London: Bloomsbury Academic, 2014).

26   Atina Grossman, 'Family Files: Emotions and Stories of (Non-)Restitution', *German Historical Institute London Bulletin*, 34:1 (2012), p. 62; Joanna Brooks, *Why We Left: Untold Stories and Songs of America's First Immigrants* (Minneapolis: University of Minnesota Press, 2013), p. 21; Kendra Taira Field, 'The Privilege of Family History', *American Historical Review*, 127:2 (2022), 600-633; Stephane Gerson, 'A History from Within: When Historians Write about Their Own Kin', *Journal of Modern History*, 94:4 (2022), 898-937; Laura King, *Living with the Dead: Memories, Histories and the Stories Families Tell in Modern Britain* (Oxford: Oxford University Press, 2025), p. 11.

27   Tanya Evans, 'Secrets and Lies: The Radical Potential of Family History', *History Workshop Journal*, 71 (2011), 49-73; Ashley Barnwell, 'Keeping the Nation's Secrets: "Colonial Storytelling" within Australian Families', *Journal of Family History*, 46:1 (2021), 46-61; Katie Barclay and Nina Javette Koefoed, 'Family, Memory, and Identity: An Introduction', *Journal of Family History*, 46:1 (2021), 3-12.; Tanya Evans, *Family History, Historical Consciousness and Citizenship* (London: Bloomsbury, 2021); Malcolm Allbrook and Sophie Scott-Brown (eds), *Family History and Historians in Australia and New Zealand* (New York: Routledge, 2021); Anna Green, 'Intergenerational Family Memory and Historical Consciousness', in Anna Clark and Carla L. Peck (eds), *Contemplating Historical Consciousness: Notes from the Field* (New York/Oxford: Berghahn Books, 2018), pp. 200-211; Stacey Zembrzycki, *According to Baba: A Collaborative Oral History of Sudbury's Ukrainian Community* (Vancouver: UBC Press, 2015); Laura King and Jessica Hammett, 'Family Historians and Historians of the Family: The Value of Collaboration', in Paul Ashton, Tanya Evans and Paula Hamilton (eds), *Making Histories* (Berlin: De Gruyter Oldenberg, 2020), pp. 237-250; Radmila Švarícková Slabáková, *Family Memory: Practices, Transmissions and Uses in a Global Perspective* (London: Routledge, 2021), pp. 1-24. See also: Jonathan Scott Holloway, *Jim Crow Wisdom: Memory & Identity in Black America since 1940* (Durham: University of North Carolina Press, 2013), pp. 8-13; Gaiutra Bahadur, *Coolie Woman: The Odyssey of Indenture* (London: C. Hurst & Co, 2013); Kendra Taira Field, *Growing Up*

With the Country: Family, Race, and Nation after the Civil War (New Haven: Yale University Press, 2018), pp. xv, xvii-xix.

28 See Michel-Rolph Trouillot, *Silencing the Past: Power and the Production of History* (Boston: Beacon Press, 1995), p. 26. See also: Wendy Anne Warren, '"The cause of her grief": The Rape of a Slave in Early New England', *Journal of American History*, 93:4 (March 2007), 1031–049.

29 Ivan Jablonka, *A History of the Grandparents I Never Had*, trans. Jane Kuntz (Stanford: Stanford University Press, 2016), p. 123.

30 Alison Light, *Common People: The History of An English Family* (Harmondsworth: Penguin, 2015), pp. xii; 57, 128-130; Light, 'In Defence of Family History', *The Guardian*, 11 October 2014: https://www.theguardian.com/books/2014/oct/11/genealogy-not-historys-poor-relation-family; Richard White, *Remembering Ahanagran* (New York: Hill & Wang, 1998), pp. 4-5. Discussions of women as 'kin-keepers' span disciplines. For family history, see Gloyn et al., 'The Ties That Bind'. For an excellent discussion of ways of using family histories to enrich historical understanding, see Irna Qureshi, 'Memories and Journeys of Chhachhi ex-Merchant Navy Seamen from the Chhachh to Bradford' (University of Hull: unpublished PhD thesis, 2025).

31 Louis P. Masur, 'What Will It Take to Turn Historians into Writers', in Aaron Sachs and John Demos (eds), *Artful History: A Practical Anthology* (New Haven: Yale University Press, 2020), p. 215; Robert Nelson, 'Toward a History of Rigour: An Examination of the Nasty Side of Scholarship', *Arts & Humanities in Higher Education*, 10:4 (2011), 374-387, p. 376. For critiques of academic history and writing, see: Michael Stanford, *Introduction to the Philosophy of History* (Oxford: Blackwell, 1998), p. 55; Stephen J. Pyne, *Voice & Vision: A Guide to Writing History and Other Serious Nonfiction* (Cambridge and London: Harvard University Press, 2009); Nancy F. Partner, 'Making Up Lost Time: Writing on the Writing of History', *Speculum*, 61:1 (1986), 90-117; Ann Rigney 'History as Text: Narrative Theory and History', in Nancy Partner and Sarah Foot (eds), *The Sage Handbook of Historical Theory* (New York: Sage Publications, 2013), pp. 183-201, pp. 8-10; Elizabeth Chapman Hoult, 'Recognising and Escaping from the Sham: Authority Moves, Truth Claims and the Fiction of Academic Writing about Adult Learning', *InterActions: UCLA Journal of Education and Information Studies*, 8:2 (2012), 5; Tracey Loughran, 'Blind Spots and Moments of Estrangement: Subjectivity, Class and Education in British "Autobiographical Histories"', in Dawn Mannay and Tracey Loughran (eds), *Emotion and the Researcher: Sites, Subjectivities, and Relationships* (Leeds: Emerald Publishing, 2018), 245-259; Helen Sword, *Stylish Academic Writing* (Cambridge, MA: Harvard University Press, 2012); Hayden White, 'The Value of Narrativity in the Representation of Reality', *Critical Inquiry*, 7:1 (1980), 5-27; Fraser

MacDonald, 'The Ruins of Erskine Beveridge', *Transactions of the Institute of British Geographers*, 2 (2013), 477-489; Ann Curthoys and Ann McGrath, *How to Write History that People Want to Read* (Basingstoke: Palgrave, 2011 [2009]).

32 Hayden White, 'The Public Relevance of Historical Studies: A Reply to Dirk Moses', *History and Theory*, 44:3 (2005), 333.

33 I am paraphrasing Jennifer Sinor here. For a discussion of academic history uncovering 'the means by which selves are made, but not the selves themselves', see James Bradley, 'The Colonel and the Slave Girls: Life Writing and the Logic of History in 1830s Sydney', *Journal of Social History*, 45:2 (2011), 416-435, p. 430.

34 Alexis Okeowo, 'How Saidiya Hartman Retells the History of Black Life', *The New Yorker*, 19 October 2020, https://www.newyorker.com/magazine/2020/10/26/how-saidiya-hartman-retells-the-history-of-black-life. See Saidiya Hartman, *Wayward Women and Beautiful Experiments: Intimate Histories of Riotous Black Girls, Troublesome Women and Queer Radicals* (London: Serpent's Tail, 2019); Saidiya Hartman, 'Intimate History, Radical Narrative', *Black Perspectives*, 20 May 2020, https://www.aaihs.org/intimate-history-radical-narrative.

35 Tim O'Brien, *The Things They Carried* (Boston: Houghton Mifflin, 1990), p. 179; Hilary Mantel, Reith Lectures, 2017: see https://medium.com/@bbcradiofour/hilary-mantel-bbc-reith-lectures-2017-aeff8935ab33

36 See Tom Griffith, 'The Intriguing Dance of History and Fiction', *TEXT: Special Issue 28: Fictional Histories and Historical Fictions: Writing History in the Twenty-first Century*, eds Camilla Nelson and Christine de Matos, 19:28 (2015); and Christine de Matos, 'Fictorians: Historians Who 'Lie' about the Past and Like It', in the same volume; Katherine Collins, 'Is There any Truth in Biographical Fictions?', *University of Oxford*, 12 May 2020, https://greatdev.podcasts.ox.ac.uk/content/there-any-truth-biographical-fictions?qt-episode_related_content=1. See also: Alison Twells, Will Pooley, Matt Houlbrook and Helen Rogers, 'Undisciplined History: Creative Methods and Academic Practice', *History Workshop Journal*, 96:1 (2023), 153–175.

37 Kiera Lindsey, *The Convict's Daughter* (Crows Nest: Allen and Unwin, 2017), p. 305. See also Kiera Lindsey, '"Deliberate Freedom": Exploring the Role of Informed Imagination and Speculation in Historical Biography', *TEXT: Special Issue 50: Life Narrative in Troubled Times*, eds Kate Douglas, Donna Lee Brien and Kylie Cardell, 22:50 (2018); Donna Lee Brien and Kiera Lindsey (eds), *Speculative Biography: Experiments, Opportunities*

and *Provocations* (New York and Abingdon: Routledge, 2022); Suzannah Lipscomb, 'How Can We Recover the Lost Lives of Women?" in Helen Carr and Suzannah Lipscomb (eds), *What is History, Now? How the Past and Present Speak to Each Other* (London: Weidenfeld & Nicolson), 178-196.

38   Ulrich, *A Midwife's Tale*, p. 33.

39   Maria Tamboukou, 'Feeling Narrative in the Archive: The Question of Serendipity', *Qualitative Research*, 16:2 (2016), 151-166, pp. 155-156.

40   Here I paraphrase James Goodman, 'For the Love of Stories (1998)', reprinted in Sachs and Demos, *Artful History*, p. 109. On the question of why there has been so little innovation in voice and form in history writing, Robert Rosenstone's reflections still hold true. Rosenstone, 'Experiments in Narrative: Introduction', *Rethinking History*, 5:3 (2001), 411-416.

3. Norah Hodgkinson, Schoolgirl Diarist

1   Anthony Letts, 'A History of Letts', in *Letts Keep a Diary: A History of Diary Keeping in Great Britain from 16th-20th Century* (London: Charles Letts, 1987), pp. 29-30; Brian Dobbs, *Dear Diary: Some Studies in Self-interest* (London: Elm Tree Books, 1974), pp. 224-228; Joe Moran, 'Private Lives, Public Histories: The Diary in Twentieth-Century Britain', *Journal of British Studies*, 54:1 (2015), 138-162.

2   Mary Jo Maynes, 'Age as a Category of Historical Analysis: History, Agency and Narratives of Childhood', *Journal of the History of Childhood and Youth*, 1:1 (2008), 114-124; Kristine Alexander, 'Can the Girl Guide Speak? The Perils and Pleasures of Looking for Children's Voices in Archival Research', *Jeunesse: Young People, Texts, Cultures*, 4:1 (2012), 132-145; Colin Heywood, *A History of Childhood* (Cambridge: Polity Press, 2018).

3   Selina Todd, *The People: The Rise and Fall of the Working Class, 1910-2010* (London: John Murray, 2014), p. x. 25% of free places in the grant-aided grammar schools were saved for poorer pupils. Ross McKibbin, *Classes and Cultures: England, 1918-1951* (Oxford: Oxford University Press, 1998), p. 260.

4   Richard Hoggart, *The Uses of Literacy: Aspects of Working-Class Life* (Harmondsworth: Penguin, 1957), p. 292; Pierre Bourdieu, cited in Tony Bennett, 'Habitus Clivé: Aesthetics and Politics in the Work of Pierre Bourdieu', *New Literary History*, 38:1 (2007), 201-228; Valerie Avery quoted in Worpole, 'Class of '55', *City Limits*, 29 January 1982, p. 39; Rob Colls, 'When We Lived in Communities', in Rob Colls and Richard Rodgers, *Cities of Ideas: Civil Society and Urban Governance in Britain 1800-2000*.

Essays in Honour of David Reeder (Aldershot: Ashgate, 2004); Ken Worpole, 'Scholarship Boy: the Poetry of Tony Harrison', *New Left Review*, 1:153 (Sept/Oct 1985): https://newleftreview-org.hallam.idm.oclc.org/issues/i153/articles/ken-worpole-scholarship-boy-the-poetry-of-tony-harrison. My thanks to Ken Worpole for sending me his *City Limits* piece.

5   David Storey, *Saville* (London: Jonathan Cape, 1976).

6   Mallon, *A Book of One's Own*, p. xi; Michel Foucault, 'Technologies of the Self', in L. H. Martin, H. Gutman and P. H. Hutton (eds), *Technologies of the Self: A Seminar with Michel Foucault* (Amherst: University of Massachusetts Press, 1998), pp. 16-49; James Hinton, *Nine Wartime Lives: Mass Observation and the Making of the Modern Self* (Oxford: Oxford University Press, 2010), pp. 5-6; Lejeune, 'The "Journal De Jeune Fille"; Irina Paperno, 'What Can Be Done with Diaries?', *The Russian Review*, 63:4 (2004), 561-573.

7   Giles, *Women, Identity, and Private Life*, chapter two; Sally Alexander, 'The Mysteries and Secrets of Women's Bodies: Sexual Knowledge in the First Half of the Twentieth Century', in Mica Nava and Alan O'Shea (eds), *Modern Times: Reflections on a Century of English Modernity* (London: Routledge, 1996), pp. 161-175.

8   The phrase 'hint of the Orient' reflects period language and attitudes, and appears here as part of a historically situated imaginative reconstruction. For the 'craze for all things romantically "Oriental"' which swept through film, novels and fashion in the 1920s and 1930s, see Hsu-Ming Teo, *Desert Passions: Orientalism and Romance Novels* (Austin: University of Texas, 2012).

9   J. M. Lee, 'The Rise and Fall of a Market Town: Castle Donington in the Nineteenth Century', *Transactions of Leicestershire Archaeology and History Society*, 32 (1956), 53-80, 53, 55, 57; Pamela J. Fisher and J. M. Lee, *The Victoria History of Leicestershire: Castle Donington* (London: Victoria County History, 2016).

10   Letter from Princess Chula Chakrabongse, *Motor Sport Magazine*, https://www.motorsportmagazine.com/archive/article/may-1971/76/cars-in-books-203-may-1971/

11   Interview with John Glenn, 1 August 2014.

12   Alison Ravetz, *Council Housing and Culture: The History of a Social Experiment* (London: Routledge, 2001); John Broughton, *Municipal Dreams: The Rise and Fall of Council Housing* (London: Verso, 2018).

13 Letter from the Corporation of Bristol Housing Estates on 15th June 1936, Myers-Insole Local Learning Community Interest Company, https://www.locallearning.org.uk/img_pxu733/

14 For debates about the working-class parlour in this period, see Krista Cowman, 'A Waste of Space? Controversies Surrounding the Working-Class Parlour in Inter-War Britain', *Home Cultures*, 15:2 (2018), 129-153.

15 Irene Marsh, Interview, 4 April 2015.

16 Philippe Lejeune and Catherine Bogaert, 'The Practice of Writing a Diary', in Batsheva Ben-Amos and Dan Ben-Amos (eds), *The Diary: The Epic of Everyday Life* (Bloomington: Indiana University Press, 2020), pp. 25-38, 30.

17 Anthony Carter, *Motor Racing: The Pursuit of Victory* (Dorchester: Veloce Publishing Ltd, 2011), pp. 18-19; Christopher Hilton, *Hitler's Grands Prix in England: Donington Park 1938 and 1939* (Yeovil: Haynes Manual Inc, 1999).

18 Frank Soo was born in Derbyshire in 1914 to a Chinese father and English mother. Newspaper reports frequently referred to him in terms of his Chinese heritage. See The Frank Soo Foundation, 'Frank Soo: The Forgotten Footballer', www.artsandculture.google.com/story/frank-soo-the-forgotten-footballer-the-frank-soo-foundation/agVhGPgckSpQIA?hl=en

19 Norah always wrote football results this way (4.1), rather than using a conventional dash (4-1).

4. A Poke in the Eye for Hitler

1 John Baxendale, *Priestley's England: J.B. Priestley and English Culture* (Manchester: Manchester University Press, 2007), chapter five.

2 Joan Strange, quoted in Terry Charman, *Outbreak, 1939: The World Goes to War* (London: Virgin Books, 2010), p. 15.

3 May Smith, *These Wonderful Rumours: A Young Schoolteacher's Wartime Diaries*, ed. by Duncan Marlor (London: Virago, 2012), pp. 21, 23, 30-36; Pratt, *A Notable Woman*, pp. 178-179. For mothers, see Broad and Fleming (eds), *Nella Last's War*.

4 Charman, *Outbreak*, pp. 36-38, 44; Daniel Todman, *Britain's War: Into Battle, 1937-1941* (Harmondsworth: Penguin, 2016), pp. 184-188. The WAAF: Women's Auxiliary Air Force.

5 I.e., clean the lavatory.

6   Cited in Charman, *Outbreak*, p. 50.

7   Angus Calder, *The People's War: Britain 1939-1945* (London: Pimlico, 2008 [1969]), p. 34.

8   Cited in Charman, *Outbreak*, pp. 56, 58, 60, 71.

9   In a BIPO survey of September, 89% said 'yes' to the question, 'Should we continue to fight until Hitlerism goes?' Todman, *Britain's War*, pp. 272-277.

10   Calder, *The People's War*, pp. 35-76. For the early months, see Todman, *Britain's War*, pp. 199-289.

11   Frances Partridge, *A Pacifist's War* (London: Phoenix, 1996), pp. 38-39.

12   Margaret Lindner in Jeanne Carswell (ed.), *At Home and Away* (Coalville: Coalville Publishing, 1995), pp. 14-16; Castle Donington Museum, Local Wartime Memories folder.

13   Royces: conversation with Bruce Townsend, August 2011; for the 'wizard war', see: Historic England Research Records: Starfish Bombing Decoy, https://www.heritagegateway.org.uk/Gateway/Results_Single.aspx?uid=42703a6a-4898-488a-aeae-14e9b20e3ccb&resourceID=19191.

14   For the ARP, Home Guard and WVS, see: Corinna Peniston-Bird and Penny Summerfield, *Contesting Home Defence: Men, Women and the Home Guard During the Second World War* (Manchester: Manchester University Press, 2007); James Hinton, *Women, Social Leadership and the Second World War: Continuities of Class* (Oxford: Oxford University Press, 2002), Jessica Hammett, *Creating the People's War: Civil Defence Communities in Second World War Britain* (Manchester: Manchester University Press, 2022).

15   Delia Richards, personal conversation; Geoffrey Abel, 'Evacuation to Hemington', *WW2 Peoples' War: An Archive of WW2 Memories – Written by the Public, Gathered by the BBC* (August 2005), https://www.bbc.co.uk/history/ww2peopleswar/stories/96/a5294496.shtml; Robert Mackay, *Half the Battle: Civilian Morale in Britain during the Second World War* (Manchester: Manchester University Press, 2002), p. 69.

16   *Derby Evening Telegraph*, 1/1/1940, 3/1/1940, 8/1/1940, 17/4/1940, 18/4/1940, 3/5/1940, 10/5/1940, 23/5/1940, 29/5/1940, 30/5/1940, 1/6/1940, 4/6/1940, 25/6/1940, 9/9/1940, 11/9/1940, 13/12/1940, Derby Local Studies Library. On sock knitting: *Derby Evening Telegraph*, 4/6/1940; 1/1/1940.

17   Rebecca Gill, 'Networks of Concern, Boundaries of Compassion: British Relief in the South African War', *The Journal of Imperial and Commonwealth History*, 40 (2012), 827-844, p. 828; Richard Rutt, *A History of Hand-knitting*

(London: B. T. Batsford, 1987), pp. 139-140. For discussion of knitting 'parties' in the House of Lords, 3 August 1943, *Hansard*, Vol. 128, Fifth Series, cc 958. https://api.parliament.uk/historic-hansard/lords/1943/aug/03/merchant-navy-comforts#column_958

18 CSV Action Desk/BBC Radio Lincolnshire, 'If You Can Knit – You Can Do Your Bit', *WW2 Peoples' War: An Archive of WW2 Memories – Written by the Public, Gathered by the BBC* (October, 2005) https://www.bbc.co.uk/history/ww2peopleswar/ 'on the shelf', see single women stories/26/a6041026.shtml

19 On knitting as a comfort for women, see: Hinton, *Women, Social Leadership and the Second World War*, p. 62; on male knitters: see, for example, images on blogs such as *Knitting for Victory*, http://elinorflorence.com/blog/wartime-knitting and Anika Burgess, 'The Wool Brigades of World War I', *Atlas Obsura*, 26 July 2017, https://www.atlasobscura.com/articles/when-knitting-was-a-patriotic-duty-wwi-homefront-wool-brigades; for Cary Grant: Kristin Devine, 'Knitting in WWII: A Photoessay', 29 March 2020, https://ordinary-times.com/2020/03/29/knitting-in-wwii-a-photoessay/

20 Hinda Mandell, *Crafting Dissent: Handicraft as Protest from the American Revolution to the Pussyhats* (London: Rowman and Littlefield, 2019), p. 2; Natalie Zarrelli, 'The Wartime Spies Who Used Knitting as an Espionage Tool', *Atlas Obscura*, 16 March 2022, https://www.atlasobscura.com/articles/knitting-spies-wwi-wwii

21 Keith Strange, 'Cardiff Schools and the Age of the Second World War. The Log Books: A Documentary History', https://www.scribd.com/document/2589099/Cardiff-schools-and-the-age-of-the-Second-World-War. See entries for 13/3/1941; 1/5/1942; 20/7/1942; 2/10/1942; 12/11/1942; 13/9/1943; 19/1/1944; 31/5/1944.

22 Joan Bakewell, *All the Nice Girls* (London: Virago, 2010), p. 5; Edith Wilshaw, 'Adopting ships', BBC Peoples' War, July 2005: https://www.bbc.co.uk/history/ww2peopleswar/stories/04/a4430404.shtml

23 Interview with Mary Belton, 22 June 2011.

24 See Hinton, *Women, Social Leadership and the Second World War*, p. 78. The phrase 'a poke in the eye' is taken from the film *Housewife, 49* (Gavin Millar, 2006), starring (and written by) Victoria Wood and based on Nella Last's diaries.

25 *Woman's Own*, 10/2/1940, p. 18.

5. Jim Gilbert, Royal Navy Stoker

1   The details of Jim's career come from his early letters to Norah, discussed in later chapters. The description of Portsmouth is based on W. J. Stonebridge, 'Memories of a Young Stoker, Part 3', *BBC WW2 Peoples' War* (August 2005), https://www.bbc.co.uk/history/ww2peopleswar/stories/27/a3509327. shtml The rest of this chapter is developed from: ADM 199/184 HMS Niger Minesweeping Reports Oct 1940 (Extracts), http://www.halcyon-class.co.uk/niger/sweep_reports_oct_40.htm; letter from J. J. Youngs to Jack Neale, 20 November 1974 (IWM 92/50/1); Correspondence to Capt J. J. Youngs (IWM 92/50/1); Papers of Lt Commander J. K. Neale DSC RNVR, IWM 2130 92/50/1; Raymond Card, IWM Oral History 10240; and especially, Paul Lund and Harry Ludlam, *Out Sweeps! The Story of the Minesweepers in WWII* (London: W. Foulsham and Co., 1978). The 4th minesweeping flotilla, images of the bullets bouncing off bombs, the sight of the *Simon Bolivar*, the Italian planes as grand pianos and accounts of life aboard a minesweeper, are all from Lund and Ludlam, *Out Sweeps!*, pp. 18-21, 26, 29, 48, 56, 65-69. For Royal Navy life, see Christopher McKee, *Sober Men and True: Sailor Lives in the Royal Navy, 1940-1945* (Cambridge: Harvard University Press, 2002); Glynn Prysor, *Citizen Sailors: The Royal Navy and the Second World War* (Harmondsworth: Penguin, 2012).

6. Dearest Dimples

1   Steven Banks, *The Handicrafts of the Sailor* (London: David & Charles, Ltd., 1974).

2   Calder, *The People's War*, pp. 231-232; Don Kindell, 'British and Other Navies in WWII, Day by Day', http://www.naval-history.net/xDKWW2-4104-31APR02.htm

3   On diary time and parataxis, see Judy Nolte Lensink, 'Expanding the Boundaries of Criticism: The Diary as Female Autobiography', *Women's Studies* 14 (1987), 39-53, p. 42; Hogan, 'Engendered Autobiographies', p. 103.

4   Leonora Eyles, *Woman's Own*, 3/2/1940, p. 36; Sandra Koa Wing, *Our Longest Days: A People's History of the Second World War* (London: Profile Books, 2008), p. 30.

5   Margaret Forster, *Diary of an Ordinary Woman* (London: Vintage, 2003), p. 254.

6   On love and romance in the 1920s, see: Sally Alexander, 'Becoming a Woman in London in the 1920s and 1930s', in D. Feldman and G. S. Jones (eds), *Metropolis – London: Histories and Representations since 1800* (London: Routledge, 1989) pp. 245-271; Penny Tinkler, *Constructing Girlhood: Popular Magazines for Girls Growing Up in England 1920-1950* (London: Taylor and Francis, 1995); Penny Tinkler, '"A Material Girl": Adolescent Girls and their Magazines, 1920-1958', in Mary Talbot and Maggie Morgan (eds), *All the World and Her Husband in Twentieth Century Consumer Culture* (London: Cassell, 2000); Penny Tinkler, 'Miss Modern: Youthful Feminine Modernity and the Nascent Teenager, 1930-40', in C. Clay, M. DiCenzo, B. Green and F. Hackney (eds), *Women's Periodicals and Print Culture in Britain, 1918-1939: The Interwar Period* (Edinburgh: Edinburgh University Press, 2018), 153-169; Judy Giles, *The Parlour and the Suburb* (Oxford: Berg, 2004); Adrian Bingham, *Gender, Modernity, and the Popular Press in Inter-War Britain* (Oxford: Oxford University Press, 2004); Birgitte Søland, *Becoming Modern: Young Women and the Reconstruction of Womanhood in the 1920s* (Princeton: Princeton University Press, 2000); Alys Eve Wienbaum et al, *The Modern Girl Around the World: Consumption, Modernity, and Globalization* (Durham, North Carolina: Duke University Press, 2008); Langhamer, *Women's Leisure*; Claire Langhamer, *The English in Love: The Intimate Story of an Emotional Revolution* (Oxford: Oxford University Press, 2013); Carol Dyhouse, *Glamour: Women, History, Feminism* (London: Zed Books, 2010); Carol Dyhouse, *Heartthrobs: A History of Women and Desire* (Oxford: Oxford University Press, 2017); Eva Illouz, *Consuming the Romantic Utopia: Love and the Cultural Contradictions of Capitalism* (Berkeley: University of California Press, 1997).

7   Simon May, *Love: A History* (New Haven and London: Yale University Press, 2012), p. 1.

8   J. B. Priestley, *English Journey* (Harmondsworth: Penguin, 1985 [1934]), p. 375; George Orwell, *The Road to Wigan Pier* (Harmondsworth: Penguin Modern Classics, 2001 [1937]), pp. 80-81.

9   For Deanna Durbin and the bolero, see Stacey, *Star Gazing*, pp. 200-201, 215.

10 Henry Durant, cited in Penny Tinkler, 'Cause for Concern: Young Women and Leisure, 1930-50', *Women's History Review*, 12:2 (2003), 233-262, pp. 245-246; Pearl Jephcott, *Girls Growing Up: A Study of the Lives of Some Working Girls* (London: Faber and Faber, 1942), p. 110.

11 On young women being tasked with keeping up men's morale, see: Goodman, *Women, Sexuality and War*, pp. 101-155; advertisements: *Woman's Own*, 18/6/1943, 10/2/10, 9/3/40, 10/11/1940; *Picture Post*, December 1939,

p. 66; on make-up/wartime controls: Antonia Lant, 'Prologue: Mobile Femininity', in Christine Gledhill and Gloria Swanson (eds), *Nationalising Femininity: Culture, Sexuality and British Cinema in the Second World War* (Manchester: Manchester University Press, 1996), pp. 13-32, p. 24.

12   Joshua Goldstein, *War and Gender: How Gender Shapes the War System and Vice Versa* (Cambridge: Cambridge University Press, 2001), p. 334; James Chapman, *British Comics: A Cultural History* (London: Reaktion Books, 2011), pp. 40-43; Goodman, *Women, Sexuality and War*, pp. 111-113.

13   On Norah's diaries and expressions of emotion, see: Alison Twells, '"Went into Raptures': Reading Emotion in the Ordinary Wartime Diary, 1941-1946', *Women's History Review*, 25:1 (2016), 143-160. For 'emotional communities' giving shape to expressions of emotion, see Barbara Rosenwein, 'Worrying About Emotions in History', *The American Historical Review*, 107:3 (2002), 821-845.

7. I Believe You and I Have a Few Things in Common

1   Arthur Ford and Bill Batters, quoted in McKee, *Sober Men and True*, pp. 33, 178. See also Alan Allport, *Browned Off and Bloody-Minded: The British Soldier Goes to War 1939-1945* (Yale University Press, 2015); Luke Turner, *Men at War: Loving, Lusting, Fighting, Remembering, 1939-1995* (London: Weidenfeld and Nicolson, 2023).

2   Dennis Maxted, Imperial War Museum, Oral History 18200, recorder Conrad Wood, 1/2/1999, Reel 1.

3   For letters shaped by social context, see Martin Lyons, 'New Directions in the History of Written Culture', *Culture and History*, 1 (2012), http://cultureandhistory.revistas.csic.es/index.php/cultureandhistory/article/view/8/71; the ditty box: thanks to Chris Hopkins for this insight.

4   Letters to Mollie Baker: Private Papers of Mrs M. Baker, Documents 570, 88/42/1: Bill Stewart to Mollie Baker, 27/8/1940; undated (August 1940), 12/12/1940, 25 April 1945. Sam Gibbs to Mollie Baker, 8/9/1940, 18/10/1940, 24/10/1940, 13/12/1940, 19/12/1940, 12/2/1941, 25/2/1941, 4/4/1941, 18/10/1940, 29/10/1941. NB: As with Jim, I have not used [sic] to denote the many grammatical errors in Stewart's and Gibbs' writing, as to do so feels unnecessary and disrupts the flow of their prose. ATS: Auxiliary Territorial Service.

5   'B knitters' is a play on 'knitting bee' and a reference to Stewart's playful use of the phrase the 'Blessed Knitters'. Bill Stewart to Mollie Baker, above.

6   Private Papers of Miss D. Dockrill, Documents 19147, 16/32/1, Imperial War Museum Archive: H[erbert] R[onald] Cotter, 208 A/T Battery RA, in Co. Tyrone, N. Ireland, 2/1/1942; W.C. Brown, RACS MEF, 31/5/44; Eric Bowring, env dated 10/8/1943; S. E. Ridge, 8/2/1943; Peter O'Dwyer, 26/12/1943; P. R. Hunt, 6/11/1944, 11/11/1944. A letter from A.E. Duffin reveals that Doris has discussed his letters with her father, env dated 9/10/1941.

7   See Michael Roper, *The Secret Battle: Emotional Survival in the Great War* (Manchester: Manchester University Press, 2009); Jessica Meyer, *Men of War: Masculinity and the First World War in Britain* (Basingstoke: Palgrave, 2009), pp. 2, 44-45; Carol Acton, '"You Yourself Are Here Now Looking Over My Shoulder as I Write": Emotional Dialogue and the Construction of a Shared Intimate Space in First World War Letters', *L'Atelier*, 8:1 (2016), 194-219; Martha Hanna, 'War Letters: Communication Between Front and Home Front', *International Encyclopedia of the First World War* (2014), 1-22, https://encyclopedia.1914-1918-online.net/pdf/1914-1918-Online-war_letters_communication_between_front_and_home_front-2014-10-08.pdf; Jenny Hartley, 'Letters Are Everything: Mothers and Letters in the Second World War', in Rebecca Earle (ed.), *Epistolary Selves: Letters and Letter-writers, 1600-1945* (Aldershot: Ashgate, 1999), pp. 183-195.

8   On romantic letters, see Alison Twells, 'Sex, Gender, and Romantic Intimacy in Servicemen's Letters during the Second World War', *The Historical Journal*, 63:3 (2020), 1-22; Janet Altman, *Epistolarity: Approaches to a Form* (Columbus, OH: Ohio State University, 1982), pp. 87-116. For imaginary selves, see Margaretta Jolly, *In Love and Struggle: Letters in Contemporary Feminism* (New York: Columbia University Press, 2008), pp. 6–8, 25.

9   Peter Hunt to Doris Dockrill, 11/11/1944, 10/12/1944.

8. Where Is That Photo? A Summer of Snaps and Studio Portraits

1   Martin Francis, *The Flyer: British Culture and the Royal Air Force, 1939-1945* (Oxford: Oxford University Press, 2008), pp. 14, 20, 25.

2   Joan Wyndham, *Love Lessons: A Wartime Diary* (London: Heinemann, 1985); Nevil Shute quoted in Francis, *The Flyer*, p. 25.

3   For family photography, see: Jo Spence and Patricia Holland (eds), *Family Snaps: The Meanings of Domestic Photography* (London: Virago, 1991).

4   Penny Tinkler, 'Researching Girlhood using Photo-elicitation', SAGE Research Methods Video (2017), https://methods.sagepub.com/video/researching-girlhood-using-photo-elicitation

5   See Pat Kirkham, 'Fashioning the Feminine: Dress, Appearance, and Femininity in Wartime Britain', in Gledhill and Swanson, *Nationalising Femininity*, pp. 152-174; Julie Summers, *Fashion on the Ration: Style in the Second World War* (London: Profile Books, 2015).

6   Penny Tinkler, *Using Photographs in Social and Historical Research* (London: Sage, 2013), p. 12; Pat Holland, '"Sweet it is to scan ...": Personal Photographs and Popular Photography', in Liz Wells (ed.), *Photography: A Critical Introduction* (London: Routledge, 2000), pp. 115–158, 119.

7   Roland Barthes, *Camera Lucida* (London: Vintage, 2000 [1980]), pp. 16, 42.

8   Annette Kuhn, *Family Secrets: Acts of Memory and Imagination* (London: Verso, 1995); Mette Sandbye, 'Looking at the Family Photo Album: A Resumed Theoretical Discussion of Why and How', *Journal of Aesthetics & Culture*, 6:1 (2014).

9. I'm in Love with Him and I Don't Care a Scrap

1   The Bible, King James Version, Hebrews 13:2.

10. The Erotics of War

1   Pearl Jephcott, *Rising Twenty: Notes on Some Ordinary Girls* (London: Faber and Faber, 1948), p. 68.

2   Interview with Kath Jones, 28 October 2011. For soldiers in Donington, see Hetty Carr, in Carswell (ed.), *At Home and Away*.

3   John R. Gillis, *For Better, For Worse: British Marriages 1600 to the present* (Oxford: Oxford University Press, 1986), p. 294.

4   Penny Summerfield, *Reconstructing Women's Wartime Lives* (Manchester: Manchester University Press, 1998), pp. 15, 24, 179, 285. And of course I have no idea how our acquaintance shaped Kath's responses.

5   See, for example, Kate Fisher, *Birth Control, Sex and Marriage in Britain 1918-60* (Oxford: Oxford University Press, 2006).

6   An exception is Gail Braybon and Penny Summerfield, *Out of the Cage: Women's Experiences in Two World Wars* (London: Pandora, 1987), pp. 205, 209.

7   See https://www.cwgc.org/find-records/find-war-dead/casualty-details/2054274/robert-evans/

8   Letters to John Davison from Bob Evans. Lent to me by John's daughter, my second cousin.

9   Mary Wesley, Toronto Globe and Mail, 9 May 1995, cited by Patrick Marnham, 'Siepmann [née Farmar], Mary Aline [other married name Mary Aline Eady, Lady Swinfen; pseud. Mary Wesley]', *ODNB*, 5 March 2009.

11. Poor Jim?

1   Jane Lewis, 'Women Clerical Workers in the Late Nineteenth and Early Twentieth Centuries', in Gerry Anderson, *The White-Blouse Revolution: Female Office Workers Since 1870* (Manchester: Manchester University Press, 1988), p. 34.

2   Illouz, *Consuming the Romantic Utopia*, p. 286; and Eva Illouz, *Why Love Hurts: A Sociological Explanation* (Cambridge: Polity, 2014), p. 120.

3   Adrian Bingham, '"It would be better for the newspapers to call a spade a spade": The British Press and Child Sexual Abuse, c. 1918-1990', *History Workshop Journal*, 88 (2019), 89-110; Louise Jackson, 'Child Sexual Abuse in England and Wales: Prosecution and Prevalence 1918-1970', *History & Policy* (2015), http://www.historyandpolicy.org/policy-papers/papers/child-sexual-abuse-in-england-and-wales-prosecution-and-prevalence-1918-197. See also Carol Smart, 'A History of Ambivalence and Conflict in the Discursive Construction of "the Child Victim" of Sexual Abuse', *Social & Legal Studies*, 8:3 (1998), 391-409; Carol Smart, 'Reconsidering the Recent History of Child Sexual Abuse, 1910-1960', *Journal of Social Policy*, 29:1 (2000), 55-71.

4   Bingham, '"It would be better..."'; Lucy Delap, 'Child Welfare, Child Protection and Sexual Abuse, 1918-1990', *History & Policy* (2015), p. 2, http://www.historyandpolicy.org/policy-papers/papers/child-welfare-child-protection-and-sexual-abuse-1918-1990.

5   Penny Summerfield and Nicole Crockett, '"You weren't taught that with the welding": Lessons in Sexuality in the Second World War', *Women's History Review*, 1:3 (1992), 435-454, pp. 436-438.

6   Summerfield, *Reconstructing Women's Wartime Lives*, pp. 137-138, 145-148, 272-273; Braybon and Summerfield, *Out of the Cage*, pp. 205-210; Goodman, *Women, Sexuality and War*, pp. 93-94; Jo Stanley, naval historian, personal conversation (2016); Joyce Grenfell in Patrick Deer, *Culture in Camouflage: War, Empire and Modern British Literature* (Oxford: Oxford University Press, 2009), pp. 121-122; Zelda Katin, *Clippie: The Autobiography of a Wartime Conductress* (London: Adam Gordon, 1995 [1944]), pp. 65-66, 89, 60.

7   Dorothy Williams, in Peniston-Bird and Summerfield, *Contesting Home Defence*, pp. 264-265.

12. Went over Daleacre: The Likely and the Plausible

1   Mollie Panter Downes, *London Notes, 1939-1945* (London: Longman 1972), p. 210; Calder, *The People's War*, pp. 298-302, 285-287.

2   On rationing, see Calder, *The People's War*, pp. 275-77, Todman, *Britain's War*, pp. 270-272.

3   Simon Cooke, 'Review of Hallie Rubenhold's *The Five*', *The Victorian Web*, 18 May 2019, https://victorianweb.org/history/crime/rubenhold.html

4   James Buchan, 'Search for a Legend: James Buchan Struggles to Find the Facts amid the Speculation of Natalie Zemon Davis's biography of Leo Africanus, Trickster Travels', *The Guardian*, 13 January 2007.

5   Jonathan P. Berkey, 'Featured Review: Life of an Unknown', *American Historical Review*, 112:2 (2007), 459-461.

6   Hannu Salmi, 'Cultural History, the Possible, and the Principle of Plenitude', *History and Theory*, 50:2 (2011), 171-187, pp. 187, 185, 182.

7   Frank Ankersmit quoted in Aaron Sachs, 'Letters to a Tenured Historian: History as Creative Nonfiction—Or Maybe Even Poetry', in Sachs and Demos, *Artful History*, pp. 115-131, 121.

8   Davis, *The Return of Martin Guerre*, p. 4.

9   Doreen Massey, 'Places and Their Pasts', *History Workshop Journal*, 39:1 (1995), 182-192, pp. 185-187.

10 J. Lee and T. Ingold, 'Fieldwork on Foot: Perceiving, Routing, Socializing', in S. Coleman and P. Collins (eds), *Locating the Field: Space, Place and Context in Anthropology* (Oxford: Berg, 2006), 67-86; Maggie O'Neill and Brian Roberts, *Walking Methods: Research on the Move* (London: Routledge,

2019); Richard Holmes, *Footsteps: Adventures of a Romantic Biographer* (London: Harper Perennial, 1985), p. 27.

11   Elena Ferrante, *The Story of a New Name*, trans. Ann Goldstein (New York: Europa Editions, 2015 [2012]), p. 291; Lynne Sharon Schwartz, *Leaving Brooklyn* (London: Orion, 1988), p. 74.

13. If You Love Danny He Is Yours

1   On the 'exceptional normal', see Chapter 2. For 'representativeness', see Penny Summerfield, *Histories of the Self* (London: Routledge, 2019), chapter six.

2   On 'making love': 'I here define it as including all of the normal activities of lovers towards one another short of what would provoke interference from a not excessively zealous policeman'. Mass-Observation Archive, 'Love-making in public', p. 1, quoted in Langhamer, 'Love and Courtship', p. 192.

14. Glorious Letters from My Sweetheart

1   On WJACs, see Penny Tinkler, 'At Your Service: The Nation's Girlhood and the Call to Service in England, 1939-1950', *European Journal of Women's Studies*, 4 (1997), 353-377.

2   Daisy Warren in Carswell (ed.), *At Home and Away*, pp. 21-22.

3   Dorothy Parker, 'The Lovely Leave' (1943), cited in Mackay, *Half the Battle*, p. 98. For stoicism and emotional restraint, see Lucy Noakes, 'Gender, Grief, and Bereavement in Second World War Britain', *Journal of War and Culture Studies*, 8:1 (2015), 72-85.

4   For conventions of letters and love letters, see Martin Lyons, 'Love Letters and Writing Practices: On Ecritures Intimes in the Nineteenth Century', *Journal of Family History*, 24 (1999), 232-239.

5   Lake, 'Female Desires', p. 368.

6   Helen Fisher et al., 'Intense, Passionate, Romantic Love: A Natural Addiction? How the Fields that Investigate Romance and Substance Abuse Can Inform Each Other', *Frontiers in Psychology*, 7:687 (2016); Sarah Pinto, 'Researching Romantic Love', *Rethinking History*, 21:4 (2017), 567-585.

7   Illouz, *Consuming the Romantic Utopia*, pp. 2, 16, 66; Langhamer, *The English in Love*, pp. 4, 11.

8   For feminist critiques, see: Stevi Jackson, *Heterosexuality in Question* (London: Sage, 1999), p. 96; Wendy Langford, *Revolutions of the Heart: Gender, Power and the Delusions of Love* (London: Routledge, 1999). For romance as transformative, see: Mary Evans, *Love: An Unromantic Discussion* (Cambridge: Blackwell, 2003), p. 40; Langhamer, *English in Love*, p. 38. See also Anthony Giddens, *The Transformation of Intimacy: Sexuality, Love and Eroticism in Modern Societies* (Stanford: Stanford University Press, 1992), p. 38.

15. Danny Told Me a Thing or Two

1   William Acton, *The Functions and Disorders of the Reproductive Organs, in Childhood, Youth, Adult Age, and Advanced Life, Considered in Their Physiological, Social, and Moral Relations* (London: J and A Churchill, 1875), pp. 212-214.

2   Elizabeth Blackwell, 'On the Abuses of Sex – II. Fornication', *Essays in Medical Sociology*, Vol. I (London: Ernest Bell, 1902), pp. 44-49.

3   Szreter and Fisher, *Sex Before the Sexual Revolution*, p. 322.

4   Eliot Slater and Moya Woodside, *Patterns of Marriage: A Study of the Marriage Relationships of the Urban Working Classes* (London: Cassell, 1951), p. 176; Moya Woodside, 'Health and Happiness in Marriage', *Health Education Journal* (1946), p. 148.

5   Lesley Hall, '"The wo that is in marriage": Abstinence in Practice and Principle in British Marriages, 1890-1940', in Kaat Wils, Leen van Molle and Evert Peeters (eds), *Beyond Pleasure: Cultures of Modern Asceticism* (London: Berghahn, 2011); Maureen Sutton, *We Didn't Know Aught: A Study of Sexuality, Superstition and Death in Women's Lives in Lincolnshire during the 1930s, '40s and '50s* (Stamford: Paul Watkins, 1992); Alexander, 'The Mysteries and Secrets of Women's Bodies'; Kate Fisher, '"She was quite satisfied with the arrangements I made": Gender and Birth Control in Britain 1920-1950', *Past and Present*, 169 (2001), 161-193; Steve Humphries, *A Secret World of Sex: Forbidden Fruit: The British Experience* (London: Sidgwick & Jackson, 1988), p. 94; Szreter and Fisher, *Sex Before the Sexual Revolution*, p. 123.

6   Lucinda McCray Beier, '"We were green as grass": Learning about Sex and Reproduction in Three Working-class Lancashire Communities, 1900-1970', *Social History of Medicine*, 16:3 (2003), 461-480; Humphries, *A Secret*

World of Sex, p. 106; Richard Hoggart, cited in Szreter and Fisher, *Sex Before the Sexual Revolution*, p. 82.

7   Hera Cook, *The Long Sexual Revolution: English Women, Sex and Contraception, 1800-1975* (Oxford: Oxford University Press, 2004); Tinkler, *Constructing Girlhood*, p. 166.

8   Alexander, 'The Mysteries and Secrets'; Roberts, *A Woman's Place*, pp. 15-16; Angela Davis, '"Oh no, nothing, we didn't learn anything": Sex Education and the Preparation of Girls for Motherhood, c.1930-70', *History of Education*, 37 (2008), 661-677, p. 671; Hera Cook, 'Getting "foolishly hot and bothered"? Parents and Teachers and Sex Education in the 1940s', *Sex Education*, 12:5 (2012), 555-567, pp. 557-558.

9   Szreter and Fisher, *Sex Before the Sexual Revolution*, p. 133; Penny Tinkler, *Constructing Girlhood*, pp. 137-142.

10   *Woman's Own*, 20/4/1945, p. 18; Mass Observation Archive Topic Collection 32 and *Woman's Own*, 6/1/1940, p. 3, cited in Langhamer, *The English in Love*, pp. 46, 42-43.

11   Rosita Forbes, 'Be a Success', *Woman's Own*, 27/1/1940, p. 15; *Woman's Own*, 11/9/1942, p. 18. See also Leonore Eyles, *Woman's Own*, 28/1/1943, p. 22.

12   Eustace Chesser, *The Sexual, Marital and Family Relationships of the English Woman* (London: Hutchinson's Medical Publications, 1956), pp. 311-316; Irene Clephane, *Towards Sex Freedom* (London: John Lane, 1935); Szreter and Fisher, *Sex Before the Sexual Revolution*, pp. 116, 146; Cook, *The Long Sexual Revolution*, pp. 105, 212-219, 230-231, 59-60, 321.

13   Mary Wesley, *The Camomile Lawn* (London: Macmillan, 1984), p. 244; Elizabeth Bowen, postscript to *The Demon Lover* (1945), in Hermione Lee (ed.), *The Mulberry Tree: Writings of Elizabeth Bowen* (London: Virago, 1986), pp. 94-99, 95; Elizabeth Bowen, *The Heat of the Day* (London: Vintage, 1998 [1948]), p. 172; Henry Green, *Caught* [1943], in Lara Feigel, *Love Charm of Bombs: Restless Lives in the Second World War* (London: Bloomsbury, 2014), p. 85.

14   Katherine Angel, *Unmastered: A Book on Desire, Most Difficult to Tell* (London: Penguin, 2012).

15   Lillian Rogers in Hinton, *Nine Wartime Lives*, p. 118; Pratt, *A Notable Woman*, pp. 237-238, 289-90, 327; Malcolmson (ed.), *The Mass Observation Wartime Diary of Olivia Cockett*, pp. 117, 206.

16 Bates, *Diary of a Wartime Affair*, pp. 8, 24, 47, 244.

17 William Reddy, 'Historical Research and the Self and Emotions', *Emotion Review*, 1:4 (2009), 302-315, p. 310. Reddy's comment is about mid-century America, but the same is true for Britain.

18 Marion Paul, in Summerfield, *Reconstructing Women's Wartime Lives*, p. 175.

16. Unconditional Surrender?

1 Roald Dahl, 'Death of an Old Man', cited in Francis, *The Flyer*, p. 111; Joan Wyndham, *Love Lessons*; and *Love is Blue: A Wartime Diary* (London: Flamingo, 1987).

17. Please God ... Waiting for Danny

1 Interview with Kath Jones.

2 Cited in Lucy Noakes, *War and the British: Gender and National Identity, 1939-1941* (Cambridge: Cambridge University Press, 1998), p. 69.

3 On superstition and magical thinking, see Vanessa Ann Chambers, 'Fighting Chance: Popular Belief and British Society, 1900-1951' (PhD dissertation: University of London, 2007), pp. 62-87, 246, 293.

4 André Gerolymatos, *The British and the Greek Resistance, 1936-1944: Spies, Saboteurs, and Partisans* (Washington, DC: Lexington Books, 2018).

5 Ben Wadham, 'Mogan Hunts and Pig Nights: Military Masculinities and the Making of the Arms-Corp Soldier', *TASA Conference Proceedings: Revisioning Institutions* (2004), 13; Wadham, 'Brotherhood: Homosociality, Totality and Military Subjectivity', *Australian Feminist Studies*, 28:76 (2013), 212-235.

6 See for example, Victoria Lindrea, 'Head of the Royal Navy Defends Handling of Rape Allegations', *BBC News*, 27 November 2022, https://www.bbc.co.uk/news/uk-63770307; Karl Mercer and Raphael Sheridan, 'London Fire Brigade Institutionally Misogynist and Racist – Report', *BBC News*, 26 November 2022, https://www.bbc.co.uk/news/uk-england-london-63749444; 'Newspaper Headlines: "Monster of the Met" and "Slapdown for Sturgeon"', *BBC News*, 17 January 2023, https://www.bbc.co.uk/news/blogs-the-papers-64299275

7 Langhamer, *The English in Love*, p. 102.

8   George Ryley Scott, *Sex Problems and Dangers in Wartime* (1940), quoted in Luke Turner, *Men at War*, p. 181.

18. Danny

1   Panter Downes, *London Notes*, p. 266

2   Mary Kathryn Barbier, *D-Day Deception: Operation Fortitude and the Normandy Invasion* (Westport: Praeger Security International, 2007).

3   Partridge, *A Pacifist's War*, pp. 211-212.

4   Sometimes the phrase used is 'give way'. See Humphries, *A Secret World of Sex*, p. 70.

5   H. E. Bates, *Fair Stood the Wind for France* (Harmondsworth: Penguin, 1980 [1944]), pp. 163, 158; Jess, 8 August 2019, *Goodreads*, https://www.goodreads.com/book/show/2143538.

6   Katherine Angel, *Tomorrow Sex Will Be Good Again: Women and Desire in an Age of Affirmative Consent* (London: Verso, 2021), p. 5.

7   Elizabeth Howard, *Slipstream: A Memoir* (Basingstoke: Macmillan, 2002), p. 101.

8   Littauer, *Bad Girls*, p. 44.

9   Francis, *The Flyer*, p. 63. General Patton and other prominent (US) generals saw 'fucking and fighting as complementary activities'. See Susan Carruthers, *Dear John: Love and Loyalty in Wartime America* (Cambridge: Cambridge University Press, 2022), p. 40.

10 Nesta H. Wells, 'Sexual Offences as Seen by a Woman Police Surgeon', *British Medical Journal*, 8 (1958), 1404-1408, pp. 1406-1407.

11 Private conversation.

12 Angel, *Tomorrow Sex Will Be Good Again*, chapter one; Bingham, *Family Newspapers? Sex, Private Life and the British Popular Press, 1918-1978* (Oxford: OUP, 2009), pp. 180-181.

13 *Woman's Own*, 20/4/1945, p. 9; 4/5/1945, p. 5; Julie Summers, *Stranger in the House: Women's Stories of Men Returning from the Second World War* (London: Simon & Schuster, 2009).

19. Our Night of Love

1. Cited in Laura Bissell, 'My Diary Diary', *Life Writing*, 22:1 (2023), 1–25.

2. Annie Ernaux, *A Girls' Story*, trns Alison L. Strayer (London: Fitzcarraldo Editions, 2020), p. 28.

3. Jennifer Sinor, *Ordinary Trauma: A Memoir* (Salt Lake City, Utah: University of Utah Press, 2017).

4. Shirely Jordan, 'Overstepping the Boundaries: Sexual Awakening, Trauma, and Writing in Annie Ernaux's *Mémoire de Fille* and Christine Angot's *Une Semaine de Vacances*', *Esprit Créateur*, 59:3 (2019), 5-18, p. 7.

21. Son of Danny

1. Thomas Couser, *Vulnerable Subjects: Ethics and Life Writing* (Ithaca and London: Cornell University Press, 2018) p. 201.

2. Kuhn, *Family Secrets*, p. 2.

3. Carolyn Ellis, 'Telling Secrets, Revealing Lives: Relational Ethics in Research with Intimate Others', *Qualitative Inquiry*, 13:1 (2007), p. 4; Lesley Neale, 'The Ethics and Intentionality of Writing Family', *Vitae Scholasticae* (2017), 110-126.

22. Men's Regrets

1. Twells, 'Sex, Gender, and Romantic Intimacy'; Rose, *Which People's War*, p. 196.

2. Joanna Bourke, 'Unwanted Intimacy: Violent Sexual Transfers in British and American Societies 1870s to 1970s', *European Journal of English Studies*, 9:3 (2005), 287-300; Herzog (ed.), *Brutality and Desire*, pp. 4-5; Joanna Bourke, *Rape: A History from 1860 to the Present* (London: Virago, 2007), pp. 376-378, 366. For wartime sexual violence, see: Raphaëlle Branche and Fabrice Virgili (eds), *Rape in Wartime* (Basingstoke: Palgrave, 2012); Bourke, *Rape: A History*, pp. 368-369; Joanna Bourke, 'Wartime Rape: the Politics of Making Visible', in Andrew Knapp and Hilary Footit (eds), *Liberal Democracies at War: Conflict and Representation* (London: Bloomsbury, 2013), pp. 135-156; Cynthia Cockburn, 'Why Are You Doing This to Me? Identity, Power and Sexual Violence in War', in Anna G. Jonasdottir, Valerie Bryson and Kathleen B. Jones (eds), *Sexuality, Gender and Power: Intersectional and Transnational Perspectives* (London: Routledge, 2012), pp. 189-204; John

Costello, *Love, Sex and War: Changing Values, 1939-1945* (London: Harper Collins, 1985), pp. 140-146; Goldstein, *War and Gender*, pp. 362-371, 365; Mary Louise Roberts, *What Soldiers Do: Sex and the American GI in World War II France* (Chicago and London: University of Chicago Press, 2013); J. R. Lilly, *Taken by Force. Rape and American GIs in Europe During World War II* (Basingstoke: Palgrave Macmillan, 2007); Elissa Mailänder, 'Making Sense of a Rape Photograph: Sexual Violence as Social Performance on the Eastern Front, 1939-1944', *Journal of the History of Sexuality*, 26 (2017), 489-520; Regina Mulhauser, 'Reframing Sexual Violence as a Weapon and Strategy of War: The Case of German Wermacht during the War and Genocide in the Soviet Union, 1941-1944', *Journal of the History of Sexuality*, 26 (2017), 366-401; Andrea Pető, 'Memory and the Narrative of Rape in Budapest and Vienna', in Richard Bessell and Dirk Schumann (eds), *Life after Death: Approaches to a Cultural and Social History of Europe during the 1940s and 1950s* (Cambridge: Cambridge University Press, 2003), pp. 129-148; Andrea Pető, 'The New Monument of Victims of Military Sexual Violence in Budapest', *Hungarian Studies Review*, 48:2 (2021), 209-216.

3   Pierre Nora, *Les Lieux de Mémoire* (Paris: Gallimard, 1984); Noakes and Pattinson, *British Cultural Memory and the Second World War*; Mark Connelly, *We Can Take It! Britain and the Memory of the Second World War* (Harlow: Pearson, 2004); Penny Summerfield, 'Film and the Popular Memory of the Second World War in Britain, 1950-1959', in P. Levine and S. Grayzel (eds), *Gender, Labour, War and Empire: Essays on Modern Britain* (Houndmills: Palgrave, 2009).

4   Turner, *Men at War*, pp. 10-15.

23. Still Part of Me

1   Philip Hensher, 'Smoother than Velvet: Sarah Waters Leaves Behind the Intimate Tricks and Turns of Victorian Life for a Simply Truthful Study of Wartime Alienation', *The Observer*, 8 January 2006.

2   Victoria Stewart, 'The Second World War in Contemporary Women's Fiction: Revisiting the Home Front', *Contemporary Women's Writing*, 9:3 (2015), 416-432, p. 429; Sarah Waters, *The Night Watch* (London: Virago, 2006), pp. 6, 100, 106, 108.

3   See Judy Giles, 'A Home of One's Own: Women and Domesticity in England, 1918-1950', *Women's Studies International Forum*, 16 (1993), 239-253.

4   Laurel Richardson, *Fields of Play: Constructing an Academic Life* (Brunswick: Rutgers University Press, 1997), p. 225; Ferdynand Zweig, *Women's Life and Labour* (London: Victor Gollancz, 1952), p. 122.

5   Langhamer, 'Love and Courtship', p 178; Pat Thane, 'Family Life and "Normality" in Post-war British Culture', in Bessel and Schumann, *Life after Death*, p. 198; Lorna Sage, *Bad Blood* (London: Fourth Estate, 2001), p. 89.

6   On being shunned, see Claire Langhamer, 'Adultery in Postwar England', *History Workshop Journal*, 62:1 (2006), 86-115, p. 104. For surveys: Simon Duncan, 'The World We Have Made? Individualisation and Personal Life in the 1950s', *The Sociological Review*, 59:2 (2011), 242-265, pp. 257, 252.

7   This paragraph is based on Langhamer, 'Adultery in Postwar England', p. 104.

8   Dyhouse, *Glamour*, pp. 43-45, 72-73, 29, 75, 90, 93.

9   Jill Tweedie cited in Carol Dyhouse, 'Was There Ever a Time when Girls Weren't in Trouble?', *Women's History Review*, 23:2 (2014), 272-274, p. 272.

10 Katherine Holden, '"Nature takes no notice of morality": Singleness and Married Love in Interwar Britain', *Women's History Review*, 11:3 (2002), 481-504, p. 485; *Woman's Own* letters page, 14/1/44, p. 22.

11 The International Friendship League was set up in 1931 with the lofty ideal of encouraging world peace through friendship: https://iflworld.org/history-of-ifl/

12 Interview with Dinah Cook, 4 July 2013.

13 Langhamer, 'Adultery in Postwar England', p. 107.

14 Interview with Dinah Cook.

15 Roderick Phillips, *Putting Asunder: A History of Divorce in Western Society* (Cambridge: Cambridge University Press, 1988), pp. 561-572.

16 Julia Bennet, 'Narrating Family Histories: Negotiating Identity and Belonging through Tropes of Nostalgia and Authenticity', *Current Sociology*, 66:3 (2018), 449-465; King, *Living With the Dead*.

17 Norah is making reference here ('greenery in the hedges') to a family story about her great-grandparents' wedding day on an unusually warm and spring-like 1 March 1885.

18 Vanessa May and Stewart Muir, 'Everyday Belonging and Ageing: Place and Generational Change', *Sociological Research Online*, 20:1 (2015), 72-82.

19 Philippe Lejeune, 'The Practice of the Private Journal: Chronicle of an Investigation (1986-1998)', in Jeremy D. Popkin and Julie Rak (eds), trans. Katherine Durnin, *Philippe Lejeune, On Diary* (Honolulu: The University of Hawai'i Press, 2009), p. 31.

20 Eva Hoffman, *Lost in Translation* (London: Vintage, 1998), p. 239.

21 Khadeeja Munawar, Sara K. Kuhn and Shamsul Haque, 'Understanding the Reminiscence Bump: A Systematic Review', *PLoS ONE*, 13:12 (2018): e0208595, https://doi.org/10.1371/journal.pone.0208595

22 Arlette Farge, *The Allure of the Archives* (New Haven: Yale University Press, 2015), p. 117.

23 Elizabeth Bowen, *Eva Trout* (London: Vintage, 1999 [1968]), p. 206.

24 Carol Smart, *Personal Life: New Directions in Sociological Thinking* (Cambridge: Polity, 2007).

24. A Mum's Book?

1 Turner, *Men at War*, explores the complex meanings of such behaviour to men in the forces (though might have examined issues concerning the cultural shaping of such behaviour).

2 Peggy Orenstein, *Girls & Sex: Navigating the Complicated New Landscape* (London: Oneworld, 2016); Peggy Orenstein, 'What Young Women Believe About Their Own Sexual Pleasure', *TED*, 2016, https://www.ted.com/talks/peggy_orenstein_what_young_women_believe_about_their_own_sexual_pleasure; Sara I. McLelland, 'Intimate Justice: A Critical Analysis of Sexual Satisfaction', *Social and Personality Psychology Compass*, 4:9 (2010), 663-680. See also Caitlin E. Welles, 'Breaking the Silence Surrounding Female Adolescent Sexual Desire', *Women and Therapy*, 28.2 (2005), 31-45; Cara Kulwicki, 'Real Sex Education', in Jaclyn Friedman and Jessica Valenti (eds), *Yes Means Yes! Visions of Female Sexual Power & a World Without Rape* (Cypress: Seal Press, 2008), 305-313; Julia Hirst, '"It's Got to Be about Enjoying Yourself": Young People, Sexual Pleasure, and Sex and Relationships Education', *Sex Education*, 13:4 (2013), 423-436; Rachel Wood, Julia Hirst, Liz Wilson and Georgina Burns-O'Connell, 'The Pleasure Imperative? Reflecting on Sexual Pleasure's Inclusion in Sex Education and Sexual Health', *Sex Education*, 19:1 (2019), 1-14; Eimar

McBride, *Something Out of Place: Women and Disgust* (London: Profile Books, 2021).

3   Melissa Febos, *Girlhood* (London: Bloomsbury, 2021), p. 37.

4   *Dirty Dancing* (Bergstein, Ardolino, 1987).

5   David Gates, 'Elizabeth Gilbert's 'City of Girls' Delivers a Love- and Booze-filled Romp through 1940s New York', *New York Times*, 1 June 2019.

6   Joan Jacobs Brumberg, *The Body Project: An Intimate History of American Girls* (London: Vintage, 1998), pp. xx, xxxi-xxxii, 196-197; Joan Jacobs Brumberg, 'Girl History: Social Change and Female Sexuality in the 20th Century', *Youth Studies Australia*, 19:4 (2000), 19-21, p. 21.

7   Febos, *Girlhood*, p. 23; Annie Ernaux, *A Girl's Story* (London: Fitzcarraldo Editions, 2020), p. 24.

8   Aaron Sachs, 'Letters', in Sachs and John Demos, *Artful History*, p. 124.

9   Gertie Whitfield and Alison Twells, 'Nell's Story', *Learning Creatively through History*, http://www.learningcreativelythroughhistory.org/nellsstory.html

10 John Demos, in Sachs and Demos, *Artful History*, p. 275.

11 Laura Kipnis, *Unwanted Advances* (London: Verso, 2018), p. 1; Mithu Sanyal, *Rape: from Lucretia to #MeToo* (London: Verso, 2019); Sarah Leonard and Ann Snitow, 'The Kids Are Alright: A Legendary Feminist on Feminism's Future', *The Nation*, 18 October 2016. Katherine Angel's powerful discussion of consent in *Tomorrow* led me to these texts.

12 Carole Vance, *Pleasure and Danger: Exploring Female Sexuality* (Boston and London: Routledge, 1984); Angel, *Tomorrow Sex Will Be Good Again*, p. 100.

25. Writing Norah's Story

1   Selina Todd, *Snakes and Ladders: The Great British Social Mobility Myth* (London: Chatto and Windus, 2021).

2   Illouz, *Consuming the Romantic Utopia*.

3   Carolyn Heilbrun, *Writing a Woman's Life* (New York: W. W. Norton, 1988), p. 21. See also Marguerite Duras: 'It was soon all over – public places, dancing. In my day. For women, I mean'. Duras, 'The Pleasures of the 6th Arrondisement', in *The Lover, Wartime Notebooks, Practicalities: Marguerite Duras* (London: Everyman, 2017), p. 357.

4   For men's bad behaviour as 'accepted' conduct and women's discomfort with the idea of being labelled as victims of sexual harassment, see Hannah Charnock, 'Writing the History of Male Sexuality in the Wake of Operation Yewtree and #MeToo', in Matt Houlbrook, Katie Jones and Ben Mechen (eds), *Masculinities in the Twentieth Century* (Manchester: Manchester University Press, 2023), pp. 288-298.

5   See Katherine Borland, '"That's not what I said": Interpretive Conflict in Oral Narrative Research', in Sherna Berger Gluck and Daphne Patai (eds), *Women's Words: The Feminist Practice of Oral History* (New York: Routledge, 1991), pp. 63-75. See also Katherine Borland, '"That's Not What I Said": A Reprise 25 Years On', in K Srigley, S. Zembrzycki and F. Iacovetta (eds.) *Beyond Women's Words: Feminisms and the Practices of Oral History in the Twenty-First Century* (Abingdon: Routledge, 2018), pp. 31-37.

6   Penny Summerfield, 'Culture and Composure: Creating Narratives of the Gendered Self in Oral History Interviews', *Cultural and Social History*, 1:1 (2004), 65–93.

7   Interview with Dinah Cook; Alistair Thomson, *Anzac Memories: Living with the Legend* (Victoria: Monash University, 2013 [1994]).

8   Virginia Woolf, *Orlando: A Biography* (Oxford: Oxford University Press, 1998 [1928]), p. 294.

9   Alain Corbin, *The Life of an Unknown: The Rediscovered World of a Clog Maker in Nineteenth-Century France*, trans. Arthur Goldhammer (New York, 2003), p. 212.

10 Ken Plummer, *Documents of Life 2* (London: Sage, 2001), pp. 224, 2.

11 Zembrzycki, *According to Baba*, p. 15. See also Srigley, Zembrzycki and Iacovetta (eds), *Beyond Women's Words*.

12 Brooks, *Why We Left*, p. 21; Janet Malcolm, *Sylvia Plath and Ted Hughes: The Silent Woman* (London: Granta, 2012), p. 176; Marion Rust, 'Personal History: Martha Ballard, Laurel Thatcher Ulrich, and the Scholarly Guise in Early American Women's Studies', *Legacy*, 32:2 (2015), 147-166; Jill Lepore, 'Personal History: The Prodigal Daughter', *New Yorker*, 8 July 2013.

13 Carolyn Steedman, *Master and Servant: Love and Labour in the English Industrial Age* (Cambridge: Cambridge University Press, 2007), p. 6. See also: Liz Stanley, *The Auto/Biographical I: The Theory and Practice of Feminist Auto/Biography* (Manchester: Manchester University Press, 1992); Gesa E. Kirsch and Liz Rohan (eds), *Beyond the Archives: Research as a Lived Process* (Carbondale: Southern Illinois University, 2008).

26. A Place of Dreams

1. Lake, 'Female Desires', p. 368; Illouz, *Why Love Hurts*, p. 247; *Miss Modern*, cited in Tinkler, *Miss Modern*.

2. Goodman, 'Patriotic Femininity', p. 278.

3. Lake, 'Female Desires', pp. 361, 371; for libidinal femininity, see Page Dougherty Delano, 'Making Up for War: Sexuality and Citizenship in Wartime Culture', *Feminist Studies*, 26:1 (2000), 33-68. For the impact of the war in contributing to new marital styles, see Janet Finch and Penny Summerfield, 'Social Reconstruction and the Emergence of the Companionate Marriage, 1945-1959', in D. Clarke (ed.), *Marriage, Domestic Life and Social Change: Writings for Jacqueline Burgoyne (1944-88)* (London: Routledge, 1991), pp. 7-32.

4. Hélène Cixous, 'Sorties: Out and Out: Attacks/Ways Out/Forays', in Hélène Cixous and Catherine Clement, *The Newly Born Woman*, trans. Betsy Wing (Minneapolis: University of Minnesota Press, 1986), pp. 66, 82.

5. Cecily Davey, 'Jouissance: Journeys beyond the Bed with Helene Cixous', *The Luminary*, 3:9 (2013), https://www.lancaster.ac.uk/liminary/issue3/Issue3article9.htm, pp. 63-64.

6. Hélène Cixous, 'The Laugh of the Medusa', trans. Keith Cohen and Paula Cohen, *Signs*, 1:4 (1976), 875-893.

7. Kuhn, *Family Secrets*, p. 98; Brian Jackson and Dennis Marsden, *Education and the Working Classes* (Harmondsworth: Penguin, 1964), p. 172. See also Diane Reay, 'Beyond Consciousness? The Psychic Landscape of Social Class', *Sociology*, 39:5 (2005), 911-928; Sam Friedman, 'The Price of the Ticket: Rethinking the Experience of Social Mobility', *Sociology*, 48:2 (2014), 352-368.

8. Penelope Lively, *A House Unlocked* (London: Grove Press, 2003).

9. Carolyn Steedman, *Dust: The Archive and Cultural History* (Manchester: Manchester University Press, 2001), p. 69. These final paragraphs owe much to conversations with John Baxendale and Van Gore. I thank them both.

Bibliography

Archival Sources

Private Papers

Letters from Jim and Danny Gilbert, Norah Hodgkinson's personal archive, in author's possession.

Letters to John Davison from Bob Evans, private archive, personally held.

Norah Hodgkinson's diaries, documents and artefacts, in author's possession.

Imperial War Museum Archive

Correspondence to Capt J. J. Youngs (IWM 92/50/1).

Dennis Maxted, Oral History 18200, recorder Conrad Wood, 1/2/1999, Reel 1.

Letter from J. J. Youngs to Jack Neale, 20 November 1974 (IWM 92/50/1).

Papers of Lt Commander J. K. Neale DSC RNVR, IWM 2130 92/50/1.

Private Papers of Mrs M. Baker, Documents 570, 88/42/1.

Private Papers of Miss D. Dockrill, Documents 19147, 16/32/1.

Raymond Card, Oral History 10240, https://www.iwm.org.uk/collections/item/object/80010020

Digital and Web-Based Sources

BBC Peoples' War: An Archive of WW2 Memories – Written by the Public, Gathered by the BBC

Abel, Geoffrey, 'Evacuation to Hemington' (August 2005), https://www.bbc.co.uk/history/ww2peopleswar/stories/96/a5294496.shtml

Davison, Eileen, CSV Action Desk/BBC Radio Lincolnshire, 'If You Can Knit – You Can Do Your Bit' (October 2005), https://www.bbc.co.uk/history/ww2peopleswar/stories/26/a6041026.shtml

Stonebridge, W. J., 'Memories of a Young Stoker, Part 3' (August 2005), https://www.bbc.co.uk/history/ww2peopleswar/stories/27/a3509327.shtml

Wilshaw, Edith, 'Adopting Ships' (July 2005), https://www.bbc.co.uk/history/ww2peopleswar/stories/04/a4430404.shtml

Other Web Sources

ADM 199/184 HMS Niger Minesweeping Reports Oct 1940 (Extracts), http://www.halcyon-class.co.uk/niger/sweep_reports_oct_40.htm

Burgess, Anika, 'The Wool Brigades of World War I', *Atlas Obsura*, 26 July 2017, https://www.atlasobscura.com/articles/when-knitting-was-a-patriotic-duty-wwi-homefront-wool-brigades

Devine, Kristin, 'Knitting in WWII: A Photoessay', 29 March 2020, https://ordinary-times.com/2020/03/29/knitting-in-wwii-a-photoessay/

The Frank Soo Foundation, 'Frank Soo: The Forgotten Footballer', www.artsandculture.google.com/story/frank-soo-the-forgotten-footballer-the-frank-soo-foundation/agVhGPgckSpQIA?hl=en

Goodreads, 8 August 2019, Jess, https://www.goodreads.com/book/show/2143538

Historic England Research Records: Starfish Bombing Decoy, https://www.heritagegateway.org.uk/Gateway/Results_Single.aspx?uid=42703a6a-4898-488a-aeae-14e9b20e3ccb&resourceID=19191

International Friendship League, https://iflworld.org/history-of-ifl/

Kindell, Don, 'British and Other Navies in WWII, Day by Day', http://www.naval-history.net/xDKWW2-4104-31APR02.htm

Knitting for Victory, http://elinorflorence.com/blog/wartime-knitting

Letter from the Corporation of Bristol Housing Estates on 15th June 1936, Myers-Insole Local Learning Community Interest Company, https://www.locallearning.org.uk/img_pxu733/

Letter from Princess Chula Chakrabongse, *Motor Sport Magazine*, https://www.motorsportmagazine.com/archive/article/may-1971/76/cars-in-books-203-may-1971/

Lindrea, Victoria, 'Head of the Royal Navy Defends Handling of Rape Allegations', *BBC News*, 27 November 2022, https://www.bbc.co.uk/news/uk-63770307

Mercer, Karl, and Raphael Sheridan, 'London Fire Brigade Institutionally Misogynist and Racist – Report', *BBC News*, 26 November 2022, https://www.bbc.co.uk/news/uk-england-london-63749444

'"Monster of the MET" and "Slapdown for Sturgeon"', *BBC News*, 17 January 2023, https://www.bbc.co.uk/news/blogs-the-papers-64299275

Strange, Keith, 'Cardiff Schools and the Age of the Second World War. The Log Books: A Documentary History', https://www.scribd.com/document/2589099/Cardiff-schools-and-the-age-of-the-Second-World-War

Zarrelli, Natalie, 'The Wartime Spies Who Used Knitting as an Espionage Tool', *Atlas Obscura*, 16 March 2022, https://www.atlasobscura.com/articles/knitting-spies-wwi-wwii

Government Records

Discussion of knitting 'parties' in the House of Lords, 3 August 1943, *Hansard*, Vol. 128, Fifth Series, cc 958, https://api.parliament.uk/historic-hansard/lords/1943/aug/03/merchant-navy-comforts#column_958

Newspapers and Magazines

Derby Evening Telegraph, Derby Local Studies and Family History Library.

Loughborough Echo, Loughborough Local and Family History Centre.

Picture Post, 1938-1945, British Library.

Woman's Own, 1940-1945, British Library.

Local Collections, Oral Histories and Conversations

Castle Donington Museum, Local Wartime Memories folder.

Mary Belton, interview, 22 June 2011.

Bruce Townsend, conversation, August 2011.

Kath Jones, interview, 28 October 2011.

John Davison, conversations, 28 October 2011 and many others.

Dinah Cook, interview, 4 July 2013.

John Glenn, interview, 1 August 2014.

Irene Marsh, interview, 4 April 2015.

Jean Powditch, personal conversations.

Delia Richards, personal conversations.

Published Sources

Acton, Carol, '"You Yourself Are Here Now Looking Over My Shoulder as I Write": Emotional Dialogue and the Construction of a Shared Intimate Space in First World War Letters', *L'Atelier*, 8:1 (2016), 194–219.

Acton, William, *The Functions and Disorders of the Reproductive Organs, in Childhood, Youth, Adult Age, and Advanced Life, Considered in Their Physiological, Social, and Moral Relations* (London: J and A Churchill, 1875).

Alexander, Kristine, 'Can the Girl Guide Speak? The Perils and Pleasures of Looking for Children's Voices in Archival Research', *Jeunesse: Young People, Texts, Cultures*, 4:1 (2012), 132-145, https://doi.org/10.3138/jeunesse.4.1.132

Alexander, Sally, 'Women, Class and Sexual Differences in the 1830s and 1840s: Some Reflections on Writing Feminist History', *History Workshop Journal*, 17:1 (1984), 125-149, https://doi.org/10.1093/hwj/17.1.125

Alexander, Sally, 'Becoming a Woman in London in the 1920s and 1930s', in D. Feldman and G. S. Jones (eds), *Metropolis – London: Histories and Representations since 1800* (London: Routledge, 1989) pp. 245-271, https://doi.org/10.4324/9781315446684

Alexander, Sally, 'The Mysteries and Secrets of Women's Bodies: Sexual Knowledge in the First Half of the Twentieth Century', in Mica Nava and Alan O'Shea (eds), *Modern Times: Reflections on a Century of English Modernity* (London: Routledge, 1996), pp. 161-175.

Allbrook, Malcolm and Sophie Scott-Brown (eds), *Family History and Historians in Australia and New Zealand* (New York: Routledge, 2021), https://doi.org/10.4324/9780429355899

Allport, Alan, *Browned Off and Bloody Minded: The British Soldier Goes to War* (Yale: Yale University Press, 2015).

Altman, Janet, *Epistolarity: Approaches to a Form* (Columbus, OH: Ohio State University, 1982).

Angel, Katherine, *Unmastered: A Book on Desire, Most Difficult to Tell* (London: Penguin, 2012).

Angel, Katherine, *Tomorrow Sex Will Be Good Again: Women and Desire in an Age of Affirmative Consent* (London: Verso, 2021).

Avery, Valerie, *London Morning* (London: Kimber, 1964).

Bahadur, Gaiutra, *Coolie Woman: The Odyssey of Indenture* (London: C. Hurst & Co, 2013), https://doi.org/10.7208/chicago/9780226043388.001.0001

Bailey, Jenna (ed.), *Can Any Mother Help Me?* (London: Faber, 2007).

Bakewell, Joan, *All the Nice Girls* (London: Virago, 2010).

Banks, Steven, *The Handicrafts of the Sailor* (London: David & Charles, Ltd., 1974).

Barbier, Mary Kathryn, *D-Day Deception: Operation Fortitude and the Normandy Invasion* (Westport: Praeger Security International, 2007), https://doi.org/10.5040/9798400636622

Barclay, Katie, and Nina Javette Koefoed, 'Family, Memory, and Identity: An Introduction', *Journal of Family History*, 46:1 (2021), 3-12, https://doi.org/10.1177/0363199020967297

Barclay, Katie, 'Falling in Love with the Dead', *Rethinking History* 22:4 (2018), 459-473, https://doi.org/10.1080/13642529.2018.1511105

Barnwell, Ashley, 'Keeping the Nation's Secrets: "Colonial Storytelling" Within Australian Families', *Journal of Family History*, 46:1 (2021), 46-61, https://doi.org/10.1177/0363199020966920

Barthes, Roland, *Camera Lucida* (London: Vintage, 2000 [1980]).

Basu, Paul, *Highland Homecomings: Genealogy and Heritage Tourism in the Scottish Diaspora* (London: Routledge, 2007), https://doi.org/10.4324/9780203945506

Bates, Doreen, *Diary of a Wartime Affair: The True Story of a Surprisingly Modern Romance* (Harmondsworth: Penguin, 2016).

Bates, H. E., *Fair Stood the Wind for France* (Harmondsworth: Penguin, 1980 [1944]).

Baxendale, John, *Priestley's England: J.B. Priestley and English Culture* (Manchester: Manchester University Press, 2007), https://doi.org/10.7765/9781847791320

Beier, Lucinda McCray, '"We were green as grass": Learning about Sex and Reproduction in Three Working-class Lancashire Communities, 1900-1970', *Social History of Medicine*, 16:3 (2003), 461-480, https://doi.org/10.1093/shm/16.3.461

Bennet, Julia, 'Narrating Family Histories: Negotiating Identity and Belonging Through Tropes of Nostalgia and Authenticity', *Current Sociology*, 66:3 (2018), 449-465, https://doi.org/10.1177/0011392115578984

Bennett, Tony, 'Habitus Clivé: Aesthetics and Politics in the Work of Pierre Bourdieu', *New Literary History*, 38:1 (2007), 201-228, https://doi.org/10.1353/nlh.2007.0013

Berkey, Jonathan P., 'Featured Review: Life of an Unknown', *American Historical Review*, 112:2 (2007), 459-461.

Bingham, Adrian, *Gender, Modernity, and the Popular Press in Inter-War Britain* (Oxford: Oxford University Press, 2004).

Bingham, Adrian, *Family Newspapers? Sex, Private Life and the British Popular Press, 1918-1978* (Oxford: Oxford University Press, 2009), https://doi.org/10.1093/acprof:oso/9780199279586.001.0001

Bingham, Adrian, '"It Would Be Better for the Newspapers to Call a Spade a Spade": The British Press and Child Sexual Abuse, c. 1918-1990', *History Workshop Journal*, 88 (2019), 89-110, https://doi.org/10.1093/hwj/dbz006

Blackwell, Elizabeth, 'On the Abuses of Sex – II. Fornication', *Essays in Medical Sociology*, Vol. I (London: Ernest Bell, 1902).

Bloom, Lynn Z., '"I Write for Myself and Strangers": Private Diaries as Public Documents', in Suzanne L. Bunkers and Cynthia A. Huff (eds), *Inscribing the Daily: Critical Essays on Women's Diaries* (Amherst: University of Massachusetts Press, 1996), pp. 23-38.

Borland, Katherine, '"That's Not What I Said": Interpretive Conflict in Oral Narrative Research', in Sherna Berger Gluck and Daphne Patai (eds), *Women's Words: The Feminist Practice of Oral History* (New York: Routledge, 1991), pp. 63-75, https://doi.org/10.4324/9780203435960-33

Borland, Katherine, '"That's Not What I Said": A Reprise 25 Years On', in K Srigley, S. Zembrzycki and F. Iacovetta (eds.) *Beyond Women's Words: Feminisms and the Practices of Oral History in the Twenty-First Century* (Abingdon: Routledge, 2018), pp. 31-37, https://doi.org/10.4324/9780203435960-33

Born, A. M., 'The Price of the Ticket Revised: Family Members' Experiences of Upward Social Mobility', *The Sociological Review*, 72:2 (2024), 394-411, https://doi.org/10.1177/00380261231167748

Bourke, Joanna, 'Unwanted Intimacy: Violent Sexual Transfers in British and American Societies 1870s to 1970s', *European Journal of English Studies*, 9:3 (2005), 287-300, https://doi.org/10.1080/13825570500363534

Bourke, Joanna, *Rape: A History from 1860 to the Present* (London: Virago, 2007).

Bourke, Joanna, 'Wartime Rape: the Politics of Making Visible', in Andrew Knapp and Hilary Footit (eds), *Liberal Democracies at War: Conflict and Representation* (London: Bloomsbury, 2013), pp. 135-156, https://doi.org/10.5040/9781350041837.ch-007

Bowen, Elizabeth, *The Heat of the Day* (London: Vintage, 1998 [1948]).

Bowen, Elizabeth, *Eva Trout* (London: Vintage, 1999 [1968]).

Bradley, James, 'The Colonel and the Slave Girls: Life Writing and the Logic of History in 1830s Sydney', in *Journal of Social History*, 45:2 (2011), 416-435, https://doi.org/10.1093/jsh/shr064

Branche, Raphaëlle and Fabrice Virgili (eds), *Rape in Wartime* (Basingstoke: Palgrave, 2012), https://doi.org/10.1057/9781137283399

Braybon, Gail and Penny Summerfield, *Out of the Cage: Women's Experiences in Two World Wars* (London: Pandora, 1987).

Brien, Donna Lee, and Kiera Lindsey (eds), *Speculative Biography: Experiments, Opportunities and Provocations* (New York and Abingdon: Routledge, 2022), https://doi.org/10.4324/9781003054528

Brooks, Joanna, *Why We Left: Untold Stories and Songs of America's First Immigrants* (Minneapolis: University of Minnesota Press, 2013), https://doi.org/10.5749/minnesota/9780816681259.001.0001

Broad, Richard and Suzie Fleming (eds), *Nella Last's War: The Second World War Diaries of 'Housewife, 49'* (London: Profile Books, 2006).

Broughton, John, *Municipal Dreams: The Rise and Fall of Council Housing* (London: Verso, 2018).

Brumberg, Joan Jacobs, *The Body Project: An Intimate History of American Girls* (London: Vintage, 1998).

Brumberg, Joan Jacobs, 'Girl History: Social Change and Female Sexuality in the 20th Century', *Youth Studies Australia*, 19:4 (2000), 19-21.

Buchan, James, 'Search for a Legend: James Buchan Struggles to Find the Facts Amid the Speculation of Natalie Zemon Davis's Biography of Leo Africanus, Trickster Travels', *The Guardian*, 13 January 2007.

Bunkers, Suzanne L., and Cynthia A. Huff (eds), *Inscribing the Daily: Critical Essays on Women's Diaries* (Amherst: University of Massachusetts Press, 1996).

Bunkers, Suzanne L., *Diaries of Girls and Women: A Midwestern American Sampler* (Madison: University of Wisconsin Press, 2001).

Burton, Antoinette, *Dwelling in the Archive: Women Writing House, Home, and History in Late Colonial India* (Oxford: Oxford University Press, 2003), https://doi.org/10.1093/acprof:oso/9780195144253.001.0001

Burton, Antoinette (ed.), *Archive Stories: Facts, Fictions, and the Writing of History* (Durham: Duke University Press, 2005), https://doi.org/10.2307/j.ctv11smn7b

Calder, Angus, *The People's War: Britain 1939-1945* (London: Pimlico, 2008 [1969]).

Carruthers, Susan, *Dear John: Love and Loyalty in Wartime America* (Cambridge: Cambridge University Press, 2022), https://doi.org/10.1017/9781108913867

Carswell, Jeanne (ed.), *At Home and Away* (Coalville: Coalville Publishing, 1995).

Carter, Anthony, *Motor Racing: The Pursuit of Victory* (Dorchester: Veloce Publishing Ltd, 2011).

Carter, Kathryn, 'An Economy of Words: Emma Chadwick Stretch's Account Book Diary, 1859-1860', *Acadiensis*, 29:1 (1999), 43-56.

Carter, Kathryn, *The Small Details of a Life: Twenty Diaries by Women in Canda, 1830-1996* (Buffalo: University of Toronto Press, 2002), https://doi.org/10.3138/9781442682375

Chapman, James, *British Comics: A Cultural History* (London: Reaktion Books, 2011).

Charman, Terry, *Outbreak, 1939: The World Goes to War* (London: Virgin Books, 2010).

Charnock, Hannah, 'Writing the History of Male Sexuality in the Wake of Operation Yewtree and #MeToo', in Matt Houlbrook, Katie Jones and Ben Mechen (eds), *Masculinities in the Twentieth Century* (Manchester: Manchester University Press, 2023), pp. 288-298, https://doi.org/10.7765/9781526174703

Chesser, Eustace, *The Sexual, Marital and Family Relationships of the English Woman* (London: Hutchinson's Medical Publications, 1956).

Cixous, Hélène, 'Sorties: Out and Out: Attacks/Ways Out/Forays', in Hélène Cixous and Catherine Clement, *The Newly Born Woman*, trans. Betsy Wing (Minneapolis: University of Minnesota Press, 1986).

Cixous, Hélène, 'The Laugh of the Medusa', trans. Keith Cohen and Paula Cohen, *Signs*, 1:4 (1976), 875-893.

Clephane, Irene, *Towards Sex Freedom* (London: John Lane, 1935).

Cockburn Cynthia, 'Why Are *You* Doing This to *Me*? Identity, Power and Sexual Violence in War', in Anna G. Jonasdottir, Valerie Bryson and Kathleen B. Jones (eds), *Sexuality, Gender and Power: Intersectional and Transnational Perspectives* (London: Routledge, 2012), pp. 189-204, https://doi.org/10.4324/9780203834916-23

Cohen, Deborah, *Family Secrets: Shame and Privacy in Modern Britain* (Oxford: Oxford University Press, 2013).

Cohen, Patricia Cline, et al., 'Dialogue. Paradigm Shift Books: *A Midwife's Tale* by Laurel Thatcher Ulrich', *Journal of Women's History*, 14:3 (2002), 133-161, https://doi.org/10.1353/jowh.2002.0066

Collins, Katherine, 'Is There any Truth in Biographical Fictions?', *University of Oxford*, 12 May 2020, https://greatdev.podcasts.ox.ac.uk/content/there-any-truth-biographical-fictions?qt-episode_related_content=1

Collins, Katherine, '"A Man of Violent and Ungovernable Temperament": Can Fiction Fill Silences in the Archives?', *Life Writing*, 2019, https://doi.org/10.1080/14484528.2018.1564215

Colls, Rob, 'When We Lived in Communities', in Rob Colls and Richard Rodgers (eds), *Cities of Ideas: Civil Society and Urban Governance in Britain 1800-2000. Essays in Honour of David Reeder* (Aldershot: Ashgate, 2004).

Connelly, Mark, *We Can Take It! Britain and the Memory of the Second World War* (Harlow: Pearson, 2004).

Cook, Hera, *The Long Sexual Revolution: English Women, Sex and Contraception, 1800-1975* (Oxford: Oxford University Press, 2004), https://doi.org/10.1093/acprof:oso/9780199252183.001.0001

Cook, Hera, 'Getting "Foolishly Hot and Bothered"? Parents and Teachers and Sex Education in the 1940s', *Sex Education*, 12:5 (2012), 555-567, https://doi.org/10.1080/14681811.2011.627735

Cooke, Simon, 'Review of Hallie Rubenhold's *The Five*', *The Victorian Web*, 18 May 2019: https://victorianweb.org/history/crime/rubenhold.html

Corbin, Alain, *The Life of an Unknown: The Rediscovered World of a Clog Maker in Nineteenth-Century France*, trans. Arthur Goldhammer (New York: Columbia University Press, 2003).

Costello, John, *Love, Sex and War: Changing Values, 1939-1945* (London: Harper Collins, 1985).

Couser, Thomas, *Vulnerable Subjects: Ethics and Life Writing* (Ithaca and London: Cornell University Press, 2018). https://doi.org/10.7591/9781501723551

Cowman, Krista, 'A Waste of Space? Controversies Surrounding the Working-Class Parlour in Inter-War Britain', *Home Cultures*, 15:2 (2018), 129-153, https://doi.org/10.1080/17406315.2018.1610610

Cox, Pamela, *Bad Girls in Britain: Gender, Justice and Welfare, 1900-1950* (Basingstoke: Palgrave, 2003).

Curthoys, Ann, and Ann McGrath, *How to Write History that People Want to Read* (Basingstoke: Palgrave, 2011 [2009]), https://doi.org/10.1007/978-0-230-30496-3

Davey, Cecily, 'Jouissance: Journeys Beyond the Bed with Helene Cixous', *The Luminary*, 3:9 (2013), https://www.lancaster.ac.uk/liminary/issue3/Issue3article9.htm

Davis, Angela, '"Oh No, Nothing, We Didn't Learn Anything": Sex Education and the Preparation of Girls for Motherhood, c.1930-70', *History of Education*, 37 (2008), 661-77, https://doi.org/10.1080/00467600701727730

Davis, Natalie Zemon, *The Return of Martin Guerre* (Cambridge, MA: Harvard University Press, 1983).

Deer, Patrick, *Culture in Camouflage: War, Empire and Modern British Literature* (Oxford: Oxford University Press, 2009), https://doi.org/10.1093/acprof:oso/9780199239887.001.0001

Delano, Page Dougherty, 'Making Up For War: Sexuality and Citizenship in Wartime Culture', *Feminist Studies,* 26:1 (2000), 33-68, https://doi.org/10.2307/3178592

Delap, Lucy, 'Child Welfare, Child Protection and Sexual Abuse, 1918-1990', *History & Policy* (2015), http://www.historyandpolicy.org/policy-papers/papers/child-welfare-child-protection-and-sexual-abuse-1918-1990

Demos, John, *The Unredeemed Captive: A Family Story from Early America* (London: Macmillan, 1996 [1994]).

Dobbs, Brian, *Dear Diary: Some Studies in Self-interest* (London: Elm Tree Books, 1974).

Downes, Mollie Panter, *London Notes, 1939-1945* (London: Longman 1972).

Duncan, Simon, 'The World We Have Made? Individualisation and Personal Life in the 1950s', *The Sociological Review,* 59:2 (2011), 242-265, https://doi.org/10.1111/j.1467-954x.2011.02001.x

Duras, Marguerite, 'The Pleasures of the 6th Arrondisement', in *The Lover, Wartime Notebooks, Practicalities: Marguerite Duras* (London: Everyman, 2017).

Dyhouse, Carol, *Glamour: Women, History, Feminism* (London: Zed Books, 2010), https://doi.org/10.5040/9781350220409

Dyhouse, Carol, *Girl Trouble: Panic and Progress in the History of Young Women* (London: Bloomsbury, 2014).

Dyhouse, Carol, 'Was There Ever a Time when Girls Weren't in Trouble?', *Women's History Review,* 23:2 (2014), 272-274, https://doi.org/10.1080/09612025.2014.894752

Dyhouse, Carol, *Heartthrobs: A History of Women and Desire* (Oxford: Oxford University Press, 2017).

Ellis, Carolyn, 'Telling Secrets, Revealing Lives: Relational Ethics in Research with Intimate Others', *Qualitative Inquiry* 13:1 (2007), 3-29, https://doi.org/10.1177/1077800406294947

Ernaux, Annie, *Shame,* trans. Tanya Leslie (New York: Seven Stories Press, 1998).

Ernaux, Annie, *A Girl's Story* (London: Fitzcarraldo Editions, 2020).

Evans, Tanya, 'Secrets and Lies: The Radical Potential of Family History', *History Workshop Journal,* 71 (2011), 49-73, https://doi.org/10.1093/hwj/dbq065

Evans, Tanya, *Family History, Historical Consciousness and Citizenship* (London: Bloomsbury, 2021), https://doi.org/10.5040/9781350212091

Evans, Mary, *Love: An Unromantic Discussion* (Cambridge: Blackwell, 2003).

Farge, Arlette, *The Allure of the Archives* (New Haven: Yale University Press, 2015), https://doi.org/10.12987/9780300180213

Febos, Melissa, *Girlhood* (London: Bloomsbury, 2021).

Ferrante, Elena, *The Story of a New Name*, trans. Ann Goldstein (New York: Europa Editions, 2015 [2012]).

Feigel, Lara, *Love Charm of Bombs: Restless Lives in the Second World War* (London: Bloomsbury, 2014).

Field, Kendra Taira, *Growing Up With the Country: Family, Race, and Nation after the Civil War* (New Haven: Yale University Press, 2018), pp. xv, xvii-xix, https://doi.org/10.12987/yale/9780300180527.001.0001

Field, Kendra Taira, 'The Privilege of Family History', *American Historical Review*, 127:2 (2022), 600-633,https://doi.org/10.1093/ahr/rhac151

Finch, Janet and Penny Summerfield, 'Social Reconstruction and the Emergence of the Companionate Marriage, 1945-1959', in D. Clarke (ed.), *Marriage, Domestic Life and Social Change: Writings for Jacqueline Burgoyne (1944-88)* (London: Routledge, 1991), pp. 7-32.

Fisher, Kate, '"She Was Quite Satisfied with the Arrangements I Made": Gender and Birth Control in Britain 1920-1950', *Past and Present*, 169 (2001), 161-193, https://doi.org/10.1093/past/169.1.161

Fisher, Kate, *Birth Control, Sex and Marriage in Britain 1918-60* (Oxford: Oxford University Press, 2006), https://doi.org/10.1093/acprof:oso/9780199267361.001.0001

Fisher, Helen, Xu X, Aron A, L.L. Brown, 'Intense, Passionate, Romantic Love: A Natural Addiction? How the Fields that Investigate Romance and Substance Abuse Can Inform Each Other', *Frontiers in Psychology*, 7:687 (2016), https://doi.org/10.3389/fpsyg.2016.00687

Fisher, Pamela J., and J. M. Lee, *The Victoria History of Leicestershire: Castle Donington* (London: Victoria County History, 2016).

Flem, Lydia, *The Final Reminder: How I Emptied my Parent's House*, trans. Elfreda Powell (London: Souvenir Press, 2005).

Forster, Margaret, *Diary of an Ordinary Woman* (London: Vintage, 2003).

Francis, Martin, *The Flyer: British Culture and the Royal Air Force, 1939-1945* (Oxford: Oxford University Press, 2008).

Friedman, Sam, 'The Price of the Ticket: Rethinking the Experience of Social Mobility', *Sociology*, 48:2 (2014), 352-368, https://doi.org/10.1177/0038038513490355

Fussell, Paul, *Wartime: Understanding and Behaviour in the Second World War* (Oxford: Oxford University Press, 1989).

Gammerl, Benno, 'Emotional Styles – Concepts and Challenges', *Rethinking History*, 16:2 (2012), 161-175, https://doi.org/10.1080/13642529.2012.681189

Gates, David, 'Elizabeth Gilbert's 'City of Girls' Delivers a Love- and Booze-filled Romp through 1940s New York', *New York Times*, 1 June 2019.

Gebhardt, Miriam, *Crimes Unspoken: The Rape of German Women at the End of the Second World War*, trans. Nick Somers (Cambridge: Polity, 2016).

Gerolymatos, André, *The British and the Greek Resistance, 1936-1944: Spies, Saboteurs, and Partisans* (Washington, DC: Lexington Books, 2018).

Gerson, Stephane, 'A History from Within: When Historians Write about Their Own Kin', *Journal of Modern History*, 94:4 (2022), 898-937, https://doi.org/10.1086/722420

Giddens, Anthony, *The Transformation of Intimacy: Sexuality, Love and Eroticism in Modern Societies* (Stanford: Stanford University Press, 1992).

Giles, Judy 'A Home of One's Own: Women and Domesticity in England, 1918-1950', *Women's Studies International Forum*, 16 (1993), 239-253.

Giles, Judy, *Women, Identity, and Private Life in Britain, 1900-1950* (Basingstoke: Palgrave, 1995).

Giles, Judy, *The Parlour and the Suburb* (Oxford: Berg, 2004).

Gill, Rebecca, 'Networks of Concern, Boundaries of Compassion: British Relief in the South African War', *The Journal of Imperial and Commonwealth History*, 40 (2012), 827-844, https://doi.org/10.1080/03086534.2012.730836

Gillis, John R., *For Better, For Worse: British Marriages 1600 to the Present* (Oxford: Oxford University Press, 1986).

Ginzburg, Carlo, and Carlo Poni, 'The Name and the Game: Unequal Exchange and the Historiographic Marketplace', in Edward Moore and Guido Ruggiero (eds), *Microhistory and the Lost Peoples of Europe* (Baltimore: John Hopkins University, 1991).

Gloyn, Liz, Vicky Crewe, Laura King, and Anna Woodham, 'The Ties that Bind: Materiality, Identity, and the Life Course in the "Things" Families Keep', *Journal of Family History*, 43:2 (2018), 164-165, https://doi.org/10.1177/0363199017746451

Goldman, Ronald (ed.), *Breakthrough: Autobiographical Accounts of the Education of Some Socially Disadvantaged Children* (London: Routledge, 1968).

Goldstein, Joshua, *War and Gender: How Gender Shapes the War System and Vice Versa* (Cambridge: Cambridge University Press, 2001).

Goodman, James, 'For the Love of Stories', reprinted in Aaron Sachs and John Demos (eds), *Artful History: A Practical Anthology* (New Haven, CT: Yale University Press, 2020), pp. 189-212, https://doi.org/10.12987/9780300252040-015

Goodman, Philomena, *Women, Sexuality and War* (Basingstoke: Palgrave, 2002), https://doi.org/10.1057/9781403914132

Green, Anna and Kayleigh Luscombe, 'Family Memory, "Things" and Counterfactual Thinking', *Memory Studies* 12:6 (2017), 646–59, doi:10.1177/1750698017714837

Green, Anna, 'Intergenerational Family Memory and Historical Consciousness', in Anna Clark and Carla L. Peck (eds), *Contemplating Historical Consciousness: Notes from the Field* (New York/Oxford: Berghahn Books, 2018), pp. 200-211, https://doi.org/10.2307/j.ctvw04bhk.19

Griffiths, Tom, 'The Intriguing Dance of History and Fiction', *TEXT: Special Issue 28: Fictional Histories and Historical Fictions: Writing History in the Twenty-first Century*, eds Camilla Nelson and Christine de Matos, 19:28 (2015), https://doi.org/10.52086/001c.27284

Griffiths, Tom, *The Art of Time Travel: Historians and Their Craft* (Melbourne: Black, Inc., 2016).

Grossman, Atina, 'Family Files: Emotions and Stories of (Non-)Restitution', *German Historical Institute London Bulletin*, 34:1 (2012).

Hall, Lesley, '"The Wo That Is in Marriage": Abstinence in Practice and Principle in British Marriages, 1890-1940', in Kaat Wils, Leen van Molle and Evert Peeters (eds), *Beyond Pleasure: Cultures of Modern Asceticism* (London: Berghahn, 2011), https://doi.org/10.1515/9781845459871-008

Hallam, Elizabeth and Jenny Hockey, *Death, Memory and Material Culture* (Berg, 2000).

Hämmerle, Christa, '"Waiting longingly…" Love Letters in the First World War – a Plea for a Broader Genre Concept', *History of Emotions – Insights into Research*, 2 (2014), https://doi.org/10.14280/08241.24

Hamlett, Jane, 'Mothering in the Archives: Care and the Creation of Family Papers and Photographs in Twentieth-Century Southern England', *Past & Present*, 246:15 (2020), 186–214, https://doi.org/10.1093/pastj/gtaa036

Hammett, Jessica, *Creating the People's War: Civil Defence Communities in Second World War Britain* (Manchester: Manchester University Press, 2022), https://doi.org/10.7765/9781526162427

Hampsten, Elizabeth, *'Read this Only to Yourself': The Private Writings of Midwestern Women, 1880-1910* (Bloomington, IN: Indiana University Press, 1982).

Hanna, Martha, 'War Letters: Communication between Front and Home Front', *International Encyclopedia of the First World War* (2014), 1-2, https://encyclopedia.1914-1918-online.net/pdf/1914-1918-Online-war_letters_communication_between_front_and_home_front-2014-10-08.pdf

Hansen, Lulu Anne, '"Youth Off the Rails": Teenage Girls and German Soldiers – A Case Study in Occupied Denmark, 1940-1945', in Dagmar

Herzog (ed.), *Brutality and Desire: War and Sexuality in Europe's Twentieth Century* (Basingstoke: Palgrave, 2011 [2009]), pp. 135-167, https://doi.org/10.1057/9780230234291_1

Harris, Kirsten, *Walt Whitman and British Socialism: The Love of Comrades* (London: Routledge, 2016), https://doi.org/10.4324/9781315757988

Hartley, Jenny, 'Letters Are Everything: Mothers and Letters in the Second World War', in Rebecca Earle (ed.), *Epistolary Selves: Letters and Letter-writers, 1600-1945* (Aldershot: Ashgate, 1999), pp. 183-195.

Hartman, Saidiya, *Lose Your Mother: A Journey Along the Atlantic Slave Route* (Farrar, Straus & Giroux, 2007).

Hartman, Saidiya, *Wayward Women and Beautiful Experiments: Intimate Histories of Riotous Black Girls, Troublesome Women and Queer Radicals* (London: Serpent's Tail, 2019).

Hartman, Saidiya, 'Intimate History, Radical Narrative', *Black Perspectives*, 20 May 2020, https://www.aaihs.org/intimate-history-radical-narrative/

Hegarty, Marilyn E., *Victory Girls, Khaki-Wackies, and Patriotutes: The Regulation of Female Sexuality during World War II* (New York: New York University Press, 2008), https://doi.org/10.18574/nyu/9780814790823.001.0001

Heilbrun, Carolyn, *Writing a Woman's Life* (New York: W. W. Norton, 1988).

Heilbrun, Carolyn, *The Last Gift of Time: Life Beyond Sixty* (New York: Random House, 1998).

Hensher, Philip, 'Smoother than Velvet: Sarah Waters Leaves Behind the Intimate Tricks and Turns of Victorian Life for a Simply Truthful Study of Wartime Alienation', *The Observer*, 8 January 2006.

Herzog, Dagmar (ed.), *Brutality and Desire: War and Sexuality in Europe's Twentieth Century* (Basingstoke: Palgrave, 2011 [2009]), https://doi.org/10.1057/9780230234291

Heywood, Colin, *A History of Childhood* (Cambridge: Polity Press, 2018).

Hilton, Christopher, *Hitler's Grands Prix in England: Donington Park 1938 and 1939* (Yeovil: Haynes Manual Inc, 1999).

Hinton, James, *Women, Social Leadership and the Second World War: Continuities of Class* (Oxford: Oxford University Press, 2002), https://doi.org/10.1093/acprof:oso/9780199243297.001.0001

Hinton, James, *Nine Wartime Lives: Mass Observation and the Making of the Modern Self* (Oxford: Oxford University Press, 2010), https://doi.org/10.1093/acprof:oso/9780199574667.001.0001

Hinton, James, *The Mass Observers: A History, 1937-1949* (Oxford: Oxford University Press, 2013), https://doi.org/10.1093/acprof:oso/9780199671045.001.0001

Hirsch, Marianne, *Family Frames: Photography, Narrative and Postmemory* (Cambridge, MA: Harvard University Press, 1997).

Hirst, Julia, '"It's Got to Be about Enjoying Yourself": Young People, Sexual Pleasure, and Sex and Relationships Education', *Sex Education*, 13:4 (2013), 423-436, https://doi.org/10.1080/14681811.2012.747433

Hoffman, Eva, *Lost in Translation* (London: Vintage, 1998).

Hogan, Rebecca, 'Engendered Autobiographies: The Diary as a Feminine Form', *Prose Studies*, 14.2 (1991), 95-107.

Hoggart, Richard, *The Uses of Literacy: Aspects of Working-Class Life* (Harmondsworth: Penguin, 1957).

Holden, Katherine, '"Nature takes no notice of morality": Singleness and Married Love in Interwar Britain', *Women's History Review*, 11:3 (2002), 481-504, https://doi.org/10.1080/09612020200200332

Holland, Pat, '"Sweet it is to scan ...": Personal Photographs and Popular Photography', in Liz Wells (ed.), *Photography: A Critical Introduction* (London: Routledge, 2000), pp. 115–158, https://doi.org/10.4324/9780429274183-4

Holloway, Jonathan Scott, *Jim Crow Wisdom: Memory & Identity in Black America Since 1940* (Durham: University of North Carolina Press, 2013), pp. 8-13, https://doi.org/10.5149/9781469610719_holloway

Holmes, Richard, *Footsteps: Adventures of a Romantic Biographer* (London: Harper Perennial, 1985).

hooks, bell, *Where We Stand: Class Matters* (London: Routledge, 2000)

Houlbrook, Matt, Katie Jones, and Ben Mechen (eds), *Men and Masculinities in Modern Britain: A History for the Present* (Manchester: Manchester University Press, 2024), https://doi.org/10.7765/9781526174703

Houlbrook, Matt, 'Sexing the History of Sexuality', *History Workshop Journal*, 60:1 (2005), 216-222.

Houlbrook, Matt, *Prince of Tricksters: The Incredible True Story of Netley Lucas, Gentleman Crook* (Chicago: University of Chicago Press, 2016).

Hoult, Elizabeth Chapman, 'Recognising and Escaping from the Sham: Authority Moves, Truth Claims and the Fiction of Academic Writing about Adult Learning', *InterActions: UCLA Journal of Education and Information Studies*, 8:2 (2012), https://escholarship.org/uc/item/2164s2gc

Howard, Elizabeth, *Slipstream: A Memoir* (Basingstoke: Macmillan, 2002).

Huff, Cynthia A., 'Reading as Re-vision: Approaches to Reading Manuscript Diaries', *Biography*, 23:3 (2000), 504-523, https://doi.org/10.1353/bio.2000.0032

Humphries, Steve, *A Secret World of Sex: Forbidden Fruit: The British Experience* (London: Sidgwick & Jackson, 1988).

Hurdley, Rachel, *Home, Materiality, Memory and Belonging: Keeping Culture* (Basingstoke: Palgrave, 2013), https://doi.org/10.1057/9781137312952

Illouz, Eva, *Consuming the Romantic Utopia: Love and the Cultural Contradictions of Capitalism* (Berkeley: University of California Press, 1997).

Illouz, Eva, *Why Love Hurts: A Sociological Explanation* (Cambridge: Polity, 2014).

Jablonka, Ivan, *A History of the Grandparents I Never Had*, trans. Jane Kuntz (Stanford: Stanford University Press, 2016), https://doi.org/10.1515/9780804799386

Jackson, Brian, and Dennis Marsden, *Education and the Working Classes* (Harmondsworth: Penguin, 1964).

Jackson, Louise, 'Child Sexual Abuse in England and Wales: Prosecution and Prevalence 1918-1970', *History & Policy* (2015), http://www.historyandpolicy.org/policy-papers/papers/child-sexual-abuse-in-england-and-wales-prosecution-and-prevalence-1918-197

Jackson, Stevi, *Heterosexuality in Question* (London: Sage, 1999).

Jephcott, Pearl, *Girls Growing Up: A Study of the Lives of Some Working Girls* (London: Faber and Faber, 1942).

Jephcott, Pearl, *Rising Twenty: Notes on Some Ordinary Girls* (London: Faber and Faber, 1948).

Jolly, Margaretta (ed.), *Dear Laughing Motorbyke: Letters from Women Welders in the Second World War* (London: Scarlet Press, 1997).

Jolly, Margaretta, *In Love and Struggle: Letters in Contemporary Feminism* (New York: Columbia University Press, 2008).

Jones, Ben, *The Working Class in Mid-Twentieth Century England: Community, Identity and Social Memory* (Manchester: Manchester University Press, 2018), https://doi.org/10.7765/9781526130303

Katin, Zelda, *Clippie: The Autobiography of a Wartime Conductress* (London: Adam Gordon, 1995 [1944]).

King, Laura, *Living With the Dead: Memories, Histories and the Stories Families Tell in Modern Britain* (Oxford: Oxford University Press, 2025), https://doi.org/10.1093/9780191915697.001.0001

King, Laura, 'Family Historians, Collaboration and a New History from Below Methodology – or, Sharing History over a Cup of Tea', *History Workshop Online*, 6 March 2019, https://www.historyworkshop.org.uk/family-childhood/family-historians-collaboration/

King, Laura and Jessica Hammett, 'Family Historians and Historians of the Family: The Value of Collaboration', in Paul Ashton, Tanya Evans, and Paula Hamilton eds, *Making Histories* (Berlin: De Gruyter Oldenbourg, 2020), 237–50, https://doi.org/10.1515/9783110636352-020

Kipnis, Laura, *Unwanted Advances* (London: Verso, 2018).

Kirkham, Pat, 'Fashioning the Feminine: Dress, Appearance, and Femininity in Wartime Britain', in Christine Gledhill and Gloria Swanson (eds), *Nationalising Femininity: Culture, Sexuality and British Cinema in the Second World War* (Manchester: Manchester University Press, 1996), pp. 152-174.

Kirsch, Gesa E., and Liz Rohan (eds), *Beyond the Archives: Research as a Lived Process* (Carbondale: Southern Illinois University, 2008).

Kramer, Anne-Marie, 'Kinship, Affinity and Connectedness: Exploring the Role of Genealogy in Personal Lives', *Sociology*, 45:3 (2011), 379-395, https://doi.org/10.1177/0038038511399622

Kuhn, Annette, *Family Secrets: Acts of Memory and Imagination* (London: Verso, 1995).

Kulwicki, Cara, 'Real Sex Education', in Jaclyn Friedman and Jessica Valenti (eds), *Yes Means Yes! Visions of Female Sexual Power & a World Without Rape* (Cypress: Seal Press, 2008), pp. 305-313.

Laite, Julia, 'The Emmet's Inch: Small History in a Digital Age', *Journal of Social History* 53: 4 (2020), 979–80, https://doi.org/10.1093/jsh/shy118

Lake, Marilyn, 'Female Desires: The Meaning of World War II', in Gordon Martel (ed.), *The World War Two Reader* (London: Routledge, 2004 [1990]), pp. 359-376.

Lake, Marilyn, 'The Desire for a Yank: Sexual Relations between Australian Women and American Servicemen during World War 2', *Journal of the History of Sexuality*, 2:4 (1992), 621-633.

Langford, Wendy, *Revolutions of the Heart: Gender, Power and the Delusions of Love* (London: Routledge, 1999).

Langhamer, Claire, *Women's Leisure in England, 1920-1960* (Manchester: Manchester University Press, 2000).

Langhamer, Claire, 'Adultery in Postwar England', *History Workshop Journal*, 62:1 (2006), 86-115, https://doi.org/10.1093/hwj/dbl004

Langhamer, Claire, *The English in Love: The Intimate Story of an Emotional Revolution* (Oxford: Oxford University Press, 2013).

Langhamer, Claire (ed.), *A Cultural History of Love in the Modern Age* (London: Bloomsbury Academic, 2025). https://doi.org/10.5040/9781350119772

Lant, Antonia, 'Prologue: Mobile Femininity', in Christine Gledhill and Gloria Swanson (eds), *Nationalising Femininity: Culture, Sexuality and British*

Cinema in the Second World War (Manchester: Manchester University Press, 1996), 13-32.

Lawrence, Jon, *Me, Me Me?: The Search for Community in Post-war England* (Oxford: Oxford University Press, 2019).

Lee, Hermione (ed.), *The Mulberry Tree: Writings of Elizabeth Bowen* (London: Virago, 1986).

Lee, Jo, and Tim Ingold, 'Fieldwork on Foot: Perceiving, Routing, Socializing', in S. Coleman and P. Collins (eds), *Locating the Field: Space, Place and Context in Anthropology* (Oxford: Berg, 2006), 67-86, https://doi.org/10.4324/9781003085904-4

Lee, J. M., 'The Rise and Fall of a Market Town: Castle Donington in the Nineteenth Century', *Transactions of Leicestershire Archaeology and History Society*, 32 (1956), 53-80.

Lejeune, Philippe, 'The "Journal de Jeune Fille" in Nineteenth-Century France', in Suzanne L. Bunkers and Cynthia A. Huff (eds), *Inscribing the Daily: Critical Essays on Women's Diaries* (Amherst: University of Massachusetts Press, 1996), pp. 107-122.

Lejeune, Philippe ,'The Practice of the Private Journal: Chronicle of an Investigation (1986-1998)', in Jeremy D. Popkin and Julie Rak (eds), trans. Katherine Durnin, *Philippe Lejeune, On Diary* (Honolulu: The University of Hawai'i Press, 2009), https://doi.org/10.1515/9780824863784-004

Lejeune, Philippe, and Catherine Bogaert, 'The Practice of Writing a Diary', in Batsheva Ben-Amos and Dan Ben-Amos (eds), *The Diary: The Epic of Everyday Life* (Bloomington: Indiana University Press, 2020), pp. 25-38, https://doi.org/10.2307/j.ctvxcrxgp.5

Lensink, Judy Nolte, 'Expanding the Boundaries of Criticism: The Diary as Female Autobiography', *Women's Studies*, 14 (1987), 39-53.

Leonard, Sarah and Ann Snitow, 'The Kids Are Alright: A Legendary Feminist on Feminism's Future', *The Nation*, 18 October 2016.

Lepore, Jill, *Book of Ages: The Life and Opinions of Jane Franklin* (New York: Knopf, 2013).

Lepore, Jill, 'Personal History: The Prodigal Daughter', *New Yorker*, 8 July 2013.

Lessard, Suzannah, *The Architect of Desire: Beauty and Danger in the Stanford White Family* (New York: Delta, 1997)

Letts, Anthony, 'A History of Letts', in *Letts Keep a Diary: A History of Diary Keeping in Great Britain from 16th-20th Century* (London: Charles Letts, 1987).

Lewis, Jane, 'Women Clerical Workers in the Late Nineteenth and Early Twentieth Centuries', in Gerry Anderson, *The White-Blouse Revolution:*

Female Office Workers Since 1870 (Manchester: Manchester University Press, 1988).

Light, Alison, *Common People: The History of An English Family* (Harmondsworth: Penguin, 2015), https://doi.org/10.7208/chicago/9780226331133.001.0001

Light, Alison, 'In Defence of Family History', *The Guardian*, 11 October 2014, https://www.theguardian.com/books/2014/oct/11/genealogy-not-historys-poor-relation-family

Light, Alison, *Inside History: From Popular Fiction to Life-Writing* (Edinburgh: Edinburgh University Press, 2021), https://doi.org/10.3366/edinburgh/9781474481557.001.0001

Lilly, J. Robert., *Taken by Force. Rape and American GIs in Europe During World War II* (Basingstoke: Palgrave Macmillan, 2007).

Lindsey, Kiera, *The Convict's Daughter* (Crows Nest, Sydney: Allen and Unwin, 2017).

Lindsey, Kiera, '"Deliberate Freedom": Exploring the Role of Informed Imagination and Speculation in Historical Biography', *TEXT: Special Issue 50: Life Narrative in Troubled Times,* eds Kate Douglas, Donna Lee Brien and Kylie Cardell, 22:50 (2018), https://doi.org/10.52086/001c.25601

Littauer, Amanda H., *Bad Girls: Young Women, Sex, and Rebellion Before the Sixties* (Chapel Hill: University of North Carolina Press, 2015), https://doi.org/10.5149/northcarolina/9781469623788.001.0001

Little, Ann, *The Many Captivities of Esther Wheelwright* (New Haven and London: Yale University Press, 2016), https://doi.org/10.12987/9780300224627

Lively, Penelope, *A House Unlocked* (London: Grove Press, 2003).

Loughran, Tracey, 'Blind Spots and Moments of Estrangement: Subjectivity, Class and Education in British "Autobiographical Histories"', in Dawn Mannay and Tracey Loughran (eds), *Emotion and the Researcher: Sites, Subjectivities, and Relationships* (Leeds: Emerald Publishing, 2018), 245–60, https://doi.org/10.1108/s1042-319220180000016016

Lund, Paul, and Harry Ludlam, *Out Sweeps! The Story of the Minesweepers in WWII* (London: W. Foulsham and Co., 1978).

Lyons, Martin, 'New Directions in the History of Written Culture', *Culture and History*, 1 (2012), http://cultureandhistory.revistas.csic.es/index.php/cultureandhistory/article/view/8/71

Lyons, Martin, 'Love Letters and Writing Practices: On Ecritures Intimes in the Nineteenth Century', *Journal of Family History*, 24 (1999), 232-239.

MacDonald, Fraser, 'The Ruins of Erskine Beveridge', *Transactions of the Institute of British Geographers*, 2 (2013), 477-489, https://doi.org/10.1111/tran.12042

Mackay, Robert, *Half the Battle: Civilian Morale in Britain during the Second World War* (Manchester: Manchester University Press, 2003), https://doi.org/10.7228/manchester/9780719058936.001.0001

Magnússon, Sigurður Gylfi, and István M. Szijártó, *What is Microhistory? Theory and Practice* (London: Routledge, 2013), https://doi.org/10.4324/9780203500637

Mailänder, Elissa, 'Making Sense of a Rape Photograph: Sexual Violence as Social Performance on the Eastern Front, 1939-1944', *Journal of the History of Sexuality*, 26 (2017), 489-520, https://doi.org/10.7560/jhs26306

Malcolmson, Robert (ed.), *Love & War in London: The Mass Observation Diary of Olivia Cockett* (Stroud: The History Press, 2009 [2005]), https://doi.org/10.51644/9781554581085

Mallon, Thomas, *A Book of One's Own: People and their Diaries* (New York: Ticknor & Fields, 1984).

Mandell, Hinda, *Crafting Dissent: Handicraft as Protest from the American Revolution to the Pussyhats* (London: Rowman and Littlefield, 2019), https://doi.org/10.5040/9798881815035

Mantel, Hilary, 'The Reith Lectures', 2017, https://medium.com/@bbcradiofour/hilary-mantel-bbc-reith-lectures-2017-aeff8935ab33

Marnham, Patrick, 'Siepmann [*née* Farmar], Mary Aline [*other married name* Mary Aline Eady, Lady Swinfen; *pseud.* Mary Wesley]', *ODNB*, 5 March 2009.

Martin, L. H., H. Gutman, and P. H. Hutton (eds), *Technologies of the Self: A Seminar with Michel Foucault* (Amherst: University of Massachusetts Press, 1998).

Massey, Doreen, 'Places and Their Pasts', *History Workshop Journal*, 39:1 (1995), 182-192.

Masur, Louis P., 'What Will It Take to Turn Historians into Writers', in Aaron Sachs and John Demos (eds), *Artful History: A Practical Anthology* (New Haven: Yale University Press, 2020), pp. 213-217, https://doi.org/10.12987/9780300252040-016

de Matos, Christine, 'Fictorians: Historians Who 'Lie' about the Past and Like It', *TEXT: Special Issue 28: Fictional Histories and Historical Fictions: Writing History in the Twenty-first Century*, eds Camilla Nelson and Christine de Matos, 19:28 (2015), https://doi.org/10.52086/001c.27293

May, Simon, *Love: A History* (New Haven and London: Yale University Press, 2012), https://doi.org/10.12987/9780300177237

May, Vanessa, and Stewart Muir, 'Everyday Belonging and Ageing: Place and Generational Change', *Sociological Research Online*, 20:1 (2015), 72-82, https://doi.org/10.5153/sro.3555

Maynes, Mary Jo, 'Age as a Category of Historical Analysis: History, Agency and Narratives of Childhood', *Journal of the History of Childhood and Youth*, 1:1 (2008), 114-124, https://doi.org/10.1353/hcy.2008.0001

McBride, Eimar, *Something Out of Place: Women and Disgust* (London: Profile Books, 2021).

McCarthy, Molly, *The Accidental Diarist: A History of the Daily Planner in America* (Chicago: University of Chicago Press, 2013), https://doi.org/10.7208/chicago/9780226033495.001.0001

McKee, Christopher, *Sober Men and True: Sailor Lives in the Royal Navy, 1940-1945* (Cambridge: Harvard University Press, 2002).

McKibbin, Ross, *Classes and Cultures: England, 1918-1951* (Oxford: Oxford University Press, 1998).

McLelland, Sara I., 'Intimate Justice: A Critical Analysis of Sexual Satisfaction', *Social and Personality Psychology Compass*, 4:9 (2010), 663-680, https://doi.org/10.1111/j.1751-9004.2010.00293.x

Meyer, Jessica, *Men of War: Masculinity and the First World War in Britain* (Basingstoke: Palgrave, 2009), https://doi.org/10.1007/978-0-230-30542-7

Moran, Joe, 'Private Lives, Public Histories: The Diary in Twentieth-Century Britain', *Journal of British Studies*, 54:1 (2015), 138-162, https://doi.org/10.1017/jbr.2014.168

Motz, Marilyn Ferris, 'Folk Expression of Time and Place: 19th-Century Midwestern Rural Diaries', *The Journal of American Folklore*, 100:396 (1987), 131-147.

Mühlhäuser, Regina, 'Reframing Sexual Violence as a Weapon and Strategy of War: The Case of German Wermacht during the War and Genocide in the Soviet Union, 1941-1944', *Journal of the History of Sexuality*, 26 (2017), 366-401, https://doi.org/10.7560/jhs26302

Munawar, Khadeeja, Sara K. Kuhn, and Shamsul Haque, 'Understanding the Reminiscence Bump: A Systematic Review', *PLoS ONE*, 13:12 (2018): e0208595, https://doi.org/10.1371/journal.pone.0208595

Neale, Lesley, 'The Ethics and Intentionality of Writing Family', *Vitae Scholasticae* (2017), 110-126.

Nelson, Robert, 'Toward a History of Rigour: An Examination of the Nasty Side of Scholarship', *Arts & Humanities in Higher Education*, 10:4 (2011), 374-387, https://doi.org/10.1177/1474022211408797

Noakes, Lucy, *War and the British: Gender and National Identity, 1939-1941* (Cambridge: Cambridge University Press, 1998).

Noakes, Lucy, and Juliette Pattinson (eds), *British Cultural Memory and the Second World War* (London: Bloomsbury Academic, 2014), https://doi.org/10.5040/9781350214583

Noakes, Lucy, '"My Husband Is Interested in War Generally": Gender, Family History and the Emotional Legacies of Total War', *Women's History Review*, 27:4 (2018), 610–26. doi:10.1080/09612025.2017.1292634

Noakes, Lucy, 'Gender, Grief, and Bereavement in Second World War Britain', *Journal of War and Culture Studies*, 8:1 (2015), 72-85.

Noakes, Lucy, Claire Langhamer, and Claudia Siebrecht (eds), *Total War: An Emotional History*, Proceedings of the British Academy (London, 2020; online edn, British Academy Scholarship Online), https://doi.org/10.5871/bacad/9780197266663.001.0001

Nora, Pierre, *Les Lieux de Mémoire* (Paris: Gallimard, 1984).

O'Brien, Tim, *The Things They Carried* (Boston: Houghton Mifflin, 1990).

Okeowo, Alexis, 'How Saidiya Hartman Retells the History of Black Life', *The New Yorker*, 19 October 2020, https://www.newyorker.com/magazine/2020/10/26/how-saidiya-hartman-retells-the-history-of-black-life

O'Neill, Maggie, and Brian Roberts, *Walking Methods: Research on the Move* (London: Routledge, 2019), https://doi.org/10.4324/9781315646442

Orenstein, Peggy, *Girls & Sex: Navigating the Complicated New Landscape* (London: Oneworld, 2016).

Orenstein, Peggy, 'What Young Women Believe about Their Own Sexual Pleasure', *TED*, 2016, https://www.ted.com/talks/peggy_orenstein_what_young_women_believe_about_their_own_sexual_pleasure.

Orwell, George, *The Road to Wigan Pier* (Harmondsworth: Penguin Modern Classics, 2001 [1937]).

Pamuk, Orhan, 'My Father's Suitcase', Nobel lecture, *The New Yorker*, 17 December 2006.

Paperno, Irina, 'What Can Be Done with Diaries?', *The Russian Review*, 63:4 (2004), 561-573, https://doi.org/10.1111/j.1467-9434.2004.00332.x

Partner, Nancy F., 'Making Up Lost Time: Writing on the Writing of History', *Speculum*, 61:1 (1986), 90-117.

Partridge, Frances, *A Pacifist's War* (London: Phoenix, 1996).

Peniston-Bird, Corinna, and Penny Summerfield, *Contesting Home Defence: Men, Women and the Home Guard during the Second World War* (Manchester: Manchester University Press, 2007).

Pető, Andrea, 'The New Monument of Victims of Military Sexual Violence in Budapest', *Hungarian Studies Review*, 48:2 (2021), 209-216, https://doi.org/10.5325/hungarianstud.48.2.0209

Pető, Andrea, 'Memory and the Narrative of Rape in Budapest and Vienna', in Richard Bessell and Dirk Schumann (eds), *Life after Death: Approaches to a Cultural and Social History of Europe during the 1940s and 1950s* (Cambridge:

Cambridge University Press, 2003), pp. 129-148, https://doi.org/10.1017/cbo9781139052344.006

Phillips, Roderick, *Putting Asunder: A History of Divorce in Western Society* (Cambridge: Cambridge University Press, 1988).

Pinto, Sarah, 'Researching Romantic Love', *Rethinking History*, 21:4 (2017), 567-585, https://doi.org/10.1080/13642529.2017.1333288

Plamper, Jan, *The History of Emotions: An Introduction* (Oxford: Oxford University Press, 2015).

Plummer, Ken, *Documents of Life 2* (London: Sage, 2001), https://doi.org/10.4135/9781849208888

Pratt, Jean Lucey, *A Notable Woman: The Romantic Journals of Jean Lucey Pratt* (London: Canongate, 2016).

Priestley, J. B., *English Journey* (Harmondsworth: Penguin, 1985 [1934]).

Prysor, Glynn, *Citizen Sailors: The Royal Navy and the Second World War* (Harmondsworth: Penguin, 2012).

Pyne, Stephen J., *Voice & Vision: A Guide to Writing History and Other Serious Nonfiction* (Cambridge and London: Harvard University Press, 2009), https://doi.org/10.2307/j.ctvjnrv08

Ravetz, Alison, *Council Housing and Culture: The History of a Social Experiment* (London: Routledge, 2001), https://doi.org/10.4324/9780203451601

Reay, Diane, 'Beyond Consciousness? The Psychic Landscape of Social Class', *Sociology*, 39:5 (2005), 911-928, https://doi.org/10.1177/0038038505058372

Revel, Jacques, 'Scale and Discontinuity in History', in Sebastian Jobs and Alf Lüdtke (eds), *Unsettling History: Archiving and Narrating in Historiography* (Frankfurt: Campus Verlag, 2010).

Richardson, Laurel, *Fields of Play: Constructing an Academic Life* (Brunswick: Rutgers University Press, 1997).

Rigney, Ann, 'History as Text: Narrative Theory and History', in Nancy Partner and Sarah Foot (eds), *The Sage Handbook of Historical Theory* (New York: Sage Publications, 2013), pp. 183-201, https://doi.org/10.4135/9781446247563

Roberts, Elizabeth, *A Woman's Place: An Oral History of Working-Class Women, 1890-1940* (London: John Wiley and Sons, 1995).

Roberts, Mary Louise, *What Soldiers Do: Sex and the American GI in World War II France* (Chicago and London: University of Chicago Press, 2013), https://doi.org/10.7208/chicago/9780226923123.001.0001

Robinson, Emily, 'Touching the Void: Affective History and the Impossible', *Rethinking History*, 14:4 (2010), 503–20, https://doi.org/10.1080/13642529.2010.515806.

Robinson, Jane, *In the Family Way: Illegitimacy Between the Great War and the Swinging Sixties* (London: Viking, 2015).

Roper, Michael, *The Secret Battle: Emotional Survival in the Great War* (Manchester: Manchester University Press, 2009).

Rose, Sonya O., *Which Peoples' War? National Identity and Citizenship in Britain 1939-1945* (Oxford: Oxford University Press, 2003), https://doi.org/10.1093/oso/9780199255726.001.0001

Rosenstone, Robert, 'Experiments in Narrative: Introduction', *Rethinking History*, 5:3 (2001), 411-416.

Rosenwein, Barbara, 'Worrying About Emotions in History', *The American Historical Review*, 107:3 (2002), 821-845, https://doi.org/10.1086/ahr/107.3.821

Rust, Marion, 'Personal History: Martha Ballard, Laurel Thatcher Ulrich, and the Scholarly Guise in Early American Women's Studies', *Legacy*, 32:2 (2015), 147-166, https://doi.org/10.5250/legacy.32.2.0147

Rutt, Richard, *A History of Hand-knitting* (London: B. T. Batsford, 1987).

Sachs, Aaron, 'Letters to a Tenured Historian: History as Creative Nonfiction—Or Maybe Even Poetry', in Aaron Sachs and John Demos (eds), *Artful History: A Practical Anthology* (New Haven: Yale University Press, 2020), pp. 115-131, https://doi.org/10.2307/j.ctvwcjf57.19

Sage, Lorna, *Bad Blood* (London: Fourth Estate, 2001)

Salmi, Hannu, 'Cultural History, the Possible, and the Principle of Plenitude', *History and Theory*, 50:2 (2011), 171-187, https://doi.org/10.1111/j.1468-2303.2011.00575.x

Sandbye, Mette, 'Looking at the Family Photo Album: A Resumed Theoretical Discussion of Why and How', *Journal of Aesthetics & Culture*, 6:1 (2014), https://doi.org/10.3402/jac.v6.25419

Sanyal, Mithu, *Rape: from Lucretia to #MeToo* (London: Verso, 2019).

Scheck, Raffael, *Love Between Enemies: Western Prisoners of War and German Women in World War II* (Cambridge: Cambridge University Press, 2021), https://doi.org/10.1017/9781108894821

Scheer, Monique, 'Are Emotions a Kind of Practice (and Is That What Makes Them Have a History)? A Bourdieuian Approach to Understanding Emotion', *History and Theory*, 51 (2012), https://doi.org/10.1111/j.1468-2303.2012.00621.x

Schwartz, Lynne Sharon, *Leaving Brooklyn* (London: Orion, 1988).

Sheridan, Dorothy (ed.), *Among You Taking Notes: The Wartime Diary of Naomi Mitchison* (London: Gollancz, 2000 [1985]).

Sherman, Stuart, *Telling Time: Clocks, Diaries, and English Diurnal Form, 1660-1785* (Chicago: University of Chicago, 1996).

Sinor, Jennifer, *The Extraordinary Work of Ordinary Writing: Annie Ray's Diary* (Iowa City: University of Iowa, 2002), https://doi.org/10.1353/book6925

Sinor, Jennifer, 'Reading the Ordinary Diary', *Rhetoric Review,* 21:2 (2002), 123-149, https://doi.org/10.1353/book6925

Sinor, Jennifer, *Ordinary Trauma: A Memoir* (Salt Lake: University of Utah Press, 2017), https://doi.org/10.1353/book56639

Slabáková, Radmila Švarícková, *Family Memory: Practices, Transmissions and Uses in a Global Perspective* (London: Routledge, 2021), https://doi.org/10.4324/9781003156048

Slater, Eliot, and Moya Woodside, *Patterns of Marriage: A Study of the Marriage Relationships of the Urban Working Classes* (London: Cassell, 1951).

Sleeter, Christine, 'Critical Family History: An Introduction', *Genealogy,* 4:2 (2020). https://doi.org/10.3390/genealogy4020064

Sleeter, Christine, 'Critical Family History', https://www.christinesleeter.org/critical-family-history

Smart, Carol, 'A History of Ambivalence and Conflict in the Discursive Construction of "the Child Victim" of Sexual Abuse', *Social & Legal Studies,* 8:3 (1998), 391-409.

Smart, Carol, 'Reconsidering the Recent History of Child Sexual Abuse, 1910-1960', *Journal of Social Policy,* 29:1 (2000), 55-71, https://doi.org/10.1017/s0047279400005857

Smart, Carol, *Personal Life: New Directions in Sociological Thinking* (Cambridge: Polity, 2007).

Smith, May, *These Wonderful Rumours: A Young Schoolteacher's Wartime Diaries*, ed. by Duncan Marlor (London: Virago, 2012).

Søland, Birgitte, *Becoming Modern: Young Women and the Reconstruction of Womanhood in the 1920s* (Princeton: Princeton University Press, 2000), https://doi.org/10.2307/j.ctv1h9djjc

Spence, Jo, and Patricia Holland (eds), *Family Snaps: The Meanings of Domestic Photography* (London: Virago, 1991).

Srigley, Katrina, Stacey Zembrzycki and Franca Iacovetta (eds), *Beyond Women's Words: Feminisms and the Practices of Oral History in the Twenty-First Century* (London: Routledge, 2018), https://doi.org/10.4324/9781351123822

Stacey, Jackie, *Star Gazing: Hollywood Cinema and Female Spectatorship* (London: Routledge, 1994).

Stanford, Michael, *Introduction to the Philosophy of History* (Oxford: Blackwell, 1998), https://doi.org/10.2307/j.ctvwcjf57

Stanley, Liz, *The Auto/Biographical I: The Theory and Practice of Feminist Auto/Biography* (Manchester: Manchester University Press, 1992).

Steedman, Carolyn, *Landscape for a Good Woman* (London: Virago, 1986).

Steedman, Carolyn 'The Space of Memory: In an Archive', *History of the Human Sciences*, 11:4 (1998), 65-83.

Steedman, Carolyn, *Dust: The Archive and Cultural History* (Manchester: Manchester University Press, 2001).

Steedman, Carolyn, *Master and Servant: Love and Labour in the English Industrial Age* (Cambridge: Cambridge University Press, 2007), https://doi.org/10.1017/cbo9780511618949

Steedman, Carolyn, *An Everyday Life of the English Working Class: Work, Self and Sociability in the Early Nineteenth Century* (Cambridge: Cambridge University Press, 2013).

Stewart, Victoria, 'The Second World War in Contemporary Women's Fiction: Revisiting the Home Front', *Contemporary Women's Writing*, 9:3 (2015), 416-432, https://doi.org/10.1093/cww/vpv025

Storey, David, *Saville* (London: Jonathan Cape, 1976).

Summerfield, Penny, *Reconstructing Women's Wartime Lives* (Manchester: Manchester University Press, 1998).

Summerfield, Penny and Nicole Crockett, '"You weren't taught that with the welding": Lessons in Sexuality in the Second World War', *Women's History Review*, 1:3 (1992), 435-454, https://doi.org/10.1080/09612029200200015

Summerfield, Penny, *Histories of the Self* (London: Routledge, 2018), https://doi.org/10.4324/9780429487217

Summerfield, Penny, 'Culture and Composure: Creating Narratives of the Gendered Self in Oral History Interviews', *Cultural and Social History*, 1:1 (2004), 65–93, https://doi.org/10.1191/1478003804cs0005oa

Summers, Julie, *Fashion on the Ration: Style in the Second World War* (London: Profile Books, 2015).

Summers, Julie, *Stranger in the House: Women's Stories of Men Returning from the Second World War* (London: Simon & Schuster, 2009).

Sutton, Maureen, *We Didn't Know Aught: A Study of Sexuality, Superstition and Death in Women's Lives in Lincolnshire during the 1930s, '40s and '50s* (Stamford: Paul Watkins, 1992).

Sword, Helen, *Stylish Academic Writing* (Cambridge, MA: Harvard University Press, 2012), https://doi.org/10.4159/harvard.9780674065093

Szreter, Simon, and Kate Fisher, *Sex Before the Sexual Revolution: Intimate Life in England 1918-1963* (Cambridge: Cambridge University Press, 2010), https://doi.org/10.1017/cbo9780511778353

Tamboukou, Maria, 'Feeling Narrative in the Archive: The Question of Serendipity', *Qualitative Research*, 16:2 (2016), 151-166, https://doi.org/10.1177/1468794115569563

Tebbutt, Melanie, *Being Boys: Youth, Leisure and Identity in the Inter-war Years* (Manchester: Manchester University Press, 2012), https://doi.org/10.7228/manchester/9780719066139.001.0001

Tebbutt, Melanie, 'Imagined Families and Vanished Communities: Memories of a Working-Class Life in Northampton', *History Workshop Journal*, 73:1 (2012), 144–69. https://doi.org/10.1093/hwj/dbr025

Teo, Hsu-Ming, *Desert Passions: Orientalism and Romance Novels* (Austin: University of Texas, 2012), https://doi.org/10.7560/739383

Thane, Pat, 'Family Life and "Normality" in Post-war British Culture', in Richard Bessel and Dirk Schumann (eds), *Life after Death: Approaches to a Cultural and Social History of Europe During the 1940s and 1950s* (Cambridge: Cambridge University Press, 2013), pp. 193-210, https://doi.org/10.1017/cbo9781139052344.009

Thomson, Alistair, *Anzac Memories: Living with the Legend* (Victoria: Monash University, 2013 [1994]).

Tinkler, Penny, *Constructing Girlhood: Popular Magazines for Girls Growing Up in England 1920-1950* (London: Taylor and Francis, 1995).

Tinkler, Penny, 'At Your Service: The Nation's Girlhood and the Call to Service in England, 1939-1950', *European Journal of Women's Studies*, 4 (1997), 353-377.

Tinkler, Penny, '"A Material Girl": Adolescent Girls and their Magazines, 1920-1958', in Mary Talbot and Maggie Morgan (eds), *All the World and Her Husband in Twentieth Century Consumer Culture* (London: Cassell, 2000), pp. 97-112, https://doi.org/10.5040/9781472545411.ch-007

Tinkler, Penny, 'Cause for Concern: Young Women and Leisure, 1930-50', *Women's History Review*, 12:2 (2003), 233-262, https://doi.org/10.1080/09612020300200695

Tinkler, Penny, *Using Photographs in Social and Historical Research* (London: Sage, 2013), https://doi.org/10.4135/9781446288016

Tinkler, Penny, Stephanie Spencer and Claire Langhamer, *Women in Fifties Britain: A New Look* (London: Routledge, 2017), https://doi.org/10.4324/9781315102146

Tinkler, Penny, 'Researching Girlhood Using Photo-elicitation', SAGE Research Methods Video (2017), https://methods.sagepub.com/video/researching-girlhood-using-photo-elicitation, https://doi.org/10.4135/9781473964624

Tinkler, Penny, 'Miss Modern: Youthful Feminine Modernity and the Nascent Teenager, 1930-40', in C. Clay, M. DiCenzo, B. Green and F. Hackney (eds), *Women's Periodicals and Print Culture in Britain, 1918-1939: The Interwar*

Period (Edinburgh: Edinburgh University Press, 2018), pp. 153-116, https://doi.org/10.3366/edinburgh/9781474412537.003.0013

Todd, Selina, *Young Women, Work, and the Family in England, 1918-1950* (Oxford: Oxford University Press, 2005).

Todd, Selina, *The People: The Rise and Fall of the Working Class, 1910-2010* (London: John Murray, 2014).

Todd, Selina, *Snakes and Ladders: The Great British Social Mobility Myth* (London: Chatto and Windus, 2021).

Todman, Daniel, *Britain's War: Into Battle, 1937-1941* (Harmondsworth: Penguin, 2016).

Trouillot, Michel-Rolph, *Silencing the Past: Power and the Production of History* (Boston: Beacon Press, 1995).

Turner, Luke, *Men at War: Loving, Lusting, Fighting, Remembering, 1939-1995* (London: Weidenfeld and Nicolson, 2023).

Twells, Alison, '"Went into Raptures": Reading Emotion in the Ordinary Wartime Diary, 1941-1946', *Women's History Review,* 25:1 (2016), 143-160, https://doi.org/10.1080/09612025.2015.1047250

Twells, Alison, 'Sex, Gender, and Romantic Intimacy in Servicemen's Letters during the Second World War', *The Historical Journal*, 63:3 (2020), 1-22, https://doi.org/10.1017/s0018246x19000311

Twells, Alison, Will Pooley, Matt Houlbrook and Helen Rogers, 'Undisciplined History: Creative Methods and Academic Practice', *History Workshop Journal*, 96:1 (2023), 153–175, https://doi.org/10.1093/hwj/dbad012

Ugolini, Wendy, and Juliette Pattinson (eds), *Fighting for Britain? Negotiating Identities in Britain During the Second World War* (Edinburgh: Peter Lang, 2015), https://doi.org/10.3726/978-3-0353-0704-7

Ulrich, Laurel Thatcher, *A Midwife's Tale: The Life of Martha Ballard based on her Diary, 1785–1812* (New York: Alfred A. Knopf, 1990).

Ulrich, Laurel Thatcher, 'The Significance of Trivia', *Journal of Mormon History*, 19:1 (1993), 52-66.

Usborne, Cornelie, 'Female Sexual Desire and Male Honour: German Women's Illicit Love Affairs with Prisoners of War during the Second World War', *Journal of the History of Sexuality*, Special Issue: Transgressive Sex, Love, and Violence in World War II Germany and Britain, 26:3 (2017), 454-488, https://doi.org/10.7560/jhs26305

Vance, Carole, *Pleasure and Danger: Exploring Female Sexuality* (Boston and London: Routledge, 1984).

Wadham, Ben, 'Mogan Hunts and Pig Nights: Military Masculinities and the Making of the Arms-Corp Soldier', *TASA Conference Proceedings* (2004).

Wadham, Ben, 'Brotherhood: Homosociality, Totality and Military Subjectivity', *Australian Feminist Studies*, 28:76 (2013), 212-235, https://doi.org/10.1080/0 8164649.2013.792440

Waters, Sarah, *The Night Watch* (London: Virago, 2006).

Wells, Nesta H., 'Sexual Offences as Seen by a Woman Police Surgeon', *British Medical Journal*, 8 (1958), 1404-1408.

Welles, Caitlin E., 'Breaking the Silence Surrounding Female Adolescent Sexual Desire', *Women and Therapy*, 28.2 (2005), 31-45, https://doi.org/10.1300/ j015v28n02_03

Wesley, Mary, *The Camomile Lawn* (London: Macmillan, 1984).

White, Hayden, 'The Value of Narrativity in the Representation of Reality', *Critical Inquiry*, 7:1 (1980), 5-27.

White, Hayden, 'The Public Relevance of Historical Studies: A Reply to Dirk Moses', *History and Theory*, 44:3 (2005), https://doi.org/10.1111/j.1468-2303.2005.00327.x

White, Richard, *Remembering Ahanagran* (New York: Hill & Wang, 1998).

Whitfield, Gertie and Alison Twells, 'Nell's Story', *Learning Creatively Through History*, http://www.learningcreativelythroughhistory.org/nellsstory.html

Wienbaum, Alys Eve, Lynn M. Thomas, Priti Ramamurthy, Uta G. Poiger, Madeleine Yue Dong and Tani E. Barlow (eds), *The Modern Girl Around the World: Consumption, Modernity, and Globalization* (Durham: Duke University Press, 2008), https://doi.org/10.1515/9780822389194

Wing, Sandra Koa, *Our Longest Days: A People's History of the Second World War* (London: Profile Books, 2008).

Wood, Rachel, Julia Hirst, Liz Wilson and Georgina Burns-O'Connell, 'The Pleasure Imperative? Reflecting on Sexual Pleasure's Inclusion in Sex Education and Sexual Health', *Sex Education*, 19:1 (2019), 1-14, https://doi.org/10.1080/14681811.2018.1468318

Woodside, Moya, 'Health and Happiness in Marriage', *Health Education Journal* (1946).

Worpole, Ken, 'Class of '55', *City Limits*, 29 January 1982, 39.

Worpole, Ken, 'Scholarship Boy: The Poetry of Tony Harrison', *New Left Review*, 1:153 (Sept/Oct 1985).

Woolf, Virginia, *Orlando: A Biography* (Oxford: Oxford University Press, 1998 [1928]).

Woolf, Virginia, *A Room of One's Own* (Herts: Granada, 1983).

Wyndham, Joan, *Love Lessons: A Wartime Diary* (London: Heinemann, 1985).

Wyndham, Joan, *Love is Blue: A Wartime Diary* (London: Flamingo, 1987).

Zembrzycki, Stacey, *According to Baba: A Collaborative Oral History of Sudbury's Ukrainian Community* (Vancouver: UBC Press, 2015), https://doi.org/10.59962/9780774826976

Zweig, Ferdynand, *Women's Life and Labour* (London: Victor Gollancz, 1952).

Unpublished Sources

Chambers, Vanessa Ann, 'Fighting Chance: Popular Belief and British Society, 1900-1951' (unpublished PhD thesis: University of London, 2007).

Qureshi, Irna, 'Memories and Journeys of Chhachhi ex-Merchant Navy Seamen from the Chhachh to Bradford' (unpublished PhD thesis: University of Hull, 2025).

Index

absence and silence 6, 15, 25–26, 29–30, 141–142, 147, 175, 191, 197–202, 214–215, 248–249
   in the historical record 29–30, 141–142
adultery 225, 227–228, 234
advice columns/agony aunts 98, 166
air raids 73, 79–81, 91, 98, 110, 266
Allies 177, 179–181, 188, 194
Ancestry (website) 206–207, 211, 215
Angel, Katherine 166, 190, 261
Ankersmit, Frank 142
archive vii, 12, 24, 26, 28–29, 31–33, 65–66, 69, 79, 230, 272, 274
Army, British 20, 91, 98, 110, 123, 135, 140, 161, 168, 172, 176–177
ARP (Air Raid Precautions, later Civil Defence) 70, 75
Atlee, Clement 193
audience 25, 31, 46, 65, 83, 267
Australia 20, 37, 46, 126, 241, 272
   women, sex and romance in WW2 20, 126, 166, 272
Avery, Valerie 40

Baker, Mollie 102–104
Bakewell, Joan 78
Baldwin, Stanley 38, 40
Barthes, Roland 113
Bates, Doreen 167
Bates, H. E. 189–190
Battle of Britain 75
BBC People's War 77–78
Belton, Mary 79–82
Berlin 71, 177, 188–189, 191
Bible 13, 54, 181, 274
Bingham, Adrian 191
biography. *See* life writing/memoir

Bira, Prince 43–46, 57
Blitz 74, 76, 140, 166, 193, 219, 221
bombing 68, 72–73, 75, 88, 95, 158, 212, 218
Bourdieu, Pierre 40
Bowen, Elizabeth 166
Bristol 21, 52, 59, 71, 95, 172, 258, 272
Brumberg, Joan Jacobs 258–259

Castle Donington 8, 28, 35, 44, 47, 68, 76, 96, 100, 118, 123, 130, 157, 169, 177, 192, 198, 244, 248, 263, 274
   aerodrome 110, 124, 127, 130, 192
   Daleacre 67, 139, 144–146, 154, 158, 162–163, 168, 170, 173, 202, 223, 246, 272, 274
   Donington Park 39, 43–44, 46, 53, 58, 123, 176, 263
   Hill Top 29, 35, 44, 46–51, 53, 83, 130, 240, 274
   Lady's Close 144, 146, 162, 274
   Moira Dale 12, 26, 51–53, 56, 67–68, 71, 92, 150, 173, 193, 205, 207, 224, 235–236, 238, 240, 245, 272–273
Chamberlain, Neville 38, 58, 69, 72, 74, 86
Christadelphians 13
Churchill, Winston 65, 70, 74–75, 95–96, 110, 140, 178–179, 182, 191
cinema 39, 73, 77–78, 82, 97–98, 169, 204
Cixous, Hélène 272
class (socio-economic) 5, 25, 30–31, 33, 40–41, 52, 70, 97, 164, 256–257, 263–264, 273
Cockett, Olivia 167
Colls, Rob 40
consumer capitalism 97, 264

council housing 12, 36, 51–53, 56, 126, 205, 263, 273
courtship 96–97, 142, 149, 160, 162, 165, 227, 264, 271
   Danny and Norah 142, 146, 153, 162, 172
   letters from servicemen 105, 107, 136
creative history 32–33
cricket 37, 46, 49, 153, 156, 222, 229, 263

Daily Herald 38, 61
Daily Mirror 98
Daily Telegraph 70
dances 96, 123, 126–128, 130, 179, 224, 241
Davis, Natalie Zemon 141–142
Davison, John 124, 126–130, 151, 256
D-Day 188
demobilisation 16, 194–195, 202, 204
Demos, John 260
Denmark 20–21, 126
   women, sex and romance in WW2 20–21, 126, 272
Derby 7, 10–11, 39, 43–44, 54–55, 59, 69–72, 74–76, 80, 92, 100, 109, 111–113, 117, 119–120, 124, 129–132, 143, 147–148, 151, 153, 158, 162, 170, 175–176, 178, 195–196, 204–205, 218, 222, 227–228, 230, 233, 235–236, 238, 245, 263
Derby County Football Club 39, 92, 228, 263
Derby Evening Telegraph 69, 74
Derby Library 195, 245
dialogue. *See* life writing/memoir
diary-writing
   interpretations 19, 23–26, 31, 33
   interwar diary craze 36
   Letts's School-girl's Diary 11, 25, 35, 39–41, 265
   Mass Observation diaries. *See* Mass Observation
   ordinary diaries 23
   pocket diaries 5, 12, 24, 201, 274
   private diaries 25
Dirty Dancing 257
divorce 207, 226–227, 229, 235, 237–238
Dockrill, Doris 105–107
domesticity, postwar 271
domestic service 20, 24, 77, 264, 271
Dönitz, Admiral Karl 191
double standards. *See* sexuality: sexual double standards
Dunkirk 65, 75–76, 83, 88, 124, 179
Durbin, Deanna 91, 97, 171, 229

Eastbourne 151–152, 169–170, 176, 195, 203–205, 207, 217, 238, 242, 245, 248
Eddy 6–8, 12, 15, 26, 29, 202, 232, 234–239, 241–246, 248, 265–267
Eden, Anthony 57, 182
education 2, 7, 13, 17, 20, 23, 26, 28–29, 35–37, 40–42, 46, 54, 56–58, 61, 68, 73–74, 77–78, 80–83, 89, 91–92, 95–96, 103, 110, 113, 116, 124, 130, 132–135, 162, 165, 172, 176–177, 183, 200, 223, 226, 240, 243, 245, 248, 253–254, 259, 263–265, 273
   class and education/scholarship boys and girls 12, 28–29, 31, 40, 80, 82, 91, 205, 248, 264
   Loughborough Girls High School. *See* Loughborough Girls High School
   Oxford School Certificate 27, 37, 80, 110
Egypt 86, 202, 235
ENSA (Entertainments National Service Association) 136, 182
Ernaux, Annie 201, 209, 259
ethical considerations 109, 213–215, 249
Evans, Robert 128–129
Eyles, Leonora 96, 228

fact/fiction 32
family history 8, 13, 15, 29–30, 206, 211, 241, 243

and academic historians 29
doing of 29–30
heirlooms 14, 273
photographs 9–10, 14, 29, 212
stories 13, 26, 29–30, 38
Febos, Melissa 259
femininity 20, 22, 97, 184, 189, 256, 259, 261, 265, 271–272, 274
feminism 24, 33, 135, 160, 163, 257, 260–261, 265–266, 268
Follick, Dr Mont 192
football 39, 71, 73–74, 86, 222, 229
Forbes, Rosita 166
Forster, Margaret 96
France 10, 25, 77, 160, 170, 172, 179–180, 188, 191, 201, 261, 268
Francis, Martin 190
functions of history. *See* history: functions of

'genealogical imaginary' 13
genealogy. *See* family history
Germany 10, 20, 72, 124, 126, 132, 177, 233, 235, 239. *See also* Nazis women, sex and romance in WW2 21
Gibbs, Sam 102–104
Gilbert, Danny 11, 16–17, 19, 22–23, 26, 33, 55, 68, 92, 109–110, 115–121, 123, 127, 130–133, 135, 137–163, 165, 167–173, 175–185, 187–189, 191–207, 211–212, 214–215, 217–223, 228–229, 232, 237–239, 242, 244–248, 253–256, 261, 265–266, 272–274
Gilbert, Elizabeth 257
Gilbert, Jim 1–2, 10–11, 16–17, 19, 22, 25, 32–33, 55, 68, 78, 82, 85–96, 99–101, 105, 109–111, 113, 115–117, 120–121, 130–134, 136–139, 142–143, 147–157, 159, 170, 173, 175, 177–179, 181–185, 188, 194, 204–207, 211–212, 214, 217–219, 222, 238, 242, 244–246, 248, 253–255, 259–261, 266, 272, 274
'giving in' 154, 189, 191, 198, 257

glamour 12, 20, 97–98, 120, 124, 146, 196, 203, 253–254, 259
Glenn, John 46–47
Goodman, Philomena 20
'good-time girls' 22, 258
Gothard, Marjorie 71
Grant, Cary 77
Greece 85, 96, 179, 181–183, 194
Green, Henry 166
Grenfell, Joyce 136
Grimsby 59, 103, 117
grooming. *See* sexual grooming

Hall, Vivienne 71
Hampsten, Elizabeth 26
Hansen, Lulu Anne 22
Hartman, Saidiya 3, 32
Harwich 1, 58, 87
Heilbrun, Carolyn 264–265
history
  academic history 29–31
  and fiction 32–33, 68, 141
  and life writing 32, 214
  functions of 23, 30–31, 142, 259–260
  'history from below' 31
  nature of 30
Hitler, Adolf 42, 57–58, 65, 69–72, 83, 87–88, 188, 240
HMS *Challenger* 204–205
HMS *Collingwood* 101, 136
HMS *Dunoon* 88, 92
HMS *Elgin* 1–2, 85–86, 88, 92, 95, 143
HMS *Ganges* 106
HMS *Gazelle* 177
HMS *Wishart* 180
HMT *John Stephen* 102
Hodgkinson
  Dennis 28–29, 37, 41, 49, 71, 140, 193, 240–242, 248, 274
  Frank 37, 49, 52, 55–56, 58–59, 68, 72, 74, 76, 118, 121, 130, 132, 140, 176, 178, 182, 191, 195–196, 199–204, 224, 230, 241–242, 248
  Helen 11, 26, 28–29, 36–37, 44–46, 49–52, 54, 69–73, 92–93, 117,

123, 140, 161–162, 171, 176–177, 180, 200, 224–225, 232, 238, 242, 273–274
   Milly (Marsie) 9–10, 13, 16, 27–29, 35, 37, 43–44, 46, 49, 51–52, 54–56, 71, 73–74, 79, 83, 111, 115, 118–120, 132, 140, 143–145, 155, 158, 161–162, 170, 172, 176–178, 193, 197–200, 202–203, 223, 226–227, 230, 233–235, 239, 242, 246, 253–254, 256, 259, 274
   Richard (Birdy) 27–28, 37, 42, 49, 52, 54, 57, 65, 71, 76, 118–119, 121, 140–141, 161, 176, 198, 203–204, 223, 228, 232–233, 236, 241–242, 245, 248, 274
   Tom 9–10, 38, 44, 56, 120
Hoggart, Richard 40, 164
holidays 7, 37, 42, 60, 70–71, 132, 185, 192, 203, 205, 222, 232–234, 236, 239, 242, 244, 248, 254, 257, 273
Holland 128, 180, 194
Home Guard 68, 76, 91, 285
Housing and Town Planning Act (1919). *See* council housing
Howard, Elizabeth 190–191

'I' in history writing. *See* history: academic history
Illouz, Eva 160, 264
ILP (Independent Labour Party) 13
Imperial War Museum 71
International Friendship League 233
interviews. *See* oral history
Italy 75, 172, 177, 179, 188, 220

Jablonka, Ivan 29
Jackson, Brian 273
Jane (*Daily Mirror* cartoon) 98
Japan 99
Jephcott, Pearl 98, 123
Jones, Kath 123–126, 179, 241

Katin, Zelma 136
Kelly, Grace 7, 229, 234, 266
King Farouk 61
Kipnis, Laura 261

knitting 1, 17, 26, 49, 68, 77–79, 81–83, 85, 89, 96–97, 102–103, 105, 156, 173, 176, 204, 212, 228, 232, 255, 265
Kuhn, Annette 214, 273

Labour Party 13, 38, 53, 127, 192–193, 204
Lake, Marilyn 159, 271
Landis, Carole 20
Leadbetter, Arthur and Harriet 8, 13
Leadbetter, Frank and Mary 52, 59
Leicester 44, 59, 71, 80, 125, 238
   Leicestershire County Council Education Committee 27
Lejeune, Philippe 24, 172
Lepore, Jill 269
letters
   from Bob Evans to John Davison 128–130
   from Danny 10, 55, 115–119, 123, 131–132, 139, 149–150, 155, 157, 159, 162, 169–173, 187, 189, 192, 194, 199, 219, 228–229, 245, 255
   from Jim 1, 10, 17, 19, 22, 25, 32–33, 55, 82, 85, 90–93, 95, 100, 105, 109–110, 115–117, 131, 133–134, 137, 139, 143, 147, 149–153, 155–157, 177–178, 181–183, 185, 188, 204–207, 217, 222, 238, 244–245, 254–255, 259, 261, 274
   letter writing/scribal culture in the Forces 101–102, 104, 106, 149
   letter writing to servicemen 1–2, 17, 107, 158
life writing/memoir 32–33, 38, 69, 104, 201, 214, 259, 267
Light, Alison 30
Littauer, Amanda 22, 190
Lively, Penelope 273
'living in sin' 14, 19, 236
LMS (London, Midland and Scottish) Railway 120, 131–132, 142
London 1, 10, 19–20, 36–37, 40, 45, 71, 73, 76, 88–89, 92, 105, 131, 139, 143,

161, 166–167, 182, 184, 193, 207, 222, 228, 243
Long Eaton 70
Loughborough Girls High School 27, 80
Loughborough Grammar School 28

MacDonald, Ramsay 38
Maidenhead 102–103, 105
Mantel, Hilary 32
marriage 12, 22, 29, 54, 97, 126, 132, 158–160, 163–165, 170–171, 207, 211, 219, 227, 230, 235, 238, 241, 244, 255–257, 267, 271
Marsden, Dennis 273
Marsh, Irene 55, 124, 193–194, 204
masculinity 102, 123, 148, 156, 184
Mass Observation 23, 37, 165, 167, 227, 234
Meadows, Maureen 21
memoir. *See* life writing/memoir
memory 11, 29–30, 34, 51, 56, 66, 76, 78, 81, 85, 126, 152, 209, 214, 219–220, 222, 240, 242, 244–245, 247, 251, 268
#MeToo 260, 268
microhistory 25
minesweeping 1–2, 85, 87, 94–95, 102, 120, 217, 266
morale 20, 76, 95, 98, 105, 189, 271
motherhood 66, 230, 260–261
Munich 58, 69, 79, 86
Mussolini, Benito 69, 85, 88, 177, 188
myths 220–221, 272

narrative. *See* history: academic history
Nazis 21, 74, 76, 179, 191, 240, 256
Nazi-Soviet Pact 179
night school/evening classes 265
nonfiction. *See* creative history
Norway 74, 188–189, 191–194, 215, 218
nostalgia 244–245, 273
Nottingham 44, 46, 78, 103, 130, 171

novels 31, 37, 41, 65, 91, 166, 226, 232, 258, 264
and history. *See* history: and fiction
Norah's reading 38, 73, 158, 243

O'Brien, Tim 32
'on the shelf'. *See* single women
Operation Fortitude 187, 215
oral history 2, 22, 32–33, 101, 111, 120, 125–126, 164, 213, 215, 240
Belton, Mary 79–82
Glenn, John 46–47
Jones, Kath 123–126, 179, 241
Marsh, Irene 55, 124, 193–194, 204
Orwell, George 97

Pamuk, Orhan 15
pantomime 161
Paris 75, 81, 180
Partridge, Frances 74, 188
patriotism 22, 185, 190
'patriotic femininity' 20, 189, 271
photography 37, 40, 111, 113
studio portraits 7, 11, 17, 109, 111, 113
Picturegoer 43, 263
Picture Post 70, 98
Plummer, Ken 268
Poland 71–73, 180, 240
politics 38, 58, 65, 70, 263
post-war Britain 53, 125, 130, 194, 205, 211, 217, 222–223, 225, 235, 271
poverty 49, 205, 217, 274
POWs (prisoners of war) 21, 78, 192–193, 235
Pratt, Jean Lucey 70, 177
prayer 8, 16, 200
predatory men 134–135
Priestley, J. B. 38, 65, 97
propaganda 98, 219
PSHE (Personal and Social Health Education) 259

RAF (Royal Air Force) 11, 17, 74, 88, 91–92, 109–110, 116–117, 124, 128,

132, 146, 149, 151, 177–178, 184, 188, 190, 194, 201, 217
RAF Carnaby 129
RAF Filey 117–118
RAF Macmerry 187–188
RAF Scampton 128–129
RAF Skeabrae 162, 169, 188, 215
RAF Spitalgate 182
rape and sexual violence 107, 136, 184, 191, 219–220, 261
rationing 27, 74, 79, 81, 140, 204
reconstruction 204
Rolls Royce 46, 75–76, 158
romance 17, 19, 25, 77, 95, 97–98, 105, 108, 120, 125–126, 141, 145, 147, 155, 159–160, 162–163, 165, 167, 179, 190–191, 204, 217, 223, 233, 254–256, 258, 265, 267, 271
romantic love 133, 159–160, 256, 264, 271
Rome 177, 179, 232–233, 265
Royal Navy 2, 11, 61, 79, 85, 88, 91, 93–94, 98, 101–102, 109, 134, 149, 159, 184, 207, 212, 217
  Comforts Fund 1, 61, 76–78, 83, 89, 102, 106–107, 176, 184, 212, 271
  dockyard 85
  mess culture 86, 100–101, 105, 136, 153, 155, 184
RSHE (Relationships, Sex and Health Education). *See* PSHE (Personal and Social Health Education)
Rubenhold, Hallie 141
Russia. *See* Soviet Union

sailors 1, 16, 17, 19, 68, 78, 82–83, 86, 96, 98, 100–102, 105–106, 109, 111, 113, 116, 121, 134, 138, 149, 155, 173, 190, 193, 204, 212, 265. *See also* Royal Navy
Salmi, Hannu 142
sewing 10, 13–14, 27, 94
sexual education 162, 165, 167, 256–257, 259–260
sexual grooming 98, 134, 214, 219, 254–255, 259, 268

sexual harassment. *See* predatory men; *See* rape and sexual violence
sexuality 22, 165, 256, 259–261
  desire and pleasure 20, 22, 29, 31–33, 101, 116, 120, 123, 126, 152, 159–160, 163–164, 166–167, 173, 189–190, 201, 206, 219, 221, 236, 256–262, 267, 272
  premarital sex 22, 135, 164
  sexual double standards 22
  sexual knowledge/ignorance 101, 135, 165, 167, 191
  sexual manuals 101, 166. *See also* sexual education
Sheffield 7, 16, 57, 60, 74, 136, 191, 213
shorthand 11, 158, 204
Shute, Nevil 110
single women 6, 26, 104, 202, 223, 227, 229–230, 243, 256
Sinor, Jennifer 24
Slater, Eliot 164
Smart, Carol 249
Smith, May 70
Snitow, Ann 261
socialism 38, 240
Soo, Frank 42, 59, 74
Soviet Union 140, 175, 180, 188–189, 204, 240
Spain 86, 241–242
Stainless Stephen 74
Stalin, Joseph 71
Steedman, Carolyn vii, 269, 274
Stewart, Bill 102–105
Stoke City Football Club 39, 42, 59, 71–72, 74
Stopes, Marie 164
Storey, David 41
stories 3, 11, 13–15, 19, 21–22, 25–26, 28–34, 38, 46, 58, 65, 68, 105, 126, 141, 145, 152–153, 155, 179, 189, 191–192, 198, 201, 213–215, 217, 219, 221, 228, 230, 235, 238, 241–242, 248, 256, 258–261, 263–264, 267–269, 274. *See*

also history: academic history; *See also* family history; *See also* life writing/memoir
Strange, Joan 71
Summerfield, Penny 125
superstition 180
Switzerland 179, 233, 265

Tamboukou, Maria 33
Tinkler, Penny 111
Tobruk 140
Townsend, Ernest 75
Tweedie, Jill 229
Twells
   Jean (Powditch; also referred to as my mother etc.) 6–18, 28, 51–55, 59, 65, 67, 118, 121, 130, 157, 162, 172, 193, 199, 201–202, 207, 223–226, 228, 232, 241–242, 244, 248, 254, 263
   Joe and Helen 46, 52, 71, 72, 123, 141, 171, 176, 273, 274. *See also* Hodgkinson: Helen
   Mary and John (Davison) 71, 73, 123–127, 130, 171, 182, 195, 244

Ulrich, Laurel Thatcher 24–25, 269
uniform 7, 11, 17, 20, 29, 37, 40, 63, 85, 124–125, 134–136, 146, 158, 185, 212, 240, 245
Union Jack 98
USA 19–22, 25, 32, 78, 128, 160, 166, 180, 188, 190–191, 198, 257–258, 272
   women, sex and romance in WW2 19–22, 190–191, 257–258
Utility Wear 141

Vance, Carole 261
VE Day 189, 191, 220, 241–242
virginity 166, 190, 258
VJ Day 193, 220

WAAF (Women's Auxiliary Air Force) 70, 97, 110, 129, 132, 157, 169, 193, 218
Wadham, Ben 184

walking 13, 20, 53, 85, 93, 101, 119, 133, 146, 234, 246
   as a research method 145–146
   local walks 106, 119, 144–146, 158, 170, 172–173, 202
Walpole, Hugh 73, 158
Wandsworth 105
war graves 128
Waters, Sarah 221
weddings 54, 70–71, 92–93, 96–97, 111, 123, 125–126, 152–153, 159, 202, 212, 230, 234, 242–243, 258, 261
Wells, Nesta 191
Wesley, Mary 63, 130, 166
White, Hayden 31
White, Richard 30
Winter, W. W. 111–113, 115, 121, 128, 195–196
Woman's Own 83, 96, 98, 165–166, 179, 195, 228, 230
women and WW2
   concerns about impact of war on domestic life 20, 22
   in the forces. *See* Women's Auxiliary Territorial Service (ATS); *See* WAAF (Women's Auxiliary Air Force); *See* Women's Royal Naval Service (WRNS); *See* Women's Voluntary Services (WVS)
   sexual morality 22–23, 135, 156, 165, 219
   transformative effects 221, 271–272
   wartime employment 20, 37
Women's Auxiliary Territorial Service (ATS) 103, 135, 167, 180
women's history 24, 33, 163, 220, 249
Women's Junior Air Corps (WJACs) 157
Women's Land Army (WLA) 135
Women's Royal Naval Service (WRNS) 135–136
Women's Voluntary Services (WVS) 61, 76–77, 83

women's work, white collar 28, 132
Woodside, Moya 164
Woolf, Virginia 15, 268
Worpole, Ken 40
Wyndham, Joan 110, 169

Yugoslavia 85, 178, 180, 194, 233, 265

Zweig, Ferdynand 223

Acknowledgements

This book has been very many years in the making. I have been extremely fortunate to have received the support of Humanities colleagues at Sheffield Hallam University as I worked on what seemed to them to be a never-ending project. A special 'thank you' to Chris Hopkins, Charles Mundye, Suzanne Spiedel and Matt Stibbe for (varying combinations of) support, research time and generous line management; and to the late Nicola Verdon, with whom I shared teaching, the head of history role and very much more.

One reason for the lengthy gestation is that for a long time, I was unsure what kind of book this should or could be. When Norah's diaries first came my way, all I knew was that traditional academic history was at odds with my desire to capture Norah's voice and tell a story that she would recognise as her own. My thanks, then, to Mary Peace, for suggesting I sign up for the life-writing module on Sheffield Hallam University's MA in Creative Writing, and to Conor O'Callaghan, Jane Rogers and Harriet Tarlo, for taking me back to basics and enabling me to think afresh about how history can be written. I haven't always followed their advice, but the MA was a mid-life adventure and being supervised by a poet was a rare treat.

Issues of accessibility – questions of how we explore 'obscure' histories, how we 'hear' our subjects' voices and bring them to life, and for whom, as academics, we write – have been central to this project. I am immensely grateful to Alessandra Tosi, Director at OBP, for her commitment to the accessibility of academic research and for allowing me to write the book I wanted to write. My thanks to Jeevanjot Kaur Nagpal for her attentiveness and patience in cover design and Adèle Kreager for being such careful and sympathetic editor. It was my supremely good fortune that Justin Smith reviewed the manuscript and gave me such engaged, astute and clarifying feedback. I thank him, and the second anonymous reviewer, warmly.

While Norah's diaries and wider archive are in my possession, I am extremely grateful for the help and attentiveness of librarians and archivists at Derby and Loughborough Local Studies Libraries, the British Library, the Imperial War Museum Archive, Sheffield Hallam University and The Keep, University of Sussex. Thanks also to volunteers at Castle Donington Museum, the headteacher at Loughbrough High School for access to archives, the editor of the LGHS Old Girls' Association newsletter, and recent residents of 18 Moira Dale for allowing me to nose around. Thank you to Rachael Richardson for diary-scanning, Cath Feely for double-checking some Derby details, Gertie Whitfield for sharing her expertise regarding sexual grooming and Eileen Yeo for an enjoyable 'research trip' to Eastbourne.

Sadly, many of my interviewees have passed away in the last few years, but I remain immensely grateful to Irene Marsh, the late Mary Belton, the late John Glenn, the late Kath Jones and the late John Davison, for lovely afternoons spent drinking tea and reminiscing about Norah, Loughborough Girls' High School, sock-knitting, Hill Top, Moira Dale, wartime dances and romances, VE and VJ Days, and life in the Royal Navy and the RAF. Dinah Cook very generously welcomed me into her home and shared her girlhood memories of Norah. Thank you also to Margaret Lindner, the late Lilian Newall, Delia Richards, Bruce Townsend, and everyone else who has shared memories of wartime Castle Donington. Family history is of course a family affair, and Anne Davison, Elaine Hodgkinson and Darina Kelly have been supportive of this project and have kindly allowed me to use family stories and documents.

I sent this book out to readers – friends, family and colleagues – far too early; again, I think, because I wasn't sure what kind of book it was, and I hoped they might tell me. Usually they didn't, but they did read parts of it, or the whole of it, sometimes more than once, and offer thoughtful and challenging criticisms, enlightenment on important details, and/or warm encouragement that kept me believing in its value. Thank you to Chris Allen, Nick Ball, June Balshaw, Dagmar Bere, Barbara Bloomfield, Fiona Cosson, Sarah Cullen, Anne Cumley, Carol Dyhouse, Stavros Flouris, Jane Haggis, Ingrid Hanson, Graham

Hofmann, Elaine Hodgkinson, Elizabeth Holloway, Sarah Jack, Marjorie Jack, Darina Kelly, Ruth Johnson, Mike Lewis, Tracey Loughran, Donald McLean, Clare Midgley, Will Pooley, Michelle Rawlins, Helen Rogers, Matt Stibbe, Penny Tinkler, Gertie Whitfield and Eileen Yeo. (I apologise if I have forgotten anyone; it is undoubtable that I have.) My warmest and most heartfelt appreciation goes to John Baxendale, Van Gore, Chris Hopkins and Matt Houlbrook, who 'got' the project from the outset and have read various drafts over the years. Their insightful criticisms and ongoing encouragement has been absolutely crucial at various stages of writing and rewriting and I am immensely grateful to them all.

As might be apparent, I have both loved writing this book and, at times, felt very adrift. The responses of audience members and conversations with fellow speakers at numerous events, conferences and research seminars where I have talked about Norah have boosted my confidence at critical times. Events at the University of Greenwich and Flinders University, Adelaide, hold special places in my memory: thank you June Balshaw, Jane Haggis and Ella York. Unofficial Histories gatherings in Huddersfield and Manchester were very affirming, not least a conversation about council house front doors with Ian Waites. I am grateful also to book club members Shelagh Chambers, Doreen Haydon, Maggie Hayes, Heather Howarth, Hilda Milne, Delphine Price, Nancy Tomlinson, Barbara West and especially Pat Rogers, and to the late Suzanne Boudjada and friends, for thoughtful and challenging feedback on an early draft and stimulating discussions of the themes of this book. I have had the pleasure of teaching many fabulous students over the years, but in terms of this project, my dissertation group during COVID gave me such heartfelt feedback on Norah and their own experiences of young womanhood. Finally, thank you to Molly Aitken and Sophie Nield-Parkes for inviting me to share a session at Sheffield's Off the Shelf festival on writing the lives of obscure women in history; their enthusiasm and thoughtful feedback, and that of audience members, reaffirmed for me that this book does have a natural home.

Thank you to Liz, Ingrid, Sarah, Hayley, Helen and Eileen for friendship and inspiration, as well as lots of Norah chat, over many years; and to Nicola, gone but never forgotten, for the same; and to Chris, for all of the above, and more besides.

This book is dedicated to my mum, Jean Powditch, without whose memories it couldn't have been written and whose enthusiasm and humour made for a very enjoyable collaboration; and to my daughters, Ruby Mancini and Maddy Mancini, who have lived with this project for longer than they knew their great-great-aunt Norah, for allowing me to write about them, and for their sharp-witted, stimulating engagement, wry commentary and general fabulousness and fun.

Two points of clarification: firstly, in case anyone from South Yorkshire Housing is reading, my sub-letting neighbours have long since moved on (as have I, but they went first). And secondly, while my grandad, Joe Twells, was as I represent him here – a profoundly uncommunicative husband to my gran – he was a good man and I loved him dearly.

About the Team

Alessandra Tosi was the managing editor for this book.

Adèle Kreager proof-read this manuscript and compiled the index.

Jeevanjot Kaur Nagpal designed the cover. The cover was produced in InDesign using the Fontin font.

Annie Hine typeset the book in InDesign. The main text font is Tex Gyre Pagella and the heading font is Californian FB.

Jeremy Bowman produced the PDF, paperback, and hardback editions and created the EPUB.

The conversion to the HTML edition was performed with epublius, an open-source software which is freely available on our GitHub page at https://github.com/OpenBookPublishers

Hannah Shakespeare was in charge of marketing.

This book was peer-reviewed by Justin Smith, The Monfort University, and an anonymous referee. Experts in their field, these readers give their time freely to help ensure the academic rigour of our books. We are grateful for their generous and invaluable contributions.

This book need not end here...

Share

All our books — including the one you have just read — are free to access online so that students, researchers and members of the public who can't afford a printed edition will have access to the same ideas. This title will be accessed online by hundreds of readers each month across the globe: why not share the link so that someone you know is one of them?

This book and additional content is available at
https://doi.org/10.11647/OBP.0461

Donate

Open Book Publishers is an award-winning, scholar-led, not-for-profit press making knowledge freely available one book at a time. We don't charge authors to publish with us: instead, our work is supported by our library members and by donations from people who believe that research shouldn't be locked behind paywalls.

Join the effort to free knowledge by supporting us at
https://www.openbookpublishers.com/support-us

We invite you to connect with us on our socials!

BLUESKY	MASTODON	LINKEDIN
@openbookpublish.bsky.social	@OpenBookPublish @hcommons.social	open-book-publishers

Read more at the Open Book Publishers Blog

https://blogs.openbookpublishers.com

You may also be interested in:

The Birds That Wouldn't Sing
Remembering the D-Day Wrens
Justin Smith

https://doi.org/10.11647/OBP.0430

No Life Without You
Refugee Love Letters from the 1930s
Edited by Franklin Felsenstein; introduction by Rachel Pistol

https://doi.org/10.11647/OBP.0334

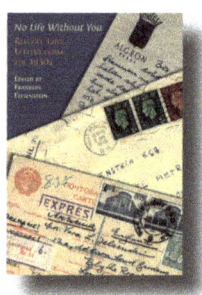

Breaking Conventions
Five Couples in Search of Marriage-Career Balance at the Turn of the Nineteenth Century
Patricia Auspos

https://doi.org/10.11647/OBP.0318

www.ingramcontent.com/pod-product-compliance
Lightning Source LLC
Chambersburg PA
CBHW041457020526
44114CB00057B/2925